Latino Los Angeles

Latino Los Angeles

Transformations, Communities, and Activism

Edited by Enrique C. Ochoa and Gilda L. Ochoa

The University of Arizona Press   Tucson

The University of Arizona Press
© 2005 The Arizona Board of Regents
All rights reserved

Library of Congress Cataloging-in-Publication Data
Latino Los Angeles : transformations, communities, and activism /
edited by Enrique C. Ochoa, Gilda L. Ochoa.
p. cm.
Includes bibliographical references and index.
ISBN-13: 978-0-8165-2466-2 (hardcover : alk. paper)
ISBN-10: 0-8165-2466-1 (hardcover : alk. paper)
ISBN-13: 978-0-8165-2468-6 (pbk. : alk. paper)
ISBN-10: 0-8165-2468-8 (pbk. : alk. paper)
1. Hispanic Americans—California—Los Angeles—Social
conditions. 2. Hispanic Americans—California—Los Angeles—
Politics and government. 3. Hispanic Americans—California—
Los Angeles—Economic conditions. 4. Immigrants—California—
Los Angeles—Social conditions. 5. Community life—California—
Los Angeles. 6. Ethnicity—California—Los Angeles. 7. Los
Angeles (Calif.)—Emigration and immigration. 8. Latin America—
Emigration and immigration. 9. Los Angeles (Calif.)—Ethnic
relations. 10. Los Angeles (Calif.)—Economic conditions.
I. Ochoa, Enrique. II. Ochoa, Gilda L., 1965–
F869.L89S7537 2005
979.4'9400468—dc22
                                                            2005017394

Publication of this book is made possible in part by the proceeds of a permanent endowment
created with the assistance of a challenge grant from the National Endowment for the
Humanities, a federal agency.

For our parents,

Henry José Ochoa (1935–89) and Francesca Palazzolo Ochoa,

who from Nicaragua and New York

made Los Angeles County home.

And to all others who have struggled for a more just Los Angeles.

Contents

Review of Contemporary Latina/o Scholarship and Resources

List of Illustrations and Tables

Latina/o Los Angeles

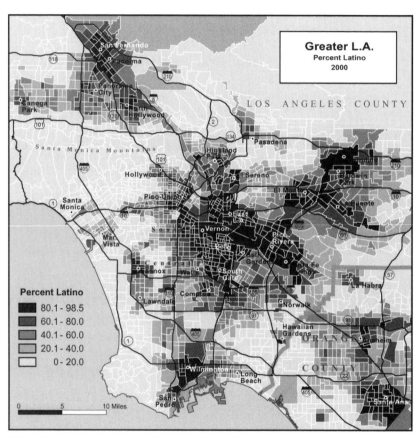

Map showing percentages of Latina/o population in greater Los Angeles area cities and towns, 2000. (Courtesy of James P. Allen and Eugene Turner)

1 Latina/o Los Angeles in Context

Enrique C. Ochoa and Gilda L. Ochoa

On May 1, 2002, more than twelve thousand people took to the streets of Los Angeles demanding general amnesty for immigrant workers. The march was organized by MIWON (the Multi-ethnic Immigrant Worker Organizing Network) and included an impressive array of grassroots organizations, labor unions, and students. Salvadorans marched alongside Mexicanas/os from Zacatecas, indigenous Mexicans from Oaxaca and U.S.-born Chicanas/os and Latinas/os. In the midst of a growing backlash against immigrants that included the firing of noncitizens in U.S. airports and increased efforts to close the border as part of the proclaimed "war on terrorism," the ability of MIWON to mobilize a large and diverse group on May Day is indicative of years of grassroots organizing in immigrant communities. It also underscores the changing nature of immigration that has tapped into new sending communities propelled by global economic restructuring. However, there has been little willingness on the part of the city's establishment to recognize the magnitude of the demographic transformations. The day after the demonstration, the *Los Angeles Times* printed a picture of a screaming Latino demanding amnesty. No article on the march or on the issues raised was included in the newspaper.

This division between Los Angeles's power brokers and the majority of Los Angeles residents reflects significant rifts. A report issued by the United Way of Greater Los Angeles found that "extremes of income characterize Los Angeles County, with rates of wealth and poverty higher than the state or nation. Closely related to shifts in the area's basic industries, increases in poverty and wealth suggest a trend toward a polarized society with a shrinking middle class" (2000). This growing economic chasm is what sparked some to march on May 1, 2002, and it is causing many to question divisive rhetoric and policies.

Currently, Latinas/os comprise 45 percent of the residents of Los Angeles County, making them the largest racial/ethnic group in the region. The Mexican-origin population constitutes the majority of this population, accounting for nearly three-quarters (72 percent) of

Latinas/os in the county (U.S. Bureau of the Census 2001). Although the Mexican-origin population remains the majority, the diversity has grown significantly to include established U.S.-born residents, urban professionals, and indigenous migrants. Likewise, Central Americans have experienced such significant population growth that in 2000 they were an estimated 13 percent of the Latina/o population in Los Angeles County. Thus, after Mexicans, Salvadorans and Guatemalans, who numbered 340,229 and 186,496, respectively, were the next two largest Latina/o nationalities (Allen and Turner 2002, 21).

The growth in this diverse Latina/o population has occurred in conjunction with global economic transformations. Industrial restructuring led to the movement of manufacturing jobs from the United States to countries throughout Latin America as well as to other regions in the United States. The North American Free Trade Agreement (NAFTA), implemented in 1994, hastened the movement of factories into Mexico as companies sought to maximize their profits. Such capitalist restructuring has increased wealth gaps, further destabilizing communities in Latin America and fostering immigration (J. Gonzalez 2000). In cities throughout Los Angeles County, the shift from an economic base of durable goods manufacturing to a service-based economy has contributed to a decline in high-wage, stable, full-time, and unionized manufacturing and industrial jobs and decreases in middle management and white-collar jobs, significantly impacting working class families.

These demographic and economic transformations have been met with a backlash that has included state propositions directly impacting Latinas/os, an escalation in anti-immigrant rhetoric, and a growing militarization of the U.S.-Mexico border. During the 1990s, California voters endorsed Proposition 187, which attempted to exclude undocumented immigrants from receiving public education and other social services; Proposition 209, which resulted in the elimination of affirmative action; and Proposition 227, which sought the eradication of bilingual education. Shifts in border patrol policies such as Operation Gatekeeper have resulted in the deaths of numerous migrants who have been forced to cross the border in more difficult terrain and weather. More recently, there have been summary roundups in L.A.-area neighborhoods and a growing vigilante movement aimed at undocumented immigrants.

As was apparent during the May Day march, Latinas/os have conveyed their dissatisfaction with such economic transformations and political backlashes. Los Angeles is replete with illustrations of Latina/o resistance. For example, while proponents of Proposition 187 sought to criminalize undocumented immigrants, Latinas/os across generations and nationalities raised their voices in protest by applying for U.S. citizenship, voting, and participating in demonstrations. In a powerful display of solidarity, nearly one hundred thousand people marched in downtown Los Angeles against the proposition. Hundreds more organized community demonstrations, and over ten thousand students walked out of their Los Angeles-area schools in protest (Acuña 1996, 158–59). More recently, community mobilizations have been instrumental in winning key victories in the state legislature that have granted California's undocumented high school graduates the right to pay in-state tuition at public colleges and universities and undocumented adults the right to hold driver's licenses. However, a divisive gubernatorial recall campaign and the election of Arnold Schwarzenegger as governor led to the repeal of the driver's license bill.

Despite the growth in the Latina/o population, there remain significant gaps in knowledge that this book addresses. As George Sánchez (2002) and Gilbert Gonzalez and Raul Fernandez (2003) have argued, the development of Chicana/o and Latina/o history has been framed within the context of U.S. history, with relatively little connection to Latin America. Likewise, until recently, most sociological research on the experiences of Latinas/os in the United States has been removed from a discussion of historical and contemporary dynamics in Latin America (for exceptions, see Hamilton and Chinchilla 2001 and Vélez-Ibañez and Sampaio 2002). Furthermore, scholars of Latin America have generally stopped their analysis at the border and have only recently begun to transnationalize their studies. Moving beyond the compartmentalization of the study of Latinas/os in the United States or the study of Latin America, this volume adds to the contemporary scholarship on transnationalism by rooting Los Angeles in the larger political economy of globalization and U.S. imperial conquest.

The recent growth of academic scholarship on Los Angeles has often either overlooked the historical presence of Mexicanas/os or has obscured significant forms of inequality by trumpeting L.A.'s multiethnic communities (for exceptions, see Valle and Torres 2000 and López-Garza and Diaz 2001). By bringing together scholars from a range of disciplines, this volume combines historical perspectives on Mexican Americans and

Mexican immigrants with an analysis of power and inequality. It also considers how the exclusionary ideologies and practices encountered by Mexican Americans have influenced the experiences of Latinas/os more recent to Los Angeles.

Finally, the mainstream press and some scholars have tended to ignore the multiple forms of Latina/o activism and organizing. This invisibility stems from stereotyped assumptions that undocumented residents or immigrants in general are too fearful to organize, are unaware of their rights, or lack a history of organizing in their home communities. Likewise, some scholars have been more concerned with questions of assimilation than with forms of resistance. In particular, a number of neoconservative scholars, who have often been successful in having their publications and ideas widely disseminated, have used the traditional assimilationist paradigms of race and ethnic relations to compare Southern and Eastern European immigrants at the turn of the twentieth century with Latinas/os (see Chavez 1991; Skerry 1993). This has typically resulted in a situation where Latinas/os are blamed for their position in society or are scapegoated for society's ills.

To address these gaps and misperceptions, this volume examines Latina/o Los Angeles in the context of historical, economic, and social factors that have shaped the region and that have fueled migration. It is organized around three basic themes: the global, economic, and historical context of Latina/o migration; the settlement and the (re)construction of Latin American communities and identities throughout the Los Angeles area; and the ways that political and economic concerns have resulted in political activism. These themes provide both a structural analysis and context as well an emphasis on how different communities have sought to create and shape their own experiences in Los Angeles.

Part 1: Globalization and Latina/o Migration to Los Angeles

The four chapters in this first section of the volume provide historical and macroscopic contexts for understanding Latina/o migration to Los Angeles. They locate contemporary immigration patterns in historical and structural factors, such as U.S. economic and military domination, labor and economic integration in the Americas, and Los Angeles's economic history.

Latina/o Los Angeles, along with the U.S. Southwest in general, needs to be analyzed within the context of U.S. empire and U.S. relations with Latin America. As Juan Gonzalez (2000) and Gilbert Gonzalez and Raul Fernandez (2003) have argued, there is a direct connection between U.S. empire and migration to the United States. According to Juan Gonzalez (2000),

> the Latino migrant flows were directly connected to the growth of a U.S. empire, and they responded closely to that empire's needs, whether it was a political need to stabilize a neighboring country or to accept its refugees as a means of accomplishing a broader foreign policy objective (Cubans, Dominicans, Salvadorans, Nicaraguans), or whether it was an economic need, such as satisfying the labor demands of particular U.S. industries (Mexicans, Puerto Ricans, Panamanians) (xiv).

U.S. dominance has played an important role in integrating Mexico into the U.S. economy. Mexico and the U.S. Southwest have a long relationship that stretches back centuries. These historic ties have been deepened since the nineteenth century through U.S. imperial policies, capitalist expansion, migration, and cultural transmission. The U.S war against Mexico (1846–47) and the subsequent conquest of nearly half of Mexico's territory, including the present-day states of Arizona, California, New Mexico, Nevada, Texas, Utah, and parts of Colorado, profoundly shaped relations with Mexico as well as with individuals of Mexican descent in the United States. U.S. capitalist expansion in the Southwest and in the Mexican north led to the development of an integrated labor market, with Mexicans working in U.S.-owned railroads, mines, and agricultural industries in both Mexico and in the United States (G. Gonzalez and Fernandez 2003; Raat 1992).

Throughout the twentieth century, the U.S. government and capitalists engaged in patterns of recruitment and deportation of Mexicans depending on the economy and labor market conditions. When there has been a need for laborers, as during World Wars I and II, the United States has actively recruited workers from Mexico. However, during economic downturns Mexican immigrants and Mexican Americans have oftentimes been scapegoated and deported.

Martin Valadez Torres's chapter, "Indispensable Migrants," focuses precisely on this history. He outlines the important political and economic factors in Mexico and in the United States that have influenced

Mexican migration. However, rather than ending with this history, Valadez Torres considers the dynamic ways that Mexicans have shaped the economy, culture, and politics of Los Angeles, a topic typically overlooked in the narratives of Los Angeles.

U.S. citizens and governmental policy have also played a dominant role in the political and economic history of Central America since the 1840s and 1860s. U.S. entrepreneurs such as Cornelius Vanderbilt colluded with Central American governments and worked with U.S. mercenaries to advance their economic interests. The most overt example of this was William Walker, who ruled Nicaragua between 1855 and 1857 and received recognition from the United States.

U.S. interests competed with European powers to build railways and control waterways, with the United States finally winning out with the building of a canal in Panama. These efforts to dominate Central America led to significant flows of U.S. capital into the isthmus. By 1897, U.S. financiers had invested 21 million dollars in the region, and less than two decades later, on the eve of World War I, investment increased to 93 million dollars (LaFeber 1984, 35). Along with this investment came the watchful eye of the U.S. government to protect its investments.

During the turn of the century, the United States greatly expanded its empire in the Caribbean and in Central America. The marines were used throughout the region to quell uprisings and to prop up governments favorable to U.S. capital. U.S. invasions and occupations occurred in Haiti, the Dominican Republic, Cuba, Puerto Rico, Panama, and Nicaragua, with intense political and military threats hovering over other countries. By the 1930s, the U.S. military had overtly withdrawn from the region after it had installed dictators who upheld U.S. economic and political interests.

Since World War II, efforts to maintain U.S. hegemony in Central America have escalated. Through covert operations, the United States has added to the political instability of the region. The cold war policies of the United States led to significant meddling in the affairs of Central American republics that included the support of authoritarian dictators, covert actions to overthrow a popularly elected president in Guatemala in 1954, overt efforts to destabilize the Nicaraguan revolution throughout the 1980s, and the support of military regimes in Guatemala, El Salvador, and Honduras to squelch revolutionary armies and popular movements during the 1980s. Coupled with these political policies, U.S. economic policies have led to the erosion of subsistence agriculture, resulting in campesinos being pushed off of their lands for U.S. production of cotton in the 1950s and 1960s and beef in the 1970s and 1980s (Williams 1986; Vilas 1995). As campesinos lost access to their lands, many migrated to cities, whereas others became dependent as temporary migrant laborers at the whim of the world economy. As the price for cotton fell in the 1960s, with the polyester/synthetic fiber fashion revolution, many peasants had few alternatives but to migrate, whereas others joined guerrilla and revolutionary movements (Williams 1986). Hence, U.S. political meddling and economic domination exacerbated and prolonged Central American social conflicts in ways that further devastated the area and led to significant migration within the region and to the United States.

Shifts in the global economy, beginning in the 1960s, have resulted in a restructuring of U.S industry, greatly impacting the labor market in Los Angeles and in Latin America. Specialized crafts and skills have led to a decline in mass production of products that typified industrial countries in the postwar era. Simultaneously, the expansion of the service sector, the demise of heavy industry, and the growth of light industry have accelerated migration and the incorporation of third world women into the labor force (Sassen 1998). Hence, Latina/o migration to the United States has been closely intertwined with U.S. imperialism and capitalist expansion in the region for nearly two centuries. It is, as Juan Gonzalez has aptly stated, part of the "harvest of empire" (2000).

The chapter by Edur Velasco Arregui and Richard Roman and the one by Kristine M. Zentgraf center on those macrostructural factors influencing the experiences of Central Americans. In "Perilous Passage," Velasco Arregui and Roman examine how U.S. interventions and Mexico's immigration policies have severely limited mobility, leading to large numbers of deaths, accidents, and other abuses against Central American migrants. This continental dimension of migration is rarely discussed, and it has a profound impact on the relationships between Central American and Mexican immigrants in Los Angeles.

Drawing on in-depth interviews with Salvadoran and Guatemalan women, Zentgraf demonstrates how macrolevel social and economic forces combine with household and individual factors to influence migration decisions. In "Why Women Migrate," she provides an important gendered analysis to illustrate how a restructuring of U.S. industry resulted in a demand for female labor in the Southern California economy, encouraging the migration of Salvadoran and Guatemalan women in the 1970s and 1980s.

Through a case study of the industrial belt of Los Angeles, Myrna Cherkoss Donahoe's "Economic Restructuring and Labor Organizing" focuses on the impacts of industrialization, deindustrialization, and re-industrialization on labor struggles and community organizing in the 1930s and 1990s in Southeast Los Angeles. Donahoe illustrates how, though the residents and workers have changed, the area remains a heartland of manufacturing and a residential neighborhood for blue-collar workers. It continues to be an industrial sector with great potential for community organizing.

Part II: Settlement and (Re)Constructing Identities and Communities

The five chapters in this section focus on established and recent communities, the ways that they are remaking Los Angeles, and how dynamics in Los Angeles are influencing racial/ethnic identities. They examine how various Latina/o groups have formed communities and interacted with the existing Mexican-origin populations in a rapidly globalized world and in the context of an often hostile reception.

From its inception as a Mexican pueblo in 1781, Los Angeles has been a multiethnic and cosmopolitan city. The first census demonstrates that Spaniards of diverse racial backgrounds, including blacks, whites, and native people, were among the original settlers. They settled in the region that had been inhabited for centuries by indigenous populations, and they sought to create a society that was connected to the centers of power—Mexico City, Spain, and the rest of Europe. The initial settlers came from the nearby Mexican regions of Sonora and Sinaloa, reinforcing bonds with other Mexican communities. In addition, conquest led to *mestizaje* (mixing of indigenous and Spanish peoples) and other efforts to dominate indigenous peoples (Monroy 1990; Rios-Bustamante 1992).

By the 1820s, European American merchants, many from the East Coast, began to settle in Los Angeles and worked to connect the region to the emerging economic power—the United States. Trade and cultural contact between Los Angeles and the United States grew during the 1830s and 1840s. With trade and travel by U.S. citizens came ideas of Manifest Destiny that sought to transform the region's people and "up-lift" them. The numerous U.S. travelers of the day wrote travel books and articles for an East Coast audience that often characterized the local population as indolent and half-civilized. Colonel Philip Edwards, commenting on San Francisco, argued that "It is inhabited by a half dozen families, too indolent to do anything to arrest the progress of decay" (Monroy 1990, 166). These attitudes were used to justify the U.S. conquest of northern Mexico and have endured.

Over the past two centuries, the Los Angeles area has experienced significant economic and demographic expansion, being transformed from a remote colonial outpost of a waning empire to an international economic and commercial center in the heart of the vast U.S. empire. The California gold rush, the building of the transcontinental railroad, and the market revolution in the United States led to the further integration of Los Angeles and the now-U.S. West into the U.S. economy and polity (Gonzalez and Fernandez 2003). As this occurred, the Mexicana/o population lost its control over politics and the economy and by the 1880s was increasingly marginalized (Pitt 1966). Expensive litigation used to defend land grants, unlawful squatting, and sales of land for debts reduced many Mexicans in the Southwest to a landless group that became powerless and had a foreign language and culture imposed on them (Weber 1973; Almaguer 1994). As Camarillo (1979) has described, Southern California was transformed "from Mexican pueblos to American barrios."

Mexican migrants fleeing the economic, political, and social upheaval of the Mexican Revolution (1910–20) and responding to the labor shortages during World War I joined the established Mexican population of Los Angeles. As a result of this large wave of immigration, in many areas immigrants outnumbered Mexican Americans (Barrera 1979; Gutiérrez 1995; Ruiz 1998). In Los Angeles, the Mexican population grew from five thousand in 1900 to an estimated twenty-nine thousand in 1910 and fifty thousand in 1920 (Gutiérrez 1995).

As Los Angeles was transformed from a Mexican pueblo to an important economic sector, racism and segregation in housing, the workplace, schools and public facilities, already existent in the Spanish and Mexican periods, were exacerbated. As early as the 1920s, neighborhoods were publicly advertising that they were White communities, free of Mexicans and Blacks. The Mexicana/o community developed around the historical central plaza—Olvera Street—and then developed east of the Los Angeles River (Romo 1983). Racial covenants and segregated schools actually increased between 1920 and 1950 (Camarillo 1979), with the proportion of Los Angeles area municipalities maintaining exclusionary racial covenants that prevented Mexicans and other people of color from purchasing homes rising from 20 percent in 1920 to 80 percent in 1946 (Ruiz 1998, 68). In the labor market, Mexican Americans and Mexican immigrants were segregated into jobs that were dangerous, labor intensive, seasonal, and poorly remunerated (Guerin-Gonzales 1994). Segregated schools and classrooms focused on teaching Mexican-origin youth manual labor and the English language, and instilling a sense of U.S. patriotism (G. Gonzalez 1990; Ochoa 2004). The economic depression of the 1930s resulted in more overt anti-Mexican sentiment, as mass deportations of Mexicans led to nearly one million Mexicans leaving the United States (Balderrama and Rodriguez 1995).

During the post-World War II period, federal investment in the U.S. West led to the development of massive public works projects, the expansion of industry and agriculture, and the development of the defense industry. This economic growth resulted in significant demographic shifts since Mexico was experiencing a rapid modernization process that was displacing Mexican campesinos from the countryside and the United States was recruiting Mexicans to work as *braceros*.

Since the 1960s, however, there has been a significant transformation in the composition of the Latina/o population. The profile of Mexican immigrants has changed. Due to larger economic restructuring, shifting priorities of the Mexican government, and Mexico's profound economic crisis of the 1980s and 1990s, immigrants have come from nontraditional sending areas, such as Mexico City, Oaxaca, and Puebla, to areas as diverse as New York, Arkansas, Georgia, North Carolina, Iowa, and the state of Washington. In addition, larger numbers of immigrants have been urban college graduates, women, and indigenous Zapotecos and Mixtecos from Oaxaca.

The first chapter in this section, "Indigenous Mexican Migrants in a Modern Metropolis," by Daniel Melero Malpica, focuses on this newer wave of immigrants. Malpica's ethnographic research offers a case study of Zapotec Mexican incorporation. Contrary to the expectations of many social scientists and the general public, settlement for Zapotec Mexicans has not been a comprehensive process of assimilation, or even an approximation of it. Instead, by highlighting the adaptive strategies that Zapotec migrants are devising as a means of coping with their new environment, Malpica documents how they continue to find substantial inspiration in the resources of their own cultural and ethnic heritage, which they are actively and creatively reinterpreting as they rebuild their lives in Los Angeles.

In the context of the economic and demographic changes in Los Angeles, Zulema Valdez's article, "Two Sides of the Same Coin?" considers one avenue that some Mexican Americans and Mexican immigrants have used in their struggle for economic integration: self-employment. Using the 2000 Census of Population and Housing, Valdez compares self-employment participation rates among Mexican Americans, Mexican immigrants, and U.S.-born Whites and finds that entrepreneurship may not only provide an alternative to limited labor market opportunities for the Mexican-origin community but that it may also facilitate assimilation.

Although Mexicans constitute the majority of Latinas/os in Los Angeles, U.S. policies in Latin America, changes in U.S. immigration laws, and the restructuring of the economy have led to geographically, racially, and economically diverse populations. This diversity is most apparent in the growing Central American population, largely from El Salvador. Drawing on her extensive research, Susan Bibler Coutin examines "The Formation and Transformation of Salvadoran Community Organizations in Los Angeles" over the past two decades. By focusing on groups that struggle for immigrant rights, Coutin's study demonstrates the creative organizing and legal strategies employed by community activists in their effort to legalize the status of Central Americans in the United States.

Along with the growth of Central Americans in Los Angeles, there is also a growing presence of South Americans; after New York and Miami, Los Angeles County is the third most popular area of destination (Allen and Turner 2002, 21). These populations have developed their own communities, yet they have interacted with the predominantly Mexican populations. As each new Latina/o group settles in Los Angeles, its experiences are influenced by the historical and contemporary presence of Mexicans.

Bernadete Beserra's "Negotiating Latinidade in Los Angeles" uses ethnographic data with two Brazilian communities to explore the patterns of Brazilian immigrant integration and identity formation. Beserra argues that the construction of a Brazilian identity in Los Angeles must be understood within the broader context of a Latin American identity that has been constructed in the milieu of globalization where Latin Americans particularly, and Third World people in general, have become the "other" in U.S. domestic and international politics. It is in this ambiguous space that Brazilians both distinguish themselves from and align themselves with other Latinas/os.

The diversity of recent Latina/o migration to Los Angeles has helped to challenge dominant views of a homogenous Latina/o population, or even of a homogenous Mexican population. Once thought of as mestizos, Catholics, and Spanish-speakers, recent Latino/a migrants are challenging these facile notions.

In "Black Face, Latin Looks," Anulkah Thomas uses in-depth interviews to investigate how Afro-Latina/o young adults are negotiating their racial and ethnic identities in Los Angeles, where a normative conception of Latina/o may exclude them. Thomas's respondents reveal how Spanish language competency, geographical positioning, appearance, and situation are significant in shaping their identities. Her findings suggest the limitations of the racial and ethnic categories in the United States that are based on the rule of hypodescent and binary either/or Black-White constructions.

Part III: Labor Organizing and Political Activism

For Latinas/os, struggle and resistance have often accompanied the process of identity formation and community building. Current organizing is part of a long history of resistance. As early as the 1780s, indigenous Tongvas and mestizos organized to reclaim their lives and freedom at the Mission San Gabriel from the Spanish priests and soldiers (see Monroy 1990). Such resistance continued in various forms throughout Mexican and then Anglo rule.

Under U.S. domination, the more well-off Californio population in Los Angeles organized opposition to Anglo power and racism. In 1855, Francisco Ramírez began publishing *El Clamor Público* to publicize the injustices committed by the new California government and Los Angeles's local power structure (Pitt 1966). It served as an effective means of galvanizing the Californio population to protect their rights. Meanwhile, working-class Mexicana/o and indigenous populations developed their own strategies of resistance, which included supporting social bandits such as Joaquín Murrieta, Tiburcio Vásquez, and Juan Flores. Although these social bandits operated outside of Anglo law and often robbed cattle and openly defied Anglo authorities, they were popularly seen as heroes in an unjust system.

Organizing throughout the late nineteenth and early twentieth centuries continued. Together, Mexican Americans and Mexican immigrants developed mutual aid organizations to provide social benefits such as death and unemployment benefits to their members. Such organizations often included community activists and labor leaders who organized cultural events and built community among Mexicanas/os (Gómez-Quiñonez, 1994). One example of such a coalition was El Congreso de Pueblos de Habla Española (the Congress of Spanish-Speaking Peoples), established in 1938 by the efforts of Guatemalan immigrant Luisa Moreno. This organization is credited with shaping future generations of activists, endorsing the rights of immigrants, and emphasizing cultural and class solidarity among members of the Mexican-origin community (Garcia 1989; Gutierrez 1995; Ruiz 1998). Within such organizations, women had important leadership and activist roles, drawing on their kin and community networks in the struggle for social justice (Ruiz 1998).

Since the 1960s, economic transformations and demographic and gender makeup have rendered traditional forms of labor organizing ineffectual. The AFL-CIO concentrated on heavy industry and did not exert significant effort to organize new sectors, so workers began organizing themselves. One of the most visible examples of this effort was the organization of drywall workers that culminated in a 1992 strike and paralyzed the construction industry. Once on strike, they turned to the California Immigrant Workers Association, an organization affiliated with the AFL-CIO, and they were successful at improving their working conditions (De Paz 1993).

Throughout the 1990s, many community-based immigrant rights organizations also began to work with individuals in industries where no unions existed, such as among domestic workers and day laborers. These organizations have been crucial in mobilizing workers and educating them on various work-related issues (Hamilton and Chinchilla 2001; Hondagneu-Sotelo 2001). Such movements have been particularly strong among janitors and in the hotel and restaurant sector, where Chicana labor leader María Elena Durazo heads the local chapter of HERE (Hotel and Restaurant Employees Union).

The role of Latina/o immigrants in revitalizing the labor movement is made explicit in the first chapter in this section—"Justice for Janitors Latinizing Los Angeles," by Maria A. Gutierrez de Soldatenko. Soldatenko considers the role of Latinas in Justice for Janitors and their success in organizing a large number of documented and undocumented residents. Key to their organizing campaigns are the ways that workers have claimed public space by engaging in street performances and civil disobedience, speaking in Spanish, and including children in their demonstrations.

Just as the organizing efforts of Latinas/os have been critical in impacting changes in the labor market, within the educational system, the Mexican-origin community and other Latina/o panethnic groups have mobilized in opposition to school segregation, curriculum tracking, Eurocentric course curriculum, and the elimination of bilingual education. Preceding the 1954 Supreme Court desegregation decision, *Brown v. the Board of Education*, Mexican-origin parents in Southern California successfully organized against de jure segregation in the 1930 *Lemon Grove* case, the first successful desegregation case in the United States, and the 1947 *Mendez v. Westminster* decision, which was an important and often unacknowledged precursor to the elimination of *Plessy v. Ferguson* (Gonzalez 1990).

Whereas Mexican immigrant and Mexican American parents were crucial in these two desegregation cases, in the 1960s and early 1970s Mexican American high school and college students were increasingly voicing their dissatisfaction with discrimination and inferior schools. During this period, students formed organizations, participated in protests and school strikes, and adopted a Chicano identity to emphasize cultural pride, ethnic solidarity, and self-determination. Students involved in this Chicana/o movement argued for increasing the educational opportunities of Mexicans and for establishing educational programs on Chicana/o history and experiences. In Los Angeles, more than ten thousand students "blew out" of high schools to raise awareness of the racist attitudes and behaviors of the largely White teaching staff, the course curriculum that ignored Chicanas/os, and the poor quality of education that Mexican students were receiving (Acuña 1988).

The two chapters by Michael Soldatenko and José Z. Calderon, Suzanne F. Foster, and Silvia L. Rodriguez offer complementary examples of the contemporary role of students in political activism. By focusing on UCLA student activism during the 1990s, Soldatenko's chapter, "Constructing Chicana and Chicano Studies," offers examples of some of the struggles against exclusionary educational policies and practices. As well as analyzing the actions and responses of university officials to the demands for Chicana/o studies, Soldatenko considers how the chance for an inclusively defined and cross-racial movement reflecting the changing demographics of Los Angeles was lost to patriarchy and nationalism.

Whereas Soldatenko's chapter suggests the problems that may arise in nationalist movements, Calderon, Foster, and Rodriguez present a case study of coalition building among college students, faculty, and day laborers in "Organizing Immigrant Workers." The authors focus on a campus/community partnership that emerged in the city of Pomona to oppose an anti-day laborer ordinance and resulted in the establishment of a day labor center. Through this center, the collaborative has established job and health referral programs, computer classes, and literacy projects as a means of organizing day laborers. This chapter illustrates how workers within the informal economy are organizing and the roles that college students and faculty may have in advancing social change.

This volume concludes with a review of some of the most recent scholarship on Latinas/os in Los Angeles. In this chapter, Ester E. Hernández discusses significant books, articles, and videos on immigration, the economy, schools, neighborhoods, gender, and activism as they relate to Central American and Mexican immigrants. This chapter is designed for scholars new to these topics and for those interested in learning more. By combining the themes of this volume into one review, Hernández provides an important synthesis and a guide for increasing our understanding of the continuity and change present in Latina/o Los Angeles.

References

Acuña, Rodolfo. 1988. *Occupied America: A History of Chicanos*. 5th ed. New York: HarperCollins.

——. 1996. *Anything but Mexican: Chicanos in Contemporary Los Angeles*. London: Verso.

Allen, James P., and Eugene Turner. 2002. *Changing Faces, Changing Places: Mapping Southern Californians*. Northridge: Center for Geographical Studies, California State University, Northridge.

Almaguer, Tomas. 1994. *Racial Fault Lines: The Historical Origins of White Supremacy in California*. Berkeley: University of California Press.

Balderrama, Francisco, and Raymond Rodriguez. 1995. *Decade of Betrayal: Mexican Repatriation in the 1930s*. Albuquerque: University of New Mexico Press.

Barrera, Mario. 1979. *Race and Class in the Southwest: A Theory of Racial Inequality*. Notre Dame, Ind.: University of Notre Dame Press.

Camarillo, Albert. 1979. *Chicanos in a Changing Society: From Mexican Pueblos to American Barrios in Santa Barbara and Southern California, 1848–1930*. Cambridge, Mass.: Harvard University Press.

Chavez, Linda. 1991. *Out of the Barrio: Toward a New Politics of Hispanic Assimilation*. New York: Basic Books.

De Paz, José. 1993. "Organizing Ourselves." *Labor Research Review* 20:25–32.

García, Mario T. 1989. *Mexican Americans: Leadership, Ideology, and Identity, 1930–1960*. New Haven: Yale University Press.

Gimenéz, Martha E. 1992. "U.S. Ethnic Politics: Implications for Latin Americans." *Latin American Perspectives* 19(4): 7–17.

Gómez-Quiñonez, Juan. 1994. *Mexican American Labor, 1790–1990*. Albuquerque: University of New Mexico Press.

Gonzalez, Gilbert G. 1990. *Chicano Education in the Era of Segregation*. Philadelphia: Balch Institute Press.

Gonzalez, Gilbert G., and Raul A. Fernandez. 2003. *A Century of Chicano History: Empire, Nations, and Migration*. New York: Routledge.

Gonzalez, Juan. 2000. *Harvest of Empire: A History of Latinos in America*. New York: Viking.

Guerin-Gonzales, Camille. 1994. *Mexican Workers and the American Dreams: Immigration, Repatriation, and California Farm Labor, 1900–1939*. New Brunswick, N.J.: Rutgers University Press.

Gutiérrez, David G. 1995. *Walls and Mirrors: Mexican Americans, Mexican Immigrants, and the Politics of Ethnicity*. Berkeley: University of California Press.

Hamilton, Nora, and Norma Stoltz Chinchilla. 2001. *Seeking Community in a Global City: Guatemalans and Salvadorans in Los Angeles*. Philadelphia: Temple University Press.

Hondagneu-Sotelo, Pierrette. 2001. *Doméstica: Immigrant Workers Cleaning and Caring in the Shadows of Affluence*. Berkeley: University of California Press.

LaFeber, Walter. 1984. *Inevitable Revolutions: The United States in Central America*. New York: W.W. Norton.

López-Garza, Marta, and David R. Diaz. 2001. *Asian and Latino Immigrants in a Restructuring Economy: The Metamorphosis of Southern California*. Stanford, Calif.: Stanford University Press.

Monroy, Douglas. 1990. *Thrown among Strangers: The Making of Mexican Culture in Frontier California*. Berkeley: University of California Press.

Nelson, Candace, and Marta Tienda. 1997. "The Structure of Hispanic Ethncity." In *Challenging Fronteras: Structuring Latina and Latino Lives in the U.S.*, edited by Mary Romero, Pierrette Hondagneu-Sotelo, and Vilma Ortiz. New York: Routledge.

Ochoa, Gilda L. 2004. *Becoming Neighbors in a Mexican American Community: Power, Conflict, and Solidarity*. Austin: University of Texas Press.

Pitt, Leonard. 1966. *The Decline of the Californios: A Social History of the Spanish-Speaking Californios, 1846–1890*. Berkeley: University of California Press.

Raat, Dirk W. 1992. *Mexico and the United States: Ambivalent Vistas*. Athens: University of Georgia Press.

Rios-Bustamante, Antonio. 1992. *Mexican Los Ángeles: A Narrative and Pictorial History*. Encino, Calif.: Floricanto Press.

Romo, Ricardo. 1983. *East Los Angeles: History of a Barrio*. Austin: University of Texas Press.

Ruiz, Vicki L. 1998. *From Out of the Shadows: Mexican Women in Twentieth-Century America*. New York: Oxford University Press.

Sánchez, George J. 2002. "'Y tú,¿Qué?' (Y2K): Latino History in the New Millennium." In *Latinos Remaking America*, edited by Marcelo M. Suárez-Orozco and Mariela M. Páez. Berkeley: University of California Press.

Sassen, Saskia. 1998. *Globalization and Its Discontents: Essays on the New Mobility of People and Money*. New York: New York University Press.

Skerry, Peter. 1993. *Mexican Americans: The Ambivalent Minority*. New York: Free Press.

United Way of Greater Los Angeles. 2000. "A Tale of Two Cities: Promise and Peril in Los Angeles." State of the county 1998–1999, executive summary.

U.S. Bureau of the Census. 2001. *U.S. Census American Fact Finder*. Available at http://facfinder.census.gov/servlet.

Valle, Victor M., and Rodolfo D. Torres. 2000. *Latino Metropolis*. Minneapolis: University of Minnesota Press.

Vélez-Ibañez, Carlos G., and Anna Sampaio. 2002. *Transnational Latina/o Communities: Politics, Processes, and Cultures*. Lanham, Md.: Rowman and Littlefield.

Vilas, Carlos. 1995. *Between Earthquakes and Volcanoes: Market, State, and the Revolutions in Central America*. New York: Monthly Review Press.

Weber, David J. 1973. *Foreigners in Their Native Land: Historical Roots of the Mexican Americans*. Albuquerque: University of New Mexico Press.

Williams, Robert. 1986. *Export Agriculture and the Crisis in Central America*. Chapel Hill: University of North Carolina Press.

Part I   Globalization and Latina/o Migration to Los Angeles

La Cucaracha cartoon strip by Lalo Alcaraz, from August 1, 2004.
(Courtesy of Universal Press Syndicate)

2   Indispensable Migrants

Mexican Workers and the Making of
Twentieth-Century Los Angeles

Martin Valadez Torres

In 1920 Ramón and Petra Sánchez left their village of San Julián, in the Los Altos
region of the Mexican state of Jalisco, for the United States. After arriving in Los
Angeles the couple began working in the berry farms in Buena Park and saving
money for their eventual return to Mexico. And all seems to have gone well. The
couple returned to San Julián in 1923 ready to live out their years in their native
land. But things were not to be. That same year Ramón and Petra decided that
they must go back to the United States and by late 1924 the couple was once again
working in the fields in the greater Los Angles area, but this time it was in Knott's
Berry Farms   *(Ruiz 1998, 4).*

The story of the Sánchez family is part of the history of Mexican migration to Los Angeles and to the United States in general. Although Mexican immigrants have not always been as numerous or visible as they are
at the beginning of the twenty-first century, it is difficult to deny their
role in the making of twentieth-century Los Angeles. During the beginning of the last century, Mexican labor was crucial in the city's railways,
agricultural fields, and nascent light industry. Today, although Mexicans
do not occupy the most prestigious positions in Hollywood or the city's
financial center, it is difficult to imagine how people in leadership positions would function without the immigrants who, among other things,
clean their office buildings, take care of their children, tend their lawns
and gardens, harvest much of the food they eat, cook and pick up after
them at restaurants, and help them build and maintain their homes.
Without this source of inexpensive and readily available labor from Mexico, the lives of the city's middle and upper classes would be much more
difficult and expensive. Indeed, the presence of cheap Mexican labor subsidizes the lavish lifestyles of the city's wealthier residents.

Although Mexican migrants have been a crucial part of the city's
growth and development, their stories are not well known. Thus, the
purpose of this chapter is to demonstrate the essential role that Mexican

migrant workers have played in the development of the city since the beginning of the twentieth century. And, although workers from Mexico have been coming to Los Angeles continuously since the early 1900s, this chapter will concentrate on several key periods of the migrant experience. Also, whenever possible, the chapter will discuss the lives of specific individuals, such as Ramón and Petra Sánchez. Migration and labor, after all, are about people and the process is more easily understood when they are given a name and a face.

Roots of Mexican Immigration to Los Angeles, 1900–1930

Although both Spain and Mexico controlled the region now occupied by the city of Los Angeles, during their rule neither country was able to populate the region successfully. A semiarid land and the absence of a large sedentary population to mobilize for labor attracted few Spaniards and, later, Mexicans to California. Significant Mexican migration to the United States would have to await the important political, economic, and structural transformations that took place in both Mexico and the United States in the late nineteenth and early twentieth centuries.

During the first fifty years after achieving independence from Spain in 1821, Mexico had a difficult time establishing peace and stability. Civil strife combined with foreign invasions, occupations, and wars led to the loss of over half of the nation's territory to the United States (including the land now occupied by Los Angeles) and negligible levels of economic growth. Economic growth and stability in Mexico, however, characterized the presidency of General Porfirio Díaz (1876–1911).

As soon as Díaz arrived in the presidential palace, he began making the necessary changes to industrialize and modernize the nation. To consolidate his power, the general made several military maneuvers to weaken the strength of various generals and of the army as a whole. Given the scarcity of native capital and the previously risky conditions for investors, Díaz made a series of changes to convince foreigners to invest in the country's industries and infrastructure. A combination of tax exceptions, subsidies, land grants, and changes to the country's legal codes eventually attracted much-needed foreign investment into Mexico.

The result of this inflow of foreign capital was dramatic. By 1910, Mexico, which in 1876 could count only 476 miles of track, had an extensive railway network system nearly 20,000 miles long that passed through the country's most important cities, mines, industrial zones, agricultural regions, and ports. Many regions of the country were now connected to the United States at various points along the border. The construction of the railway system combined with the establishment of a nascent industrial sector, the revival of many mines, and the development of an export-oriented agricultural sector eventually brought Mexico what it had been seeking for nearly a century: economic growth and political stability.

As the eruption of the Mexican Revolution in 1910 would make clear, not everyone in Mexico gained equally from Porfirian prosperity. In fact, the construction of the railways as well as the development of new industries and commercial agriculture displaced a significant number of people and created a pool of available and reserve labor. Artisans, once the primary source of the nation's manufacturing, now found themselves out of work, unable to compete with the more inexpensively produced wares of the newly established factories. In addition, peasant farmers and indigenous communities were now constantly under attack by *hacendados* eager to take their fertile land to grow export products for the new markets opened up by the railways. Thus, just as the nation as a whole was modernizing and reaching previously unprecedented levels of growth, an increasing number of people, particularly displaced peasants and artisans, found themselves looking for work.

While Mexico's political and economic transformations were creating a small and growing pool of reserve labor, economic changes in Los Angeles and the Southwest were increasing the region's need for workers. The growth of the region's railway, mining, and agricultural sectors created constant need for labor that had to compete with the new but increasingly important service, manufacturing, and construction sectors appearing in cities like Los Angeles (Camarillo 1984, 36). However, as several industries, particularly agribusiness and railways, were increasing their demand for workers, immigration laws were making it difficult to recruit workers from abroad. Pressure from nativist groups beginning in the late nineteenth century forced the federal government to close off many of the country's traditional sources of immigrant labor. The Chinese Exclusion Act of 1882 and the "Gentlemen's Agreement" (1907) with Japan effectively cut off immigration from Asia by the beginning of the twentieth century. Subsequently, a series of immigration acts between 1917 and 1924 placed quotas and other requirements (such as head taxes and literacy tests) that considerably decreased the number of immigrants from southern and eastern Europe. In light of the increasing restrictions on immigration from Europe and Asia, southwestern employers quickly turned their gaze south. The completion of the railway system connecting the two countries facilitated travel to the north and transformations in Mexico created a pool of available labor for the United States. In addition, although employers in the United States were unable to block the passage of restrictive immigration acts in the 1920s, they were nevertheless able to exclude Mexicans from the quota system and to exempt them from some of the tests and taxes.

Southwestern railways were the most important recruiters, and often the first employer, of Mexican workers. Companies like the Santa Fe and Southern Pacific railways established recruiting agencies along the border (particularly in El Paso) and, even though it was illegal, in Mexico to hire and maintain a fully employed line. Their recruiting efforts were quite successful. By the beginning of the 1920s, Mexican workers made up the bulk of the maintenance crews on most of the railroads in the Southwest. Railway work, however, was difficult, dangerous, and nonstationary, and did not always pay the highest wages. As a result, many Mexican workers eventually left track work for the more stationary and sometimes better-paid jobs in cities like Los Angeles. Pablo Mares was one such worker. Mares arrived in Ciudad Juárez in 1915 and soon crossed the border into neighboring El Paso. There, Mares contracted to work on the track until he arrived in California. Once in Los Angeles, Mares abandoned his railroad job and began working in the cement industry, which was providing materials for the quickly growing city (Camarillo 1984, 33; Cardoso 1980).

Although, as Mares's case suggests, Mexican migrants in the early 1900s labored in both the railways and various sectors of the construction industry, workers from our southern border contributed even more significantly to another industry. Ramón and Petra Sanchez, whose story begins this chapter, were just two of many migrants who contributed to what was, up to the 1930s, the city's most important sector: agriculture. Mexicans often worked during the harvesting season. In addition to working on modern, labor-intensive farms, which McWilliams (1939) called "factories in the field," Mexicans also comprised a significant proportion of the workforce in the related packing and canning industries (Laslett 1996). Without the labor provided by the men and women from

Mexico, it is unlikely that the agricultural fields and packing and canning houses in the Los Angeles area would have been able to survive and grow. As one historian has noted, "By the late 1920s Mexican workers accounted for eighty percent of farm workers in southern California and were the preferred laborers on the vast majority of farms throughout the state" (Camarillo 1984, 35). The importance of Mexican workers is made more evident when we remember that until 1940 the agricultural producing regions "provided Los Angeles County with its most important source of wealth" (Laslett 1996, 50).

In addition to being the most important source of labor in the city's richest industry, Mexican immigrants also contributed their labor to other important sectors of the Los Angeles economy. Mexican men were especially employed in construction-related industries, on the urban railways, and in other manual jobs. Pablo Mares, discussed above, gained employment in a cement company, whereas Carlos Almazán, who had also come to Los Angeles after going to El Paso, worked and labored for the Simon Brick Company. Women, in comparison, were likely to find employment in the packing houses, canneries, garment industry, and laundries (Camarillo 1984, 39–40). Some Mexican women, like their African American counterparts, labored as domestics in the homes of the city's more affluent people. Jesusita Torres, for instance, who migrated to the United States with her mother from Durango in 1923 and who had previously picked berries in El Monte, eventually found a job as a live-in housekeeper. Torres, however, was forced to leave her two children with her mother while she worked as a live-in domestic. Torres recalled, "I went to do housework and they did not pay me too much and I had to stay there so I did not like it" (quoted in Ruiz 1998, 19). After her son died and Torres realized that the money her employer had offered her to bury her child was an advance, not a gift, Jesusita quit her job and returned to work in the city's fields and orchards.

Thus, it is clear that by the 1930s Mexican workers were an essential part of the city's labor force and a growing portion of the city's population. Although it is estimated that no more than five thousand Mexicans resided in Los Angeles in 1900, by 1930 the city's Mexican population, both immigrant and citizen, had risen to about one hundred fifty thousand. The city's Mexican population was also increasing compared to that of other southwestern regions. By 1930, Los Angeles had the largest concentration of Mexicans of any city in the United States, surpassing that of El Paso, Texas. Much of this increase was due to migration. Scholars of Mexican migration have estimated that in addition to the migrants that left during the Porfiriato (1876–1911), an additional one million people left Mexico for the United States between 1910 and 1930 and an increasing proportion moved to Los Angeles, attracted by the city's growing employment opportunities (Ruiz 1998; Cardoso 1980).

The Great Depression, Deportation, and Repatriation

Despite the importance of Mexican workers to the economy of Los Angeles, and of the Southwest in general, the economic troubles brought about by the depression of the 1930s and the xenophobia and nativism that it engendered led to a reversal of this previously important immigrant stream. After the stock market crash of 1929, local, state, and federal agencies began to enact a series of programs to aid American workers. The federal government began a number of public works programs designed to employ thousands of unemployed Americans, while local and state governments expanded their welfare and other roles in order to ensure that the population had access to basic foods. In addition to these employment and relief programs, President Herbert Hoover and other government officials decided to begin deporting or encouraging foreigners to return to their countries of origin because they were seen as taking jobs away from Americans. Although this encouragement was directed at all immigrants, Mexicans received special attention from the government since they were increasingly being viewed as taking away jobs from needy Americans and disproportionately depending on government assistance (Camarillo 1984).

Since the city had the largest concentration of people of Mexican origin by 1930, Los Angeles received the most attention from the forces of repatriation. Thus, between 1931 and 1933, the U.S. Labor Department, along with welfare agencies and local governments, carried out an organized effort to forcefully deport or convince Mexicans to "voluntarily" return to Mexico. These agencies rarely differentiated between those who were in the country "illegally" and individuals who were U.S. citizens or documented residents. Citizen or not, if you were Mexican, you were subject to deportation or repatriation during this period. In Los Angeles, in fact, the Chamber of Commerce estimated that 60 percent of repatriated children were U.S. citizens (Takaki 2000, 92; Hoffman 1974).

In addition to the government-organized efforts to repatriate Mexicans, some left on their own. Some left because they, like many other people in the United States, were unable to find employment. Their departure from the United States was further encouraged by the fact that Mexicans, even those born or legally residing in the country, were often denied access to the relief and services available to others. In addition, local papers scared Mexicans away by printing articles about the joint efforts by both the federal and city governments to round up and deport "aliens" (Camarillo 1984, 49; Hoffman 1974). Local governments often offered men and women free fare to the U.S.-Mexican border to make their decision to leave easier. The Mexican government, furthermore, contributed to the repatriation by offering to pay for the returnees from the border to reach their desired destinations and promising land or other opportunities upon their arrival in Mexico. Although these promises never came true for most, at least they were something to look forward to and they appeared better than starving or continuing to live in hostile and insecure conditions in the United States.

Government efforts eventually succeeded in forcing many to Mexico. It is estimated that approximately five hundred thousand people of Mexican origin moved to Mexico between 1929 and 1939; seventy-five thousand to one hundred thousand were from California. It has also been estimated that during the 1930s Los Angeles lost one-third of its Mexican residents (Sánchez 1993, 12; Hoffman 1974).

Welcome Back: World War II and the Return of the Mexican Migrant

Though over half a million people of Mexican origin were deported or encouraged to return to Mexico, the United States government would soon forget this history and would once again look south of the border to meet its labor needs. With the United States' entrance into World War II after the attack on Pearl Harbor on December 7, 1941, more and more of the nation's men were shipped off to Europe and the Pacific to fight in the war. Many jobs once occupied by these men were left vacant. To meet this demand, the government encouraged women to leave their homes and to take jobs in industries once reserved for men. Although each of these "Rosie the Riveters" contributed in important ways to the war effort, particularly in the shipyards and aircraft plants, there was not enough "native" manpower (or womanpower) to sustain the economy. Agriculture, in particular, was suffering from the labor scarcity. As a result, the United States once again looked toward Mexico.

This time, however, rather than coming on their own or being lured by private companies, this new migration stream was to be managed by a series of agreements, which are now collectively called the Bracero Program, between the United States and Mexico. These *braceros*, so-called because they came to work with their arms (*brazos*), were to labor in the United States under contract for a specified period, after which they were to return to Mexico. In exchange for their labor, the migrants would receive a minimum wage, housing, and free round-trip transportation, and they were to be protected from discrimination (Galarza 1964; Camarillo 1984).

The first fifteen hundred braceros arrived by train in California on September 29, 1942, and by the end of the year a total of four thousand had come to the United States. These totals grew significantly during the coming years: fifty-two thousand in 1943, sixty-two thousand in 1944, and one hundred twenty thousand in 1945. By the end of the war, a total of one hundred fifty thousand braceros had labored in the United States. Braceros would eventually be employed in twenty-one states and, in addition to their crucial labor in agriculture, would also be employed on railways and in a select number of urban industries (Takaki 2000, 93; Camarillo 1984, 75).

The men who came to work in Southern California as part of the Bracero Program, however, were not the only Mexicans to benefit from the labor shortages resulting from World War II. The labor scarcity in the 1940s led to a renewal of undocumented migration from our southern border (Rolle 1981). For example, an advertisement by the Martin Ship Service Company in *La Opinión*, the city's most important Spanish-language daily, called for Mexican workers to apply for openings in its repair and maintenance shops. The announcement declared that potential employees did not have to be U.S. citizens or speak English; "We speak Spanish," it stated (Takaki 2000, 96). Other companies hired even more Mexicans. *La Opinión*, for instance, indicated that in 1944 the Douglas Aircraft plant in Southern California alone employed twelve thousand Mexicans. Although it is likely that many of these Mexicans were women who were long-term residents like Alicia Medeola Shelit and Julia Luna Mount, who had left their jobs in the fields and the canneries for the better-paid positions in the defense industry, it is also likely that a significant number were neither citizens nor long-time residents of the United States (Ruiz 1998, 82–83). As the advertisement by the Martin Ship Service Company suggests, these firms were aware that the English-speaking, second-generation Mexican Americans would not be numerous enough to meet their labor needs; thus, they cast their net wider to also attract noncitizen, non-English speaking, and probably more recently arrived people from Mexico.

Post-World War II Braceros, Operation Wetback, and Non-Bracero Workers from the 1950s to the 1970s

Although the Bracero Program began as an "emergency wartime" agreement between Mexico and the United States, it did not end with the war. Agribusiness convinced the U.S. government to continue the contracts after the war. But the way the program was administered changed considerably. Whereas at the beginning of the program all braceros were to be recruited in Mexico and the program itself was to be managed by the two governments, by the end of the 1940s the employers gained a larger say in the hiring process. Southwest growers, in fact, had begun to encourage Mexican workers to come to the United States and assured them employment. As Acuña notes, "Between 1947 and 1949 alone 142,000 undocumented workers were certified [as part of the Bracero Program], whereas only 74,600 *braceros* were hired by contract from Mexico" (Acuña 1988, 264). The program was finally institutionalized in 1951 with the passage of Public Law 78, and during that decade an average of 336,000 braceros participated in the program every year. Despite opposition from southwestern growers and railway firms, increased protests on the part of labor unions and civil rights groups finally convinced the U.S. government to end the Bracero Program when the last agreement expired in 1964.

In addition to these braceros, noncontracted immigrants also continued arriving in Los Angeles in the postwar years. As several scholars have argued, the Bracero Program restarted migration, particularly unauthorized migration, to the United States. Southwestern growers continued hiring Mexicans, both documented and undocumented, who sought work during the postwar years. Some growers preferred hiring workers outside of the confines of the Bracero Program because then they did not have to provide the workers with the minimum wages, housing, and transportation that the contracts required. Beyond agriculture, Mexican immigrants during the postwar years continued to labor in the same sectors that had previously provided them with much of their work such as construction, light industry, and, particularly for women, the garment industry.

The renewed migration stream that had begun with World War II and the Bracero Program, however, would not continue uninterrupted. Though the Korean War had, like World War II, increased demand for Mexican workers, the recession that followed the end of the war in 1952 would lead to renewed attack on these immigrants. Mexican migrants were again seen as one of the primary causes of the nation's economic woes, which led the Immigration and Naturalization Service (INS), in conjunction with local law enforcement officials, to carry out raids in rural labor camps, Mexican barrios, and other places frequented by Mexicans. This mass deportation campaign, called Operation Wetback, not only instilled fear in the Mexican community but also resulted in the expulsion of more than one million Mexicans in just three years (1953–55) (Camarillo 1984, 84; Garcia 1989).

Despite the "success" of Operation Wetback, Mexicans continued migrating, both with and without governmental approval, to the United States from the late 1950s and into the 1970s. As long as jobs were available and employers were willing to hire them, men, women, and children crossed into the United States. During this period, an increasing proportion chose California, and especially Los Angeles, as their place of residence. It is estimated that by 1980 there were approximately eight hundred fifty thousand Mexican immigrants (both documented and undocumented) living in the state, with over 50 percent of them residing in Los Angeles County (Camarillo 1984, 107). The booming economy of Southern California continued to create new jobs and the immigrants were filling many of those positions. My parents, Maria Elena Torres de Valadez and José Isabel Valadez, were typical immigrants of this period. In 1972, they decided to leave their two young sons in Tepatitlán, Jalisco, to seek work in Los Angeles. Like many Mexican migrants during this period, although neither had previously worked in the United States, they had established connections in the city that facilitated their search for work. The couple decided to move to Los Angeles because friends had assured José that there was plenty of work for a Mexican musician in Los Angeles. By the early 1970s, the Mexican community in Los Angeles had grown to such an extent that not only was there an increasing number of specialized restaurants, markets, and record stores in places like East Los Angeles, but there was also a growing need for live musicians to entertain at weddings, baptisms, birthday parties, restaurants, bars, and nightclubs. Thus, soon after arriving in Los Angeles, my father began playing with a local mariachi band while my mother found a job ironing, and later sewing, in a factory in the downtown garment district.

Immigration, Mexican Workers, and Government Policy since the 1980s

Migration from Mexico to Los Angeles from the mid-1960s to the late 1970s continued and grew over time, and it was characterized by a considerable amount of return migration. Many immigrants came, worked for a few years, saved money to pay off debts, bought a home, started a business, and/or married and eventually returned to Mexico. Although Mexico did not provide peasant- and working-class Mexicans who migrated to the United States with ways to accumulate enough money to cover large expenses such as those mentioned above, once a person had his home, family, and a steady job or small business, the Mexican economy appears to have been stable enough for the average Mexican to live, if only modestly. This, however, changed dramatically in the early 1980s.

The economic crisis that struck Mexico in 1982 significantly transformed the Mexican immigrant population in Los Angeles and, indeed, the entire United States. The number of Mexicans crossing the border increased dramatically and eventually led to the 1986 Immigration Reform and Control Act. The immigrant stream was transformed not only in size but also in composition. Whereas the majority of Mexican migrants prior to the 1980s had come primarily from the states close to the U.S. border (such as Chihuahua, Sonora, and Durango) and several others in central Mexico (particularly Jalisco, Guanajuato, and Michoacan), after the crisis, migrants from states like Oaxaca that were distant from the U.S.-Mexico border and that did not have a long history of migration to the United States began arriving in large numbers in California. As Daniel Melero Malpica explains in this volume, Oaxaqueños have settled in Venice, Santa Monica, North Hollywood, and South Central, and so many of them reside in the area known as Koreatown that some, like Fernando Lopez Mateos, now call the area "Oaxacatown" (Quinones 2001, 120). Unlike the previous migrants, who were primarily Spanish-speaking mestizos, these new migrants are indigenous Mexicans who speak languages such as Zapotec and Mixtec.

The severity of the economic crisis also hit residents of Mexico's major cities. Whereas the majority of Mexico's immigrants up to the 1970s came primarily from the countryside or from small towns, since the 1980s an increasing number of people are coming from urban centers such as Mexico City and Guadalajara. Many of these new immigrants, or their parents or grandparents, had previously left their Mexican villages and headed to Mexico's largest cities in search of better-paying industrial and service sector jobs. But after 1982, these urban jobs, for those fortunate enough to still have them, were not enough to keep many in Mexico. Although urban Mexicans do not represent a large percentage of the immigrant population, they have nevertheless had an impact on the Mexican community in the United States. One sign of their presence may be seen in the growing importance of *rock en español*, or Latin rock, in Los Angeles and the United States as a whole. Since in the past the great majority of the city's Mexican residents traced their heritage to the Mexican countryside and to states in the northern part of the country, the most popular forms of music were *corridos, rancheras*, and *norteñas*. Although certainly not the only factor, we must nevertheless acknowledge that the growing number of migrants from Mexico's largest cities, particularly *chilangos*, as residents of Mexico City are typically called, has certainly contributed to the growing number of Spanish-language radio shows specializing in rock en español music and the increasing number of concerts by Mexican and Latin American rock bands, such as Café Tacuba and Maldita Vecindad.

The 1980s also saw the arrival of another type of immigrant: the college-educated Mexican. With the exception of the few middle- and upper-class Mexicans who migrated for political reasons during the turmoil of the Mexican Revolution (1910–20), for most of the twentieth century migrants were primarily peasants and workers with little or no formal education. Mexico's economic crisis, however, has also pushed a significant number of people who have attended or completed college to seek work in the United States. Many of these Mexicans come from lower-middle-class families and are often the first, or the first generation, to attend college. Because of Mexico's shrinking economy the number of jobs in both the private and public sectors shrank and the people most likely to get such jobs were those with either familial or other connections. One of my cousins, José Niño (Pepé), who graduated from the Universidad de Guadalajara with a degree in agronomy, looked for a job in Mexico but was unable to find a suitable position. He eventually became frustrated and decided to move to Los Angeles to try his luck. Unfortunately, because the United States does not easily recognize, or revalidate, degrees from Mexican universities, Pepe was forced to compete for unskilled or semiskilled jobs with the rest of the immigrant population. He eventually found himself working, among other places, in a garment factory, liquor store, and tire repair shop. Although his university training has undoubtedly helped him at times move into supervisory and entry-level white-collar positions like real estate, it is unfortunate that neither Mexico nor the United States is taking advantage of Pepe's specialized university training.

The increasing migration from Mexico that began in the early 1980s eventually led to U.S. government attempts to stem the tide. The number of border patrol agents has been increased, and the border has been militarized in other ways. In addition, in 1986 the U.S. government passed the Immigration Reform and Control Act (IRCA), which allowed those living "illegally" in the United States since 1982 to regularize their status. Although IRCA calls for sanctions against employers who knowingly hire undocumented workers, much of the emphasis of the new law is focused on the workers. But in the long run, IRCA has done little to stem the flow of migration from Mexico, and it is unlikely to end without a significant improvement in that country's economy. What IRCA *has* managed to do is to criminalize migrants who are seeking employment and has driven an increasing number of them to work in the informal economy. As José Z. Calderon, Susan F. Foster, and Silvia L. Rodriguez discuss in this volume, the growing number of day laborer sites that have sprung up throughout the country are the most visible sign of this. Also, an increasing number of Mexican and Central American women are responsible for cleaning the homes and taking care of the children of the city's wealthy. With the decline of the Los Angeles industrial base beginning in the 1970s, furthermore, many Mexican immigrants have also begun to search for jobs in the service sector. They comprise the majority of the cooks, dishwashers, and busboys in the city's restaurants, and, as Maria A. Gutierrez Soldatenko's chapter in this volume recounts, they also form the bulk of the janitorial staff in West Side and downtown office buildings.

Mexican Migrants and the City's Future

Today, it is difficult to think of Los Angeles without Mexican migrants. Although most of them are employed in the lowest-paid and most menial positions, the city would not function without them; homes and offices would not be cleaned, lawns would be overgrown, restaurants would be unable to serve their customers, and many other sectors and industries would be unable to function. Therefore, it is in the interest of migrants and all the residents of the city who benefit from their labor to let them work. Given Mexican workers' historical and contemporary contributions to the city's wealth, the question is whether the city's wealthier residents and city officials will continue to keep these workers as second-class citizens, or whether they are willing to make the economic, structural, and legal changes that will allow Mexican migrants to have greater access to the wealth that they help create.

References

Acuña, Rodolfo. 1988. *Occupied America: A History of Chicanos*. 3d ed. New York: HarperCollins.

Camarillo, Albert. 1984. *Chicanos in California: A History of Mexican Americans in California*. San Francisco: Boyd and Fraser.

Cardoso, Lawrence A. 1980. *Mexican Emigration to the United States, 1897–1931*. Tucson: University of Arizona Press.

Galarza, Ernesto. 1964. *Merchants of Labor: The Mexican Bracero Story*. Charlotte, N.C.: McNally and Loftin.

Garcia, Juan Ramon. 1989. *Operation Wetback: The Mass Deportation of Mexican Undocumented Workers in 1954*. Westport, Conn.: Greenwood Press.

Hoffman, Abraham. 1974. *Unwanted Mexican Americans in the Great Depression: Repatriation Efforts, 1929–1939*. Tucson: University of Arizona Press.

Laslett, John H. M. 1996. "Historical Perspectives: Immigration and the Rise of a Distinctive Urban Region, 1900–1970." In *Ethnic Los Angeles*, edited by Roger Waldinger and Mehdi Bozorgmehr. New York: Russell Sage Foundation.

McWilliams, Carey. 1939. *Factories in the Field: The Story of Migrant Farm Labor in California*. Boston: Little, Brown and Company.

Monroy, Douglas. 1999. *Rebirth: Mexican Los Angeles from the Great Migration to the Great Depression*. Berkeley: University of California Press.

Niño, José. 2003. Interview by Martin Valadez Torres. Los Angeles, Calif., June 20.

Quinones, Sam. 2001 *True Tales from Another Mexico: The Lynch Mob, the Popsicle Kings, Chalino and the Bronx*. Albuquerque: University of New Mexico Press.

Rolle, Andrew. 1981. *Los Angeles: From Pueblo to City of the Future*. San Francisco: Boyd and Fraser.

Ruiz, Vicki L. 1998. *From Out of the Shadows: Mexican Women in Twentieth-Century America*. New York: Oxford University Press.

Sánchez, George J. 1993. *Becoming Mexican American: Ethnicity, Culture and Identity in Chicano Los Angeles, 1900–1945*. Oxford: Oxford University Press.

Takaki, Ronald. 2000. *Double Victory: A Multicultural History of Americans in World War II*. Boston: Little, Brown and Company.

Torres de Valadez, Maria Elena. 2004. Interview by Martin Valadez Torres. Los Angeles, Calif., Mar. 20.

3 Perilous Passage

Central American Migration through Mexico

Edur Velasco Arregui
Richard Roman

The face of the United States, Los Angeles more specifically, is changing with the dramatic increase in immigration. The number of new immigrants increased from 6.9 million to almost 15 million from the 1980s to the 1990s. Immigration represented almost 50 percent of the net growth of persons residing in the United States in the last years of the twentieth century. The most dramatic increase has been that of the Latino population. Despite notable undercounting, the Latino population increased from 21.9 million to 35.3 million people in only one decade, an unprecedented increase of almost 60 percent. The percentage of the U.S. resident Latino population born outside of the United States increased from 27 percent in 1980 to 43 percent in 2000. Nearly 20 million people born in Latin America or the Caribbean now live in countries other than their country of birth. And one-half of these individuals migrated in the 1990s, most heavily to the United States (CEPAL/ECLAC 2002b). The Latino population tripled in the most dynamic regions of the United States— the Southwest and South. Within these areas, California represents a paradigmatic case—Latinos now make up one-third of the population of the state.

Central Americans have been of growing importance within this immigration—though Mexicans continue to be the most significant by far. The great increase in Central American immigration has been propelled by U.S. military intervention, persisting poverty, and rapid population growth. These immigrants, along with other Latino and non-Latino immigrants, play an important role in the supply of cheap and "flexible" labor for U.S. capital. The role of foreign labor in the development of the U.S. economy is not new. It has been present throughout U.S. history, from slavery to the massive immigration of Europeans in the nineteenth and twentieth centuries to Third World immigration today. The role of direct force in the "recruitment" process has varied over time and place. Although there are fundamental differences between the slave trade of early U.S. history and the "voluntary" immigration of Europeans and Latin Americans, there are also similarities. All these immigrants served to provide necessary labor that was more affordable to key interests in the United States. But there are basic differences among the three experiences. Although forces similar to those that stimulated European migration propel Central American migration, the journey to the immigrants' new countries is distinct. Although European immigrants suffered great hardships in their journeys, they did not face a state-inflicted system of brutality and exploitation, as Central Americans do in their passage through Mexico. And although the brutality of this experience does not approach that of the African slaves in scale and horror, it is brutal nonetheless. This Central American middle passage has remained largely hidden from the world.

The term *middle passage* refers to the forcible transport of Africans to the Americas as slaves. Millions of Africans were killed, and untold numbers raped and maimed in body and soul as they were transported across the Atlantic in what was known as the middle passage. Although coercion is not the main direct mechanism in the "recruitment" of Central American labor, it is present at a variety of levels, from the use of force to impose the market relations that destroy traditional ways of earning a livelihood to the experience of coercion in the journey north. And, in both cases, it was the middle passage that was most dangerous.

Central American immigrants must pass through—or along—the coast of Mexico to get to the United States. This middle passage is the most perilous part of their journey. The Mexican state plays the role of gatekeeper for these immigrants. The Mexican government can make this already perilous passage more difficult through a variety of actions. The behavior of officials and agencies of the Mexican state is shaped by cues from the United States as part of a series of understandings that developed along with the North American Free Trade Agreement (NAFTA) and were elaborated in other bilateral and multilateral meetings. Issues of social control at the borders also shape their behavior. But Mexico is not only a gatekeeper. Sections of the Mexican state (police and migration authorities)—as well as associated or autonomous criminal bands—siphon off significant amounts of money from the desperate Central Americans heading for the United States through various mechanisms of extortion, as well as direct robbery. In contrast, some local officials in the Mexican south have aided migrants in their journeys.

Violations of the human rights of Central Americans in their middle passage by some Mexican authorities is facilitated by the role of the Mexican state at its various levels in the regulation of the flow of Central Americans. Mexicans, especially indigenous Mexicans, also experience these violations. Analysis of the struggle for the human rights of Central Americans seeking to immigrate to the United States must address this middle passage as well as their situations in Central America and in the United States.

The Massive Growth of Central American Migration and the New Face of Latino Los Angeles

The long-term and large-scale flow of Mexican immigration to the United States has shaped the traditional image that equates Latino immigration with Mexico. But that reality and, more slowly, that image has been changing. There is a growing significance of Central Americans in the flow of Latino immigrants. Recent cultural celebrations in Los Angeles have vividly displayed this new reality.

Traditionally, the big Latina/o celebration was on May 5, the Cinco de Mayo celebration of the Mexican victory over the French interventionist forces that invaded Mexico in the nineteenth century. This was one of various indications of the predominance of Mexicans in the Latina/o community. However, several years ago, Central Americans began to mobilize to their own civic calendar. Central American celebrations in Los Angeles in September 2000 were the most overwhelming proof of their emergence as distinct parts of the Latino community with their own self-organizing capacities:

> Hundreds of thousands of Latinos who live in Southern California enjoyed the culmination of the patriotic festivities of their respective countries of origin yesterday, including: Mexico, El Salvador, Costa Rica, Honduras, Nicaragua, Guatemala and Chile, in different parks and streets of the region. Mexican independence was celebrated in Plaza Olvera, in Whittier Narrows Park and East Los Angeles. Central Americans celebrated their liberation on Alvarado Street and in Mac-Arthur Park and Chileans celebrated their Independence in San Fernando Valley. Another Latino festival celebrated a common festival of unity and brotherhood in Virginia Park Avenue in Santa Monica. One

of the most widely attended celebrations was the parade of Central American Independence. First were the flags of the different Latin American countries that fluttered throughout the length of Alvarado Street, followed by floats and a military band drumming loudly, and then the shouts of ¡Viva Centroamérica! (Vega 2000)

Carlos Escorcia described the same parade vividly:

This population of refugees brought their customs, their idiosyncrasy, their history, and their rich cultural heritage with themselves. Last month, we saw an impressive demonstration of cultural pride from this population. Over one hundred thousand people came together in the Angelino district called "Little Central America" in the annual parade celebrating the independence of the countries of that region, which has become the largest Central American event in the whole of the United States. In addition to typical floats, the beautiful cheer-leaders and beauty queens from Belize, Guatemala, El Salvador, Nicaragua, and Panama, notable Los Angeles politicians were part of the ceremony, among them Antonio Villaraigosa. . . . The groups of local dancers have multiplied in Los Angeles. The Salvadorian pupusas, Nicaraguan nacatamales, and Guatemalan and Honduran dishes can be found in hundreds of restaurants throughout the city. . . . The customs, the idiosyncrasy, and the culture of Central America have been transported to California. (Vega 2000)

In 1970, Central Americans made up 5 percent of the U.S. Latinas/os born outside of the United States. By the year 2000, they represented approximately 25 percent, and their levels of community cohesion gave them a character of their own. The growth of the Central American population in the United States in absolute numbers was dramatic. It increased from 925 thousand people in 1990 to 3.7 million in 2000, quadrupling in a ten-year period with an increase of 3 million new immigrants!

An examination of remittances of Central Americans in comparison to those of Mexican immigrants shows the growing importance of Central Americans in the composition of Latino immigrants to the United States (see Table 3.1). Most remittances—money transfers from the immigrants to home—are done through bank machines and debit cards or money orders. The remittances of Central Americans amounted to one-third of those of Mexican workers in 1992 ($1.2 billion compared to more

Table 3.1.   Remittances Home from Central Americans and Mexicans Living Abroad
(in millions of U.S. dollars)

Country	1992	1993	1994	1995	1996	1997	1998	1999	2000	2002	2003	2004[b]
Guatemala[a]	291.3	251.7	358.2	478.4	457.9	517.1	601.1	614.3	988.4	1,959.0	2,413.7	2,757.4
El Salvador	602.0	754.7	964.3	1,062.6	1,086.6	1,201.8	1,338.3	1,373.0	1,750.0	1,935.2	2,105.3	2,413.9
Honduras[a]	216.0	218.3	210.9	264.0	276.7	312.0	487.5	736.9	805.0	968.7	1,091.6	1,229.6
Nicaragua	10.0	25.0	50.0	75.0	95.0	150.0	200.0	300.0	310.0	376.5	438.8	555.4
Costa Rica[c]												
Panama[a]	81.7	80.1	81.6	85.0	85.9	89.1	90.1	93.6	97.2	112.1	134.5	141.2
Central America Total	1,201.0	1,329.8	1,665.0	1,965.0	2,002.1	2,270.0	2,717.0	3,117.8	3,950.6	5,351.5	6,183.9	7,097.5
Mexico[a]	3,404.0	3,656.0	3,822.0	3,995.0	4,560.0	5,272.0	6,039.0	6,340.0	6,730.0	10,268.0	13,873.0	16,256.0

Source: Sistema de Información Estadística sobre Migraciones Centroamericanas (2004), Informe sobre Migraciones Internacionales en Centro América, San Salvador, El Salvado.

[a]Remittances from workers account for almost all of the funds transferred, but the figures also include other transfers such as private donations or pension payments.

[b]Annual estimate based on data for the first semester of 2004.

[c]In the case of Costa Rica, the transfer account is the difference between Costa Rican workers living abroad and non-Costa Rican workers living in Costa Rica, and the total is not significant.

than $3.4 billion), according to official statistics. But by the year 2000, the gap between Central American and Mexican remittances had been sharply reduced. The remittances of Central Americans rose to 58 percent the size of that of Mexicans (almost $4 billion to slightly more than $6.7 billion). In the year 2003, the remittances of the Central Americans surpassed $6 billion, and those of Mexicans were almost $14 billion. The projections for 2004, based on the first semester, are that Central American remittances will rise above $7 billion and that those of Mexicans will increase to $16 billion. Although both sets of remittances grew impressively in absolute terms, the decline in the ratio of Central American to Mexican remittances may reflect a differential impact of responses to the the September 11 terrorist attacks on the two migration groups. Nevertheless, the growth of both sets of remittances between 2000 and 2003 continued to be spectacular—Central American remittances grew by 57 percent and those of Mexicans doubled in these three years. And the remittances played an even more important role in the economies of Central America than they did in Mexico. Looking at Guatemala, El Salvador, Honduras, and Nicaragua as a whole, remittances accounted for 10 percent of the region's GNP in the year 2000 (CEPAL/ECLAC 2002a). In the Mexican case, remittances accounted for only 2 percent of the GNP in 2000 (Banco de México 2004).

The Roots of Central American Emigration

People migrate for a variety of reasons. Persistently extreme poverty and inequality, rapid population growth, and the absence of significant job growth have combined to produce powerful pressures in Central America to emigrate. The horrors and dislocations of military interventions by the United States against regimes in Nicaragua and insurgent movements in El Salvador and Guatemala combined with these long-term factors to propel large-scale emigration. Furthermore, immigration networks both facilitated emigration and became another factor promoting immigration. Migration flows are shaped by political, economic, military, and social factors within which people carve out strategies of survival or improvement. The processes bear little resemblance to the crude economicist perspective in which the migratory process is seen as a spontaneous search for labor market equilibrium in a transnationalized world, with the invisible hand of the market guiding the process. People are part of social collectivities; the decision to migrate is not simply an individual decision, but the historical result of the construction of regional migration networks that nourish and provide the necessary resources that resupply the flows between communities of origin and communities of destination (Brettell and Hollifield 2000, 106–108).

The demographic growth of the region—within the specific economic context—is central to understanding the historical formation of immigration patterns. Central America (Belize, Costa Rica, El Salvador, Guatemala, Honduras, Nicaragua, and Panama) has a population of 36 million people in an area of only 487,946 square kilometers. Population density is 75 persons per square kilometer, which is three times greater than the rest of the continent. El Salvador is one of the most densely populated countries in the whole continent, with 300 persons per square kilometer. The density of Guatemala is close to 250 habitants per square kilometer—if we don't include the fragile Petén, the sparsely populated jungle region. This tendency toward a densely populated Pacific coast and the very inhospitable Atlantic coast is repeated in almost all of the Central America isthmus. If we take into account the presence of the most important tropical forests of the northern region of the hemisphere, from Petén to the jungle region of Darién, the real inhabitable territory is greatly reduced, which would significantly modify the gross data of habitants per square kilometer.

The rate of population growth in Central America—2.5 percent per annum during the decade of the 1990s—was the most rapid in the Americas. This was the case even taking into account the loss of population through migration. The rate of population growth in the rest of the continent is only 1.3 percent annually (CEPAL/ECLAC 2000). If present growth rates continue, the demographic density of Central America will be 30 percent greater than at present, and the isthmus will have a population of 44 million people in 2010. According to the projections of the Comisión Económica para América Latina y el Caribe (CEPAL), this means that there will be a population density of almost 100 people per square kilometer in 2010, double the density of Mexico and triple that of the United States. The relative weight of Central American emigration will sharply increase during this period due to this tremendous population growth, as compared to that of Mexico, whose population expansion has slowed. Moreover, the lack of jobs in Central America is more severe. Comparing Central America and Mexico with similar criteria, it has been shown that Central America has twice the rate of unemployment as Mexico, which itself has the very high rate of 15 percent (CEPAL/ECLAC 2001, 230, 265).

The ferocious civil wars of the 1970s and 1980s provided the push for the departure of the first flow of refugees. These U.S.-sponsored "dirty wars" had the paradoxical result of promoting the flow of Central Americans to the United States as well as developing genuine solidarity within sectors of the North American civilian population in favor of the victims of U.S. imperialism. The violence forced thousands of Central Americans to migrate to the United States in an attempt to rebuild their lives. Severe poverty has a long history among the people of the Mesoamerican region, but the horrors of the wars were the central dynamic that propelled the growth of the Central American population in the United States from one hundred thousand in the 1970s to three hundred thousand in the 1980s and close to one million in the 1990s.

Emigration did not cease with the peace accords reached in the late 1980s and early 1990s. The accords began the process of ending the internal wars and U.S. military intervention in Central America. But peace did not bring authentic change in the prospects for social and economic development in these countries. The violence simply changed from centralized political violence toward more diffuse violence, involving various organized crime networks developed by paramilitary groups that had participated in repression and human rights violations during the 1980s and, with impunity, continued to terrorize the population.

The peace accords did not bring about significant social reform or better distribution of wealth. The crisis of unemployment will continue to grow because the number of people seeking jobs is expected to greatly exceed job creation, given the projected growth of the economically active population from 11.2 million to 16 million in the next ten years (CEPAL/ECLAC 2000). This growth of almost 50 percent will be a result of expected increases in the participation of women in the labor force and the migration of peasants to the cities, both seeking work in a region of lagging job creation that presently has only one million industrial jobs, according to the data from the International Monetary Fund. At the same time, the rest of the population will continue to languish on the highly concentrated agricultural estates and in the saturated and precarious informal urban labor market.

The rate of unemployment in urban areas presently exceeds 15 percent for all these countries, with the exception of Costa Rica. As high as this figure appears, it underestimates the real number because a great amount of unemployment is hidden in the precarious employment of the informal sector. High rates of unemployment exist despite the "exceptional decade" of economic growth in the 1990s, during which part of the losses caused by the military conflagration of the 1980s were regained. Costa Rica, spared major military intervention and civil war, had high growth rates in the 1970s, 1980s, and 1990s, and even attracted immigrants from other Central American countries for work in the agricultural and service sectors. In contrast, high growth rates in the other Central American countries during the 1990s came only after the lost decade of the 1980s, in which there was almost no economic growth. When recuperation came, it was achieved at the cost of very risky financial engineering since the rate of savings in the region, with the exception of Costa Rica, was only 10 percent of GNP. Thus, high rates of growth were achieved through unprecedented increases in external indebtedness.

The first three years of the new millennium have seen Central America, and Latin America in general, return to the scenario of the lost decade of the 1980s. While some countries drift in stagnation, others have experienced dramatic recessions, their economies experiencing double-digit contraction in levels of production and per capita income. But the severity of economic crisis in the new millennium contrasts sharply with that of the 1980s. The recession of the 1980s was preceded by three decades of economic growth that contributed to a strengthened public infrastructure and social patrimony. The recession of the new millennium has hit a society whose public infrastructure has been hollowed out by privatization and cutbacks, and whose national wealth has been depleted by twenty years of austerity, debt servicing, and neoliberal reforms. At present, there are few remaining public assets to sell off.

The U.S. government has argued that peace and market reform will solve the endemic problems of poverty and income inequality in Central America. However, the economic growth of the 1990s did not resolve these problems. Instead, neoliberal policies and austerity programs have deepened them. This particular form of economic growth has generally increased poverty and inequality in the third world. Economic growth that produces jobs and redistributes income and resources is required for these expanding populations. However, a policy shift in this direction would require significant changes in power relations that could come about only through a major change in social and political power in the region.

The economic outlook for Central America is grim. It entered the twenty-first century with a latent and potentially explosive financial crisis, without the possibility of substantially increasing external funding, and with untenable fiscal deficits. The next ten years will see a decrease in economic growth and job creation in the absence of a major—and unlikely—change in the economic parameters. All of this will occur at a time when, according to the statistics of CEPAL, hundreds of thousands of young adults will enter the labor force annually throughout the next two decades. This growing unemployment, combined with the demographic tendencies and the migration networks created by the war, will be a driving force for increased migration. Currently, the implacable poverty and the inequality of Central America are appalling. Although the devastation of the civil wars and U.S. interventions had a damaging impact on the economy, it was the continuing legacy of severe inequality that largely determined who would most suffer the costs of the damages. Income concentration has been increasing. On average, the richest 10 percent receive 35 percent of income and own 85 percent of the wealth, whereas the poorest 20 percent of the Central American population receives 5 percent of income (CEPAL/ECLAC 2000). The CEPAL data also show that 80 percent of Nicaraguans, 75 percent of Hondurans, and 65 percent of Guatemalans live below the poverty line. Poverty in El Salvador affects 48 percent of the population and 20 percent in the relatively prosperous nations of Costa Rica and Panama.

The large migration flows of the 1990s—in which three million Central Americans came to the United States—will be even stronger in the next ten years. This desperate journey of hundreds of thousands of Central Americans has to pass through the crucible of Mexico.

The Mexican Gateway and Binational Policing

This geographical fact has led to increasing efforts to coordinate migration policies between the United States and Mexican governments, on the one hand, and between both of them and the governments of Central America, on the other. This is another facet of the integration of Mexico into the American empire. Mexico has become the gatekeeper of migration to "El Norte" from Central America as well as from other parts of Latin America—and even from Asia—in the last decade. In fact, state control of these migration flows appears to constitute part of the new responsibilities of Mexico, as part of the unwritten agreements of NAFTA. The Mexican state's attempt at coercive regulation of this flow has developed concurrently with the intensification of the flow. While Mexican society continued to be the main supplier of cheap, flexible, and vulnerable labor to the United States throughout the 1990s, Mexican territory has come to be the giant gateway for Central and Latin American migration.

Regional conferences on migration as well as bilateral meetings between Mexico and the United States have been at the center of attempts to coordinate policy. The U.S. government has initiated regional conferences on migration in which Canada and all the nations of Central America, including Belize and Panama, have participated along with Mexico and the United States. Recently, the Dominican Republic also joined these meetings. The first meetings took place in Puebla, Mexico, on March 13–14, 1996. In years of relative prosperity and low unemployment in the United States, the focus of these meetings was on the amelioration of the conditions of migration. A statement issued by the conference said: "Migration is caused by different income levels among different countries. It is a complex phenomenon as a result of the asymmetries between the economies and the labor markets." The statement also condemned the violations of the human rights of migrants and called for the eradication of their maltreatment and for respecting their dignity (Instituto Nacional de Migración 1996, 2).

There have been a total of seven meetings, the most recent taking place in Antigua, Guatemala, on May 30 and 31, 2002. There has been a significant shift in the tone of the resulting declarations. The theme of the conference was "Regional Solidarity in Security and Migration" (Solidaridad Regional en Seguridad y Migración), and migration was viewed as a security problem because it was alleged to be propitious for terrorism. Undocumented migration had been further criminalized and linked to security by definition. The seventh Regional Conference on Migration asked member countries to "ratify the Convention to prevent, repress and penalize illicit traffic of migrants" and to create a Network of Migration Functionaries charged with developing the battle against "irregular" migratory movements (Instituto Nacional de Migración 2002, Punto 10). In the post-9/11 world, undocumented migration was reduced to a problem of "national security" in line with parallel transformations in the administrative structure of the U.S. federal government itself. The earlier view of the complex, multifaceted character of migration disappeared into the shadows.

The collaboration of the government of President Vicente Fox of Mexico with this U.S. focus became clearer after September 11, 2001. In March 2002, the two governments agreed to form the Alliance between Mexico and the United States on Secure Frontiers (Alianza entre México y Estados Unidos sobre Fronteras Seguras). Joint work between the INM (Instituto Nacional de Migración) of Mexico and the INS (Immigration and Naturalization Service) of the United States, which had begun after that start of NAFTA, was deepened. Their collaborative attempts to dismantle illegal networks in the trafficking of undocumented migrants became permanent. These accords, in which the war against terrorism was intertwined with security on the Mexican frontier, were ratified in the nineteenth Reunion of the Comisión Nacional México Estados Unidos (Meeting of the Mexico-U.S. National Commission) held on November 26, 2002.

The Perilous Passage by Land and Sea

The bilateral and multilateral conferences and processes of coordination have defined undocumented immigration as primarily a national security problem within the framework of the war on terrorism. This shift in emphasis and growth in interstate coordination under U.S. leadership has further criminalized migration. It has given a go-ahead to increased harassment and human rights violations and is forcing people into more dangerous migration routes.

Migrants travel through one of two land routes or by sea. They may be forcibly returned to their starting points, after having been despoiled of family savings, and often beaten, abused, imprisoned, and, in some cases, raped. Or they may even lose their lives in this perilous passage.

Mexico is the gateway for this modern-day middle passage. Tecún Umán—a town of only several hundred houses on the Guatemala-Mexico frontier—has become a little Tijuana in the last ten years. During those times of the year when many transmigrants gather there, the town has as many as twenty thousand people. This transient population is composed of immigrants heading north or those who have been deported by the Mexican authorities.

A national government organization that provides social assistance to these migrants has carried out interviews and surveys to learn more about their experiences. These investigations reported that 2,889 human rights violations were committed against migrants, and that 85 percent of these violations were committed in Mexican territory (Godínez 1999). Father Ademar Barrilli, a Brazilian priest who runs the Casa de Atención al Migrante (Migrant Assistance House), stated:

> A permanent persecution exists against Central American migrants throughout their travel through Mexico, the abuses by the authorities and the attacks by criminal gangs make the travel through Mexico hell. . . . In the detention centers Central Americans are held for many days without food nor even water. . . . This was the case where dozens of migrants were held in a cell with a dead body for four days. . . . [T]here are rapes, robberies, beatings. . . . [B]ribery and extortion spread like a plague in their trajectory towards the northern frontier. (Martín 1999)

After entering Mexico, Central American migrants take one of three main routes to try to reach the United States. One route is to jump on the Southern Railway freight trains as they slowly depart from Ciudad Hidalgo, Chiapas, and travel along the coast of Chiapas, crossing the Isthmus of Tehuantepec toward the Gulf of Mexico, then heading toward the high altitudes of the central plateau on through the cities of Orizaba and Córdoba, and from there toward Mexico City. These freight cars, loaded with agricultural products, also carry a hidden human cargo. To avoid being detected and arrested, migrants board and get off these trains before they reach the stations and immigration checkpoints. They need to pass four migration checkpoints in Chiapas and two more in Oaxaca. If they are successful in getting to Mexico City, they then hop on other trains heading for the northern border. It is a long and dangerous journey (Pickard 1999).

A second route north goes along the frontier between Belize and the state of Quintana Roo, Mexico. The networks are more sophisticated here: they use special vehicles, some of them freight cars that have been adapted to carry dozens of undocumented workers in their interiors. There are numerous deaths by asphyxiation in these containers of human cargo, as they lack proper ventilation and temperatures can rise to 95 degrees Fahrenheit or more (Adelson 2001). And many are maimed on these journeys—with the loss of arms and legs, as well as other injuries (Cano 2003).

The unsafe manner in which Central American migrants are transported results in many deaths, even while they are being deported back to their home countries. In April 2001, a bus contracted by the Mexican government to deport undocumented workers rolled over on the Mexico-Querétaro highway, killing five migrants in the crash (Berrones 2001). Also, on these routes, many died of asphyxia, as was the case with three undocumented Guatemalans who died aboard a truck covered with a tarp. They were packed in like sardines with forty-three other migrants (Enciso 2000a).

Organized crime preys on Central American migrants who travel by land routes through Mexico. These gangs kill dozens of migrants each year. For instance, four undocumented migrants were shot and killed by a criminal gang in Huixtla, a municipality of Chiapas (Villalba 2000).

The CNDH (Comisión Nacional de Derechos Humanos—National Commission on Human Rights) has recorded numerous denunciations of human rights violations of migrants in Mexico. In March 2004, the former commissioner of INAMI (Instituto Nacional de Migración), Felipe de Jesús Preciado, affirmed that during his administration one-half (one thousand functionaries) of INAMI had to be removed for participating in irregularities related to the traffic in immigrants. The judicial authorities intervened only in the most extreme cases to arrest those involved. Fifty functionaries of INAMI were arrested in March 2004 for their ties to gangs of traffickers in undocumented migrants. The behavior of the judicial police of the states generally is even more brutal and violent (Guerrero 2004).

The Mexican federal government has created the Grupo Beta Sur, a force intended to protect Central American migrants from abuses by other authorities. There have been many abuses, as reported in *La Opinion*. Through 2001, at least 551 police and migration functionaries had been formally denounced in Mexico to the Secretaria de Contraloría y Desarrollo Administrativo (Secretary of the Comptroller and Administrative Development) for irregularities that extend from extortion of undocumented people to mistreatment of detainees. As a result of actions taken by INAMI to combat these human rights violations, twenty-eight of the country's thirty-two regional delegates to the Instituto have been relieved of their duties in the first stage of the present administration. Although the INAMI and the PGR (Procuraduría General de la República) have revealed data on the abuse of migrants by functionaries, experts believe that the Federal Preventive Police could have carried out similar illicit acts (Robles 2002).

The Grupo Beta Sur is very weak and inefficient and, in fact, makes this middle passage even more dangerous. Its efforts to disrupt the networks of human smuggling do not stop these journeys of desperation but make them follow even more perilous routes:

> In reality the real function of the group Beta Sur is different. Its task is to infiltrate and dismantle the network of human traffickers that smuggle undocumented migrants across Mexico toward the United States. . . . [A]t the end of the story the human traffickers provide a service demanded by the migrants. . . . [T]he routes that they use, the guarantee of the delivery of their passengers, the multiple contacts, accomplices, and corruption are the grease that lubricate the network of transportation through thousands of kilometers. (Pickard 1999)

Even if its real intention was to protect migrants, the Grupo Beta Sur has too little capacity to deal with the enormity of the problem of victimization of migrants.

The actions of the police and migration authorities against undocumented migrants increase sharply in response to cues from the United States. The repression worsens along the southern border of Mexico as the number of migrants deported by the United States increases and the northern border becomes saturated with undocumented non-Mexicans. This is a tacit accord that regulates the passage through this dangerous route.

As can be seen in Table 3.2, the number of deportations and rejections (deportations within a week of entry into Mexico) rose continuously from almost 106,000 in 1995 to 187,000 in 2003, and, based on preliminary data, reached 224,348 in 2004 (INAMI 2005). The year 1997 was an exception to this clear ascending tendency as entry restrictions to the United States were relaxed because of increased demand for workers as the U.S. economy expanded. More than thirty thousand Central Americans were detained in the migration stations in Chiapas alone, according to Javier Jimenez Herrera of the National Institute of Migration of Mexico (*Notimex* 2001a).

Table 3.2. Deportations and Rejections of Central Americans and Citizens of Other Countries by the Mexican Federal Government, 1995–2004

Country of Origin	1995	1996	1997	1998	1999	2000	2003	2004[a]
Guatemala	52,051	50,497	37,837	45,690	53,432	78,819	85,931	99,456
Honduras	27,236	31,055	24,890	35,056	47,007	45,604	61,756	77,724
El Salvador	19,526	20,904	18,857	25,588	26,998	37,203	29,188	38,108
Nicaragua	2,521	1,878	1,172	1,853	1,507	1,938	2,155	2,320
Ecuador	829	587	440	622	643	2,416	1,840	1,792
Brazil	200	84	100	163	56	163	1,722	1,486
Costa Rica	167	91	68	158	69	75	227	214
Colombia	315	229	235	152	153	273	273	154
Peru	238	133	172	89	77	294	338	360
Bolivia	84	53	62	55	—	—	173	166
Dominican Republic	224	252	182	54	43	181	254	184
Venezuela	74	47	36	15	—	—	190	184
Argentina	27	16	20	6	—	—	180	150
Subtotal	103,492	105,826	84,071	109,501	129,985	166,966	184,227	222,298
Other Countries	2,448	1,292	1,000	1,308	1,507	1,799	3,310	2,050
Total	105,940	107,118	85,071	110,809	131,492	168,765	187,537	224,348

Source: Instituto Nacional de Migración (2004), Estadisticas Migratorias, editado por la Secretaria de Gobernación del Poder Ejecutivo Federal de los Estados Unidos Mexicanos, en la Ciudad de México.

[a]Annualized with data for first semester of 2004.

When the transmigrants are detained, they are held in migration stations for periods of thirty days to six months, depending on the availability of resources that the Mexican government possesses for their deportation, or the time it takes the authorities to verify their nationality. They are kept in decrepit, overcrowded facilities that lack proper electricity, toilet facilities, and medical attention, and food is not prepared in a sanitary manner. The main detention center is located in Iztapalapa, Mexico

City. In April 2001, it held more than 500 people in terrible conditions in a facility with a designated capacity of 140 (González 2001).

Recently, these deplorable conditions have led to several revolts in detention centers. The most well-known revolt happened in Iztapalapa, on May 27, 2000, where immigrants took over the facilities until they were crushed by a strong contingent of the federal police forces.

The treatment of Central American and other transmigrants by the Mexican government represents a serious violation of human rights. The gravity of the human rights violations in this middle passage has been so great that various Latin American governments have lodged protests against the Mexican government. Moreover, the president of Mexico's national commission on human rights, José Luis Soberanes, has on various occasions criticized the double standards of various Mexican authorities who speak out for dignified treatment of Mexicans in the United States while hundreds of Central Americans face abuse and death in passing through Mexican territory. On one occasion he said:

> We are very preoccupied that there are deaths of migrants in Mexican territory. We are preoccupied that these people leave Central America and encounter death here, especially because our commission has always said that we cannot insist that the U.S. does what we are not disposed to do in Mexico. We complain of the mistreatment of our migrants on the other side of the frontier and we have not treated Central American migrants with dignity right here, and worse yet, they lose their lives. That, for the CND, is intolerable. (Nelly Torres 2002)

Asian immigrants are treated in an even more humiliating manner by Mexican authorities. In one instance in 1994, the authorities of a detention center painted the hair of Chinese immigrants, claiming that this would make them more noticeable if they escaped (Comisión Nacional de Derechos Humanos 1997, 42). This type of aggression prompted Soberanes to state the following in May 2000:

> In Mexico the Undocumented are treated as criminals, they are jailed without adequate food and families are separated. . . . [T]he Mexican authorities should make a good example in their territory, not to act the same way that North American authorities behave with Mexican citizens. . . . [W]e must see that the Mexican authorities have a digni-

fied and respectful attitude toward the Central American immigrants. (Enciso 2000b)

Mexicans also suffer from the same kind of extortion and arbitrary detentions at the hands of Mexican authorities when they try to migrate northward. For example, the Mexican army detained forty-eight people from Chiapas as they passed through Oaxaca en route to Tijuana and the border. The army officials insisted that their documents were false (*Notimex* 2001b). Mexican authorities at the airport of Tijuana routinely detain every person of brown complexion who has scant funds on the grounds that they might be Central Americans trying to enter the United States:

> An infallible method used by the Policía Federal Preventiva [Federal Preventive Police—PFP] in the International Airport of Mexico City [is] to detect undocumented people: to interrogate . . . those of brown complexion and with humble aspect. . . . [W]ithout apparent reason, a group of 17 Guerrerenses [people from the Mexican state of Guerrero] were stopped by the PFP, under the suspicion of being undocumented. They were traveling to Tijuana to look for work and alleviate their precarious economic situation a little. The motive: all were brown skinned and were wearing old clothes. (Sevilla 2001)

The detainee is forced to sing a stanza of the Mexican national anthem or answer questions about significant dates in Mexican history to determine whether the person is a Mexican or a foreigner. However, there are many Mexicans who cannot sing a stanza of the national anthem or identify historical dates. Many of Mexico's ten million indigenous people would also have difficulty answering these questions. The government's hunting of Central American immigrants contributes to a melding of xenophobia with racism that leads to serious violations of the human rights of Mexican citizens as well as Central Americans.

There have been important expressions of solidarity from within Mexican society that contrast sharply with the brutal treatment that Central Americans receive from Mexican authorities and criminals. Some local authorities in the southern states of Chiapas, Tabasco, and Oaxaca have aided migrants by issuing false papers and documents. A vivid example of solidarity took place on April 5, 2001, in the town of Tepeapulco in the state of Hidalgo. Members of the INM discovered undocumented people hiding in a freight train near the town of El Hirolo. Before they could detain them, the immigrants escaped with the help of local people, who then hid them in their homes and prevented the police from entering. The representative of the INM, Jorge Luis Mireles, stated: "Those who gave refuge to the Central Americans violated article 138 of the General Migration Law . . . and they would be dealt with by the Attorney General" (*Notimex* 2001c). In the following days, the Central Americans left the homes, furtively made their way along the pathways, and continued their journey. With the solidarity of the local Mexican community, they avoided detention. It is said that they were carrying the image of the Virgin of Guadalupe among their possessions when they left.

Mexicans are aware of the high risks of solidarity with Central American migrants. The government seeks to prevent expressions of solidarity by creating a climate of terror in train stations and other typical stops along the migration route. Mexicans who aid hungry and thirsty migrants face draconian punishments (Alcantara 2003b). The villagers of Tenosique, Tabasco, could be accused of trafficking in illegal immigrants and fined twenty thousand pesos and receive a jail sentence of thirty years if they give food or water to migrants. Domotila Méndez Narváez, a diminutive Tabasquena, realizes the risks and therefore gives aid clandestinely:

> One has fear of the migra (the Mexican migration police) but the migrants are people and they arrive asking for water and something to eat as the coyotes [extortionists of immigrants] have already taken all their money. I give them food secretly.

Her son-in-law did not escape the migra and received a thirty-year prison sentence when he was charged with being a *pollero* for having given immigrants food (Alcantara 2003b).

The third route is to travel by sea along the west coast of Mexico, a highly dangerous route but one that avoids migration checkpoints in Chiapas and Oaxaca, as well as other locations that Mexican authorities frequent. However, many of the boats on this voyage are not seaworthy, so shipwrecks are very common. Also, pirate gangs assault and sometimes sink light craft that come from Central America. Additionally, U.S. and Mexican naval forces collaborate to police and intercept these ships.

The interception of boats in international waters is illegal unless a competent tribunal has authorized it and there has been a flagrant violation of the laws of maritime transit. The United States has not received any authorization to hunt down "boat people" on the high sea. Nevertheless, in clear violation of international law, the U.S. Coast Guard intercepted two ships, the *San Jacinto* and the *Ronaldo*, flying the Ecuadorian flag in international waters in May 2002. They seized the 535 immigrants on board (533 Ecuadorians and 2 Africans) and turned them over to the Mexican marines of PC209 *Guzmán* on the high sea. The commander of the naval sector of Puerto Madero, Chiapas, Rear Admiral Carlos Martínez de Anda, then turned them over to Mexican immigration authorities on May 18, 2002. The Ecuadorians had paid up to eight thousand dollars each to the *chiqueros*, as the traffickers in undocumented labor are called in Ecuador, for the trip, which was to take them to Los Cabos, Baja California, where they would disembark and continue to the United States. They had sailed from the port of Manta, Ecuador, and spent two arduous weeks at sea before their interception. Many had mortgaged their homes to raise the money for the trip (Egremy 2002). There were two similar episodes in February 2002. Patrol boats of the U.S. Coast Guard, the *Boutwell* and *Midget*, intercepted two other boats sailing under the Ecuadorian flag in the same zone of international waters. These boats had a total of 378 undocumented immigrants from Ecuador and three from China. These episodes show the collaboration between the U.S. and Mexican naval authorities in blocking immigration from Latin America to the United States (Egremy 2002).

The minister of foreign relations of El Salvador, Maria Eugenia Brizuela, spoke with the Mexican authorities in February 2002 about the numerous complaints of harassment and maltreatment of Central American migrants in their journey through Mexico. She pointed out that, in January 2002, there were two shipwrecks of Salvadorans, one on January 11 in front of the beach at Cocos in the state of Chiapas and the other some days later in the river of Usumacinta on the border between Guatemala and the state of Tabasco, Mexico. Two people died in each incident and, in the second incident, the bodies of eleven people were never recovered.

The shipwreck of July 2000 near San Francisco del Mar, Oaxaca, where more than twenty-four people died, is a dramatic example of this horror. The story of the only survivor vividly illustrates how hope and

tragedy can combine in these desperate flights toward a new life. Miguel
Juan Francisco was a twenty-two-year-old indigenous Guatemalan from
the village of Sticultaj, state of Huehuetenango.

> [T]his peasant had no familiarity with the sea until the day he de-
> parted on a fragile boat for the North. His life revolved around the
> routine of the coffee harvest and the planting of corn until one day,
> invited by his uncle Hugo Domingo Matías and with the blessing of
> his parents he left for the United States, in search of making some
> money to be able to have a wife. . . . "[W]hen we embarked," re-
> counted Miguel Juan, "I was very scared, it was dark, we went forward
> for some hours, then a wave sunk us, and I held onto a gasoline can,
> and the current took me toward the coast. No one wore life jackets and
> none of my fellow countrymen knew how to swim." (Rios 2000)

In another incident, the bodies of sixty undocumented workers washed
up on the coast of Oaxaca in 1998 (Rios 2000).

The tragedies on the southern border usually involve large numbers,
whereas at the northern border most of the deaths of undocumented
workers are among those in small, isolated groups. The exact number of
deaths is impossible to determine because many "disappear" in their
passage north. The Central American migrants destroy their identity
papers when they cross Mexico to avoid having their undocumented
status discovered. It is difficult, if not impossible, to find out who they are
if they are injured or killed. In July 2002, the director of Central American Resources in El Salvador, a nongovernmental organization (NGO),
reported to an international meeting in Tapachula, Chiapas, that almost
twenty-five thousand Central Americans who were trying to cross Mexico for the United States appeared on the lists of missing persons. There
were ten thousand reports of missing people filed by citizens of El Salvador since the signing of the peace treaty in January 1992 between the
government of El Salvador and the rebel forces. As well, all traces of eight
thousand Hondurans have been lost. Father Ademar Barrilli of the Casa
de Atención al Migrante (Migrant Attention House) in Tecún Umán, has
reported that about six hundred fifty undocumented Latin Americans
were assassinated on the southern frontier between 2000 and 2003 and
that it has not been possible to find out anything about what happened to
another five thousand.

The process of undocumented migration is a perilous one throughout the world. The passage through Mexico or along its coasts has its own distinctive features. The contiguous border of Mexico with the United States has always made it a gateway to the United States and a security concern. The terrorist attacks of September 11, 2001, have magnified that security aspect dramatically. Controlling the border has become a high priority of the United States. This concern has put pressure on the Mexican government to coordinate its efforts of controlling the flow of immigrants through Mexico with the United States. The increasingly U.S.-defined, militarized view of migration is congruent with the violently repressive culture of Mexico's policing institutions.

There are also financial gains made through the process of repression and control, something that has also long been a part of Mexico's policing institutions. The income generated from the migrants through extortion and robbery is significant for the Mexican economy and an important source of income for a variety of Mexican authorities. These journeys are generally financed through great sacrifices by relatives already living in the United States. Each trip costs about three thousand dollars, much of which ends up in the hands of authorities at many of the police checkpoints throughout Mexico. If we estimate that two transmigrants successfully make it to the U.S. border for each one caught and detained, the total of transmigrants that cross Mexico annually add up to four hundred thousand. On the basis of this estimate, we could project that six hundred million dollars are siphoned off annually from immigrants into the pockets of Mexican authorities in diverse payments. And officials at various levels have the possibility of financial gain because all Mexican authorities—civil, police, and military—have the power to detain and turn in any undocumented foreigner to the Mexican migration authorities.

Thus, what has long been a perilous passage has become more so in this age of counterterrorism and an increasingly militarized view of social issues. As discussed earlier, processes of expulsion, attraction, and existing social networks power the migration flow. The attempts to escape misery and repression and find a better life in "El Norte" will continue. But the already perilous passage through Mexico has intensified.

Toward a Conclusion

The Central American presence in Los Angeles specifically and the United States more generally is growing significantly. There is a growing literature on the experience of the new immigrants as well as the factors pushing them out of their homelands. However, there has been a neglect of the perilous passage of Central Americans—and other Latin Americans—through Mexico or along its coast. Mexico has become the gateway and the Mexican state the gatekeeper for entry into the United States. The dreams and hopes of these migrants are often shattered in this middle passage.

Mexico remains the major exporter of labor power to the United States. The Mexican government often pleads for the interests of these Mexican workers and appropriately denounces human rights abuses against Mexican migrants. Nevertheless, various levels of the Mexican government carry out similar abuses against Central American migrants—as well as against indigenous Mexican migrants. Many of these policies and practices of the Mexican state are carried out in cooperation with the U.S. government. The migration process of Central Americans and Mexicans can only be adequately understood if we bring this middle passage into the picture. And the struggle for social justice and an end to human rights abuses against migrants must include a struggle against these policies and practices in Mexico.

As we were finishing this chapter, the Zapatistas issued their first statement ever on these very issues and practices (*La Jornada* 2004). Some of the routes for the migrants pass through Zapatista-controlled areas in the state of Chiapas, which borders Guatemala. In their declaration, the Zapatistas state their opposition to the exploitation of migrants by polleros and by local people who sell food or supplies to migrants. Their policy and practice is to seize the pollero, distribute his money equally among the people being transported, and aid them in planning the continuation of their journey without the polleros. As well, they ban selling food or supplies to the migrants. Rather, they say, as the migrants are poor people like themselves, the people in Zapatista territories should aid them in solidarity.

This could be an important step in the development of links and a common struggle between Mexicans and Central Americans, among whom there has often been suspicion. Although in the past there have been spontaneous community expressions of solidarity in spite of the legal risks, and although local officials occasionally have helped migrants, the most common experience of Central American migrants has been one of exploitation by Mexicans. The Zapatista declaration and practice, some examples of which are described in their statement, offers a strategy of solidarity from below that challenges the practices of the Mexican state, practices that involve widespread human rights violations of migrants. It could also be a step toward wider solidarity between Mexicans and Central Americans in Mesoamerica as well as Los Angeles.

References

Adelson, Naomi. 2001. "La Migra Mexicana." *La Jornada*, Oct. 1. Suplementos de La Jornada.
Alcantara, Liliana. 2003a. "Centroamericanos y Mexicanos son victimas de abusos de autoridades." *La Jornada*, Apr. 13, Sección Estados.
———. 2003b. "Frontera Sur: Discriminación a Migrantes." *El Universal*, Feb. 9, Sección Estados.
Banco de México. 2004. *Informe Anual del Banco de México para el Ano 2003*. México City: Banco de México.
Berrones, Ruth. 2001. "Mueren cinco migrantes en choque." *Reforma*, Apr. 10, Sección Estados.
Brettell, Caroline, and James Hollifield. 2000. *Theorizing Migration Theory in Anthropology*. New York: Routledge.
Cano, Arturo. 2003. "Los mutilados por los trenes." *La Jornada*, Apr. 20, Suplementos de La Jornada.
Comisión Económica para América Latina y el Caribe (CEPAL)/Economic Commission for Latin America and the Caribbean (ECLAC). 2000. *Anuario Estadístico de América Latina*. Santiago, Chile: CEPAL/ECLAC.
———. 2001. *Panorama Social de América Latina*. Santiago, Chile: CEPAL/ECLAC.
———. 2002a. *Informe Económico de América Latina*. Santiago, Chile: CEPAL/ECLAC.
———. 2002b. *La Migración Internacional y la Globalización*. Santiago, Chile: CEPAL/ECLAC.
Comisión Nacional de Derechos Humanos. 1997. "Informe Sobre Violaciones de Los Derechos Humanos de los Inmigrantes en México." México City.
Davis, Mike. 1990. *City of Quartz, Excavating the Future in Los Angeles*. London: Verso.
Egremy, Gonzalo. 2002. "Entrego la armada a 535 ilegales." *El Universal*, May 8, Sección Estados.
Enciso, Angélica. 2000a. "Han Muerto 872 personas desde 1993." *La Jornada*, June 12, Sección Estados.
———. 2000b. "México Trata a Indocumentados como delincuentes." *La Jornada*, May 30, Sección Estados.

Godínez, Marvin. 1999. "Para que amanezcan sueños y realidades." *La Hora*, Sept. 9, Sección Nacional.

González, Maria de la Luz. 2001. "Registran sobrecupo estaciones migratorias." *Reforma*, Apr. 11, Sección Estados.

Guerrero, Claudia. 2004. "Piden explicación diputados al INAMI." *Reforma*, Mar. 25, Sección Estados.

Instituto Nacional de Migración. 1996. "Primera Conferencia Regional Sobre Inmigración." México City.

——. 2002. "VII Conferencia Regional sobre Migración, Comunicado Conjunto." México City.

——. 2005. "Boletín de Estadísticas Migratorias." México City.

La Jornada. 2004. "Leer un video: Quinta parte: Cinco decisiones de buen gobierno," Sección Politica, Aug. 24.

Martin, María. 1999. "La Otra Frontera." Center for Mexican American Studies, Austin, Texas.

Multilateral Investment Fund. 2001. *Remittances to Latin American and the Caribbean from All Sources*. Washington D.C.

Nelly Torres, Diana. 2002. "Reclaman Ataques a Migrantes." *Reforma*, Dec. 17, Sección Estados.

Notimex. 2001a. "Aumenta Número de Migrantes Centroamericanos Asegurados en Chiapas," Apr. 9, Sección Estados.

——. 2001b. "Detienen a Chiapanecos confundidos con centroamericanos," Apr. 5, Sección Estados.

——. 2001c. "Detienen a solo 9 indocumentados en Hidalgo," Apr. 5, Sección Estados.

Pickard, Miguel. 1999. "La Migración en Chiapas y en México," Centro de Investigaciones Económicas y Políticas de Acción Comunitaria (CIEPAC), *Chiapas al Día*, Boletín Número 157, May.

Ríos, Guadalupe. 2000. "Peligroso el camino hacia los Estados Unidos." *La Jornada*, July 17, Sección Estados.

Robles, Francisco. 2002. "Cruel trato a los inmigrantes: organismos de derechos humanos." *La Opinión*, Mar. 4.

Sevilla, Ramón. 2001. "Confunden a Morenos con Ilegales." *Reforma*, Apr. 10, Sección Estados.

Vega, Miguel. 2000. "Desfile de la Independencia Centroamericana: culiman celebraciones patrias." *La Opinión*, Sept. 18.

Villalba, Rodolfo. 2000. "Matan a 4 centroamericanos en Chiapas." *La Jornada*, July 2, Sección Estados.

4 Why Women Migrate

Salvadoran and Guatemalan Women in Los Angeles

Kristine M. Zentgraf

During the decades of the 1980s and 1990s, the Los Angeles region became host to an unprecedented number of Guatemalan and Salvadoran immigrants and their families. Although the migration of Central Americans to the region was not a new phenomenon, their presence prior to this upsurge had been relatively unnoticed by urban researchers, politicians, and social service providers. As the numbers increased, Central American migrants became a visible presence, not simply as individuals, but also as groups that engaged in community formation and facilitators of social change.

Less discussed is the fact that a significant percentage of Central American migrants were women and that prior to the dramatic increase in the 1980s the gender gaps were quite significant. According to 1990 census data, women constituted a significant proportion of Salvadorans and Guatemalans who came to the Los Angeles region in the pre-1950 and 1970–74 periods. In the 1970–74 period, for example, 63 percent of Salvadorans and 60 percent of Guatemalans were women (Zentgraf 1998). This gender gap did not begin to disappear until the upsurge in migration from El Salvador and Guatemala in the 1980s.

Although women may share with men their general motivations for migration—political, economic, familial, or personal—it is logical to assume that these motives may also have gender-specific dimensions and that women's relation to households, families, and the gender ideologies that surround them may have a conscious or unconscious influence on their decisions to migrate.

The gender disparity in the numbers of Salvadorans and Guatemalans who have migrated to the greater Los Angeles region provides an interesting opportunity to examine the motivations and experiences of married and single female migrants. The goal of this chapter is to view women within particular social, economic, and political contexts in an effort to understand how and why they choose to migrate to the United States, more specifically to the greater Los Angeles region. This chapter analyzes, first, how a gender-specific demand for Latina immigrant labor, related to the economic restructuring of the Southern California economy, encouraged the migration of Salvadoran and Guatemalan women in the 1970s and 1980s. Second, it explores the factors that explain why certain Guatemalan and Salvadoran women are more available, willing, and able to migrate, including women's relations to household and families, gender ideologies, and the social context in which migration decisions are made.

Guatemalan and Salvadoran Migration

The forces that shape the size and character of migration flows, push migrants out of their home countries, and pull them to a particular destination are diverse and multidimensional. In the case of Salvadoran and Guatemalan migration, these push factors include declining economic opportunities, the need to escape from political violence, and the desire to satisfy personal needs or resolve personal situations, among others. The pull factors include potential employment or better employment and family reunification.

During different periods, this multitude of larger social processes and individual circumstances combine in different ways and to different degrees to generate migration. During the 1940s, 1950s, and early 1960s, Salvadoran and Guatemalan migrants to California, usually of urban upper- or middle-class origin, came mainly for business or personal reasons. Often they arrived intending to make a short visit—to learn English or visit relatives—but ended up staying when they received job offers or other business opportunities, enrolled in a university, or got married (Chinchilla and Hamilton 1992).

A second wave of migrants, more likely to be middle- or working-class than the first, but still predominantly urban (at least at the time of migration) came as the direct or indirect result of economic changes in Central America in the 1960s and 1970s (Hamilton and Chinchilla 2001). These changes included the expansion of capitalism in agriculture, the relative decline of small- and medium-size family farming, greater dependence on a cash consumer market for daily necessities, and the replacement of home manufacturing crafts and consumer goods by manufactured ones. As a result of these changes, economic opportunities declined and inequality increased. Although these migrants were generally not as well off as those in the first wave, they were still better educated and had more access to resources than the majority of their compatriots back home (Wallace 1986).

Whereas most Salvadorans and Guatemalans who arrived in the United States prior to 1975 presumably came for economic reasons, by the second half of the 1970s many were also escaping the political violence that had begun to escalate. The emergence of armed and unarmed revolutionary groups pressuring for social change in the 1970s was met with violence by military and government security forces. This counter-insurgency war against the armed revolutionary ("guerrilla") groups resulted in attacks on unarmed civilians in urban and rural areas and massacres of village populations suspected of sympathizing with the guerrillas (Hamilton and Chinchilla 2001). By the early 1980s, the United States had become deeply involved in conflicts in El Salvador, Nicaragua, Honduras, and Guatemala, contributing to the increased militarization of the region (Leach, Miller, and Hatfield 1985). A dramatic indicator of this fact is that direct U.S. military assistance to El Salvador went from zero in 1980 to $424 million in the 1981–84 period (Lopez, Popkin, and Telles 1996). The civil war in Guatemala also escalated, indirectly aided by the United States. The relationship between immigration and political violence is evident in the fact that almost one-quarter of foreign-born Salvadorans and one-sixth of all foreign-born Guatemalan immigrants living in the United States in 1990 arrived in the 1980–81 period, when the levels of violence in El Salvador and Guatemala were very high.

Politically motivated migration from Central America continued during the 1980s and into the early 1990s, aggravated by economic instability and decline related to the war. This "new" third wave of immigrants was much larger and more diverse than the one before, and it began to disperse throughout many U.S. locations (in particular, Chicago, Houston, Washington, D.C., Boston, New York, Miami, and New Orleans). Despite this dispersion, California, and the greater Los Angeles region in particular, remained the preferred destination, with over one-half of the foreign-born Guatemalan (59 percent) and Salvadoran (53 percent) population in 1990 (Lopez, Popkin, and Telles 1996). This represented a fivefold increase over 1980, with 300 thousand Salvadorans and 159 thousand Guatemalans living in the area by 1990. Immigration and Naturalization Service statistics estimate that there were an additional 258

thousand undocumented Salvadorans and Guatemalans in the greater
Los Angeles area in 1992 (Lopez, Popkin, and Telles 1996).

The arrival of large numbers of Central American immigrants to
Southern California in the 1980s and 1990s did not, therefore, occur by
chance. Although some Latina immigrant women, particularly Mexicans,
have historically migrated to work in agriculture or garment production
in California, economic restructuring of the greater Los Angeles economy during the 1970s and 1980s created an unprecedented number of
opportunities for Latina immigrant women in garment and electronics
industries and services such as child care, elder care, housecleaning, and
maintenance. Any explanation of migration must include a consideration
of the specific economic, political, and social conditions on both sides of
the border.

Explaining Migration

In individual conversations, immigrants describe the circumstances surrounding their decision to migrate and the manner in which the decision was made with relative clarity. Even in the case of war and political
upheaval many migrants articulate how economic, political, household
and/or personal factors interacted to cause their departure. Depending on their assessment of the sympathies of the listener, however,
they may emphasize certain motives over others in the retelling of the
story (economic over political, or personal over economic factors, for
example) and they may find it difficult or impossible to rank the factors in
importance.

For immigration researchers, the explanations of why certain numbers of people with certain characteristics (age, gender, ethnicity, marital
status, and so forth) migrate to a particular location at a particular time
often involve a complex interplay of individual, household, and macrolevel social and economic forces. Some of these forces may not be visible
to individual actors, yet they provide the larger context for their stories.

Traditional social science perspectives on migration focused on either
an individual's decision to migrate (Lee 1966; Todaro 1976; Borjas 1990)
or on the structural factors that link migration to world patterns of un-
even development (Castles and Kosack 1973; Castells 1975; Petras 1981;
Piore 1979; Portes and Bach 1985; Cheng and Bonacich 1984; Sassen
1978). Over the last two decades, however, critics of these perspectives

have begun to document the importance of the role of social networks and family/household structures in migration, adaptation, and settlement. Despite these insights, the implicit (or explicit) assumption of much immigration research in the United States was that immigrants were typically young, economically motivated males who "paved the way" for family members or who migrated and worked to support families in their home countries. This characterization persisted relatively unchallenged in the discipline of sociology until the 1980s, despite statistics showing women immigrants' predominance in U.S. immigration since the 1930s (Houstoun, Kramer, and Barrett 1984). During the 1990s, feminist scholars began to argue that gender must be a central organizing principle of immigration research (Gabaccia 1992; Grasmuck and Pessar 1991; Hondagneu-Sotelo 1994; Friedman-Kasaba 1996). They argued that at the individual level gendered social realities (different roles and responsibilities for physical and social reproduction) might lead to different evaluations of "costs and benefits." They also pointed to the need to pay explicit attention to gender within households and social networks, as well as within other social processes and structures (production/ reproduction, division of labor, power relations, and so forth).

As Hondagneu-Sotelo (1994) argues, the strength of patriarchal family relations is an important factor in determining which household member migrates, why, and under what circumstances. In the case of Mexican migration to the United States, Hondagneu-Sotelo suggests that patriarchal family relations generally facilitate the selection of males for international migration while restraining the migration of wives and daughters. In traditional Mexico-U.S. migration, men–husbands or young boys—are characteristically the economic migrants who are expected to send money back home while women remain to carry out their reproductive or family related roles. When women do migrate, it is usually for family reunification by joining the male economic migrant.

These same patriarchal relations may favor the rural-to-urban migration of an otherwise un-waged daughter to augment the household's income. When patriarchal family relations weaken, women's migration, especially solo migration, can be expected to increase. Alternatively, women may undertake migration as a path of resistance to patriarchal family ties. Even in the latter case, however, women's migration may be justified to family members who stay behind on grounds of the need to fulfill family responsibilities through greater access to cash income.

Central American Female Migration

As new theoretical approaches for the study of immigration emerged, researchers also began to call for more dynamic methods of study. An overreliance on quantitative data to understand various aspects of migration can result in a conceptualization of migration as a static process. It is one thing to know, for example, that a woman was motivated to migrate for economic reasons, but quite another to understand how she decided to migrate and how this might be related to gender and family structures. Thus, results derived from qualitative analysis can enhance our understanding of patterns derived from survey and census data (Patton 1990).

The goal of this research is to place women at the center of the study in an effort to understand their migration decision-making processes. To this end, a snowball sampling technique was used to interview thirty Salvadoran and Guatemalan women who migrated to the United States in the 1970s and 1980s, and to learn about their motivations to migrate, their premigration experiences, their financial and social resources and networks, and their beliefs about and expectations of the United States. The face-to-face interviews were guided by a predetermined set of questions with enough flexibility in their administration to allow interviewees to influence the order, type, and length of answers. By utilizing an open-ended interview format and allowing women to speak of their lived experiences, the format permitted respondents to construct their own categories and meanings of the topics discussed. The interviews took place at the convenience of the respondents, in their private residences or the homes of friends. At the request of the interviewees, all of the interviews were conducted in Spanish, and ranged in length from one and one-half to three hours. The interviews were tape-recorded and subsequently transcribed and translated.

Politically Motivated Migration

The intensification of the war between the government and the guerrillas in El Salvador and Guatemala in the 1980s is generally accepted as the main reason for the dramatic upsurge in migration to the United States during those years. Despite a widespread stereotype of Latin American women as passive (Chinchilla 1977, 1993; Thomson 1986), women as well as men were combatants in and civilian supporters of the armed revolutionary movement as well as participants and leaders in many unarmed civilian organizations. As such, they were direct as well as indirect targets of the violence, although not to as great a degree as men, who served as the majority of combatants for both sides. Some women suffered persecution as suspected members of right-wing intelligence-gathering organizations (such as ORDEN in El Salvador); others were targeted for their activities on behalf of disappeared relatives, as nuns and lay religious personnel working on behalf of the poor, or as militant market vendors, teachers, and union activists protesting repression and demanding rights. Whereas many women and men were innocent victims of the conflict or indirectly put in danger by their relationships to male family members or boyfriends, many others were social movement actors and protagonists for change.

Not surprisingly, all of the women interviewed for this study who cited political violence as their main reason for migration (ten out of thirty) came to the United States during the 1980s. In some cases, this was after receiving death threats resulting from their own direct political participation. Beatriz, for example, decided to leave El Salvador with her husband after receiving threats because of her association with a revolutionary organization. Others felt (or were told) they were in danger because of their attachments to politically involved or implicated men. As one of my informants observed:

> Even women who know little about their husbands', sons', or brothers' political activity may be targeted with repression as a way of making others pay for the political involvement of the activist or as a supposed deterrent to his further activity. Women who are close to a male who is involved may also be a target but for different reasons, i.e., because of what she might know.

Rene's decision to come to the United States is an example of migration motivated by ties to a family member targeted by political repression. By her own account, Rene never thought about leaving her country, nor did she want to. But Rene came in 1985 after she, her siblings, and her parents began receiving death threats. As she explains:

> The main reason that I came to the U.S. was because my brother was murdered. After his death, anonymous notes began coming to my

parents' house saying that we would all be killed. Because of this fear, I decided to come here, leaving my husband and children in El Salvador.

Similarly, Maria Delores explained that her decision to move her family out of El Salvador came after "death squads" shot at her house "because of my son's political beliefs."

In other cases, the line between personal and political violence is not always clear. Selma, for example, migrated at the age of eighteen because she was afraid of being kidnapped and raped, as was the case with many other young women in her neighborhood. She and her mother made the decision that she should leave the country for her personal safety, despite the fact that she knew only one person in the United States and would have to make the trip alone. When asked who was committing the violence she responded, "I can't really say because I did not witness it, but people said that it was the guerrillas that took them away to be raped." Although a couple of years after this original interview Selma expressed doubts that it was the guerrillas who had done the kidnappings, this fear of violence was significant.

Women who had children also expressed fears that their daughters, in particular, might be the victims of kidnapping and/or rape. Raquel explains her decision to migrate:

[I also came because I was afraid.] . . . I had my little girl that was ten years old and during these times they went into the houses and raped the little girls . . . my cousin was taken out of the house by the death squads in the month of July. . . . Well, from that point, everyone helped me out so that I could come here. They told me to go, to leave. Also, because at times they persecuted an entire family that shared the same name, and so they persecuted everybody. There were people killed in the supermarket and some of them were friends, and then it seemed as if I was just going to funerals. And I worked in the city the year that the mayor was killed, and although I was never threatened, there were certain isolation problems.

Ramona feared that her twelve-year-old son would be "picked up and taken to war." To prevent this, she sent her son to the United States to live with her brother. Shortly thereafter she and her other two other children migrated to be with her son. Milena was motivated to migrate by similar fears for the safety of her children:

It was the soldiers chasing after the young people. I was living practically alone with just my children. I got very scared and in every letter I sent to my sister, who was here [in the United States], I told her that I was scared, I wanted to go. The bombs would explode in the morning when I got up. People would tell you that they had killed an entire family in other towns. They would bury seven people every day. Because of that I became terrorized.

Women in countries such as El Salvador and Guatemala during the 1980s thus may have had very direct political motivations for international migration and may have left their countries with or without their families. Unlike a traditional model, where men are the fighters and women are the unarmed civilians, revolutionary upheavals in Central America in the 1970s and 1980s typically involved and affected a cross section of ages, social groups, and social classes, and women as well as men. But unlike classical political migrations that typically involve whole family units, politically motivated migration from El Salvador and Guatemala during this period often resulted in family separation, with women or men migrating first or with sons of draft age or adolescent daughters being sent to live with relatives in the United States.

Economic and Household-related Migration

Over half of the women in this study (sixteen of thirty) migrated to the United States for what they identified as primarily economic reasons. Belen, who migrated in 1976, for example, "couldn't get a job," and despite having no family members living in the United States migrated alone as a single woman. At the time of migration, Isabel was living with her children, mother, and siblings. Because she couldn't find a job that paid enough to support herself and her children, her "job" was to stay at home to care for her children and siblings while her mother worked. Hoping eventually to establish herself as financially independent, Isabel made the decision to migrate to Los Angeles in search of what she hoped would be better economic opportunities.

Celia decided to migrate to the United States in 1988 after losing her previously successful clothing business. Like a number of women who attributed their migration to deteriorating economic conditions, Celia believed El Salvador's growing economic problems were related to the war. She explains how these problems affected her personally before she decided to migrate:

> Well, I realized that the economic situation in El Salvador was such that the inflation was rising all the time, and I was definitely not going to finish my university studies, and I needed to have some capital in order to start a new business. The money that I had was already running out.

As can be seen in the examples above, economic pressures resulting in migration were not always clearly distinguishable from political and/or familial ones. Raquel, for example, lost her job as the accountant and municipal treasurer for a city in the Guatemalan highlands shortly before migrating. Although Raquel cited unemployment as the main reason for migrating, she also feared for her life because other government workers had been killed. Political instability affected the viability of the national economy, resulting in a damaged infrastructure (blown-up bridges, electricity and water shortages, fragile communication and transportation systems, and so forth) and scared off foreign and domestic investors. Warlike conditions also had effects on local and regional economies, resulting in concentrated pockets of higher-than-average unemployment (Hamilton and Chinchilla 1991).

Household Composition and Migration

In contrast to the Mexican case discussed earlier, migration from El Salvador and Guatemala consists of a high proportion of females, and in this sample, a significant number of women who were single, separated, or divorced at the time of migration. More than two-thirds (thirteen out of sixteen) of those who said they migrated primarily for economic reasons (and over half—eighteen out of twenty-six—when political and economic migrants are combined) were single, separated, or divorced at the time of their migration, and all but two of these had children for whom they were the primary caretakers and economic providers. This trend seems to confirm Hondagneu-Sotelo's (1994) hypothesis that women are most likely to migrate when patriarchal familial ties are weak or nonexistent.

What may be unusual about recent Salvadoran and Guatemalan migration to the United States, if this sample is an indication of trends in the larger population, is a relatively high degree of female household-head migration and family separation in which children are left behind while one or both parents migrate. The perception of this family separation pattern has been confirmed by community informants who worked as social service providers and activists in Los Angeles during the decade of the 1980s. The extent of this female migration pattern is unknown because few large studies, including the U.S. Census, record immigrants' marital status prior to migration. But relatively high estimates for female-headed households in El Salvador (27 percent) (and even higher rates for San Salvador) in the late 1980s (Garcia and Gomariz 1989) seem to support the hypothesis of high rates of migration among unmarried females, especially among those who cite economic reasons as their primary motives for migration. Female-headed households in Guatemala, although not as high, represented 15 percent of all households in the country and 21 percent in urban areas (Garcia and Gomariz 1989).

The combination of a nontraditional household, inadequate economic or emotional support from fathers or partners, and women's responsibilities for children in the context of high female unemployment rates and inadequate wages made migration seem a viable option for many women despite the risks and dangers. Maria Elena, for example, explains that at the time of migration, she had sole responsibility for the material, physical, and emotional support of her child. She, like other women, chose to leave her partner by migrating and had nothing more to do with him afterward. She explains the difficulties that she had with her son's father:

> I left this man, my boyfriend, because he was irresponsible and a drunk. Because of this, I decided to leave him and move here. If I had stayed there, I would never have gotten him off my back. This man made my life impossible.

She continues:

> [T]he problems that I had with the father of my son gave me the strength and will to decide to come here. There were so many economic problems that confronted me that I couldn't take it. Each day it became more difficult.

Similarly, Patricia, who had ended a relationship with her abusive husband, found herself solely responsible for the well-being of her three children:

I always thought that my country, instead of progressing, was getting worse. Every day there was more poverty, and my children were growing, and I thought to myself, how am I going to give a better future to my children? So I had to choose, my country or the United States.

Single women with children could not always assume that aid from their families of origin would be forthcoming. Families did sometimes mobilize to help each other through difficult times by providing housing, food, child care, emotional support, and so forth, but a family's class position might preclude significant amounts of economic aid. Miriam, who worked as a vendor selling "anything that I could" to support herself and her children in El Salvador, described why she came to Los Angeles:

because I didn't have any work, and since I left the father of my children, and I had to see about the best path for my children, [and] because I didn't have anyone to help me. I was alone with my children. Although I had my father, he didn't help me in the economic aspect because he didn't have anything either.

Single women were not the only ones burdened with primary responsibility for their children; married women, too, sometimes were saddled with that burden, including economic support. Mona lived a comfortable life and, by her account, had a good marriage until her husband suddenly stopped bringing his paycheck home. "Instead of bringing the money home, he would spend it in other places," she said. Her efforts to change his behavior were fruitless, and she alone had to provide for her children. Migration, she felt, would provide her with economic opportunities and allow her to draw on help and economic support from her in-laws, who were living in the United States. Eventually, she migrated with her children to the United States, leaving her husband behind.

Married women who migrate with their husbands to provide economically for children left behind may still be saddled with the job of finding care for the children as a condition of their migration. Marta's husband assumed, for example, that it was her (as opposed to their) responsibility to find care for the children (that he approved of) as a condition for her migrating with him without the children. Men who migrate alone, on the other hand, generally do so assuming that the care and maintenance of the household and children are automatically taken care of by wives who remain behind.

In extreme cases, patriarchal authority can manifest itself in familial or gender-based violence (incest, domestic violence, sexual repression, or homophobia), contributing to women's adoption of migration as a survival strategy. In such cases, women may give a socially acceptable account of their migration motives to family and friends and reveal the real motive only to someone they trust to be sympathetic (Arguelles and Rivero 1993). Belen, for example, maintained that she left her country because of economic insecurity but made repeated references to her husband's violent behavior throughout her interview with me. Late in the interview, she connected her husband's violence to her reasons for migration. "A friend encouraged me to come to the U.S.," she said, because "she saw how he was." Arguelles and Rivero (1993) argue that gender-based violence as a motive for migration rarely emerges in superficial discussions of migration motives because stigma, shame, or fear of retaliation inhibit discussions of such issues with friends and family.

Individuals may also use migration as a form of "escape" from gender-based familial and/or societal expectations. Lesbian or bisexual women who feel subjected to rigid definitions of sexuality or women who are bound to traditional expectations (wives, widows, or young daughters, and so forth), for example, may consider migration in an effort to attain more social options and freedoms.

Gender, Immigration, and the Economic Restructuring of Los Angeles

As discussed above, Salvadoran and Guatemalan women typically join the ranks of international migrants primarily out of economic need and/or in search of safe haven, both of which are often gender specific. Their economic need is influenced not only by individual and household circumstances, but also changes in the global economy that affect the kind of work available to them and the wages they can earn in their home country. Equally important, however, their decisions to migrate to Southern California are influenced by the economic and political conditions of the region, which may also be shaped by global restructuring. The Southern California economy has historically maintained a high gender-specific demand for Latina immigrant laborers, employing them, in the 1980s and 1990s, in some of the fastest growing (albeit lower-skilled, lower-paid, and labor-intensive) sectors, in particular, garment, electronics, and services. From this view, the Los Angeles economy is an important pull factor that influences the size and character of female immigrant flows.

Economic restructuring in the greater Los Angeles region has resulted in significant increases in the employment of Latina immigrant women in sectors where they have been historically concentrated (garment and service), as well as inroads into newer labor-intensive industries, in particular, electronics. Guatemalan and Salvadoran female immigrants, in particular, are concentrated in some of the fastest-growing sectors of the Los Angeles regional economy. In 1990, 23 percent of Salvadoran and 18 percent of Guatemalan women worked as operatives (textile machine operators and assemblers), and 44 percent of Salvadoran and 50 percent of Guatemalan women worked in services (preparing food or working as janitors or maids or in private households)(Zentgraf 2001). In fact, these two groups represent 36 percent of all personal service workers and 17 percent of all maids in the greater Los Angeles area (Lopez, Popkin, and Telles 1996).

The apparel industry is a major component of the Los Angeles economy, and until recent declines was one of the largest and fastest-growing manufacturing employers. Between 1975 and 1985, while overall employment in the U.S. garment industry shrunk by 25 percent, in Los Angeles the workforce in the same industry expanded by 20 percent (from about 62,000 to approximately 75,000). By 1994, an estimated 119,400 people held fashion-related jobs in the Southern California region, representing $15 billion of the regional economy (Torres 1995). In 1990, immigrant labor constituted 93 percent of all personnel in the Los Angeles garment manufacturing industry (Light, Bernard, and Kim 1999), up to 80 percent of whom were Latino immigrants, primarily from Mexico but also from El Salvador and Guatemala (Loucky et al. 1994). According to the 1990 U.S. Census, about 75 percent of all garment workers in Los Angeles were women (Bonacich and Appelbaum 2000).

Fueled by the expansion of government spending in defense and aerospace programs, the electronics industries also thrived in Los Angeles at a time when traditional manufacturing was in crisis. In 1968, for example, there were fewer than 20 electronics firms in Los Angeles; by the end of 1984 there were 486 (Fernandez-Kelly and Garcia 1988, 207). This growth trend continued into the 1980s, when Los Angeles County emerged as home to one of the largest concentrations of electronics companies in the nation (Castells 1985). Orange County also became a pre-ferred location for a number of electronics plants, which, along with the aerospace and defense industry, has accounted for an estimated four-teen thousand high-technology firms established since the mid-1960s (Soja, Heskin, and Cenzatti 1985, 7). An estimated one hundred thou-sand Latinas, many undocumented, were employed as low-skilled, low-paid assemblers and solderers, and in a variety of other low-level posi-tions in electronics production in Southern California in the late 1980s (Fernandez-Kelly and Garcia 1988, 266).

Finally, economic restructuring of the Los Angeles economy is also evident in the growth of the service sector over the past four decades. The service sector had its highest rate of increase during the 1960s and 1970s, surpassing employment in manufacturing to become the largest employ-ment sector in the regional economy, a position it had last held in the 1920s (Soja 1989, 197–98). Although relatively few studies describe the role of female labor in this service sector of the Los Angeles economy, there are many indications that Latina immigrant workers comprise a large and growing segment of the workforce that cooks, cleans, and cares for children, the sick, and the elderly, in public as well as in private institutions (such as hospitals and nursing homes), and in private homes. Their labor partially subsidizes that of other working women (particu-larly middle- and high-income women workers with children) and fills a critical underserved area in public and/or private human services that were once performed "for free" by married women and daughters as part of the household division of labor.

Immigrant women constitute the bulk of cleaning crews for hotels and office buildings and engage in a host of other low-wage service ac-tivities destined for the high-income labor market. These include food preparation for specialty shops, sewing and alterations, shampooing, manicuring, and other entry-level beauty and banquet services. In addi-tion, women provide services for the immigrant community itself (baby-sitting, food preparation, sewing, and so forth). According to the 1990 U.S. Census, 20 percent of foreign-born Mexican women, and 25 percent of Salvadoran and Guatemalan women worked in the service sector in Los Angeles (Zentgraf 1998). It is interesting to note that private house-hold employment is and has been more important for Salvadoran and Guatemalan than for Mexican women, with 25 percent of Guatemalan women and 20 percent of Salvadoran women employed here, compared to only 5 percent of foreign-born Mexican women. In 1980, these numbers were similar (Zentgraf 2001).

Female immigrants are not, therefore, an undifferentiated reserve army of labor. In globalized, restructuring economies like Los Angeles, the labor of Latina immigrants is in high demand. Before migrating, Salvadoran and Guatemalan women typically have some understanding that economic opportunities are available and that the labor of immigrant women is actively sought by certain employers. For a poor or working-class Central American woman, employment in the United States (albeit typically low paid and labor-intensive) may be viewed as an opportunity to provide a better life or increased life chances for herself, her children, and/or her family. Thus, when women make decisions to migrate, they are motivated by social, economic, and political conditions on both sides of the border.

Conclusion

Salvadoran and Guatemalan female immigrants to Southern California can no longer be viewed simply as migrants who leave their countries as a result of relationships of economic dependence on a male provider or for the purpose of family reunification. Rather, women must be seen as immigrants in their own right who, whether they migrate as family members or as single women, are responding to gendered social structures, ideologies, and opportunities on both sides of the border.

Patriarchal household and family relations can be one factor that determines if and when female migration takes place. Women may be more likely to migrate when patriarchal family bonds loosen or are absent, as in the case of female-dominated household units, but women may also migrate in spite of strong opposition by male family members. Weak patriarchal bonds undoubtedly facilitate female migration, but in times of economic and political crisis, household relations and structures may be modified by the larger political-economic (macro) context, as well as mediate their effects on individuals. Single mothers who have sole or primary responsibility for their children, for example, may view migration as a viable economic option that, in their eyes, provides them the opportunity to ensure a more secure life for their children than what they could have offered them back home. Finally, women may migrate for individual as well as household-related reasons, and their decisions to migrate may be shaped by gender-specific as well as more general factors.

Women, however, are not simply making decisions to migrate, but they are also choosing their destinations. Here again, gender emerges as an important analytical category. The concentration of Central American immigrants in Los Angeles is no accident. For women in particular, the Southern California economy has offered Latina immigrant women employment opportunities in some of the fastest-growing sectors of the regional economy. They fulfill specific labor demands in a globalized economy and their earnings are typically essential to the survival of their family units (whether a married or single-headed household). The new immigration to Southern California, therefore, must be understood within the context of global economic forces that affect the size, composition, and destination of migration flows across national boundaries to developed countries.

The words and experiences of the women interviewed dramatically illustrate that women are actors and protagonists in the migration decision-making process. This same persona is carried over into their experiences in Los Angeles. In their daily lives as mothers, wives, daughters, community members, and workers, Guatemalan and Salvadoran women not only create lives for themselves and/or their families, but also affect the economies and societies of which they become a part. Despite this, their contributions to and impact on the Los Angeles landscape are not always visible to the general public or adequately acknowledged by immigrant communities themselves. Immigrant men are more likely to be in the public eye and are assumed to be the community spokespersons and representatives as they tend to hold leadership positions in formal organizations such as hometown associations and labor unions. Although often limited by survival and gendered responsibilities (and ideologies), immigrant women are active and essential participants in labor struggles (the day laborers movements, Justice for Janitors campaign, and street vendor campaigns) and in community formation, maintenance, and education. Through activities in churches and community organizations and institutions, immigrant women are involved in campaigns to ensure neighborhood safety, the promotion of health information and education (HIV/AIDS education, antismoking campaigns, and literacy campaigns), and efforts to link other immigrants to social resources and services.

How successful Salvadoran and Guatemalan immigrant women are in this country (or whether they feel that their migration was beneficial) is largely dependent on the economic conditions of the Los Angeles region—something that is largely out of their control. Nonetheless, those who choose migration and survive the difficult process continue to actively shape their own lives, their communities, and the region.

References

Arguelles, Lourdes, and Anne Rivero. 1993. "Gender/Sexual Orientation Violence and Transnational Migration: Conversations with Some Latinas We Think We Know." *Urban Anthropology and Studies of Cultural Systems and World Economic Development* 22(fall/winter): 259–75.

Bonacich, Edna, and Richard Appelbaum. 2000. *Behind the Label: Inequality in the Los Angeles Apparel Industry*. Berkeley: University of California Press.

Borjas, George. 1990. *Friends or Strangers*. New York: Basic Books.

California Employment Development Department. 2000. *Los Angeles County—Occupations with Greatest Growth 1995–2002*. Sacramento: California Employment Development Department.

Castells, Manuel. 1975. "Immigrant Workers and Class Struggle in Advanced Capitalism: The Western European Experience." *Politics and Society* 5(1): 353–66.

——. 1985. "Towards the Informational City, High Technology Economic Change and Spatial Structure: Some Exploratory Hypotheses." Working Paper No. 430, Institute of Urban and Regional Development, University of California, Berkeley.

Castles, Stephen, and Godula Kosack. 1973. *Immigrant Workers and Class Structure in Western Europe*. London: Oxford University Press.

Cheng, Lucie, and Edna Bonacich. 1984. "Introduction: A Theoretical Orientation to International Labor Migration." In *Labor Immigration under Capitalism: Asian Workers in the United States before World War II*, edited by Lucie Cheng and Edna Bonacich. Berkeley: University of California Press.

Chinchilla, Norma Stoltz. 1977. "Mobilizing Women: Revolution in the Revolution." *Latin American Perspectives* 4: 83–102.

——. 1993. "Women's Movements in the Americas: Feminism's Second Wave." *NACLA: Report on the Americas* 27(1): 7–23.

Chinchilla, Norma Stoltz, and Nora Hamilton. 1992. "Seeking Refuge in the City of Angels: The Central American Community." In *City of Angels*, edited by Gerry Riposa and Carolyn Dersch. Dubuque, Iowa: Kendall/Hunt.

Fernandez-Kelly, Maria Patricia, and Anna Garcia. 1988. "Invisible amidst the Glitter: Hispanic Women in the Southern California Electronics Industry." In *The Worth of Women's Work: A Qualitative Synthesis*, edited by Anne Statham, Eleanor M. Miller, and Hans O. Mauksch. Albany: State University of New York Press.

———. 1990. "Power Surrendered, Power Restored: The Politics of Home and Work among Hispanic Women in California and Florida." In *Women, Politics and Change*, edited by Louise Tilly and Patricia Guerin. New York: Russell Sage Foundation.

Friedman-Kasaba, Kathie. 1996. *Memories of Migration: Gender, Ethnicity, and Work in the Lives of Jewish and Italian Women in New York 1870–1924*. Albany: State University of New York Press.

Gabaccia, Donna. 1992. Introduction to *Seeking Common Ground: Multi-disciplinary Studies of Immigrant Women in the United States*, edited by Donna Gabaccia. Westport, Conn.: Greenwood.

Garcia, Ana I., and Enrique Gomariz. 1989. *Mujeres Centroamericanas: Ante la Crisis, La Guerra y el Proceso de Paz*. Vol. 1, *Tendencias Estructurales*. San Jose, Costa Rica: FLACSO.

Grasmuck, Sherri, and Patricia Pessar. 1991. *Between Two Islands: Dominican International Migration*. Berkeley: University of California Press.

Hamilton, Nora, and Norma Stoltz Chinchilla. 1991. "Central American Migration: A Framework for Analysis." *Latin American Research Review* 26(1): 75–103.

———. 2001. *Seeking Community in a Global City: Guatemalans and Salvadorans in Los Angeles*. Philadelphia: Temple University Press.

Hondagneu-Sotelo, Pierrette. 1994. *Gendered Transitions: Mexican Experiences of Immigration*. Los Angles: University of California Press.

Houstoun, Marion F., Roger G. Kramer, and Joan Mackin Barrett. 1984. "Female Predominance in Immigration to the United States since 1930: A First Look." *International Migration Review* 18(4): 908–63.

Kibria, Nazli. 1993. *Family Tightrope: The Changing Lives of Vietnamese Americans*. Princeton, N.J.: Princeton University Press.

Leach, Jim, George Miller, and Mark O. Hatfield. 1985. *U.S. Aid to El Salvador: An Evaluation of the Past, a Proposal for the Future*. Report to the Arms Control and Foreign Policy Caucus, U.S. Congress. Washington, D.C.

Lee, Everett. 1966. "A Theory of Migration." *Demography* 3:47–57.

Light, Ivan, Richard B. Bernard, and Rebecca Kim. 1999. "Immigrant Incorporation in the Garment Industry of Los Angeles." *International Migration Review* 33(1): 5–25.

Lopez, David, Eric Popkin, and Edward Telles. 1996. "Central Americans: At the Bottom, Struggling to Get Ahead." In *Ethnic Los Angeles*, edited by Roger Waldinger and Mehdi Bozorgmehr. New York: Russell Sage Foundation.

Loucky, James, María Soldatenko, Gregory Scott, and Edna Bonacich. 1994. "Immigrant Enterprise and Labor in the Los Angeles Garment Industry." In *Global Production: The Apparel Industry in the Pacific Rim*, edited by Edna Bonacich, Lucie Cheng, Norma Chinchilla, Nora Hamilton, and Paul Ong. Philadelphia: Temple University Press.

Patton, Michael Quinn. 1990. *Qualitative Evaluation and Research Methods*. 2d ed. Newbury Park, Calif.: Sage.

Petras, Elizabeth. 1981. "The Global Labor Market in the Modern World Economy."

In *Global Trends in Migration*, edited by M. M. Kritz and C. B. Keely. Staten Island, N.Y.: Center for Migration Studies.

Piore, Michael. 1979. *Birds of Passage: Migrant Labor and Industrial Societies*. Cambridge, Eng.: Cambridge University Press.

Portes, Alejandro, and Robert Bach. 1985. *Latin Journey*. Berkeley: University of California Press.

Repak, Terry. 1994. "Labor Market Incorporation of Central American Immigrants in Washington, D.C." *Social Problems* 41: 114–28.

———. 1995. *Waiting on Washington: Central American Workers in the Nation's Capital*. Philadelphia: Temple University Press.

Sassen, Saskia. 1978. "The International Circulation of Resources and Development: The Case of Migrant Labor." *Development and Change* 9(4): 509–45.

———. 1984. "Notes on the Incorporation of Third World Women into Wage-Labor through Immigration and Off-Shore Production." *International Migration Review* 18(4): 1144–67.

Soja, Edward. 1987. "Economic Restructuring and the Internationalization of the Los Angeles Region." In *The Capitalist City*, edited by Michael Peter Smith and Joe R. Feagin. Cambridge, Mass.: Basil Blackwell.

———. 1989. *Postmodern Geographies*. London: Verso Press.

Soja, Edward, Allan D. Heskin, and Marco Cenzatti. 1985. *Los Angeles: Through the Kaleidoscope of Urban Restructuring*. Los Angeles: UCLA Graduate School of Architecture and Urban Planning.

Thomson, Marilyn. 1986. *Women of El Salvador: The Price of Freedom*. Philadelphia: Institute for the Study of Human Issues.

Todaro, Michael P. 1976. *Internal Migration in Developing Countries: A Review of Theory*. Geneva: International Labor Organization.

Torres, Vicki. 1995. "Bold Fashion Statement." *Los Angeles Times*, Mar. 12, D1.

Wallace, Stephen P. 1986. "Central American and Mexican Immigrant Characteristics and Economic Incorporation in California." *International Migration Review* 20(3): 657–71.

Zentgraf, Kristine M. 1998. "I Came Only With My Soul": The Gendered Experiences of Salvadoran Women Immigrants in Los Angeles." Ph.D. diss., Department of Sociology, University of California, Los Angeles.

———. 2001. "Through Economic Restructuring, Recession, and Rebound: The Continuing Importance of Latina Immigrant Labor in the Los Angeles Economy." In *Asian and Latino Immigrants in a Restructuring Economy*, edited by Marta López-Garza and David R. Diaz. Stanford, Calif.: Stanford University Press.

5 Economic Restructuring and Labor Organizing in Southeast Los Angeles, 1935–2001

Myrna Cherkoss Donahoe

The southeast region of greater Los Angeles, known as Southeast L.A., is a case study of the relationship between U.S. capitalist development, expansion, economic restructuring, and labor organizing throughout the twentieth century (Donahoe 1987, 1991). This area has served as a microcosm of the economic and industrial changes transpiring in the nation, the workforce, and the labor movement. It has mirrored the developments occurring in other areas of the country, *with important exceptions*. Similarities have included its industrial inception, organizing campaigns, plant closures, and restructuring process. Exceptions have included diversification and the continuance of an industrial base, population increases, and since the 1970s a growing Latino workforce.

Eight cities comprise Southeast L.A.: Vernon, Commerce, Maywood, Bell, Huntington Park, South Gate, Lynwood, and Cudahy. Bordered on the east by the concrete bed of the Los Angeles River and on the west by the Southern Pacific tracks or Alameda Boulevard, Southeast L.A. is a junction between the twin ports of Los Angeles/Long Beach, fifteen miles to the south, and downtown Los Angeles, ten miles to the north. By 1980, it was one of the most densely populated areas in greater Los Angeles.

Since the 1930s, this area has been a center for labor/community organizing. Because the region included diversified manufacturing enterprises, Southeast L.A. has always attracted seemingly endless numbers of workers (Nelson 1983; Scott 1949; Steiner 1981). The area contained all basic industries, such as auto, steel, and rubber, and a multinational workforce consisting of skilled and unskilled men and women, young and old.

Beginning in the 1970s, Southeast L.A.'s population changed from Anglo American with a small percentage of Mexican Americans to a Latino population consisting of Mexican Americans, Mexican immigrants, and a smaller percentage of Central American and Cuban immigrants. This change coincided with a dramatic increase in population. The area's commercial zones were transformed from European American to

Latino shopping centers. The schools' demographics also changed; however, the composition of the administration, curriculum, and faculty remained the same (Soja, Morales, and Wolff 1983; *Los Angeles Times* 1982–87; U.S. Bureau of the Census 1970, 1980, 1990).

During the 1980s, the region underwent an economic restructuring familiar to other U.S. industrialized regions. The area's industrial sector changed from basic to light manufacturing. By the early 1980s the older steel, auto, and rubber plants had all closed and were replaced by garment, food, and plastic manufacturing. The new industries were mainly nonunion, offering low pay and few, if any, benefits. The changes in the industrial sector greatly affected the overall economic and social sectors.

Aging European American males who had been in power for years controlled the political structure. They did not speak Spanish, did not have children in the schools, and utilized few of the services in the region. Since the local governments did not represent or understand their interests, the Latino workforce and residents had considerably less political clout than the Anglo American blue collar workers they replaced.

In the mid-1980s the Latino population became more vocal about its needs and began to challenge the political structure. This was manifested in the struggle against locating toxic waste sites near schools and residential areas. Because Latino community leaders were able to mobilize the populace and call for support from political leaders such as Gloria Molina and Lucille Roybal Allard, they were successful in keeping the toxic waste plants out of their region. Community organizers in the region looked to groups such as Mothers of East Los Angeles and Uno as leadership models. (Labor/Community Strategy Center 1994; *L.A. Village View* 1994).

From a cursory examination of history, it appears that working people and the labor movement suffer endless defeats. But if we dig deeper we discover small but hardy pockets of resistance. These pockets of resistance may not appear to succeed at the moment, but they sow the seeds for larger movements, which in turn build upon their legacy. For decades, workers in the United States have banded together with community organizers, religious leaders, academics, and local politicians to build labor/community coalitions to improve the lives of working people and their communities. Historic examples of these alliances include the Knights of Labor, the Industrial Workers of the World (IWW), and the early Congress of Industrial Organizations (CIO). Modern examples of these labor/

community coalitions are the Southern California campaigns created by Justice for Janitors, Hotel Employees Restaurant Employees (HERE) Local 11, the Drywall Workers, Common Threads, and the Los Angeles Manufacturing Action Project (LAMAP). Latino/a workers, who recognized the importance of learning from labor history to build a better tomorrow, led these modern struggles. A historical analysis of these campaigns reveals that the more inclusive the organizing effort, the greater the potential for creating economically, socially, and politically viable working class communities.

To explain how and why Southeast L.A. is a microcosm of U.S. economic restructuring and labor organizing, this chapter examines the history of the Southeast L.A. communities. It will consider how workers challenged discriminatory practices in Southeast L.A. industries, specifically Bethlehem Steel and General Motors, and then explores the economic restructuring in Southeast L.A., the movement against plant closures, and the Los Angeles Manufacturing Action Project (LAMAP).

History of Southeast L.A. Communities

The area was once home to Native Americans, who were displaced by Californios and other members of Spanish society. They settled on giant land grants, or *ranchos*, bestowed upon them by the Spanish monarchy, despite the presence of the original inhabitants. The Californios became Mexican citizens in 1821, when Mexico won its independence from Spain. What was to become Southeast L.A. was Rancho San Antonio, controlled by the Lugo family until the 1870s. The road from the Lugo home to El Pueblo, downtown Los Angeles, became a major trade route and led to the settlement of the southeast region.

The United States' policy of Manifest Destiny in the 1830s had the intent of unifying the continent under U.S. rule. The United States sought to absorb California, which was rich in natural resources and harbors. After the Mexican-American War in 1848, the United States acquired the entire Southwest, including California. Railroad construction, bargain priced one-way rail tickets, and the lure of cheap fertile land, although titled to the Californios, enticed large influxes of Anglo U.S. settlers to the area.

From 1840 to 1870, Californios began selling parcels of land to bolster their decreasing incomes, which was based on a feudalistic economy. The

Californios were not schooled in U.S. property and tax laws and many of them lost their vast holdings for failure to pay small property taxes. They also began intermarrying with children of Anglo settlers, which did not forestall their financial and political demise, but hastened it. By 1880, the Californios had become a minority surrounded by the influx of Anglo U.S. settlers (Stansbury 1991), and their numbers dwindled to 20 percent of the Los Angeles population. By 1900, they represented 5 percent of the Los Angeles population. The Californios' presence and power declined under the new U.S. government.

The Mexican population began to grow again in the late nineteenth century. The newcomers were workers recruited by the railroads, mines, and agricultural growers. They were excluded from employment in the growing Southeast L.A. industries and from living in the area's communities. Restrictive covenants, forbidding the Anglo residents to sell their homes to people of color, were in place throughout the region until the mid-1960s.

The midwestern European Americans, who came during the land booms of 1880–1920, sought to preserve the small-town setting and social structure of their origins. Their original homes were similar to midwestern one-story bungalows, built upon large lots to support truck farms. Under the political leadership of the U.S. settlers, the small cities quickly incorporated in the early twentieth century to protect themselves from being devoured by their larger neighbor, Los Angeles (Mithers 1983).

The cities that comprise the area fall into three categories. First, there are two primarily industrial cities, one of which is Vernon, with 90 residents but a workforce of 250,000. Vernon is proud of this mix and proclaims through its motto that it is "exclusively industrial" (Vernon Chamber of Commerce 1984). The City of Commerce, with a higher residential population, is modeled after Vernon, but offers more amenities to its residents (*Los Angeles Times* 1982–87). Second, there are five cities that pride themselves on their commercial, residential, and industrial mix: Huntington Park, South Gate, Lynwood, Bell, and Maywood. Finally, there is tiny Cudahy, the antithesis to Vernon, with twenty-five thousand residents packed into a radius of one square mile with no industry to support them. Cudahy is among the poorest cities in the nation, ranked by a 1982 Rand Corporation study to be last among 783 cities of comparable size (U.S. Department of Housing and Urban Development 1982; Cudahy, California 1985).

The cities were predominantly European American until the late 1960s and early 1970s, although Maywood and Huntington Park had pockets of Mexican American residents. There was class stratification among the cities. Maywood's and Cudahy's residents were poorer White workers, similar to John Steinbeck's Okies, and were even designated as such by other Anglo-American residents. Huntington Park and South Gate consisted of mid- to upper-blue-collar Anglo workers. Small business owners and professionals, who catered to the industrial interests, controlled all political structures.

History of Southeast L.A. as a Diversified Industrial Sector

Southeast L.A. has been a major industrial center since the early twentieth century. Employment in the durable manufacturing sector (heavy industry such as steel, autos, and rubber) grew from these early days to the 1970s, and employment in the nondurable manufacturing sector (light manufacturing, such as food, apparel, and plastics) continues to grow.

Southeast L.A. was known as the great underbelly, or less euphemistically, the "armpit" of Los Angeles. This small corner of Los Angeles was reputed by industrialists and urban specialists to be the largest urban diversified industrial sector in the world, next to the Ruhr in West Germany (California Legislature 1982a, 1982b; Special Topics Course 239-01 Members 1981). Located within this small confine was Los Angeles's own Detroit, Pittsburgh, and Akron, all rolled into one. With Los Angeles's celebrated coastline twenty-five miles to the west and twenty-two miles to the south, the area was not cooled by ocean breezes. The residents had to endure poor air quality and withstand the putrid odors emitted by the many plants. However, from the early part of the twentieth century, thousands of Anglo-American workers sacrificed clean air, fresh smells, and ocean breezes for decent-paying jobs in the plants, which enabled them to purchase modest homes and establish economically viable blue-collar communities.

The area is flat and sits in a prime location between downtown and the twin ports of Los Angeles/Long Beach. Since the Los Angeles harbor was developed in 1922, industrialists have found it convenient to transport goods through Southeast L.A. by truck or by rail. The region was also a major railroad junction (Kidner and Neff 1945). In the early twentieth century, tax breaks, free utilities, and land grants were offered by local governments to entice industries to locate in the southeast.

The rubber industry first built plants in this region in 1919. There were four large plants: those of Uniroyal, Goodrich, Firestone, and Goodyear, which made the area second to Akron, Ohio, in rubber production. The steel plants followed when Bethlehem and United States Steel opened their largest West Coast operations there. The auto industry was reputed to be second to Detroit in assembly, with its General Motors, Ford, Chrysler, and Willys-Overland factories. The region quickly became a magnet, attracting workers from throughout the nation, who were assured jobs in one of the many industries (Reuther Labor Archives; Interviews with UAW Local 216 members and USWA Local 1845 members; UAW Local 216 Collection; Pennsylvania State Labor Archives; USWA Local 1845 Collection). Until the 1950s and 1960s the majority of workers were European American, since the industries did not hire workers of color or women. To improve their working conditions and quality of life, the workforce became part of a nationwide union organizing campaign in the 1930s.

History of Early Multiunion Organizing Campaigns

The union organizing drives followed patterns in the rest of the nation. The Los Angeles branch of the CIO was founded in 1938 and shortly thereafter located in a building at the corner of Slauson and Avalon (Interviews with Daugherty 1987–90; UCLA Oral Labor History Project; University of Pittsburgh Labor Archives). Philip "Slim" Connelly was the president of the California CIO and secretary of the Los Angeles branch. Harry Bridges, the legendary leader of the International Longshore and Warehouse Union (ILWU), was the regional director of the California CIO. Jim Daugherty, Utility Workers, served as the last president until the CIO merged with the AFL in the 1950s.

In the 1930s and 1940s, the CIO began a creative and innovative form of organizing called the Dawn Patrol. Organizers would gather at dawn to leaflet and hold rallies at various plants. This was a multiunion campaign, which had ties to the working-class communities. After winning the requisite number of votes to qualify for a National Labor Relations Board (NLRB) election, the organizers would determine, by the type of industry, which union would represent that particular plant. The unions involved were all part of the CIO and represented United Auto Workers (UAW), United Steel Workers (USW), United Rubber Workers (URW), United Electrical Workers (UE), International Longshoremen and Warehousemen Union (ILWU), and Oil, Chemical and Atomic Workers (OCAW), among others. The unions agreed that it was important for all of them to work to organize as many shops and workers as possible and to determine the jurisdictional details later. The effort was community based, as organizers enlisted the support of local businesses, politicians, and community leaders.

A wave of strikes during and following World War II were also coordinated efforts. The CIO unions held mass rallies and picnics in parks around the Southeast L.A. area to publicize their issues and to ensure that workers supported each other. The unions sought to build solidarity across occupational and union lines. During strikes, the CIO locals organized committees to visit workers' landlords, creditors, and utility companies to request moratoriums on rent, bills, and utilities. They solicited the aid of local merchants and religious and community leaders to donate food and to set up charge systems for the workers. The unions were not content simply mailing letters to these people but sent worker delegates to speak with them to educate the public about labor's cause. These activities remained joint efforts involving many workers and unions. They were also training grounds for worker organizers, as the unions strove to create more rank-and-file leaders and politicize workers. The economic outcome of these strikes was to secure union wages and decent living conditions for the workers, who were able to buy a bungalow and perhaps a camper and a boat, and to send their children to college. It was a good life for union workers and their communities flourished for many years (Reuther Archives; Interviews with UAW 216 and USWA 1845 members).

The workers and their communities were predominantly Anglo-American, despite being surrounded by the South Central Los Angeles African American community to the west and the East Los Angeles Mexican-origin community to the north. Although the union leaders were politically astute in many respects, they were Anglo-American males concerned primarily with organizing their counterparts within the plants, and their unionization efforts did not involve organizing women and workers of color, who were excluded from the plants. However, the lessons of multiunion/community organizing for political, social, and economic gains would be continued by organizers in the coming decades. By the late 1940s, labor organizers, although still Anglo, recognized the importance of including workers of color in the industries.

Fighting Discriminatory Practices in Southeast L.A. Industries

Militants and leftists within the various CIO unions in the post-World War II era demanded that companies hire workers of color (Reuther Labor Archives; Interviews with UAW Local 216 members). Economic expansion in the 1950s led to a demand for an expanded workforce, and African Americans and Latinos were hired by many Southeast L.A. facilities.

After the hiring barriers in steel and auto were overcome, upgrading and job placement presented other major obstacles. Workers of color were concentrated in the most difficult departments and positions. Many were placed in dead-end jobs, as indicated in the following examples of work practices at Bethlehem Steel and General Motors.

Discrimination at Bethlehem Steel

At Bethlehem Steel, although Latinos were hired as early as 1946, they were trapped in the dirtiest, most dangerous, and lowest-paying positions. There was not plant-wide seniority. If a worker was located in the Bolt Shop, it was impossible for him to bid on a better-paying job in the Furnace. Also, each department at Bethlehem Steel had different progression lines through which workers could upgrade. Workers could not transfer from one progression to another. For example, the majority of Latinos were located in the Bolt Shop. Although the Bolt Shop was part of the Machine Shop, there were separate lines of progression for the two. The Machine Shop offered cleaner work and higher pay and consisted of predominantly Anglo-Americans (Interviews with USWA 1845 members).

There was a hierarchy of jobs based on ethnicity. At Bethlehem Steel, Anglo-Americans held management positions and all skilled jobs, such as millwright, electrician, and crane operator. Latinos and African Americans were either in labor gangs, the pits of the Furnace, the Bolt Shop, or the Wire Mill. These jobs were lower paying and offered less or no incentive pay to produce more. Bricklaying was the only classification not organized in a hierarchy. This job, located in the furnaces, was especially dirty, dangerous, and not desired by Anglo workers. The majority of bricklayers were African Americans (Stone 1973; Interviews with USWA 1845 members).

Job placement and upgrading is best explained by Cruz "Monty" Montemayor, who was hired in 1946:

> Let me explain how discrimination used to work. They had lines of progression. If you started on the floor in the Furnace Department, you could work from floorman to supervisor. Then, on the crane, you could work from the smallest crane to the biggest crane. Then you had the ladle line of progression and the pit line of progression. Say there was an opening on the floor for a second helper and I was in the pit, I couldn't bid on it. You were frozen in the line of progression until we fought for and won plant-wide seniority; we broke it in the mid-sixties. This is how discrimination worked, because minorities were on certain progressions and couldn't get off. The Bolt Shop was the worst and that's where most of the Chicanos were. They worked hard and couldn't make the money that we did in the Furnaces. (Interview with Montemayor 1981–87).

Likewise, the local union leadership was predominantly Anglo-American and did not reflect the changing workforce until a minority slate ran in the early 1960s (Pennsylvania State University Labor Archives; Inverviews with USWA 1845 Members). By the mid-1960s, 50 percent of the workforce were people of color, but their ability to secure better-paying jobs was thwarted by obstacles to upgrading. A suit filed under the 1964 Civil Rights Act by workers of color was initiated in 1965 charging that these workers had been systematically denied access to more skilled jobs for a ten- to fifteen-year period. Illustrative in cases of such systematic exclusion, this suit dragged on for years, and was never successfully resolved by the time the plant closed in 1982 (*Bratton et al. v. Bethlehem Steel Corp. et al.*).

One of the plaintiffs, Guadalupe Galvan Jr., a millwright, argued in his deposition that:

I put in for my first test (for Millwright C) on September 2, 1969. I was not tested until 11½ months later despite a six-month requirement established by a company union agreement. The test was administered by two whites and was very technical; two parts were blueprint reading and micrometer reading. Millwrights do not have to use micrometers; this task is always given to machinists. A number of white millwrights did not have to take these tests. On June 1, 1971, I put in for another test. I did this again on June 25, 1972. Although there were a number of job openings, the company did not give me another test until July 1974. Other whites were promoted to Class A and B, and I was finally upgraded to C in 1974 and to B in 1975. On September 23, 1975, I put in for an upgrade to Millwright A, a job which I had already filled in on at times. Fourteen months later, in November 1975, I was finally tested. The tests again included micrometer reading and blueprint reading, which is seldom done in the department. Three white men all had less seniority than me and were tested and promoted before me. There were openings during this time because a number of men were promoted. This harassment and unequal treatment and comments go on all the time and have continued right up to the present (Galvan 1982).

There were examples of cross-racial alliances that challenged discriminatory practices. One important struggle involved a coalition of workers fighting to move the Scarfing Yard. This department consisted of mainly African American workers who had to burn and grind defects off steel slabs. It was one of the dirtiest areas in the plant and the workers had to breathe in high amounts of dust and oxides, since it was located near the furnaces. A group of workers that included Anglo-Americans, African Americans, Latinos, and Native Americans joined together in 1969 to demand the moving of the Scarfing Yard. They won over a majority of the workforce to their cause through petitions, rallies, and social gatherings. Charles Bratton, an African American worker who had fought Bethlehem Steel's discriminatory practices for years, used the struggle as part of his campaign for the local union presidency. Bratton won the presidency, but it took ten years to force Bethlehem Steel to move the Scarfing Yard (USWA Local 1845 Collection; Interviews with USWA 1845 members).

In 1975, in another example of cross-racial alliances, Bethlehem Steel workers successfully won plantwide seniority, enabling them to transfer to different departments and to upgrade to better positions. This especially affected workers of color. But, due to the economic crisis, layoffs over the next seven years prevented most men of color from taking advantage of the newly won opportunities before the plant closed down permanently in 1982. Workers of color and women, who had entered the plant beginning in 1975, had the least seniority and consequently were among the first workers to be permanently furloughed. Similar discriminatory hiring and upgrading practices existed at General Motors.

Discrimination at General Motors

Prior to World War II, there was one African American at the South Gate General Motors Plant, and he was a janitor. In the early 1950s, militant UAW Local 216 shop stewards went into the nearby African American and Latino communities to encourage journeymen electricians, carpenters, and plumbers to apply for General Motors positions in response to General Motors' claim that there were no qualified skilled workers of color to fill those positions. General Motors had separate hiring practices for White and non-White workers. For example, it would hire only workers of color who were high school graduates and who had five references. The same restrictions or qualifications did not apply to Anglo-American recruits (Reuther Labor Archives; Interviews with UAW 216 members). This double standard effectively excluded workers of color, despite the union's efforts to challenge the practice.

By 1955, as at Bethlehem Steel, General Motors' high production required an expanded labor force, and it began to hire men of color to meet the demand. Unfortunately, these workers were also placed in the worst departments, such as the Body, Chassis, and Paint Shops. However, Local 216 won plantwide seniority years before Bethlehem Steel granted it, which helped workers of color advance to better positions.

UAW Local 216's leadership, which had organized the plant in the 1930s, included political radicals, who were concerned to break racial imbalances in terms of plantwide job opportunities. UAW Local 216 had a more militant history than USWA Local 1845. The leadership and other workers supported many walkouts led by workers of color in their efforts to win upgrading. In 1975, a bid for the local union leadership, called the All-American Team, was led by a Native American and included a

Chinese American, African Americans, Latinos, and Anglos. This slate, more representative of the changing workforce, included some of the old-time Anglo-American militants (Reuther Labor Archives; Interviews with UAW 216 members).

Throughout the 1970s, there were many General Motors UAW job actions against discriminatory practices. There was an Equal Employment Opportunity Committee (EEOC), but as at Bethlehem Steel, it was ineffective because it could only advise and not make policy. By the time men of color and women were being hired and able to win promotion to better-paying jobs, the plant was on the verge of closing, which led to the loss of all gains. The General Motors and Bethlehem Steel plant closures and relocations followed the pattern of industrial closures and relocations in the United States' Rust Belt.

Economic Restructuring in Southeast L.A.

Ironically, as the civil rights struggles of the 1950s and 1960s finally resulted in high-paid industrial union employment for people of color and women, by the late 1970s and early 1980s the plants began to close or relocate. Although U.S. multinationals had been exporting jobs to Mexico under the *maquiladora* program since the mid-1960s, this pattern intensified in the 1970s. Thousands of workers of color and women found themselves once again in nonunion, lower-paying service or light manufacturing jobs. Some Anglo-American workers were able to retire, since they had been employed in the industries for many years. Other Anglo workers had the economic means to follow jobs to the suburban areas. But others, along with workers of color and women, remained stranded in an economy that faced a job loss of forty thousand high-wage union manufacturing jobs.

Generally, economists and urban analysts have agreed that plant closures were symptomatic of a global economic crisis that began in the late 1960s, but they disagree as to the causes of this crisis (Interview with Magdoff 1986; Magdoff and Sweezy 1981; Weisskopf 1981). One group has contended that the basic industrial sector was being moved offshore in a deindustrialization or disinvestment process as capital sought to move to areas—both industrially and geographically—that offered the highest rate of profit (Bluestone and Harrison 1982; Interviews with Bluestone 1980–81). Other analysts have argued that what was emerging was the elimination of unprofitable industries and the emergence of reindustrialization based on newer, more profitable industries (Etzioni 1980; Rohatyn 1981; *Los Angeles Times* 1982–87). According to a third group of economic and urban analysts (Block 1984; Soja, Morales, and Wolff 1983; Soja 1984; Interviews with Soja 1981–87, R. Morales 1981–85, and Wolff 1981–98), reindustrialization and deindustrialization were occurring simultaneously, both part of a global economic process, defined as restructuring. This last analysis best explains the phenomena transpiring in the United States' industrial sectors, including Southeast L.A. Both reindustrialization and deindustrialization represented U.S. capital's attempt to continue capital accumulation and reverse falling rates of profit.

Restructuring meant that capital was freed by significantly reducing labor costs. Restructuring represented a comprehensive corporate attempt to discipline labor and weaken the organized labor movement, a process already underway for decades (Moody 1988; Brecher and Costello 1989). This translated into plant closures, movement of plants offshore, and permanent layoff for thousand of workers. Gains won in the previous four decades were systematically eroded. Contracts were negotiated over the value of concessions workers were willing to relinquish and a new term *concessionary contracts* was coined (Metzgar 1980; Weisskopf 1981).

Wage decreases in lieu of increases were negotiated. Previously high-paid union workers were happy to keep a job or secure a new job, albeit at a far lower salary, often at half their former level. Two-tier contracts, in which entry-level employees were paid dramatically lower than senior employees, were also negotiated. In this manner, labor costs were significantly reduced, the labor movement was disciplined, and capital was freed for the pursuit of higher profits. Restructuring resulted in increased centralization, concentration of capital, acceleration of capital mobility, and the growth of government subsidies for large corporations.

Plant closures resulted in the majority of previously higher-paid industrial workers descending into the lower-skilled, lower-wage, nonunion reservoir of labor. Restructuring proponents challenged the concept that the United States was in a postindustrial period. They argued that the industrial sector had not been replaced by a service sector, but that the industrial sector itself was being transformed. The industrial labor force was not shrinking, but growing. It was growing in two areas: high technical and nondurable goods. Since these industries were nonunion and low paying, this had the effect of reducing labor costs and freeing capital significantly. This analysis was, in fact, being borne out in Southeast L.A., but this would not be recognized for a number of years.

Many viewed the basic industrial closures in the early 1980s as the end of an era, comparable to the industrial revolution. Analysts, claiming that the United States was moving toward a service economy, failed to see that in place of the durable industries, growth was occurring in the non-durable sector, which included production of food, apparel, and plastics. These manufacturing enterprises were nonunion and low paying, which resulted in a decline of the overall standard of living for the majority of working people. Economic restructuring represented the corporate attempt to eliminate gains and eradicate the progress won after the Great Depression (Moody 1988; Brecher and Costello 1989). Based on a long history of labor/community organizing, Southeast L.A. workers and residents mobilized to resist the newest challenge.

Movement against Plant Closures

In addition to experiencing job losses, Southeast L.A. continued to change demographically. Anglo-Americans began to move further east and south to escape the perceived turbulence of the inner cities, especially after the Watts uprising of 1965. Latinos/as, seeking affordable housing, moved into the region. By 1980, the demographics of the Southeast L.A. cities had changed dramatically. Latinos then comprised 63 percent of Bell, 58 percent of South Gate, and 80 percent of Huntington Park, City of Commerce, and Maywood (U.S. Bureau of the Census 1980).

In the restructuring era, some workers headed for cities with brighter futures, but others stayed to resist change. In the late 1970s, the USW and the UAW spearheaded a movement to forestall additional plant closures/relocations (Californians Against Plant Shutdowns 1983). Aware that plants were closing nationwide and that they, too, were in danger, Southeast L.A.'s union locals began working with community, religious, and local and state government leaders, and with academics to keep the plants open.

Once again, Southeast L.A. was the site of a multiunion effort, not to organize the plants, but to keep them open. The situation was more acute, as men of color and women had finally secured high-paying union jobs in these plants. Consequently, these workers were in the forefront of these struggles. By this time, Latinos played a major role in the leadership of both the UAW and USW Locals. Wilfred "Andy" Anderson was one of the first Latinos hired at Bethlehem Steel and served as Local 1845's president from 1975 to 1982. Al Belmontez, who was hired at General Motors in the mid-1950s, was Local 216's president from 1975 to 1981. Both men were active in challenging discriminatory practices and played leading roles in the antiplant closure movement (Interviews with Anderson 1986 and Belmontez 1986).

On March 1980, workers from the USW, UAW, ILWU, and OCWA Locals formed a multinational labor/community coalition to stop additional plant closures. Workers had already witnessed the closure of U.S. Steel, Ford, and Chrysler plants. A Labor Day march and rally in a South Gate park was attended by four hundred representatives from various unions and community, religious, political, and academic organizations. The local papers reported that South Gate had not experienced as much excitement since the opening of the General Motors plant forty-four years earlier. The movement was predicated on the historic importance of mobilizing both the industrial workforce and the primarily Latino community.

In November 1981, the group calling itself Los Angeles Coalition Against Plant Shutdowns (LACAPS) held a conference to establish a statewide organization, Californians Against Plant Shutdowns (CAPS). The goals of CAPS were to educate workers regarding the causes of closures, to offer them options such as worker community ownership, to strengthen contacts with other such groups, to support direct action campaigns, and to work for statewide plant closure legislation. CAPS established chapters throughout the state, from the depressed Northern California redwood logging regions to the San Diego canneries. Organizers in Southeast L.A. continued to spearhead the movement (Plant Closure Project 1982; Californians Against Plant Shutdowns 1983; California Legislature 1980).

In 1982, CAPS lobbied for a state antiplant closure measure, AB 2839. This bill, introduced in the California Legislature by Assemblywoman Maxine Waters, called for a twenty-month advance notification for reduction of operations for workplaces that employed 500 workers, sixteen months for workplaces that employed 100 to 499, and one year for workplaces that employed 50 to 99. The bill mandated compensation for the furloughed workforce and penalties against companies that failed to provide advance notification. The Assembly Labor and Employment Committee passed the bill by a 6–4 vote in April 1982.

CAPS intensified its lobbying efforts by taking busloads of members and supporters to Sacramento to testify at hearings held by the Assembly Ways and Means Committee, which was to vote on the measure in June. Once again, workers were involved in multiunion activities, such as rallies, picket lines, and press conferences, and in conducting research. Since many of the workers had limited formal education, this was an educational and a politicizing experience that bolstered their self-esteem. They learned that they had far more expertise in labor and community issues than those deemed "experts."

The main demand of CAPS was for corporations to be accountable to the workforce and to the communities in which they were located. Although the Assembly Ways and Means Committee was primarily composed of Democrats, many abstained from voting and the remainder of the committee voted to shelve the bill, effectively burying it (Haas 1985; Interviews with Haas 1994–98).

Within an eleven-year period, 1971–82, most of the area's basic industries closed or relocated. The local paper called 1982 the "year of the plant closures," since ten major steel, rubber, and auto plants closed in that year alone. Residents remembered 1982 as the year the bottom fell out of their local economy. The Southeast L.A. region entered the 1980s with the highest unemployment rate in California. By March 1982, the area had forty thousand unemployed residents. At the end of 1982, the unemployment rate was 15 percent, with a projected figure of 17 percent by early 1983, well over the state and county rate of 11 percent. Thousands more lost their jobs in industries dependent upon and related to rubber, steel, and autos. By 1983, the region, which had always been a microcosm of traditional industrial regions, came to resemble Rust Belt cities more than ever due to plant closures and relocations (Mithers 1983; *Daily Signal* 1982; California Legislature 1982a).

Although CAPS was not able to keep the major plants open, Southeast L.A. union locals continued to build solidarity and educate workers. USWA Local 1845 turned its union hall into a food bank, feeding over ten thousand area families per month. The hall also became a site for solidarity action as workers from throughout the country and the world came to share their stories, learn from each other, and strategize. With the help of a sympathetic theater group, former male steel workers consisting of three Latinos, one African American, one Native American, and one Anglo-American, created their own play, *Lady Beth*. The Theatre Workers Project toured the country, especially the depressed Rust Belt cities, urging workers to band together and rebuild the labor movement. *Lady Beth* was performed on Capitol Hill for hearings regarding federal antiplant closure legislation (*Los Angeles Times* 1982–87; Graumann 1987; *Steelabor* 1986; Interviews with Theatre Workers members and Tanner 1981–87).

Approximately one thousand workers from the closed General Motors South Gate plant transferred to the General Motors Van Nuys plant and offered guidance from their experience, helping to keep that plant open ten years beyond the projected closure date. This enabled the plant's five thousand workers, mainly men of color and women, to receive benefits and education packages when the plant closed (Mann 1987; Interviews with UAW Van Nuys members; Goldman and Mann 1984).

These efforts by Southeast L.A.'s union locals set an example for the rest of the state and for the continuing nationwide struggle to pass anticlosure legislation. A federal law was finally passed in 1988, mandating that corporations give advance notification to workers regarding closures. All these struggles led to unions demanding that anticlosure language be incorporated into collective bargaining agreements. In addition, the solidarity apparent in early organizing activities such as the Dawn Patrol, the multiunion organizing drives, and coordinated strike waves, which had been seen for many years, began to be rebuilt. As meager as it might appear, efforts of working people moving across occupational, union, racial, ethnic, and gender lines broke down the barriers of isolation. This enabled workers to begin rebuilding solidarity in the labor movement on a more political and multinational level.

Southeast L.A. continued to change as durable manufacturing decreased and nondurable manufacturing grew (LAMAP 1994–95; Interviews with Olney 1981–98, Wolff 1981–98, and Haas 1994–98). By the late 1980s and early 1990s, the area was still known for its diversification, but it had become known primarily for light manufacturing, which employed a nonunion, low-paid, mostly Latino immigrant labor force. The area still provided between five hundred thousand and seven hundred thousand jobs. Unlike the experience of the depressed industrial sectors of Detroit, Pittsburgh, and Akron, new global businesses rushed in to take advantage of tax incentives, cheap leases, and the seemingly never-ending supply of immigrant labor in Southeast L.A. A new sweatshop economy developed, with apparel, furniture, and food production in the lead. The Firestone Tire plant became a furniture factory; the Bethlehem Steel plant, a complex where food and furniture is produced; and Uniroyal Rubber plant, a designer label outlet center (Donahoe 1995). Southeast L.A. came to resemble a newly industrializing nation. Labor/community coalitions began to research the area with the goal of creating a new multiunion cross-racial coalition organizing drive.

Los Angeles Manufacturing Action Project

The loss of thousands of high-paying union jobs led to a socio-conomic crisis, which was partially responsible for the Los Angeles uprisings of 1992 (LAMAP 1994–1995). The loss of these jobs seriously undermined the economic viability of the working-class community's social infrastructure and led to dissatisfaction expressed through uprisings. The government responded with the Rebuild Los Angeles agency, a nonprofit corporation launched by Mayor Tom Bradley after the 1992 civil uprisings. It sought to revitalize Los Angeles, assess the needs of low-income communities, and attract job-creating investment (Labor/Community Strategy Center 1993). Although it was clear to some analysts that there was a relationship between low wages and depressed and consequently unstable communities, Rebuild Los Angeles did not recognize this relationship, and consequently did not develop measures to deal with the underlying cause, namely, a lack of jobs that provided living wages.

To counter this ineffective policy, some analysts viewed union organizing as a key economic community developmental strategy. They argued that union organizing would help alleviate the socioeconomic crisis by improving wages, benefits, and working conditions, especially for the thousands who labored in the nondurable industrial sector of Southeast L.A.

A new multiunion organizing campaign called the Los Angeles Manufacturing Action Project (LAMAP) was created based on the analysis that deindustrialization and reindustrialization were both components of economic restructuring. This analysis stressed that Southeast L.A. had been transformed from a region with unionized, high-paying, basic industrial jobs, to nonunionized, low-paying, light manufacturing jobs (LAMAP 1994–95). The industrial transformation had led to a decreased tax base. The infrastructure could no longer support the increased population due to a shortage of decent affordable housing, a substandard school system that operated on a three-track year-round basis, limited medical facilities, deteriorating parks, and declining social services.

LAMAP, created in 1994, included labor, community, religious, and academic leaders devoted to an organizing strategy to upgrade wages and working conditions and significantly increase the living standards of the region's industrial working class. LAMAP received start-up funds from the Rosenberg Foundation and then enlisted UCLA's Graduate Program in Public Policy and Social Research to analyze the potential for organizing in the region. The organizers hoped to involve fifteen unions in a regionwide organizing campaign over a three-year period. The plants organized as a result would provide significantly higher wages and transform poor working conditions. Higher wages would subsequently improve the depressed communities' infrastructures, making them economically, socially, and politically viable.

LAMAP was cognizant of the previous multiunion organizing efforts: the Dawn Patrol, the organizing drives of the 1930s and 1940s, and the 1980s movement to keep the basic industrial sites open. This new grassroots labor community coalition utilized sporting events, parks, and social and political clubs as organizing centers. The organizers discovered that Latino residents lived in clusters and had social clubs based on their geographic origins, and that many were seasoned organizers.

LAMAP determined that nondurable manufacturers could not easily move away from the area, and that these businesses could economically support union wages and benefits. For example, food production plants such as tortilla factories were tied to the predominantly Latino area. Transportation costs were minimal and the industry was economically profitable. LAMAP learned much from the Latino workers, many of whom had vast political and trade union experience in Latin America. In turn, LAMAP sought to empower the workers by training them to apply their experience to the organizing campaign.

The Latino population came to dominate the area. By the early 1990s, the Latino population, principally from Mexico and Central America, comprised 97 percent of the populations of Huntington Park, Maywood, and Bell. Latinos represented 92 percent of Southeast L.A.'s total population of four hundred thousand.

Because Latinos were not highly represented in the region prior to the

1970s, they had not built a strong political or social presence. Many were young immigrants and undocumented. Since they were excluded from the organized labor movement and the electoral process, they maintained a low profile. This was evidenced in local elections. Although by the 1980s Maywood had 25 thousand residents, 85 percent of whom were Latino, a person could be elected to the city council with only 250 votes, since the number of registered voters was low.

The old guard politicos were aging Anglo males who did not represent the interests of the changing community. They were out of tune with the changing demographics. For example, city councils recommended certain summer programs unaware that the schools operated on a year-round schedule. The political leaders voted to build tennis courts, utilized by a handful of Anglos, in lieu of soccer fields, which would have been used by thousands of local residents. The housing shortage and lack of affordable housing was not being addressed. Three families often inhabited three-bedroom homes, garages had been transformed into living units, and in some instances people were hotbedding, or sleeping in shifts in available beds. Although wages had decreased on average, the cost of living had drastically increased (U.S. Department of Housing and Urban Development 1982; *Los Angeles Times* 1985; *Huntington Park Newsletter* 1986; *Industrial Post* 1984–85; Interviews with Bell Realty 1981–89 and Jervis Realty 1981–89).

Although some unions held the mistaken notion that immigrants were fearful and unorganizable, immigrant labor has played a major role in building the U.S. labor movement. In the contemporary era, some of the greatest advances in labor organizing have taken place among Latino/a immigrant workers. Many of these workers were not novices, but had been union leaders and organizers in their own countries and had escaped from death squads and other perils before arriving in the United States. Their home countries were often devastated by U.S. foreign and economic policies and were in the throes of civil war (Olney 1993; Stansbury 1989; Interview with Stansbury 1981–98; Goldberg, Laslett, and Donahoe 1993). Many Latino immigrants, including hotel and restaurant laborers, janitors, drywall workers, and the American Racing Equipment workers, did not wait for unions to approach them, but instead organized themselves. They have set an example for the rest of the labor movement. As illustrated in Maria Soldatenko's chapter in this volume, these labor actions shared common characteristics, consisting primarily of Latino/a immigrant workers who engaged in bold and innovative tactics against large-scale industries.

Until the 1980s, the AFL-CIO leadership supported employer sanctions against the hiring of undocumented workers. This policy severely limited the organizing efforts of unions, which had finally realized the contribution made by immigrant workers to the organized labor movement. Despite the lack of financial support by the AFL-CIO, these unions began making a concerted effort to organize documented and undocumented workers. The newly elected AFL-CIO leadership of the early 1990s opposed employer sanctions and contended that organizing was a priority; it appeared that unionization campaigns such as LAMAP would now receive major support.

LAMAP presented evidence to the AFL-CIO that Southeast L.A. was still the heartland of manufacturing and the residence of blue-collar workers. It demonstrated that by the 1990s over 50 percent of the workforce were Latino immigrants. Many were unorganized, and consequently paid low wages; received no benefits; and labored under hazardous working conditions. Initial research, undertaken by LAMAP, indicated that the new industries could support unionization and still compete in the global marketplace. Southeast L.A. was the perfect location for a multinational, multiunion organizing campaign.

With the full force of capital and the state against them, working people are not always the victors in history. LAMAP, although recognizing the political potential of working people, never could secure the necessary funding from the labor movement to sustain its organizing efforts. Although a newly elected slate of the AFL-CIO leaders claimed that organizing was its number one priority, for unknown reasons it decided not to support LAMAP financially. LAMAP could not undertake the vast organizing campaign needed to turn the region around without the requisite economic resources (Interviews with Olney 1981–98 and Wolff 1981–98).

Coalition members valiantly attempted to do so with the help of a few independent unions, but they also turned their individual energies to other labor/community campaigns. Labor/community activists remain in the area educating the predominantly Latino population to become U.S. citizens to further empower them. In addition, the community has developed environmental justice projects to deal with the havoc left by the factories.

Conclusion

In the early twenty-first century certain areas of the labor movement have remained receptive to organizing efforts despite seemingly over-whelming obstacles. Often, unionizing victories in recent years have been won by Latino immigrants. Many labor and economic analysts maintain that the United States has become a service sector economy, refusing to acknowledge that for the time being capital has succeeded in reducing labor costs, weakening the labor movement, and freeing capital for maximization of profits. Economic restructuring has enabled capital to maintain its industrial base, move much of its durable sector offshore, and develop the highly technical nondurable areas, which employ thou-sands of low-paid, nonunion, primarily immigrant workers. The only limit to capital's power is a strong mass movement fighting for social change. Capital will never willingly relinquish its power or institute a policy to limit its profits on its own (Gurley 1976; Magdoff and Sweezy 1981; Interview with Magdoff 1986).

Maximization of profits involves constant expansion and leads to fur-ther creation of global or multinational corporations as capital seeks new markets and cheaper raw materials and labor. This translates into the selective deindustrialization of traditional basic industries and the selec-tive reindustrialization of high technological and other nondurable in-dustries. This does not represent a break with the basic labor process of industrial capitalism, but, instead, a continuity defined by the entire restructuring process.

The experience of the southeast region of greater Los Angeles illus-trates the process of capitalist development and restructuring and the ways that workers organize for higher wages and better working condi-tions to build economically and politically viable working-class commu-nities. The struggle continues.

Sources

Research on this chapter is based on a wealth of interviews and other archival mate-rial, much of it uncatalogued, in the following repositories. Due to lack of space not all materials consulted have been fully cited in the text.

Pennsylvania State University, Historical Collections and Labor Archives
    United Steel Workers District 38 Collection
    United Steel Workers Local 1845 Collection

University of California, Los Angeles, Oral History Program
    Labor History Project
University of Pittsburgh, Labor Archives
    United Electrical Workers Collection
Wayne State University, Walter P. Reuther Library, Archives of Labor and Union
        Affairs
    Louis Ciccone Collection
    United Auto Workers Local 216 Collection
    United Auto Workers Region Six Collection
    Virgil Collins Collection

References

Block, Fred. 1984. "The Myth of Reindustrialization," *Socialist Review* 73 (Jan.–
    Feb.): 59–76.
Bluestone, Barry, and Bennett Harrison. 1982. *The Deindustrialization of America*.
    New York: Basic Books.
*Bratton et al. v. Bethlehem Steel Corporation, and Local 1845, United Steel Workers
    of America*. 1982. CT. Case No. CV76-2131 AAH, United States District Court
    Central District of California. Mar. 18.
Brecher, Jeremy, and Tim Costello. 1989. *Building Bridges: The Emerging Coalition
    of Labor and Community*. New York: Monthly Review Press.
California Legislature. 1980. Senate Industrial Relations Committee. *Plant Closures,
    Background Material and Proposed Solutions*. Sacramento.
——. 1982a. Assembly Ways and Means Committee. *A Summary of Issues Relating
    to Plant Closures, Job Dislocation and Mass Layoffs*. Sacramento.
——. 1982b. Senate Office of Research. Report by Director Nancy Burt. Sacramento.
    June 30.
Californians Against Plant Shutdowns. 1983. "History of the Coalition Against Plant
    Shutdowns in California." N.p.
Cudahy, California. 1985. *25th Anniversary 1960–1985*. Cudahy, Calif.
Daily Signal. 1982. Jan.–Dec.
Donahoe, Myrna Cherkoss. 1987. "Workers' Response to Plant Closures: The Cases
    of Steel and Auto in Southeast Los Angeles, 1935–1986." Ph.D. diss., University
    of California, Irvine.
——. 1991. *Resolving Discriminatory Practices against Minorities and Women in
    Steel and Auto, Los Angeles, California: 1936–1982*. Los Angeles: Center for
    Labor Research and Education, Institute of Industrial Relations, UCLA.
——. 1995. "Organizing and Reorganizing in Southeast Los Angeles." Paper pre-
    sented at Southwest Labor Studies Conference, UCLA, May.
Etzioni, Amitai. 1980. "Reindustrialization: View from the Source," *New York Times*,
    June 29.
Galvan, Gaudalupe. 1982. Affidavit in *Bratton et al. v. Bethlehem Steel Corporation*.

1982. CT. Case No. CV76-2131 AAH, United States District Court Central District of California. Mar.

Goldberg, E., J. L. Laslett, and M. C. Donahoe, eds. 1993. *Picking Up the Torch*. Los Angeles: Southern California for Social Science and Research.

Goldman, Michel, and Eric Mann. 1984. *Tiger by the Tail*. [Video documentary].

Graumann, Peter. 1987. *Steel Life Drama 1987*. Los Angeles: KCET Channel 28, May 2.

Gurley, John. 1976. *Challenges to Capitalism: Marx, Lenin and Mao*. New York: Simon and Schuster.

Haas, Gilda. 1985. *Plant Closures: Myths, Realities and Responses*. Boston: South End Press.

Huntington Park Newsletter. 1986. Apr.–May.

Industrial Post. 1984–85.

Kidner, Frank, and Philip Neff. 1945. *An Economic Survey of the Los Angeles Area*. Los Angeles: Haynes Foundation.

Labor/Community Strategy Center. 1993. *Reconstructing Los Angeles From the Bottom Up*. Los Angeles: Labor/Community Strategy Center.

———. 1994. *L.A.'s Lethal Air: New Strategies for Policy, Organizing, and Action*. Los Angeles: Labor/Community Strategy Center.

L.A. Village View. 1994. "Concrete Jungle, the Fight Against Toxic Waste and Environmental Justice in Southeast L.A." Dec. 15–22.

Los Angeles Manufacturing Action Project (LAMAP). 1994–95. Collaborative project by UCLA Community Scholars, UCLA Department of Urban Planning graduate students, and Los Angeles Manufacturing Action Project.

Los Angeles Times. 1982–87.

Magdoff, Harry, and Paul M. Sweezy. 1981. *The Deepening Crisis of U.S. Capitalism*. New York: Monthly Review Press.

Mann, Eric. 1987. *Taking on General Motors*. Los Angeles: Institute of Industrial Relations, UCLA.

Metzgar, Jack. 1980. "Plant Shutdowns and Worker Response: The Case of Johnstown, PA." *Socialist Review* 53 (Sept.–Oct.): 9–49.

Mithers, Carol Lynn. 1983. "California and Bust: Laid off in a Company Town." *Voice*, Oct. 14.

Moody, Kim. 1988. *An Injury to All: The Decline of American Unionism*. London: Verso.

Nelson, Howard. 1983. *The Los Angeles Metropolis*. Dubuque, Iowa: Kendall/Hunt.

Olney, Peter. 1993. "The Rising of the Million." *Crossroads* (July/Aug.): 13–15.

Plant Closure Project. 1982. "Building a Grassroots Challenge to Plant Closings." Oakland, Calif., Oct. 20.

Rohatyn, Felix. 1981. "Putting the U.S. Economy Back On Its Toes." *Los Angeles Times*, Feb. 15, sec. 5, 1.

Scott, Mel. 1949. *Metropolitan Los Angeles: One Community*. Los Angeles: Haynes Foundation.

Soja, Edward. 1984. "LA's the Place: Economic Restructuring and the Internationalization of the Los Angeles Region." Paper presented at the Annual Meeting of the American Sociological Association, San Antonio, Texas, Aug. 27–31.

Soja, Edward, Rebecca Morales, and Goetz Wolff. 1983. "Urban Restructuring: An Analysis of Social and Spatial Change in Los Angeles." *Economic Geography* 59 (Apr.): 195–230.

Special Topics Course 239-01 Members. 1981. "A Report to the Coalition to Stop Plant Closings." School of Architecture and Urban Planning, UCLA, winter quarter.

Stansbury, Jeff. 1989. "LA Labor and the New Immigrants." *Labor Research Review* 7, no. 1 (spring): 19–31.

——. 1991. "Immigrant Labor History in Los Angeles and Environs." Unpublished paper.

Steelabor. 1986. (51) Oct.

Steiner, Rodney. 1981. *Los Angeles: The Centrifugal City.* Dubuque, Iowa: Kendall/ Hunt.

Stone, Katherine. 1973. "The Origins of Job Structures in the Steel Industry." *Radical America* 7 (Nov.–Dec.): 19–64.

U.S. Bureau of the Census. 1970. *Statistical Abstract.* Washington, D.C.

——. 1980. *Statistical Abstract.* Washington, D.C.

——. 1990. *Statistical Abstract.* Washington, D.C.

U.S. Department of Housing and Urban Development. 1982. *Troubled Suburbs: An Exploratory Study.* Washington, D.C.

Vernon Chamber of Commerce. 1984. *Facts about the City of Vernon, California.* Vernon, Calif.

Weisskopf, Thomas. 1981. "The Current Economic Crisis in Historical Perspective." *Socialist Review* 11 (May–June): 9–53.

Interviews

All interviews were conducted by the author in Southern California and remain in her possession.

Anderson, Wilfred. 1986. USWA. Apr. 25.

Astorga, Sal. 1986. UAW. Nov. 24

Balanoff, Clement. 1985. USWA. May 2.

Bell Realty. 1981–89.

Belmontez, Al. 1986. UAW. Apr. 25.

Beltram, Pete. 1982–83. UAW.

Bluestone, Barry. 1980–1981.

Brown, Charlie. 1986. UAW. Apr. 21.

Carter, Richard. 1986. USWA. Apr.8.

Chono, Cynthia. 1986. USWA. May 20.

Ciccone, Louis. 1986. UAW. Apr. 16.

Clements, Harold. 1986. UAW. Apr. 8.

Cole, George. 1981–88. USWA.

Collins, Virgil. 1986. UAW. Apr. 8.
Cook, Lewis. 1986. USWA. May 8.
Cunningham, John. 1986. USWA. Apr.30.
Daftarian, Sandy. 1986. UAW. June 8.
Daugherty, James. 1987–90. UCLA Labor Project.
Donahoe, Thomas, 1981–1986. USWA.
Douglas, Martin. 1986. UAW. May 13.
Edwards, Sam. 1986, USWA. May 22.
Franco, Jim. 1986. USWA. May 23.
Garcia, Jesse. 1986. USWA. Nov. 20.
Garcia, Tony. 1986. USWA. Nov. 20.
Haas, Gilda. 1994–98. UCLA and L.A. Manufacturing Action Project.
Hamilton, Gail. 1986. USWA. May 7.
Hamrick, Bruce. 1986. UAW. Apr. 26.
Harris, Rowena. 1986. USWA. May 21.
Hill, Evangelyn. 1986. UAW. Apr. 30.
Hollingshead, Ed. 1986. USWA. May 16.
Jenco, Kelly. 1986. UAW. Apr.
Jervis Realty. 1981–89.
Kendrick, Caren. 1986. USWA. May 15.
LaCour, Bernice. 1986. UAW. Apr. 15
Lai, Collin. 1986. UAW. Nov.24.
Magdoff, Harry. 1986. University of California, Irvine.
Mann, Eric. 1986. UAW. Apr.
——. 1991–95. Labor Community Strategy Center.
Masaoka, Mark. 1982–83. UAW.
Montemayor, Cruz. 1981–87. USWA.
Morales, Priscilla. 1986. USWA. May 21.
Morales, Rebecca. 1981–85. UCLA.
Noteboom, Peter. 1986. UAW. May 21.
Olney, Peter. 1981–98. L.A. Manufacturing Action Project.
Paiz, Hermes. 1981–86. USWA.
Perlmutter, Julius. 1986. UAW. May 14.
Salazar, Ramiro. 1986. USWA. May 1.
Seal, Kathy. 1981–86. UAW.
Sproule, Geneva. 1986. USWA. May 23.
Soja, Edward. 1981–87. UCLA.
Stansbury, Jeff. 1981–98. UCLA and L.A Manufacturing Action Project.
Sulenta, Rudy. 1986. UAW. Apr. 15.
Tanner, Susan Franklin. 1981–87. Theatre Workers Project.
Taylor, John, 1986. USWA. June 4.
Travis, Dorothy. 1986. UAW. Dec.
Underwood, Myrna. 1986. UAW. Apr. 28.
Wolff, Goetz. 1981–98. UCLA and L.A. Manufacturing Action Project.

Part II Settlement and (Re)Constructing Identities and Communities

Father and daughter at La Guelaguetza festival held in Los Angeles, California, ca. August 1998. (Photo by Daniel Melero Malpica.)

6 Indigenous Mexican Migrants in a Modern Metropolis

The Reconstruction of Zapotec Communities in Los Angeles

Daniel Melero Malpica

Artemio López was only ten when he realized he would have to leave his family in San Miguel and migrate to "el otro lado" (the other side). This did not come as a surprise to him. San Miguel is a small Zapotec-speaking village in Oaxaca, an impoverished, largely indigenous state in southern Mexico. Like other villages around this area, San Miguel offered very few work opportunities. His parents, who were subsistence farmers, could barely squeeze a living from their small plot of land. The land that was once rich enough to attract people from nearby villages had turned dry and unproductive, due to eroding environmental conditions. Carrying their few possessions and searching for a better life, men and women have migrated from this rural area to urban and rural areas in the United States because they saw no future for themselves at home. Those left behind are children and the very old. Migueleños (people from San Miguel) have migrated to a mythical place called Los Angeles where it is said there are jobs; one could make a living, prosper, and save money to assist family at home and make possible an eventual return to Mexico.

On his seventeenth birthday, Artemio finally decided that it was time for him to go to "El Norte" to "probar fortuna" (try his luck). Restless and dissatisfied with his lot in life, he informed his family of his intention to migrate. Several of his friends, of the same age, were enthusiastic about the decision and planned the trip together. His mother and other family members tried to persuade him to stay in Oaxaca, to no avail. His father, who had worked on several occasions in the United States during the Bracero Program, gave him the freedom of making his own decision but not without warning him of the dangers and difficulties he would encounter.

A couple of days after his seventeenth birthday, Artemio left his home and headed to Los Angeles. He left alone because at the last moment his friends decided against going. Upon Artemio's insistence, his father called on one of his *paisanos* (a fellow townsperson) and childhood friend, Don Carlos Cruz, who lived in Los Angeles, to send money to pay the *coyote* (professional smuggler) and to assist his son in finding work and getting settled. Three days after his arrival, Artemio found a job with the help of Don Cruz and was working as a dishwasher in an upscale restaurant on the west side of Los Angeles. Artemio also arranged to live with Don Cruz and his family. He paid very little rent and was able to start sending money to his parents and began to pay off his debt to Don Cruz.

The Cruz family treated Artemio like a son and welcomed him into the family. He missed his parents tremendously but was happy with his new life. He received emotional and economic support from his adopted family and from the newly established relationships that he had formed with distant relatives and paisanos who now lived and worked in Los Angeles. In short, upon Artemio's arrival he found himself participating in a rich community life with its own institutions, traditions, and rituals.

Artemio López's story is one I have heard many times. He is among hundreds of thousands of indigenous Mexicans who have left behind their rural roots in search of work in areas throughout the United States. Over the last two decades, as economic conditions in Mexico deteriorated with the crisis of the 1980s, Mexicans have been migrating in large numbers to the United States, not only from the historical-sending states of west-central Mexico, such as Jalisco and Guanajuato, with mestizo populations, but also from new migration streams that include greater numbers of migrants from southern Mexican states, such as Oaxaca and Guerrero, with their indigenous communities (Cornelius 1992; Durand 1998; McDonnell 1998). Indigenous peoples—Zapotecs, Chinantecs, Tarascans, Mixtecs, Otomies, Mayans, Tepehuas and others—have migrated abroad in ever-increasing numbers, and their numbers show no sign of abating (Hulshof 1991; Zabin et al. 1993; Kearney 1996; Rivera-Salgado 1999). Better job opportunities and more attractive wages coupled with severe unemployment at home have encouraged young indigenous people to migrate in search of employment. As a result, indigenous Mexicans have migrated in record numbers and have reshaped Mexican communities in the United States.

This chapter examines the "new" wave of Mexican immigrants—indigenous Mexicans as they adjust and adapt to the United States. It is motivated by the question, How do people conceive of community and work toward effecting its continued existence—to the extent that they do—in a world of movement? The key issue to be addressed is how Zapotec indigenous migrants have constructed and maintained communities consisting of networks of kinship and friendship ties and ethnic institutions in Los Angeles. This chapter forms part of a larger study that seeks to understand the processes and critical factors affecting indigenous Mexican integration into the United States. Integration is understood as a complex process of mutual adaptation of both the immigrants and the host society; it is a dialogical process, which implies two-way communication and mutual adjustment.

This study is based on ethnographic fieldwork within a community of Zapotec migrants living in Los Angeles. The migrants come from San Miguel, a pseudonym for a village in northern Oaxaca, Mexico. I studied this community in part because of the mature development of its social structure. Since the arrival of the pioneer migrants in the early 1960s, the migrants from San Miguel have developed extensive community-based networks (for example, neighborhood, housing, job, and association networks) while maintaining strong social and economic links with their village in Mexico. The data come from in-depth interviews and extensive participant observation. A total of thirty-five in-depth interviews with a socially diverse sample of Zapotec migrants were conducted. The respondents were secured through a snowball sample in which each interviewee was asked to recommend other potential interview subjects. Each interview lasted for at least two hours. To supplement the in-depth interviews, I conducted participant observation research at parties, *bailes* (Oaxacan dances), hometown association meetings, church and community events, and in people's homes. All interactions and interviews were conducted in Spanish.

In recent years, there has been a resurgence of interest in the study of community in the migration literature (for example, Gold 1992; Zhou and Bankston 1998; Hagan 1998). The ethnic community is seen as providing resources that have a significant influence on immigrants' adaptation. Sociologist Alejandro Portes and his collaborators suggest that the social structures of different ethnic communities in the United States offer diverse sources of social capital (Portes 1995; Portes 1998; Portes and Landolt 2000). By social capital, Portes refers to "the ability to secure resources by virtue of membership in social networks or larger social structures" (1995, 12). For contemporary immigrants who have insufficient financial and human capital, social capital—embodied in intra-family, kinship, ethnic ties, and the ethnic community—serves as an important form of capital. Unlike financial and human-cultural capital, social capital is available to all classes of immigrants. It is a form of capital that is spontaneously produced and reproduced within the institutions of the family and extended family group, and through recurrent social exchanges within the immigrant community.

Zapotec migrants in Los Angeles have created their own ethnic communities in response to the double exclusion to which they have been subjected. In addition to racial and ethnic disparagement from members of U.S. society in general—to which other Mexican migrants are also exposed—Zapotecs have to face the additional challenge of their mestizo Mexican compatriots continuing to subject them to equally hurtful forms of discrimination. In response, Zapotec migrants have been forced to establish and rely on their own communities as an essential survival mechanism during the incorporation process. By coming together and seeking community, Zapotec migrants have eased the settlement process through the sharing of social, cultural, and economic resources.

The "New" Mexican Migration: Indigenous Mexican Migration to the United States

Mexicans have been migrating to the United States for more than a hundred years (Massey et al. 1987). For many Mexicans, migration to the United States has become a way of life, a social and economic fact that has had important repercussions in both countries (Bustamante, Reynolds, and Hinojosa 1992). Whereas some migrate with the purpose of seeking a better standard of living for themselves, such as furthering their education or obtaining a better job and opportunities for self-actualization, the majority, especially those from rural areas, migrate to provide their families in Mexico with food and shelter and to maintain their village way of life.

By the early 1960s, with the end of the Bracero Program of contracted wage labor between the United States and Mexico, a pattern of seasonal, circular labor migration had been established. The typical Mexican worker was a young male who had worked previously in Mexico and generally sought employment in unskilled positions in agriculture (Gástelum 1991). Most were of mestizo origin and poor, although not among the poorest who migrated from the rural areas of west-central Mexico, driven by periodic economic necessity and/or desire to accumulate capital for investment in their new home (Reichert and Massey 1980). A large proportion of these migrants made one to five trips in their lifetime, and maintained their family base in Mexico (Reichert and Massey 1980). Despite the termination of the Bracero Program, migrant workers continued to cross the border in search of better opportunities.

Beginning in the 1970s, Mexican migration appears to have changed in major ways. Urban-born, semiskilled workers from Mexico's largest cities began crossing the border to work in the United States, along with unskilled, impoverished indigenous people from some of the most underdeveloped states within southern Mexico, such as Guerrero, Puebla, and Oaxaca (Cornelius 1992; Durand 1998). This recent wave of Mexican migrants has been called the "new" Mexican migration (Cornelius 1992).

Indigenous people form part of the new Mexican migration. Zapotecs, Mixtecs, Tarascans, Chinantecs, Otomies, Mayans, Tepehuas, and other indigenous groups are only the latest addition to the century-old phenomenon of Mexican immigration; they follow in the footsteps of millions of mestizo Mexicans (Cornelius 1992; COLEF 1994). An overwhelming majority of these indigenous people are from the southern Mexican state of Oaxaca (Rios Vázquez 1992; COLEF 1994; Runsten and Kearney 1994). Oaxaca is the largest state in southeastern Mexico. Its population of 3.4 million includes sixteen different indigenous groups, in addition to the mestizo population (INEGI 2000). The state is one of the most ethnically diverse in Mexico.

Oaxaca is one of the poorest states in Mexico (Clarke 2000). Health and socioeconomic indices are among the nation's lowest. Almost one-third of the population is preliterate, compared to 15 percent in the rest of Mexico. The economic backwardness of the state is evident. Most inhabitants are employed in the stagnating agricultural sector (Sorroza 1990).

The harsh socioeconomic living situations that a good number of Oaxacans experience have forced many to move to other places to earn a better living. Several studies have pointed to low income levels in local activities, the insecurity and deficiency of food production, and changing aspirations—all of which have increased the need for cash income—to explain the high rate of emigration from Oaxaca (Kearney and Nagengast 1989; Zabin et al. 1993). Until the 1970s, Oaxacans generally migrated within Mexico to such places as Veracruz, Distrito Federal, Sinaloa, and Baja California (Méndez y Mercado 1985; Nagengast and Kearney 1990; Hirabayashi 1993). Since the 1970s, however, Oaxacans have increasingly opted to migrate to the United States (Zabin et al. 1993;

COLEF 1994). Between 1950 and 1981, Oaxaca rose from thirteenth to third place among states sending migrants to the United States (Rios Vázquez 1993). Indigenous Oaxacans have become a very important Mexican migrant group, and their numbers are growing rapidly (Runsten and Kearney 1994; COLEF 1994).

Of the sixteen indigenous groups that live in Oaxaca, Zapotecs have been one of two that have participated significantly in this migration (the other group are the Mixtecs; see Kearney 1996 and Rivera-Salgado 1999). In 1995, there were 355 thousand Zapotec speakers in the state of Oaxaca (INEGI 1997). However, because of internal migration, tens of thousands of Zapotecs live in Mexico City and northern Mexico, where they may be less apt to acknowledge their indigenous heritage for the census. Moreover, due to international migration, tens of thousands more are not being accounted for in the census. Since the 1970s, Zapotecs have migrated from the central valleys and the highlands in the northwestern part of Oaxaca to cities such as New York, Chicago, and Los Angeles, where they work year-round (Vásquez 1982; Hulshof 1991; Mountz and Wright 1996).

The Village of Origin: San Miguel

Tucked away in the highlands, northeast of Oaxaca City, some fifteen hundred feet above sea level, San Miguel is a typical village of this region. The highlands of Oaxaca has a population of 163,007 (INEGI 2002). It is comprised of the districts of Ixtlán, Villa Alta, and Choapan. The village of San Miguel is a poor, homogenous indigenous Zapotec village in the district of Villa Alta. Although Zapotec is the language of everyday life in San Miguel, many speak Spanish with varying degrees of proficiency. Conditions in most villages in the region are characterized by decades of deforestation and ensuing soil erosion, lack of jobs, poverty, and powerlessness, and a weak infrastructure with poor roads, few telephones, and mediocre formal education and health services (Barabas and Barabas 1999).

The people of San Miguel rely primarily on subsistence agriculture. They cultivate maize, beans, squash, chilies, maguey, and numerous fruit trees. However, peasant farming families have only been able to gain a meager livelihood from their small unirrigated landholdings. Consequently, Migueleños look for wage work in various places throughout the region of Oaxaca and beyond to supplement family incomes.

The first major wave of labor migration from San Miguel started in the early 1930s and lasted until the late 1940s. Young unmarried men and women left the village to work seasonally in Oaxaca City. Women worked primarily as domestics, and men worked in service-related occupations.

The second important wave of migration from San Miguel occurred in the decade of the 1940s and lasted into the 1960s. Although Migueleños continued to migrate to Oaxaca City, a disproportionate number migrated to Mexico City. There was also some migration to the United States in the early 1940s, when some villagers who were living in Mexico City got temporary permits to work in the United States as braceros (Cockcroft 1983). Although the number of Migueleños who enlisted as braceros were few, proportionately they were an important number. Many of them left their village to plant and harvest crops in California and went to labor as far away as Chicago and the state of Washington.

The latest major migration from San Miguel occurred between the late 1960s and the present. The San Miguel population turned to international migration as another means of earning money. While many men and women were working hard for their families in Mexico City, others began to migrate to the United States. In the late 1960s, a small number of young unmarried males migrated from San Miguel to the United States, specifically to Los Angeles, looking for work. They worked in manufacturing and service industries. In the early 1970s, this tight network migration from San Miguel was maintained and became more systematic. There were many low-skill jobs available in the United States (Cornelius 1992), and people from San Miguel and many areas of the highlands of Oaxaca were willing to do this type of work. Migration grew steadily until the mid-1980s, when Zapotec migration to Los Angeles exploded.

Zapotecs in Los Angeles

Los Angeles has become, after Mexico City, the city with the largest number of indigenous Mexicans (Warman 2001). Among the different indigenous groups present in Los Angeles, Zapotecs are the most numerous, numbering as many as 120 thousand; the vast majority are from the highlands and the central valleys of Oaxaca (Hulshof 1991). There are also numerous Mixtecs and Triquis from the Mixtec region and a small number of Chinantecs from the highlands and central valley regions of Oaxaca (Zabin et al. 1993; Hulshof 1991).

Although Zapotecs live and work throughout greater Los Angeles, they are most visible in one of the city's poorest, most diverse areas: Westlake, just west of downtown Los Angeles. The Westlake area is bounded by Figueroa Street (near the Harbor Freeway) on the east, Washington Boulevard (roughly adjacent to the Santa Monica Freeway) on the south, Vermont Avenue on the west, and Temple Street (near the Hollywood Freeway) on the north. A smaller concentration of Zapotecs live in Mar Vista, Santa Monica, and Venice neighborhoods, on the western edge of Los Angeles (Hulshof 1991). Neither of these areas is a traditional Mexican area.

Migrants from San Miguel generally live in Westlake, which is known for its inexpensive housing, ethnic diversity, high crime, drugs, and gang activity. The growing presence of Asians, especially Koreans, in this area is evident in several Korean churches and Korean-owned buildings and stores (see Quinones 2001). In recent years, however, the Oaxacan population has made its presence felt by buying and renting buildings in this area. Oaxacan-owned businesses are burgeoning. In addition to Oaxacan restaurants, other local businesses include travel agencies, money transfer agencies, shops offering long-distance telephone services, and beauty salons.

Despite having a good number of entrepreneurs within its ranks, the Zapotec population in Los Angeles is predominantly comprised of low-skilled laborers. The majority of men and women are employed in low-paying factory or service work.

Formation and Maintenance of a Zapotec Community

Ethnic communities play a vital role in the adaptation of immigrants in the United States. As a link between the old and the new cultures, they provide practical support and guidance as well as a sense of belonging. Grouping in numbers and frequent encounters with one's fellow villagers is reassuring in an alien milieu and helps to maintain self-confidence. The community is a resource, where one can turn for help and for information about jobs, housing, the village, sending parcels, and helping relatives immigrate. In short, ethnic communities offer their members a wide variety of resources.

In Los Angeles, Zapotecs find themselves members of a multiracial and multiethnic society. For such traditional people, the diverse and dizzying world of Los Angeles at first seems incomprehensible. Few have more than a primary education, some speak only limited Spanish, much less English, and only a handful have marketable skills. In addition, Zapotecs face racial and ethnic discrimination from Americans in general as well as from mestizo Mexican immigrants, who deride them for their dark skin, short height, and "backward" culture. Because of cultural and ethnic differences and coethnic stereotyping, indigenous Mexicans do not mingle with mestizo Mexicans; instead they have built their own communities.

Zapotec migrants have formed their own vibrant and mutually supportive ethnic communities. The presence of a large number of family members and paisanos has enabled Zapotecs to establish well-structured communities. By coming together and seeking community, Zapotec migrants have eased the settlement process through the sharing of social, cultural, and economic resources.

By using the concept of community, I do not wish to imply that all members feel a sense of affinity or solidarity toward one another. The divisiveness and hierarchical nature of all social groups also characterizes ethnic communities.

There is no overarching "community" among Zapotec migrants in Los Angeles. Put differently, there is no unitary and homogeneous "majority community" of Zapotecs. Instead, what Zapotec migrants have formed is what Steven J. Gold, in his work with Soviet Jewish and Vietnamese populations in California, refers to as "segmented communities" (Gold 1992, 23–24). Gold noted that despite the image of a highly organized, unified ethnic community frequently advanced in popular and social science literature, he found little evidence of this kind of association during his research. In Gold's own words: "Both Soviet Jewish and Vietnamese populations are marked by diversity in terms of region, immigration experience, religious outlook, ideology, and background. I observed no institutions capable of unifying either of these diverse populations in a meaningful way" (Gold 1992, 24). This is not unlike what I have observed among Zapotec migrants. In the Zapotec case, individuals who come from the same village of origin form these segmented communities. Zapotec migrant communities in Los Angeles are largely extensions of communities in the country of origin. Attention to localized subcommunities probably represents the most viable framework for understanding Zapotec patterns of adaptation.

As in other segmented communities, San Miguel migrants living in the city of Los Angeles have formed a well-structured localized community. How the community is formed and maintained is at the heart of this analysis. Interaction among San Miguel migrants creates a particular dynamic that entails the emergence of specific ethnic networks and institutions, which affect the integration and adaptation processes.

Social Interaction

Interaction is the most basic level of social life, and is the activity that underlies the dynamic aspect of communities. Interaction is conceptualized as the primary basis for a community. Social interaction patterns among San Miguel migrants were observed throughout the fieldwork and many questions were asked of Migueleño migrants regarding their social life, their friends, and their leisure-time activity.

Social life is confined primarily to the family household and the community of fellow migrants. For these migrants, the continuity of social and cultural practices with their previous lives is striking. From the very beginning of my fieldwork one of the most eye-catching features of the Oaxacan communities was the exuberance of their social life. Generally speaking, most Oaxacans would agree that Oaxacans love to socialize, discussing everything from politics to basketball. Social life is centered on visits to each other's homes. In these visits, they eat, drink, and talk of Mexican politics, reminisce about the village, and discuss their hardships in Los Angeles. Through social visiting, Migueleños promote community integration.

More formal visiting and gathering occurs on Sunday, which for most of my informants is the only day of the week that they did not work. Don Baltazar, one of my closest informants, referred to these social interactions in the following way:

> Sundays are for gathering with the people that one cares for. One gets together with the family, with compadres and with friends. Well . . . one invites people so they could come over and eat or one is invited.

At these gatherings Oaxacans are very hospitable and warm. The host always provides food and drink to the guests. The guests never arrive empty-handed to these social affairs. Doing so would be considered improper behavior. Elaborate meals are served, mostly Oaxacan dishes such as *mole* (a sauce blending chocolate, nuts, and rich chilies served over chicken), *cecina* (leg of pork marinated with chile paste, thinly sliced and grilled), *tazajo* (salted beef round thinly sliced and grilled), *quesillo* (Oaxacan string cheese), mescal (the tequila-like alcoholic beverage distilled from local varieties of maguey), and other delicacies suitable for company. As people enjoy food and drink, lively conversation develops.

In addition to weekend visits, Migueleños celebrate birthdays, baptisms, first communions, *quince año* celebrations (debutante parties for fifteen-year-old girls), anniversaries, weddings, patron saint's celebrations, and funerals.

When asked who their friends are, respondents overwhelmingly state that most are San Miguel migrants and other Oaxacans, specifically from Oaxaca's highland region. For instance, Juan Castro, age forty, who came to the United States in 1986, replied eloquently:

All my friends are Oaxacan. Very few are from other parts of Mexico. How can one make friends with people that see you as somebody that is less? I ask myself. It's impossible. They look at us simply as ignorant people. As Indians! They avoid us. . . . We come from worlds that are very different. There is a different mentality, a way of being raised that is different, and a way of thinking and of living that is different.

Margarita Morales, who came to Los Angeles in 1990, described her friends:

I know people from many places. Because I work in the garment industry I meet many people from all over. Salvadorans, Nicas [short for Nicaraguans], Hondurans, Guatemalans, and from other parts of Mexico. But you know, one thing is to have acquaintances and another is to have friends. Almost all my friends are Oaxacan. Believe me I have tried to make friends with others but it is not the same. I prefer to have friends that are like myself.

Even immigrants who have lived in the United States for more than twenty-five years socialize mainly with fellow villagers or Oaxacans. San

Miguel migrants prefer to befriend paisanos or Oaxacans because they like to interact with others who are like "myself," speak Zapotec, discuss social and political events of Mexico, and share common immigrant experiences.

This is not to say that Zapotecs are completely cut off from the general American society and from mestizo Mexican immigrants. Many maintain regular contact with employers, workmates, or neighbors. But my informants consider these contacts superficial, and they do not include these individuals in the inner sphere of social relations. This is different for the second generation. They have much more contact with non-Oaxacans as a result of formal participation in American society, especially in education and the labor markets.

In terms of leisure time, Zapotecs enjoy playing sports, organizing picnics, and attending weekend bailes with paisanos or other Oaxacans. Playing basketball is without doubt one of the leisure activities that Zapotec men enjoy most. This is the most popular sport in the Oaxacan highlands, and in Los Angeles it is just as popular, if not more so. Parks and school playgrounds where Zapotecs live are filled with pickup games among Oaxacans. The popularity of the game among Zapotec migrants has been documented in a cover story in the *LA Weekly* (Quinones 2001). Oaxacan migrants in Los Angeles use basketball as an arena for social gathering by playing against each other and becoming acquainted with other Zapotecs.

Saturday and Sunday private and public evening bailes have also been an important form of entertainment and socializing (see Cruz 2001). The main attractions of these events are Oaxacan music played by a brass band and the dancing of sones and *jarabes*, a representative dance of the Oaxacan Highland region. In addition, there is usually a *banda grupera* that alternates and plays more contemporary *Norteño* (from the north of Mexico) music. The musical selections for the bailes speak volumes for Oaxacan migrants in Los Angeles. On the one hand, Oaxacan migrants want to preserve their culture partly by dancing to Oaxacan rhythms, but at the same time they are being exposed to musical rhythms of the northern part of Mexico (and the United States) and they incorporate this music into their social events. At these bailes, Zapotec migrants eat, drink, and dance into the morning, celebrating the cultural heritage of their native villages.

The bailes are organized by one of the many Zapotec communities. Most of these communities have hometown associations or *clubes* (social clubs) that resemble communal associations in villages of origin. The hometown associations usually plan the bailes. In contrast with the communal organization in Oaxaca, in which participation is mandatory, hometown associations in the city of Los Angeles are voluntary. Due to this fact, the hometown association economy depends on the voluntary participation and financial cooperation of the entire San Miguel migrant community. Thus, the most efficient way to collect money is to organize social events where San Miguel migrants participate. The most popular event is by far the bailes because it is the time to socialize with fellow paisanos and possibly to court a future spouse. Especially for migrants with little or no contact with San Miguel or with their respective villages, these bailes represent opportunities to meet fellow villagers and to pass on the latest news from the village of origin.

Networking in the Community

Zapotecs do not interact with family and friends only for social enjoyment. Social relations represent resources and are necessary for survival. This is more evident when one lives in a foreign land, where the language, customs, and ways of doing things are completely different. Newly arrived Zapotecs are completely unfamiliar with the institutions, laws, and people of the foreign country they choose as their destination. Seeing themselves alone in new surroundings and not being able to interrelate, much less seek help from mestizo Mexican migrants, Zapotec seek each other for support.

Mutual aid through social networks is a significant dimension of communities among Zapotec migrants. Communities with well-established networks provide newcomers with emotional and cultural support and various other practical resources, including aid to realize their coming to the United States, initial housing and food, knowledge of employment opportunities, and general information about U.S. culture and society, and much more (Hagan 1998). In these relationships, migrants and nonmigrants are connected to one another through a dense network of reciprocal social relations that carry mutual obligations of assistance and support.

Social networks are crucial in the adaptation of immigrants to the new society (Massey et al. 1987). These networks help to fill migrants' short-term survival needs upon arrival and their long-term needs as their duration of residence in the United States increases (Boyd 1989; Gurack and Caces 1992). Migrant networks consist of ties of kinship, friendship, and shared community of origin that link people with migrant experience to those without (Massey et al. 1987). Drawing on social ties from relatives and friends who have migrated before, nonmigrants gain access to specific resources, including information, influence, goods, and services (Boyd 1989, 641).

Aid to Migrate

Much of the literature on international migration has shown that the most common source of information for prospective migrants comes from people who migrated before them (Boyd 1989; Gurack and Caces 1992). Among Zapotecs, this is not the exception. Previous migrants provide information that serves as an incentive to migrate and enables people to learn about opportunities abroad. Zapotecs are made aware of job opportunities in Los Angeles through kin or paisanos that have already had experience working abroad. Either through letters, telegrams, phone calls, remittances, or annual visits, people in San Miguel are bombarded by news of kin or fellow villagers living in Los Angeles. Moreover, los Norteños make their presence felt by investing heavily in the village of origin, which serves as a constant reminder of employment opportunities abroad. When asked how she decided to come to Los Angeles, Candelaria, who works as a domestic worker, responded:

> When my cousin left the village I was shaken. I was seventeen years old. As she left I got this urge to migrate north. My older brother already lived there, but it was not the same thing. When I would see my aunt in the village, I would ask her how my cousin was doing over there. She would tell that she was doing well, that she worked for some Americans taking care of their child. . . . After two years, my cousin returned to the village in December and she talked to me how she was doing over there, and the work she was doing and all of the money that she was able to save. Before she left again, she promised that she would help me find work in Los Angeles. And that's how it

turned out. A month later, Juan, my brother, had arrived from Los Angeles to accompany me to the United States. We left for Los Angeles on February the 10th of 1990; I remember as it was yesterday.

Candelaria's cousin came through, as she had promised. With the help of her employer, Candelaria's cousin was able to find her a job working as a nanny with a "good family."

Another of my informants, Pedro Ramos, age fifty-five, recalled how he was told of work opportunities in the United States in the late 1970s. Pedro, who works as a breadmaker, explained:

> My brother and sister-in-law would go to San Miguel during the fiestas of the village and they would tell us how well one could earn money in Los Angeles. They told us over and over that there was work EVERYWHERE! Lupe, my sister-in-law got tired of insisting to Tere and I that we should go and that they would help us find work. During that time I worked in Mexico City, and I was earning a decent income. But when I found out that I was not going to be able to save even half the money my brother and sister-in-law had saved in a year, I thought about it more carefully. I began to ask my brother-in-law all sorts of questions about working in Los Angeles. After considering for a while, we ventured abroad.

Before migration begins, the process is marked by the flow of information from relatives and ethnic networks about the advantages of working abroad (Gurack and Caces 1992, 151). In addition to information obtained through letters, annual visits, and a mystification surrounding the earnings potential that was assumed to exist abroad, the scale of investment in Oaxaca stimulated people to seek the help of their kin and family friends. This kind of influence and support are revealed by Margarito Hernandez, a landscaping worker, who migrated in the early 1980s:

> In the village, we all know that one has to leave in order to progress. It's not easy, but one has to do it. That's how our lives are. My two older brothers already lived in Los Angeles, and they were doing very well. Both worked in a dry cleaner. The oldest, Jeremias, would send money every two weeks to my dad so he could build his house just next to ours. My other brother, the one that is younger than Jeremias—Carlos—also would send money to Dad but he bought a big piece of land for agriculture. He also bought the coolest truck!

I did not want to be left behind, and as soon as I was old enough I came to Los Angeles.

The rise in the living standard among migrants' families and the visibility of material gain evidenced by the remittances and investment assumed a decisive role in the decision-making mechanism of potential migrant workers.

In addition to providing valuable information about working conditions, family and friends already living in the United States were extremely helpful in lending money for the trip. Very few prospective migrants generated the money on their own. The trip to Los Angeles from Oaxaca is expensive due in part to the fee needed to pay for the coyote. All of my informants had to cross the border undocumented on their first trip, and in the process required the services of a professional smuggler. The money needed for covering the costs of the trip is not easily obtained in the village, so the prospective migrant usually is forced to borrow money from family or friends who already live in the United States. Thus, ties with kin and friends who already live in the United States have become even more important as the costs of migration dramatically increase.

Those who serve as sponsors of the new migrants are usually kin, predominantly brothers and sisters, cousins, uncles, and aunts. In my sample, kin were sponsors three-quarters of the time. Paisanos also served as sponsors one-quarter of the time. Such is the case of Artemio López, whose narrative opened this chapter. Artemio was sponsored by a paisano he did not even know but who was a dear friend of his father. Don López and Don Cruz grew up together in San Miguel and were *amigos entrañables* (very close friends). They had migrated together to the United States as braceros. When Don López asked Don Cruz to help his son, Don Cruz did not hesitate to offer as much help as possible. As mentioned in the opening vignette, Don Cruz generously sent Artemio López money to pay for the coyote, recommended a coyote, found Artemio a job, and provided him temporary housing. The money owed by Artemio to Don Cruz was not paid immediately but was paid in convenient installments. For the most part, my informants explained that the money they received was usually in the form of a loan, which they had to pay back once they were somewhat settled and had found a job. This is expected by the community.

Housing

A second form of aid provided to the new migrant is temporary housing and food. When new arrivals migrate to the receiving community, they have a guaranteed place to live for a few months without paying rent. Zapotec migrants understand that the sponsor is socially and financially responsible for the workers they assist in crossing the border. The sponsor will cover their expenses until the newly arrived migrants can afford to support themselves. Other migrants living with the sponsor and the newly arrived migrants must respect this arrangement, and will occasionally offer support. For the most part, housing conditions are crowded; it is not unusual for two or three families to reside together until a new family finds housing on its own. Pedro and Teresa Ramos, whose case was presented earlier, discussed with me their living arrangements in their first six months in Los Angels. Pedro explained:

> When we arrived to Los Angeles, we stayed with my sister-in-law. They were a family of four. They had a boy and a girl and lived in a small two-room apartment. The room of the children was given to us and the two children shared the room with their parents. It was rather crowded, but it worked. In a period of eight months, we had saved enough money to rent our own one-bedroom apartment in the same apartment complex.

Almost all migrants in this study depended on help finding a place to live upon first arrival. Relatives are the most important source of assistance, especially brothers and sisters who take in their siblings. To a lesser degree, but also important, was the assistance that new migrants received from paisanos. The presence of a paisano already in Los Angeles was clearly an important factor in the entry process. My informants described the process in this manner:

> I had a paisano here, and I wanted to take advantage that he was here. I came and stayed with this paisano and soon after I moved to another apartment. (José Gonzalez)

> I knew Job, a paisano of mine, who lived in Los Angeles. He was the only person I knew in the United States. I talked to Job and he was very helpful. He let me stay with him for a couple of months and found a job for me where he worked. (Eleazar Juarez)

With time, new migrants become more established, and they begin to find places of their own. Again, the assistance of previous migrants is likely to be especially important in directing the new arrivals to adequate housing. Many of the established migrants recommend apartments to the new migrants close to where they live, which leads to ethnic clustering.

Finding Work

Social networks are instrumental in finding work and acquiring the basic skill to perform the job (Massey et al. 1987; Powell and Smith-Doerr 1994; Waldinger and Lichter 2003). One of the most remarkable features of the Zapotec immigration story is the rapidity and relative ease by which Zapotecs obtain jobs. It is particularly remarkable because all the informants in this study and all the Oaxacans I have known arrived to Los Angeles without legal documentation. Despite their legal status, Zapotecs found jobs quickly, a couple of days or weeks after their arrival. This was made possible because the social networks provided reliable up-to-date information on the existence of jobs. When I asked the men and women how they had found their first jobs, the remark of Luis Perez typifies the responses:

> My brother got me my first job in Los Angeles. I had just arrived from Oaxaca, and my brother took it upon himself to find me a job. After inquiring at a number of places and asking his friends if they knew of any job openings, he found me a job at the Italian restaurant where he worked as a cook. There I started as a dishwasher, like all of us do, and then I slowly moved up.

In a similar fashion, Petra Flores explained how her friend and *comadre* had informed her of a position in the fast-food restaurant where she worked. In Petra's own words:

> Not only had she informed me exactly when there would be an opening, but she recommended me for the position. She brought me home the application for the job and helped me fill it out. I know that it was because of her that I got the job!

Powell and Smith-Doerr, who have studied the role of networks in finding work, write: "Employers have a compelling motivation not to hire complete strangers; they prefer dependable employees who have been vouched for by others. One way of insuring reliability is to hire new employees from networks that have delivered reliability in the past" (Powell and Smith-Doerr 1994, 374). Indeed, this was the case with Petra Flores's comadre. When I asked why she believed her comadre had gotten her the job, Petra explained that her comadre had worked at the fast-food restaurant for five years and that she was one of the most trusted employees. As a result, the recommendation had much weight.

In addition, social networks play a role in transmitting basic skills to perform jobs (Waldinger and Lichter 2003). Most jobs that Oaxacans perform are low skill, but they still require basic training. This is especially true for those Zapotecs who have migrated to Los Angeles with no previous migration experience. This group is less exposed to urban forms of living and has not undergone proletarization, so they require more advice and training. Even those Zapotec migrants who have lived in Mexico City or Oaxaca City and have acquired urban skills in such fields as construction, mechanics, driving, electronics, and sewing still need to be trained because of differences in such factors as work pace, tools, and language. Typically, the training is provided by the same individual who recommended them. The experiences of Gregorio Ramírez are illustrative:

> A paisano helped me find work. Hipólito Castro, my paisano, knew I was looking for work so when someone quit suddenly at the nursery where he worked, he immediately told his boss that he knew somebody that could fill the position. The boss asked Hipólito if he would be willing to train me, and he gladly accepted. I was trained and supervised by Hipólito.

There are a number of benefits for employers who use social networks to fill their labor needs. Aside from ensuring access to an ample low-cost workforce, employers can count on a certain level of control because the permanent workers can actually control the behavior of those whom they refer (Waldinger and Lichter 2003).

When Zapotecs look for work in Los Angeles, they usually concentrate on a relatively small number of occupations in such businesses as restaurants, dry cleaners, the garment industry, and domestic services. As Felix Ramirez, a dishwasher, noted, "People in our community work in three or four types of work. We work as busboys, dishwashers, or helpers to the chef in restaurants, ironing in dry cleaners, sewing in the garment industry, and as domestic workers and nannies. That's it, it's plain and simple." This concurs with the findings of Portes and Rumbaut (1996) regarding the immigrants' concentration in a small number of branches of employment. When Zapotecs look for work, they do so with the help of kin or friends. Juan Galindo found work "through paisanos in the garment industry. Migueleños help one another tremendously," he stated. When Lucas Gonzalez arrived, he worked for a restaurant that became a stepping stone for a number of Migueleños. Lucas explained: "Many of us worked at [name deleted] restaurant. There it was our first working experience in the United States for many of us. Those who worked at the restaurant would find work for other paisanos. Only Zapotec was spoken in the kitchen [laughs]. I learned a lot there and later on looked for work elsewhere where they would pay me better." Juana Martinez put it best when she noted, "Us Migueleños were taught at the pueblo that we should cooperate among members of the community. This sense of cooperation persists with us in Los Angeles."

Ethnic Institutions

In addition to social interaction and social networks among Zapotec migrants, ethnic institutions are also important in adjustment and adaptation. Among San Miguel migrants, two ethnic institutions stand out: hometown associations and religious institutions.

In the United States, immigrants from Mexico have been known to form hometown associations or clubes (Goldring 1992; González Gutiérrez 1993; Goldring 2002). It is estimated that by the late 1990s, almost 500 hometown associations had been formed by Mexican immigrants throughout the United States (Espinosa 1999). According to Zabin and Escala Rabadan, more than 170 hometown associations from 18 Mexican states were active in 1998 in the Los Angeles area (Zabin and Escala Rabadan 1998). Immigrants from Oaxaca are not the exception; they, too, have formed associations (Rivera-Salgado 1999; Zabin and Escala Rabadan 1998).

Hometown associations are important in facilitating the adjustment and adaptation of Oaxaca immigrants. Associations are typically based on identification with villages of origin, as well as the expectation among migrants that special ties and obligations exist between paisanos.

Migrants from the community of San Miguel have a well-organized hometown association. This is the most important ethnic institution among this community. The hometown association was established by San Miguel migrants living in Los Angeles in 1974. The triggering event was reportedly the reaction of the people from San Miguel in Los Angeles to the death of an elderly woman "who was respected by all." The whole community contributed money to send the body and relatives back to the village in Oaxaca.

Individuals who were among the first San Miguel migrants to settle in this area were quite surprised by the large turnout and by the overall response, and they suddenly realized that the number of their fellow paisanos living in Los Angeles had grown considerably. Only several years before, as one of these early arrivals recalled, the entire San Miguel community in Los Angeles numbered no more than a dozen families, but by this time the local San Miguel population had grown substantially, and there were strong indications that the influx of new migrants would continue. Encouraged by these developments, several individuals decided to create an association that represented all the people of San Miguel living in Los Angeles. This is how the Asociación de San Miguel was created. The association is characterized by the constitution of a ruling committee (*mesa directiva*) comprised of a president, a vice president, an executive secretary, a treasurer, and at-large members. In the case of the Association of San Miguel, no registration or financial contribution is required for membership; eligibility depends only on belonging to the same sending village.

Initially, the Association of San Miguel's main purpose was to concentrate on sponsoring projects for the village of origin. Many projects have been accomplished throughout the years, including the building and repair of major roads and streets, building appropriate infrastructure to provide water for the agricultural lands, donating different vehicles for agricultural work (one vehicle was worth thirty thousand dollars), constructing a factory that makes *tabiques* (blocks), and remodeling the town's church.

Over the years, the hometown association has gone through several stages of development. It has moved from primarily focusing on sending money for the improvement of the village to paying more attention to the needs of the community in Los Angeles. Some of the new goals include fostering a sense of community among San Miguel migrants in

Los Angeles, preserving Zapotec culture, and providing mutual aid and support among paisanos in Los Angeles. By the mid-1980s, the Association of San Miguel had subdivided into several groups based on different perceptions of their new goals. One group is devoted to athletics (for example, basketball, volleyball, and soccer). Another group is involved in cultural activities with their members (for instance, the *grupo folklórico*). A third group is responsible for an after-school program for young children. Lastly, a committee was organized to collect funds to send back the bodies of members of the San Miguel migrant community who die in the United States.

The Roman Catholic Church is an important ethnic institution among the San Miguel community in Los Angeles. Saint Anne's Church in Santa Monica and Saint Paul's and Saint Cecilia Churches in mid-Los Angeles serve indigenous Mexican migrants. Many Zapotec migrants visit one of these churches on a regular basis to pray and to receive moral support. Zapotec migrants may be married and have their U.S.-born children baptized there, and the church basement or halls are available for hometown association meetings. There are also prayer groups formed predominantly of Zapotec migrants.

Of all the Roman Catholic churches, Saint Cecilia is the most committed to Zapotec migrants. It is located on Normandie Avenue in mid-Los Angeles, and Zapotecs have adopted "Santa Cecilia" as "nuestra iglesia" (our church). It is common to hear mass accompanied by an Oaxacan brass band and patron saint festivals celebrated and Oaxacan food served after the services.

The consolidation of Saint Cecilia's as the preferred church among the Zapotecs in Los Angeles occurred in 2002 as a replica of the image of the Virgen de la Candelaria, the patron saint of all Oaxacans, was brought from Mexico and installed in the atrium of the church. This was made possible by the hard work of a group of Zapotec parishioners and the main priest of the church. I have known Zapotecs living as far away as one hundred miles who have come to this church to attend mass.

Saturday and Sunday masses at Saint Cecilia assemble large numbers of Zapotec people who come to pray and meet friends and paisanos, and some even do business. They may exchange information about available jobs, a house/apartment or rooms for rent, and information about who might leave to the village to send some money to relatives. Hence, the church does not satisfy exclusively religious needs. It acts as a communication hub—an information and meeting center. Zapotec migrants see the church as one of the few institutions where they are welcomed and respected.

Conclusion

As indigenous Zapotecs adapt to living in Los Angeles, they are confronted with the combined stresses of migration and discrimination from Americans and mestizo Mexicans. Unable to integrate into any of the mestizo Mexican communities in Los Angeles, Zapotec migrants have formed their own, emphasizing their difference and otherness. They have done so by constructing their own vibrant ethnic communities. The community that Migueleño migrants have formed offers them social capital that provides resources—economic, social, and cultural—to ease their transition and facilitate their adaptation to an alien environment.

References

Barabas, Alicia M., and Miguel A. Barabas. 1999. *Configuraciones Étnicas en Oaxaca: Perspectivos Etnográficas Para las Autonomías*. Mexico, D.F.: Instituto Nacional Indigenija.

Bartolomé, Miguel A., and Alicia M. Barabas. 1986. "Los Migrantes Étnicos de Oaxaca." *México Indígena* 13(2): 23–25.

Boyd, Monica. 1989 "Family and Personal Networks in International Migration: Recent Developments and New Agendas." *International Migration Review* 23:638–70.

Bustamante, Jorge, Clark W. Reynolds, and Raúl H. Hinojosa. 1992. *U.S.-Mexico Relations: Labor Market Interdependence*. Stanford, Calif.: Stanford University Press.

Clarke, Colin G. 2000. Class, *Ethnicity, and Community in Southern Mexico: Oaxaca's Peasantries*. New York: Oxford University Press.

Cockcroft, James D. 1983. *Mexico: Class Formation, Capital Accumulation, and the State*. New York: Monthly Review Press.

Colegio de La Frontera Norte (COLEF). 1994. *Estado Actual de la Migracion Interna e Internacional de los Oriondos del Estado de Oaxaca*. Tijuana, Mexico: COLEF.

Cornelius, Wayne. 1992. "From Sojourners to Settlers: The Changing Profile of Mexican Immigration to the United States." In *U.S.-Mexico Relations: Labor Market Interdependence*, edited by J. A. Bustamante, C. W. Reynolds, and R. A. Hinojosa Ojeda. Stanford, Calif.: Stanford University Press.

Cruz, Adriana. 2001. "Performance, Ethnicity, and Migration: Dance and Music in the Continuation of Ethnic Identity among Zapotecs from the Oaxacan Highland Village of Villa Hidalgo." Master's thesis, University of California at Los Angeles.

Durand, Jorge. 1998. "Nuevas Regiones Migratorias?" In *Población, Desarrollo y Globalización. V. Reunion de Investagación Socio-Demografica en Mexico,* edited by René Zenteno. Mexico, D.F.; Tijuana, B.C.: Somede-COLEF.

Espinosa, Victor. 1999. "La Federación de Clubes de Michoacan en Illinois." Report of the Chicago-Michoacan Project, Working Draft No. 2. Heartland Alliance for Human Needs and Human Rights, Chicago, Ill.

Gástelum, M. 1991. *La Migracion de los Trabajadores Mexicanos Indocumentados a los Estados Unidos.* Mexico, D.F.: Universidad Nacional Autónoma de Mexico.

Gold, Steven J. 1992. *Refugee Communities: A Comparative Field Study.* Newbury Park, Calif.: Sage.

Goldring, Luin. 1992. "Diversity and Community in Transnational Migration: A Comparative Study of Two Mexico U.S. Migrant Communities." Ph.D. diss., Cornell University.

———. 2002. "The Mexican State and Transmigration Organizations: Negotiating the Boundaries of Membership and Participation." *Latin American Research Review* 37(3): 55–99.

González Gutiérrez, Carlos. 1993. "The Mexican Diaspora in California: The Limits and Possibilities of the Mexican Government." In *The California-Mexico Connection,* edited by Abraham Lowenthal and Catrina Burgess. Stanford, Calif.: Stanford University Press.

Gurack, D., and F. Caces. 1992. "Migration Networks and the Shaping of Migration Systems." In *International Migration Systems: A Global Approach,* edited by M. Kritz, L. Lean Lim, and H. Zlotnick. Oxford: Clarendon Press.

Hagan, Jaqueline. 1994. *Deciding to Be Legal. A Maya Community in Houston.* Philadelphia: Temple University Press.

———. 1998. "Social Networks, Gender, and Immigrant Incorporation." *American Sociological Review* 63(1):55–67.

Hirabayashi, Lane. 1993. *Cultural Capital: Mountain Zapotec Migrant Associations in Mexico City.* Tucson: University of Arizona Press.

Hulshof, Marije. 1991. *Zapotec Moves: Networks and Remittances of U.S.-Bound Migrants from Oaxaca, Mexico.* Netherlands Geographical Studies 128. Amsterdam: KNAG.

Instituto Nacional de Estadísticas Geográficas (INEGI). 2002. *XII Censo General: Oaxaca.* Aguascalientes, Mexico.

Kearney, Michael. 1995. "The Effects of Transnational Culture, Economy, and Migration on Mixtec Identity in Oaxacalifornia." In *The Bubbling Cauldron: Race, Ethnicity, and the Urban Crisis,* edited by Michael Peter Smith and Joe R. Feagin. Minneapolis: University of Minnesota Press.

———. 1996. *Reconceptualizing the Peasantry: Anthropology in Global Perspective.* Boulder, Colo.: Westview Press.

Kearney, Michael, and Carole Nagengast. 1989. *Anthropological Perspectives on*

Transnational Communities in Rural California. Working Paper No. 3, Working Group on Farm Labor and Rural Poverty, California Institute for Rural Studies. Davis, Calif.: California Institute for Rural Studies.

Massey, Douglas, Jorge Durand, and Nolan Malone. 2002. *Beyond Smoke and Mirrors: Mexican Immigration in an Era of Economic Integration*. New York: Russell Sage Foundation.

Massey, Douglas, Rafael Alarcón, Jorge Durand, and Humberto Gonzalez. 1987. *Return to Aztlan: The Social Process of International Migration from Western Mexico*. Berkeley: University of California Press.

McDonnell, Patrick. 1998. "For Mayan Southland, Worlds Collide." *Los Angeles Times*, May 27, A1.

Méndez y Mercado, Leticia. 1985. *Migración: Decisión Involuntaria*. Mexico D.F.: Instituto Nacional Indigenista.

Mountz, Alison, and Richard A. Wright. 1996. "Daily Life in the Transnational Migrant Community of San Agustín, Oaxaca, and Poughkeepsie, New York." *Diaspora* 5:403–28.

Nagengast, Carole, and Michael Kearney. 1990. "Mixtec Ethnicity: Social Identity, Political Consciousness, and Political Activism." *Latin American Research Review* 25(2):61–91.

Portes, Alejandro. 1995. "Economic Sociology and the Sociology of Immigration: A Conceptual Overview." In *The Economic Sociology of Immigration: Essays on Networks, Ethnicity, and Entreprenuership*, edited by A. Portes. New York: Russell Sage Foundation.

———. 1998. "Social Capital: Its Origin and Application in Modern Sociology." *Annual Review of Sociology* 24:1–24.

Portes, Alejandro, and Margarita Mooney. 2002. "Social Capital and Community Development." In *The New Economic Sociology*, edited by Mauro Guillen, Randall Collins, Paula England, and Marshall Meyer. New York: Russell Sage Foundation.

Portes, Alejandro, and Patricia Landolt. 2000. "Social Capital: Promise and Pitfalls of Its Role in Development." *Journal of Latin American Studies* 32:529–47.

Portes, Alejandro, and Ruben Rumbaut. 1996. *Immigrant America*. 2d ed. Berkeley: University of California Press.

Powell, Walter W., and Laurel Smith-Doerr. 1994. "Networks and Economic Life." In *Handbook of Economic Sociology.*, edited by Neil J. Smelser and Richard Swedberg. Princeton, N.J.: Princeton University Press; New York: Russell Sage Foundation.

Quinones, Sam. 2001. "The Koreatown That Never Was." *Los Angeles Times Magazine*, June 3, 1.

Reichert, Joshua, and Douglas Massey. 1980. "History and Trends in U.S.-Bound Migration from a Mexican Town." *International Migration Review* 14:475–91.

Rios Vázquez, Othon. 1992. "Estudios de la Migración de los Trabajadores Oaxaqueños a los E.U.A." In *Migración y Etnicidad en Oaxaca*, edited by Jack Corbett et al. Nashville, Tenn.: Vanderbilt University Press.

Rivera-Salgado, Gaspar. 1999. "Migration and Political Activism: Mexican Transnational Perspective." Ph.D. diss., Sociology Department, University of California, Santa Cruz.

Runsten, David, and Michael Kearney. 1994. *A Survey of Oaxacan Village Networks in California Agriculture*. Davis: California Institute for Rural Studies.

Sorroza, Carlos. 1990. "Cambios agroproductivos y Crisis Alimentaria en Oaxaca (1940–1985)." *Estudios Sociológicos* 8(22):87–116.

Vásquez, Hector Hernández. 1982. "Migración Zapoteca. Algunos aspectos económicos, demográficos y culturales." In *Sociedad y Politica en Oaxaca*, edited by Raúl Benítez Zenteno. Oaxaca, Mexico: Instituto de Investigaciones.

Waldinger, Roger, and Michael Lichter. 2003. *How the Other Half Works*. Berkeley: University of California Press.

Warman, Arturo. 2001. "Los Indios de Mexico." *NEXOS* 23, no. 280 (Apr.).

Zabin, Carol, and Luis Escala Rabadan. 1998. "Mexican Hometown Associations and Mexican Immigrant Political Empowerment in Los Angeles." Aspen Institute Working Paper Series. Washington, D.C.

Zabin, Carol, Michael Kearney, Ana Garcia, and David Runsten. 1993. *Mixtec Migrants in California Agriculture: A New Cycle of Poverty*. Davis: California Institute for Rural Studies.

Zhou, Min, and Carl L. Bankston. 1998. *Growing up American: How Vietnamese Immigrants Adapt to Life in the United States*. New York: Russell Sage Foundation.

7 Two Sides of the Same Coin?

The Relationship between Socioeconomic Assimilation and
Entrepreneurship among Mexicans in Los Angeles

Zulema Valdez

An older Mexican man sits across from me at King Taco in East Los
Angeles, arguably the best taco stand in Los Angeles, and explains why
he went into business for himself. "Why do I want to work for someone
else, when I can work for myself and make more money? I know where to
find cheap [Mexican immigrant] workers and *I* can tell *them* what to do,
you see." Juan Mendez owns his own construction business. He explains
that when he was a factory worker at an automobile plant, he was working forty hours a week plus overtime and not making ends meet, with a
wife and four children to support. Following several failed attempts at a
promotion and waves of layoffs, his wife entered the labor force to supplement the family income, working as a nurse's assistant at a home for
the elderly. In an effort to improve his family's deteriorating economic
situation, Mr. Mendez enrolled in night school and received his contractor's license twenty-five years ago. It hasn't since been a straight-line
success story, however. During the recession in the late 1980s, he lost
everything, and his wife once again went back to work. As he's gotten
older, he's shifted from the more lucrative (if risky) housing construction
to the smaller, physically safer tasks of remodeling bathrooms or building
one-room additions. Still, Mr. Mendez claims he's happier in his current
economic situation rather than "working for somebody else for nothing,
and being passed up for the better jobs."

If Juan Mendez's labor market experience is unique, it is only because
entrepreneurship among Mexicans in the United States is rare. His work
experience up to that point, however, mirrors that of many U.S.-born
Mexican and foreign-born Mexican laborers in Los Angeles during the
last decades of the twentieth century. Massive growth in durable manufacturing (including the automobile and aerospace industries) following
World War II resulted in unprecedented economic mobility for groups
that had previously faced discrimination and inequality in the market. A
new Black middle class was formed, and Latinos in the United States were

within reach of economic parity with their Anglo-worker counterparts. However, the changing economic landscape beginning in the 1960s, coupled with an influx of "new" immigrants in numbers not seen since the arrival of Europeans on the shores of Ellis Island, has had a profound effect on the labor market situation of people of color in the United States. In Los Angeles, U.S.-born and foreign-born Mexicans now face a declining manufacturing sector, with its promise of a living wage and steady income for those with limited human capital skills (education and work experience), in favor of service sector employment that can be characterized as temporary, flexible (read insecure), and low wage.

Large increases in immigration also make economic absorption difficult. The most recent census figures show that the size of the Mexican origin population is 20.5 million in the United States (U.S. Bureau of the Census 2001). California alone accounts for 41 percent of this number (8.5 million persons). The largest Mexican population lives in Los Angeles County (3 million persons), and the largest Hispanic population (overwhelmingly Mexican) can be found in East Los Angeles (124,283) (U.S. Bureau of the Census 2001). And although Mexicans, compared to their Asian, Black, and other Latino counterparts, enjoy high participation rates in the labor force, they are disproportionately found in low-wage or minimum-wage occupations. In stark contrast to the 1960s and 1970s, earnings of Mexicans have actually declined since the 1980s (Waters and Eschbach 1995). It is in this economic context that entrepreneurship provides an interesting alternative to labor market employment.

Ethnic Entrepreneurship and Assimilation

Most scholars of ethnic entrepreneurship, simply defined as immigrant and ethnic minority business ownership, suggest that some ethnic groups rely on "ethnic resources" to facilitate business ownership. Ethnic resources include specific skills, knowledge, attitudes, and values of the group (Light 1972; Light and Bonacich 1988, 18–19; Portes and Bach 1985; Portes and Rumbaut 1990; Waldinger et al. 1990). By maintaining cultural ties in the new host country, then, ethnic members may garner economic and noneconomic support from ethnic resources that encourage business ownership.

The ethnic business is often situated within an "ethnic enclave" or "ethnic economy" (Bonacich and Modell 1980; Light et al. 1994; Portes and Zhou 1992; Waldinger et al. 1990). An "ethnic enclave" is a spatially concentrated area of business ownership, such as Little Havana, the Cuban ethnic enclave in Miami, or Koreatown in Los Angeles. A more general concept of ethnic business is the "ethnic economy." An ethnic economy may include businesses within an ethnic enclave, but also includes immigrant or ethnic minority-owned businesses outside an ethnic enclave. Such businesses may be operated by a self-employed person (one who works for him/herself without any employees), or may include coethnic employees (Bonacich and Modell 1980; Light and Bhachu 1993; Light et al. 1994). Importantly, the ethnic business, whether located in an ethnic enclave or ethnic economy, remains tied to the ethnic community.

Scholars question the benefits and detriments for those groups that engage in ethnic enterprise within an ethnic enclave or economy (Light and Roach 1996; Sanders and Nee 1987). They argue that ethnic business owners, who work in the ethnic enclave or ethnic economy, rely on ethnic ties and resources to start their businesses, and also cater to and rely on the ethnic community to provide supply and demand for the business. Therefore, ethnic business owners may have problems eventually incorporating and assimilating into the mainstream economy and society. In other words, scholars argue that incorporation into the mainstream (assimilation) is itself limited by the necessary contribution of ethnic characteristics and resources that facilitate a successful ethnic business (Alba and Nee 1997). Hence, "incorporation" in terms of assimilation is not complete. However, another consideration is that assimilation may not even be desirable, given the sometimes positive effects attributed to ethnic-oriented characteristics on an immigrant or ethnic minority group's economic activity. The assumption that ethnic entrepreneurs represent a group whose economic activity (and success) may be determined by pertinent ethnic characteristics, when brought to its logical conclusion, is that ethnic entrepreneurship limits assimilation to mainstream society (Sanders and Nee 1987).

A Reconsideration

Assimilation, in the classical sense, refers to the process by which immigrants and their descendants shed the cultural values and social institutions of their country of origin, while accumulating the skills and knowledge of the dominant cultural group in the receiving country. In the

United States, this group is the U.S.-born White population. Although questions of who the dominant cultural group is or of what the homogenous outcome consists are important (and taking on greater importance in recent social science debates), in terms of combined political, sociocultural, and economic institutions and outcomes, the U.S.-born White population continues to be the most integrated, and thus remains the barometer by which other groups are often compared. According to the classical perspective of assimilation, immigrants will ultimately integrate into American society and adopt American culture in many respects, gradually converging towards greater "homogeneity" (Lieberson 1963, 8) by learning English, becoming naturalized citizens, gaining occupational skills necessary for economic integration, and intermarrying (Borjas 1990; Lieberson 1963; Portes and Rumbaut 1990; Zhou 1997). Scholars of ethnic entrepreneurship agree that "straight-line" (Anglo-conformity) assimilation may be hindered by this economic activity, since the maintenance of ethnic ties and community is necessary for ethnic business to persist.

In contrast, I suggest that ethnic business ownership may actually indicate socioeconomic assimilation. Socioeconomic assimilation has been defined as "minority participation in institutions such as the labor market and education on the basis of parity with native groups of similar backgrounds" (Alba and Nee 1997). Variables used to capture the effects of socioeconomic assimilation (educational attainment, occupation, and earnings) usually originate from within the labor market (Borjas 1990; Lieberson 1963). In this chapter, I seek to extend the literature on socioeconomic assimilation by exploring the relationship between ethnic entrepreneurship and socioeconomic assimilation. To do so, I compare the entrepreneurial activity of foreign-born and U.S.-born Mexican men to that of U.S.-born Whites, arguably the dominant cultural group in the United States, to explore whether Mexican entrepreneurship may represent assimilation in progress. Although ethnic ties and characteristics may or may not contribute to ethnic enterprise, the assumption made by scholars that this economic activity is always connected to ethnicity may be premature or, as others have argued, overstated (Alba and Nee 1997; Aldrich and Waldinger 1990; Light et al. 1994).

Additionally, the ethnic economy literature often neglects to consider those groups that are not highly entrepreneurial. As Butler notes, "Chinese and Korean enterprises have been studied in detail, but when Afro-

Americans engage in business activities, their enterprises are called a myth by scholars" (1991, 329). To illustrate, the current general labor market literature suggests that the economic position of Mexicans in the United States is "fixed" in the secondary sector of the economy because they "do not have an ethnic economy," nor do they have the skills and education necessary to enter the primary labor market and advance their position in the general economy (Portes and Bach 1985; Portes and Zhou 1992, 495). Cursory explanations specific to the absence of entrepreneurship for certain groups range from individual shortcomings, such as a lack of education, or cultural shortcomings, such as the breakdown of an ethnic community. However, these explanations fail to account for smaller rates of entrepreneurship that exist for many immigrant and ethnic minority groups. This chapter investigates the entrepreneurial outcomes of Mexicans, a group whose entrepreneurial activity is far below that of U.S.-born Whites and many other ethnic and racial groups. In so doing, this study provides additional information on the entrepreneurial outcomes of understudied groups. In sum, I attempt to accomplish three tasks in this chapter:

1. Although social scientists consider the effects of education, earnings, and occupations on socioeconomic assimilation, the emphasis on the labor market by economists and social scientists has had the unintended consequence of omitting entrepreneurship. Therefore, entrepreneurial participation is used here as a direct indicator of socioeconomic assimilation.

2. Explanations made by scholars of ethnic entrepreneurship focus on the maintenance of ethnic ties and the ethnic community to facilitate business ownership. Therefore, ethnic business is assumed to prevent assimilation and integration in the general economy. In this chapter, entrepreneurial activity will not be assumed to limit economic integration. Rather, entrepreneurial activity among Mexican entrepreneurs will be compared with that of U.S.-born Whites, and will be used to indicate assimilation.

3. Finally, I hypothesize that the assimilation and ethnic entrepreneurship literatures may contribute to a greater understanding of each, when reconsidered as capturing a similar process. If assimilation theory is applied to ethnic entrepreneurship, I predict that differences in entrepreneurial participation should be smaller

among U.S.-born Mexicans than foreign-born Mexicans, when compared to U.S.-born Whites. Additionally, entrepreneurial participation among foreign-born Mexicans should show a small, gradual change as time in the United States increases, providing a glimpse of assimilation in progress.

Mexicans in Los Angeles

I focus on Mexicans in greater Los Angeles, where the highest concentration of U.S.-born and foreign-born Mexicans resides in the United States. Recent census figures show that the Mexican population in the United States increased by 52.9 percent from 1990 to 2000 (from 13.5 million to 20.6 million). Moreover, Mexicans are the largest Hispanic group in the United States—fully 58.5 percent of Hispanics were identified as Mexican in the 2000 census (U.S. Bureau of the Census 2001). And although Hispanics concentrate in different states, Mexicans were the largest Hispanic group in California. The highest concentration of Mexicans in California is located in Los Angeles County (3 million). Thus, the long history of immigrant settlement to California, and specifically to Los Angeles, provides an excellent opportunity to consider the relationship between self-employment and socioeconomic assimilation, since the process of assimilation takes place over time and generations.

I am interested in comparing entrepreneurial participation among foreign-born and U.S.-born Mexicans to the entrepreneurial participation of U.S.-born Whites. I posit that foreign-born and U.S.-born Mexican entrepreneurial outcomes will show a gradual increase over time and across generations and move closer to the entrepreneurial outcomes of U.S.-born Whites, as assimilation theory would predict.

Data and Methods

I use 2000 census data drawn from the Integrated Public Use Microdata Series (IPUMS) (Ruggles et al. 2004). This sample extract of the 2000 census contains specific information on U.S.-born White, U.S.-born Mexican, and foreign-born Mexican men who live in greater Los Angeles. In this chapter, U.S.-born Whites include persons who were born in the United States, and who identify themselves as "non-Hispanic" White. Mexicans are categorized into two groups: foreign-born Mexicans include all people who identified themselves as "Mexican" in response to the Hispanic-origin question, and who indicated they were either a U.S. citizen by naturalization or they were born in Mexico; U.S.-born Mexicans include persons who identified themselves as "Mexican" in response to the Hispanic-origin question and who were born in the United States.

Since much of the previous literature on ethnic entrepreneurship has focused on men and since there are gender differences in ethnic entrepreneurship, I limit this analysis to men (see Borjas 1990; Chiswick 1974; Portes and Bach 1985). The sample is further limited to men of working age (twenty-five to sixty-four years), and immigrants who entered the United States through the calendar year 2000. The sample is limited to greater Los Angeles, which includes five counties: Los Angeles, San Bernardino, Orange, Ventura, and Riverside. Greater Los Angeles constitutes a historically rich area of immigrant and ethnic minority settlement in an urban setting, which allows for variation in ethnic entrepreneurship across and among these groups.

Variable Definitions

Dependent Variable. Entrepreneurship is measured using the U.S. Census variable, "class of worker." The class of worker variable contains three categories: "not in the labor force," "self-employed," and "works for wages or salary." Thus, the class of worker variable includes people who don't work, who work for themselves, or who work for others. I use the category "self-employed" to represent those who are participating in entrepreneurship.

I conduct a statistical analysis that determines the likelihood of being self-employed, versus the likelihood of not being self-employed, given certain conditions. For instance, as a foreign-born Mexican male resides in the United States longer, what is the likelihood that he will be self-employed? The statistical procedure I employ provides the answer to this question, and is therefore, a useful method with which to explore the questions posed in this chapter.

Independent Variables. Exploring the relationship between self-employment and socioeconomic assimilation requires a consideration of important factors that capture the process of assimilation that takes place over time and generations. In the analysis of foreign-born Mexicans, if self-employment is an indicator of socioeconomic assimilation, then length of residence in the United States may influence self-employment outcomes. Therefore, length of residence is included in the analysis of the foreign-born. Length of residence in the United States is defined categorically by year of immigration (for the analysis of the foreign-born only). The reference group is recent immigrants who arrived between 1990 and 2000. The second category includes immigrant men who came to the United States between 1980 and 1990 and are labeled ten- to twenty-year residents. Lastly, the third category includes immigrant men who immigrated to the United States before 1980. This group is labeled long-term residents.

Length of residence is correlated with age; as time since migration increases, immigrants are also getting older. Age has been shown to have a positive effect on the self-employment rates for the U.S.-born (Archer 1991). Thus, it is important to control for the effect of age when examining the effect of length of residence (for the analysis of the foreign-born only). Age is measured as a categorical variable in order to observe curvilinear patterns not evident when age is used as a continuous variable. Since only a very small number of sixteen- to twenty-four-year-old men are self-employed, this analysis includes men between the ages of twenty-five and sixty-four. Men between the ages of twenty-five and thirty-four serve as the reference group. The second category includes immigrant men between the ages of thirty-five and forty-four, and the third category includes immigrant men between the ages of fifty-five and sixty-four.

Whether someone becomes self-employed may also depend upon certain background characteristics or conditions. For instance, researchers have observed that self-employment participation varies depending on such factors as education, knowledge of English, and married status. Therefore, these factors are included as controls in this analysis of self-employment. In this way, the results presented in this analysis of self-employment among foreign-born Mexicans, U.S.-born Mexicans, and U.S.-born Whites, already take into account these important background factors.

Analysis Strategy

First, I conduct a statistical analysis among foreign-born Mexican men only. I examine how age and length of residence in the United States affects the likelihood of being self-employed. I also consider the additional effects of background factors, including education, English proficiency, and married status. By comparing three groups with different lengths of residence (recent residents, ten- to twenty-year residents, long-term residents), this analysis illustrates the direction of the changes in self-employment rates within a group, as foreign-born Mexicans reside in the United States longer. If there is a relationship between self-employment and socioeconomic assimilation, I predict that as foreign-born Mexicans reside in the United States longer, they will increase their self-employment participation. I argue that this finding will provide support for the use of self-employment as an indicator of assimilation.

A second statistical analysis examines the effects of nativity on self-employment; that is, this analysis examines how being foreign-born or U.S.-born affects the likelihood of being self-employed among Mexicans. This analysis also compares the self-employment outcomes of foreign-born and U.S.-born Mexican men to those of White men. Assimilation theory would predict that the self-employment participation rate of U.S.-born Mexicans should be closer to that of U.S.-born Whites, than to foreign-born Mexicans. Furthermore, assimilation theory would predict that differences in self-employment participation should be larger among foreign-born Mexicans than U.S.-born Mexicans, when compared to U.S.-born Whites. By comparing rates of self-employment among the U.S.-born and foreign-born with that of White males, gradual convergence of self-employment rates can be observed. As in the previous analysis described above, education, English proficiency, and married status are included to capture the influence of these important background characteristics.

Findings

Descriptive Variables. Table 7.1 presents some descriptive statistics for U.S.-born Whites, and foreign- and U.S.-born Mexican males. Large differences between these groups are evident with respect to age, education, English proficiency, and married status.

Foreign-born Mexicans are the youngest group, on average, in this sample. The average age for Mexican immigrants is 36.8, approximately three years less than U.S.-born Mexicans. In contrast, the average age for U.S.-born Whites in this sample is 43.3 years old, the oldest group. Age is important for two reasons: as people get older, they are more likely to

Table 7.1. Characteristics of U.S.-Born White, U.S.-Born Mexican, and
Foreign-Born Mexican Men in Greater Los Angeles, 2000

	Whites U.S.-Born	Mexicans U.S.-Born	Foreign-Born
Percentage self-employed	17.05	9.48	8.21
Age	43.3	39.8	36.8
Education percentages			
Eighth grade or less	.73	4.48	44.30
Ninth grade through high school	23.26	43.24	41.42
Some college through bachelor's degree	61.09	47.51	12.71
Graduate/professional degree	14.92	4.77	1.58
Speaks English well	99.72	97.79	51.57
Married	59.49	54.08	61.40
Year of arrival[a]			
1970–79	—	—	26.4
1980–89	—	—	45.1
1990–2000	—	—	28.5
Sample size (unweighted N)	71,773	6,965	13,188

[a]Values for year of arrival include only foreign-born Mexicans.

Source: U.S. Census Bureau, 5 Percent Integrated Public-Use Microdata Series (IPUMS)
(Washington, D.C.: U.S. Census Bureau, 2000).

become self-employed (Archer 1991), and as people get older, they acquire human capital, such as education and work experience. Moreover,
older people are more likely to be married, and it has been shown that
married status contributes to the likelihood of entrepreneurship (Light
and Bonacich 1988).

U.S.-born Whites have the highest educational attainment, with over
60 percent holding a college degree and 15 percent holding a graduate or
professional degree. U.S.-born Mexicans lag behind, with about 48 percent reporting some college or a college degree and less than 5 percent
holding a graduate or professional degree. Foreign-born Mexicans are the
least educated, as 45 percent report an eighth-grade education or less,
whereas less than 2 percent hold a graduate or professional degree.

With respect to English proficiency, the U.S.-born groups are similar. Almost all Whites and U.S.-born Mexicans speak English "well" or "very well," however, only half of foreign-born Mexicans report this level of proficiency. Whites have the highest rate of marriage among the U.S.-born groups (59 percent). However, foreign-born Mexicans are more likely to be married (61 percent) than U.S.-born Whites (59 percent) or their U.S.-born Mexican counterparts (54 percent).

The differences between and within groups in human capital attainment (age, education, English proficiency) may partially explain differences in self-employment; thus, these variables are included in the multivariate analysis. Married status is not a human capital variable but is also included in the analysis since it is known to contribute to the likelihood of self-employment (Light and Bonacich 1988; Portes and Zhou 1992).

Industrial Classification Based on 2000 Census Codes

U.S.-born Whites, U.S.-born Mexicans, and foreign-born Mexicans also differ with respect to the kind of work they do. Since U.S.-born and foreign-born Mexicans are on average younger and lag behind in educational attainment, it is not surprising that these groups concentrate in industries that require manual labor and only limited education. Self-employed Mexicans (U.S.-born and foreign-born) are more likely to concentrate in low-skilled and/or low-paying industries, such as construction, manufacturing, and retail trade (Table 7.2). In contrast, self-employed U.S.-born Whites are more likely to work in a variety of industries, including those that require a higher level of skill and training. Specifically, U.S.-born Whites are more likely than U.S.-born or foreign-born Mexicans to concentrate in white-collar industries. For instance, U.S.-born Whites are twice as likely as U.S.-born Mexicans to concentrate in information or communication services (4.5 percent compared to 2.1 percent). U.S.-born Whites are one-third more likely than U.S.-born Mexicans to concentrate in education, health, and social service industries (6.2 percent compared to 4.4 percent), and three times more likely than foreign-born Mexicans (1.4 percent). U.S.-born Whites are also more likely than U.S.-born Mexicans (7.1 percent) or foreign-born Mexicans (3.1 percent) to be found in finance, insurance, and real estate (9.8 percent). It is important to consider that the types of industries in

Table 7.2. Industrial Concentration among Self-Employed U.S.-Born
White, U.S.-Born Mexican, and Foreign-Born Mexican Men in Greater
Los Angeles, 2000

	Whites U.S.-Born	Mexicans U.S.-Born	Foreign-Born
Agriculture	.8	.6	1.7
Mining	0	0	0
Construction	18.7	23.9	21.1
Manufacturing	6.5	5.0	6.0
Wholesale trade	3.9	3.5	2.8
Retail trade	8.9	9.7	12.2
Transportation and warehousing	2.9	5.2	6.3
Information and communication	4.5	2.1	.6
Finance, insurance, and real estate	9.8	7.1	3.1
Professional, scientific, management, administrative, and waste management	24.6	20.2	25.4
Education, health, and social services	6.2	4.4	1.4
Arts and entertainment, recreation, accommodations, and food services	8.0	5.9	1.2
Other services	6.4	12.4	13.4
Sample size (unweighted N)	13,979	660	1,083

Source: U.S. Census Bureau, 5 Percent Integrated Public-Use Microdata Series (IPUMS) (Washington, D.C.: U.S. Census Bureau, 2000).

which these groups concentrate contributes to their economic success in self-employment.

Length of Residence and Self-Employment

In order to observe gradual changes in self-employment rates among the foreign-born, I focused on length of residence. I conducted a statistical procedure that allowed me to examine how length of residence affects the self-employment participation rate of foreign-born Mexican men. I also considered important background characteristics, such as age, education, English proficiency, and married status. This analysis demonstrates changes in the direction of self-employment rates as foreign-born Mexicans reside in the United States longer.

Findings reveal that as foreign-born Mexicans reside in the United States longer, they are significantly more likely to engage in self-employment. The addition of certain background characteristics, such as human capital variables and married status, increases the effect of age on self-employment, and length of residence continues to significantly contribute to self-employment outcomes. Specific findings reveal that foreign-born Mexicans with some college education or a bachelor's degree are not markedly different from those with an eighth-grade education or less. However, Mexicans who hold a graduate or professional degree are almost twice as likely to be self-employed as foreign-born Mexicans with an eighth-grade education or less (the reference group), a large increase. Foreign-born Mexicans who speak English well or very well are also more likely to be self-employed.

Age significantly contributes to the likelihood of self-employment. As Mexicans get older, they are more likely to be self-employed. Mexicans of ages thirty-five to forty-four, forty-five to fifty-four, and fifty-five to sixty-four, are approximately one and one-half times more likely to be self-employed than twenty-five to thirty-four year olds. Turning to the effects of length of residence on self-employment, findings indicate that the likelihood of self-employment increases significantly as length of residence in the United States increases. Thus, as Mexicans get older and reside in the United States longer, and as they accumulate skills such as education (at the highest levels) and knowledge of English, self-employment within this group is more likely to occur. These results are consistent with assimilation theory, which would predict that as Mexican immigrants reside in the United States longer, rates of self-employment would begin to show a gradual increase.

Foreign and U.S.-Born Self-Employment

I conducted a second statistical analysis that considered how ethnicity (White or Mexican) and nativity (foreign-born or U.S.-born status) affect self-employment outcomes. The analysis included U.S.-born Whites, U.S.-born Mexicans, and foreign-born Mexican men in greater Los Angeles.

First, I considered how nativity affects self-employment participation by comparing the likelihood of being self-employed among U.S.-born and foreign-born Mexicans to the likelihood of being self-employed among U.S.-born Whites. The results indicate that when considering nativity as the sole factor predicting self-employment U.S.- and foreign-born Mexicans are less than half as likely to be self-employed as Whites, with U.S.-born Mexicans slightly closer to their White counterparts. When human capital variables and married status were included in the equation, as well as one interaction term (foreign-born Mexicans who are English proficient), the importance of nativity is stronger. That is, all things being equal, the effect of nativity increased slightly for both groups. U.S.-born and foreign-born Mexicans, however, remain half as likely as Whites to be self-employed.

Specific findings reveal that education contributes significantly to the likelihood of self-employment for those with a graduate or professional education, whereas those who report some high school through a bachelor's degree are not significantly different from those with an eighth-grade education or less. Among men with a graduate or professional degree, the likelihood increases to over one and one-half times more likely to be self-employed than those with an eighth-grade education or less. Additionally, the effects of age and married status illustrate that those men who are married, older, or speak English well or very well are more likely to be self-employed.

Discussion

Juan Mendez's labor market experience in greater Los Angeles provides one example of the entrepreneurial experiences of Mexican males captured here. Because Mr. Mendez realized his opportunities for employment were limited or disadvantageous, he decided to engage in entrepreneurship as an alternative avenue of economic activity. Importantly, Mr. Mendez speaks English well, but he also speaks Spanish. He benefits from living in Los Angeles, where he is able to use his ethnic membership to hire from the vast pool of Mexican immigrant workers, but also benefits from his facility in English, which allows him to work for a variety of ethnic groups—not just within his own community. Juan Mendez is not a member of a group that overwhelmingly participates in entrepreneurship, such as Koreans. Rather, he is a member of a group that is commonly perceived as a low-wage labor pool. However, he decided to try his hand at self-employment after realizing that his opportunities in the general economy were severely restricted. Thus, his own personal experience is closer to that of the assimilation perspective, which understands his participation in entrepreneurship as an avenue of economic mobility in the face of disadvantage.

In considering the entrepreneurial activity of Mexicans as a possible indicator of assimilation, I predict that entrepreneurial participation among U.S.-born and foreign-born Mexican males will gradually converge to the entrepreneurial outcomes of U.S.-born Whites, the dominant cultural group. Although this is a multigenerational process, as convergence of immigrants and their descendants with respect to a number of indicators may take place over many generations (Lieberson 1963, 10), I argue that an analysis of foreign and U.S.-born Mexicans may hint at this process.

In applying predictions of assimilation to the entrepreneurial activity of foreign-born Mexican males, I show that participation changes slowly and gradually as length of residence increases. By comparing the changes in entrepreneurship among foreign-born Mexican males as they reside in the U.S. longer, and among U.S.-born Mexicans compared to U.S.-born White males, this chapter illustrates some of the gradual process of convergence. As is shown in my analysis, rates of self-employment increase over length of residence among foreign-born Mexicans, suggesting that the accumulation of skills and experiences in the host country benefits this group in entrepreneurial participation. Furthermore, comparing U.S.-born Mexicans with their foreign-born counterparts finds this group more likely to be self-employed. Again, this supports the predictions of assimilation—entrepreneurial activity captures socioeconomic assimilation among Mexicans. Although entrepreneurial participation is partially explained by the predictions of the assimilation perspective with the factors considered here—nativity and ethnicity, the inclusion of human capital variables and married status, along with length of residence for immigrants—a consideration of the context of the immigrant and ethnic group experience itself, within the context of the U.S. economic structure, is necessary in order to fully explain the entrepreneurial activity and incorporation of Mexicans in Los Angeles.

Mexican entrepreneurship may serve as a strategy for survival, or it may provide a means to achieve economic mobility for groups not readily integrated into the general economy. This is true for U.S.-born as well as foreign-born Mexicans. Among U.S.-born Mexicans, however, it can be argued that low levels of human capital, few class and ethnic resources, and a social network of secondary sector wage labor has provided few opportunities to engage in enterprise in above-average numbers. The opportunity structure open to U.S.-born Mexicans may hinder entrepreneurial activity, as this group has historically been perceived as a low wage labor pool relegated to this sector of the labor market. U.S.-born Mexicans face limited opportunities to advance as workers in the general economy, and as a result have not been able to acquire the resources necessary to establish a firm entrepreneurial base from which to grow.

Although it has been argued that Mexicans have low rates of entrepreneurship, this chapter shows that as length of stay increases, entrepreneurship among foreign-born Mexicans increases. Interestingly, Mexicans in this sample are also more likely to be entrepreneurs as education and language proficiency increase. Upon arrival, few immigrant groups have the skills and resources necessary to engage in entrepreneurship. However, as sojourners become permanent residents, blocked mobility in the primary and secondary sectors of the labor market is realized and skills important to the host society are slowly accumulated, thus increasing the rates of foreign-born entrepreneurs. In considering nativity, my analysis suggests that as permanent immigrants integrate into the U.S. economy their entrepreneurial activity increases, and their children will become entrepreneurs in even greater numbers.

This chapter provides evidence for consideration of the assimilation perspective in understanding Mexican entrepreneurship. Whereas ethnic differences in enterprise have previously been explained by the strength of ethnic ties and the ethnic community in facilitating (or hindering) ethnic entrepreneurship (Portes and Rumbaut 1990; Waldinger et al. 1990), this chapter encourages the additional concept of socioeconomic assimilation in explaining Mexican business ownership. At the same time, this analysis also redefines and expands the concept of socioeconomic assimilation to include entrepreneurial participation. The synthesis of the ethnic entrepreneurship and assimilation literatures provides a fuller, more accurate account of both. Finally, this research may capture an increasing phenomenon—that of Mexican entrepreneurship. It is possible that as labor market opportunities continue to decline and the Mexican immigrant population continues to increase, Mexicans who have some skills, such as human capital (education and work experience) or English proficiency, may take these skills and experience and attempt business ownership. If Juan Mendez's experience in Los Angeles can be generalized—and findings presented here support such an interpretation—those Mexican males who become entrepreneurs may enjoy greater economic mobility than those who stay in the increasingly unequal U.S. labor market.

References

Alba, Richard, and Victor Nee. 1997. "Rethinking Assimilation Theory for a New Era of Immigration." *International Migration Review* 31:826–75.

Aldrich, Howard, and Roger Waldinger. 1990. "Ethnicity and Entrepreneurship." *Annual Review of Sociology* 16:111–36.

Archer, Melanie. 1991. "Self-Employment and Occupational Structure in an Industrializing City: Detroit 1880." *Social Science History* 15:67–95.

Becker, George. 1967. *Human Capital and the Personal Distribution of Income: An Analytical Approach*. Ann Arbor: University of Michigan Press.

Bonacich, Edna, and John Modell. 1980. *The Economic Basis of Ethnic Solidarity: A Study of Japanese Americans*. Berkeley: University of California Press.

Borjas, George. 1990. *Friends or Strangers: The Impact of Immigrants on the American Economy*. New York: Basic Books.

Butler, John Sibley. 1991. *Entrepreneurship and Self-Help among Black Americans: A Reconsideration of Race and Economics*. New York: SUNY Press.

Chavez, Leo. 1992. *Shadowed Lives: Undocumented Immigrants in American Society*. Fort Worth, Tex.: Harcourt, Brace, Jovanovich.

Chiswick, Barry. 1974. *Income Inequality: Regional Analyses within a Human Capital Framework*. New York: National Bureau of Economic Research.

Glazer, Nathan. 1993. "Is Assimilation Dead?" *Annals of the Academy of Political and Social Science* 530:122–37.

Lieberson, Stanley. 1963. *Ethnic Patterns in American Cities*. New York: Free Press.

Light, Ivan. 1972. *Ethnic Enterprise in America: Business and Welfare among Chinese, Japanese and Blacks*. Berkeley: University of California Press.

Light, Ivan, and Edna Bonacich. 1988. *Immigrant Entrepreneurs: Koreans in Los Angeles*. Los Angeles: University of California Press.

Light, Ivan, and Elizabeth Roach. 1996. "Self-Employment: Mobility Ladder or Economic Lifeboat?" In *Ethnic Los Angeles*, edited by Roger Waldinger and Mehdi Bozorgmehr. New York: Russell Sage Foundation.

Light, Ivan, G. Sabagh, M. Bozorgmehr, and C. Der-Martirosian. 1994. "Beyond the Ethnic Enclave Economy." *Social Problems* 41:65–80.

Light, Ivan, and Paraminder Bhachu. 1993. *Immigration and Entrepreneurship: Culture, Capital, and Ethnic Networks*. New Brunswick, N.J.: Transaction.

Portes, Alejandro, and Min Zhou. 1992. "Gaining the Upper Hand: Economic Mobility among Domestic Minorities." *Ethnic and Racial Studies* 15:491–522.

——. 1993. "The New Second Generation: Segmented Assimilation and its Variants." *Annals of the American Academy of Political and Social Science* 530:74–97.

——. 1996. "Self-employment and the Earnings of Immigrants." *American Sociological Review* 61:219–32.

Portes, Alejandro, and Richard Bach. 1985. *Latin Journey: Cuban and Mexican Immigrants in the United States.* Berkeley: University of California Press.

Portes, Alejandro, and Ruben G. Rumbaut. 1990. *Immigrant America: A Portrait.* Berkeley: University of California Press.

Ruggles, Steven, Matthew Sobek, Trent Alexander, Catherine A. Fitch, Ronald Goeken, Patricia Kelly Hall, Miriam King, and Chad Ronnander. 2004. "Integrated Public Use Microdata Series: Version 3.0." [Machine-readable database]. Minneapolis: Minnesota Population Center.

Sanders, Jimy, and Victor Nee. 1987. "Limits of Ethnic Solidarity in the Enclave Economy." *American Sociological Review* 52:745–73.

U.S. Bureau of the Census. 2001. *The Hispanic Population: Census 2000 Brief.* Washington, D.C.

Waldinger, Roger. 1986. "Immigrant Enterprise: A Critique and Reformulation." *Theory and Society* 15:249–85.

——. 1993. "The Ethnic Enclave Debate Revisited." *International Journal of Urban and Regional Research* 17:444–53.

Waldinger, Roger, et al. 1990. *Ethnic Entrepreneurs: Immigrant Business in Industrial Societies.* Newbury Park, Calif.: Sage.

Waters, Mary C., and Karl Eschbach. 1995. "Immigration and Ethnic and Racial Inequality in the United States." *Annual Review of Sociology* 21:419–46.

Zhou, Min. 1997. "Segmented Assimilation: Issues, Controversies, and Recent Research on the New Second Generation." *International Migration Review* 31:975–1019.

——. 1998. *Growing up American: How Vietnamese Children Adapt to Life in the United States.* New York: Russell Sage Foundation.

8 The Formation and Transformation of Salvadoran Community Organizations in Los Angeles

Susan Bibler Coutin

During the summer of 2000, I attended the annual awards dinner of the Association of Salvadorans of Los Angeles (ASOSAL). At a historic hotel in downtown Los Angeles, dignitaries, activists, and volunteers mingled, dined on a several-course-long meal, watched the ASOSAL folkloric dance troupe perform, listened to speeches about ASOSAL and the Central American immigrant community, and applauded the honorees who were receiving awards. One of the honorees was Anne Patterson, the U.S. ambassador to El Salvador, who received enthusiastic applause for her work in El Salvador. During the 1980s, when Salvadoran activists had complained that the U.S. government had in some ways supported or at least failed to recognize human rights abuses being committed in El Salvador, it would have been strange for a Central American community organization to honor a U.S. ambassador to El Salvador. The ambassador was not the only representative of the U.S. government at this event. In addition, though not present in person, President Bill Clinton sent a letter (which was read aloud during the event) congratulating ASOSAL for its accomplishments. Several months later, President Clinton would threaten to veto the District of Columbia appropriations bill because it did not contain legislation that would have granted legal status to Salvadorans and Guatemalans who had immigrated to the United States prior to 1995. Both the congratulatory letter and the veto threat treated Salvadorans as a valued constituency. Such treatment provided a stark contrast to the 1980s, when the Reagan administration treated Salvadoran migrants as economic immigrants who deserved to be deported to El Salvador (Bach 1990; Churgin 1996; Coutin 1993; U.S. House Committee on the Judiciary 1984; Smith 1996; Zolberg 1990).

Salvadoran immigrants' increasing political empowerment, as evidenced by the 2000 ASOSAL awards dinner, belies the widespread assumption that migrants are at the mercy of the global and national political and economic forces that compel and restrict their movements (see Coutin 1998). Migration from El Salvador to the United States has been prompted by the political violence and economic devastation of the 1981–92 Salvadoran civil war (Coutin 1993; Hamilton and Chinchilla 1991, 2001; Menjívar 2000), as well as by the transnationalization of labor markets (Harvey 1989; Sassen 1989, 1996), household economies (Hondagneu-Sotelo and Avila 1997; Schiller, Basch and Szanton Blanc 1995), and national finance (Durand, Parrado, and Massey 1996; Itzigsohn 2000; Menjívar et al. 1998; Orellana Merlos 1992; Orozco, de la Garza, and Baraona 1997; Taylor 1999). These migrants' reception in the United States has been shaped by a variety of political factors, including (1) U.S. foreign policy, which, in the 1980s, supported the Salvadoran government in its fight with insurgents; and (2) strong anti-immigrant sentiment in the 1990s, as manifested by the passage of the 1996 Illegal Immigration Reform and Immigrant Responsibility Act (IIRIRA) and by California propositions 187, 227, and 209, which, respectively, required public officials to verify the immigration status of those they served, dismantled bilingual education, and made affirmative action illegal. Nonetheless, migrants have responded to and attempted to change these conditions. The 1980s were characterized by activism in opposition to U.S. intervention in El Salvador. Moreover, Salvadoran migrants have sent remittances to family members in El Salvador, and have thus become vital to the Salvadoran economy. As a result, Salvadoran officials have urged the U.S. government to grant permanent legal status to Salvadorans living in the United States. Central American immigrants have also played important roles within the labor force of Los Angeles (Waldinger and Bozorgmehr 1996) and have transformed neighborhoods by establishing *pupuserías* (restaurants that sell Salvadoran food), Central American markets, travel agencies, courier services, and other businesses. Such transformations have enabled Central Americans to become important and visible constituencies, and have encouraged local officials to publicly support Central Americans' struggles for legal residency. Additionally, increasing naturalization rates have led U.S. politicians to court Latina/o voters, at least prior to September 2001, with a corresponding softening of anti-immigrant rhetoric. In short, the history of Central Americans in Los Angeles illustrates how relatively powerless and initially disenfranchised immigrant groups can gain political power and, to some degree, influence economic and political forces that have shaped their movements.

My account of the history of Central American community organizations in Los Angeles focuses on four periods, each of which marks a shift in strategy on the part of Salvadoran immigrants and activists. By drawing attention to these shifts, I seek to highlight the dialectic through which activists and others both respond to and bring about changes in Central Americans' economic and political circumstances. These four periods are (1) 1980–83, when organizations in solidarity with political struggles in El Salvador opposed U.S. intervention in Central America; (2) 1983–92, when refugee committees denounced U.S. involvement in the Salvadoran and Guatemalan civil wars and provided legal and humanitarian aid to Central American immigrants; (3) 1992–97, when, following the 1992 Salvadoran peace accords and facing mounting anti-immigrant sentiment, Central American organizations sought legal permanent residency in the United States; and (4) 1997–2001, when Central American groups sought rights and recognition as constituents in light of increased naturalization rates and greater attention to Latina/o voters. Although these phases are divided by key events—the 1983 shift to a prolonged strategy in the Salvadoran civil war, the 1992 peace accords, the 1997 Nicaraguan Adjustment and Central American Relief Act in 1997, and the 2001 attacks on the Pentagon and the World Trade Center in New York—these periods overlap considerably and are not rigidly demarcated.

My account of this history draws on interviews conducted with activists involved in the solidarity movement in the mid-to-late 1980s (Coutin 1993), Central Americans who founded refugee committees and who were involved in the struggle for residency in the mid-1990s (Coutin 2000), and community leaders who have continued to seek legal rights and political empowerment for Central Americans into the 2000s. In addition, from 1995 to 1997, I participated in and observed the legal services programs of three Central American community groups in Los Angeles: ASOSAL, El Rescate (The Rescue), and CARECEN (Central American Resource Center). My account of the history of these and related organizations focuses less on institutional developments within organizations than on trends within Central American community activism. I do not attempt to name every organization, but I do attempt to convey ways that the formation and transformation of Central American community organizations were linked to broader societal trends. This account suggests that Salvadoran community organizations were complexly situated; that as they have claimed space in the political mainstream, they have also maintained historic commitments to social causes.

Phase I: Solidarity (1980–1983)

> There were many organizations in Los Angeles, because the development of the movement was very strong here. Thousands of us came from El Salvador due to the war. And people came here with a political conscience, a political effervescence, a militancy. People came here with their political lines, and once they got here, they founded a series of organizations that corresponded to the organizations that existed in El Salvador.
> *Interview with Salvadoran activist, June 18, 1996*

Although Salvadorans have migrated to the United States since the early 1900s (Menjívar 2000; Poitras 1983), the numbers of immigrants began to increase dramatically in the late 1970s and early 1980s due, largely, to the onset of the Salvadoran civil war. As of 1987, over three-fourths of the Salvadoran population in the United States had arrived during the civil conflict (Montes Mozo and Garcia Vasquez 1988, 9). The Salvadoran civil war grew out of a history of societal inequities and political repression. By 1971, 20 percent of the population of El Salvador was unemployed and 40 percent was underemployed, and by 1975, 41 percent of the rural population in this heavily agricultural country was landless (Menjívar 2000, 44). Efforts to obtain social reforms encountered repression and, in 1979, the latest in a series of coups occurred. Inspired by the Sandinistas' defeat of Anastasio Somoza in 1979, guerrilla groups in El Salvador joined forces, creating the Frente Farabundo Marti para la Liberación Nacional (FMLN). Meanwhile, repression by security forces grew. In 1981, the FMLN launched its first major offensive, gaining territory and demonstrating its military capacity. Violence spread, and the Salvadoran armed forces began a systematic bombing campaign designed to drive civilians out of areas of guerrilla support (Byrne 1996; Montgomery 1995). Entire villages were massacred. Individuals who were suspected of collaborating with guerrillas were abducted, tortured, and killed, their dismembered bodies left as a warning to others. Emigration from El Salvador increased rapidly, and due to the difficulty of obtaining visas, most of those who fled to the United States did so without U.S. authorization.

As the war erupted in El Salvador, some Salvadoran immigrants in the United States founded committees in solidarity with popular struggles in El Salvador. These groups were made up of Salvadorans who had immigrated in the late 1970s and early 1980s. Some of these early immigrants had had direct involvement in the civil war. Political committees sought to raise funding for and increase the political legitimacy of their organizational counterparts in El Salvador. Participants had a strong sense of urgency, given the violence of the civil war. One activist recalled, "My priority was that lives in the country [of El Salvador] were at risk every day, so it was a personal relationship that I developed with Salvadoran, Central American problems, because part of my family remained, many of my friends remained. . . . [I thought,] 'If I don't do anything someone will die.'" This urgency was also fueled by the idea that, like the Nicaraguan revolution, the Salvadoran civil war would end quickly, enabling refugees to return home. One activist said that in the early 1980s, he and his companions believed "that the *Frente* (front-FMLN) was going to triumph militarily, that it would enter San Salvador with weapons to take over the governmental offices, that is, that then we would return. We would say, 'This will be a matter of two or three years.'" As solidarity workers, activists saw themselves as emissaries for their organizations in El Salvador. The internal rivalries that plagued the Salvadoran Left, however, also shaped relationships between political committees affiliated with different FMLN groups. One activist pointed out, "There was always this constant competition, this constant debate about who had the truth, who was the truth holder, whose political vision was the correct one. And we spent so much energy and time dealing with that that when the Salvadoran alliance was forged within the leftist groups, that didn't translate here very well."

The political committees that formed in Los Angeles were both highly organized and less established. They were less established in that they lacked funding, nonprofit numbers, and paid staff, and were, in fact, somewhat clandestine. When I interviewed activists regarding this period, some were reluctant to tell me the names of their organizations, their own posts and responsibilities, and the nature of the ties between political committees in Los Angeles and popular movements in El Salvador. Some members of these organizations used false names, noms de guerre, to protect their family members in El Salvador from reprisals. At the same time, political committees were highly organized, and took some direction from groups in El Salvador. One activist told me that the political committee that he helped to found was part of a national organization. He explained:

> We formed committees in various cities. We have here San Francisco, Los Angeles, Santa Ana. We had a small group started in Houston. We had one in Boston, Washington D.C., in New Jersey. We also had one in Philadelphia. We had one in Chicago, in New York, in Long Island. . . . In the organization, the national directorate that we had, there were twelve of us. . . . Now, every committee had a varied number. The largest committee was the one in Los Angeles; that had six hundred affiliates.

Although their founders had considerable organizational experience in El Salvador, members of solidarity committees had to learn how to do things in the United States. An Anglo Committee in Solidarity with the People of El Salvador (CISPES) member who was involved in solidarity work recalled:

> The difference between today and then is like night and day. . . . This was a community under siege. They felt bewildered by the U.S. processes, police relations, permits for marches. They needed help dramatically. . . . Arranging [a] meeting with members of Congress so they could testify, doing events where they spoke. . . . But the dynamic was so different. They did not feel empowered in this society to meet the system head-on, but needed allies to do it.

Salvadoran activists echoed this recollection of their need for allies. One man told me, "At first, the solidarity groups were formed of Salvadorans. But because everyone was illegal, they decided to seek support groups among the nationalities. . . . The North Americans in the United States, the Mexicans in Mexico, the Australians in Australia, the Canadians in Canada." Other activists pointed out that North Americans were needed to participate in the more risky activities, such as acts of civil disobedience or occupation of the Federal Building. Salvadoran activists, many of whom were undocumented and vulnerable to deportation, could not risk getting arrested. Ties were therefore forged between Salvadoran and U.S. solidarity groups, and Salvadoran political committees invited North Americans to join in their activities (Smith 1996).

The political committees that were founded by Salvadoran immigrants supported opposition groups in El Salvador, denounced violations of human rights, and opposed U.S. intervention in El Salvador. To do so, political committees organized protests at the Salvadoran consulate, public testimonies by victims of human rights abuses, action networks to denounce assassinations or abductions, and fund-raising events to support groups in El Salvador. There were caravans in which supporters traveled regionally within the United States, giving presentations and collecting donations. Mass meetings were held to publicize events in El Salvador. At these meetings, a participant explained, "We told people about the situation there, about everything, including the mass movement and we also gave out information about military things. . . . People began to come with an anxiety to know. . . . We did events to raise funds; we had working groups; we went from house to house, telling people about everything that was happening in El Salvador." Some political committees coordinated their work on a national level, organizing hunger strikes, marches, and presentations. Other groups began to work with the churches, encouraging them to declare themselves sanctuaries for Salvadoran and Guatemalan refugees (see Coutin 1993).

Despite activists' hopes for a quick end to the Salvadoran civil war, the war dragged on. By 1983, when the FMLN in El Salvador shifted to a strategy of *guerra prolongada* (prolonged warfare), Salvadorans in the United States realized that they would not be going home quickly. Upon this realization, migrants began to found refugee committees that focused on the legal, political, and humanitarian needs of the burgeoning U.S. Salvadoran population.

Phase II: Refugee Work (1983–1992)

In El Salvador there is a saying that there is no Salvadoran that does not have a relative that was killed in the war. Also in El Salvador, they say that there is no Salvadoran who does not have at least one relative in the United States.
Interview with Salvadoran activist, July 20, 1993

During the 1980s, Salvadorans and Guatemalans distinguished themselves from other immigrant groups on the ground that they were entitled to refugee status and had more compelling reasons to be in the United States. As the civil wars in El Salvador and Guatemala intensified, the needs of this growing population became more apparent. As one activist recalled, "the people who had been fleeing El Salvador at the beginning of the 1980s had political roots in the organizations there. . . . But as the war continued, it affected more of the population." Another activist linked this exodus to shifts in the Salvadoran government's military strategies: "[By 1983], there were zones where the FMLN had control over the population. The government then devised depopulation strategies. . . . Towns were bombed under the assumption that they were supporting the guerrillas and the people who lived in these towns had to flee. The government's reasoning was that the guerrillas were like fish and the people were like the water. If you remove the fish from the water, the fish will die." Newly arrived Salvadorans and Guatemalans who were victims of such strategies faced difficulty finding family members, food, work, and housing. Those who were apprehended by the U.S. Immigration and Naturalization Service (INS) faced the risk of being deported to a place where their lives were endangered. The U.S. government, which was supporting the Salvadoran and Guatemalan governments in their wars against guerrilla insurgents, denied that significant human rights violations were being committed in El Salvador and Guatemala, and argued that the vast majority of these immigrants had come for economic reasons and could safely be returned to their homelands. In fact, asylum applications filed by Salvadorans and Guatemalans were denied at a rate of 97.4 percent and 99.1 percent, respectively (USCR 1986, 9). Given these low approval rates, many Salvadorans and Guatemalans preferred to remain undocumented, applying for political asylum only as a last resort, if they were apprehended.

To address these humanitarian and legal needs, Salvadorans began to create refugee service organizations and refugee committees. In Los Angeles, CRECEN (the Central American Refugee Committee) was founded in 1981, CARECEN (the Central American Refugee Center) was founded in 1983, the Santana Chirino Amaya Refugee Committee was founded in approximately 1981, and El Rescate was founded in 1981. Related institutions, such as Clínica Monseñor Oscar A. Romero, whose initial mission was to provide health care for Central American refugees, and Casa Rutilio Grande, a shelter for refugees, were also founded during this period. Refugee committees worked closely with church groups that were outraged at human rights abuses being committed in Central America, and at U.S. involvement in these civil wars. Some congregations, such as

La Placita church in downtown Los Angeles, declared themselves sanctuaries for Salvadoran and Guatemalan refugees, and thus signaled their opposition to U.S. policies of denying the cases of Salvadoran and Guatemalan asylum seekers. The Southern California Interfaith Task Force on Central America (SCITCA), worked actively with refugee committees and with congregations that were willing to publicly house undocumented Salvadorans and Guatemalans, an action that could be considered a crime (Coutin 1995; Fiederlein 1991; Pirie 1990). By 1985, refugee committees came to replace political committees, which were beginning to disband.

Refugee service organizations focused both on the needs of the Salvadoran refugee community in the United States and on ending political violence in El Salvador. The services provided by refugee organizations included legal representation, assistance raising bond funds for detainees, presentations on U.S. immigration law, assistance locating temporary shelter, and distributions of food, clothing, and other necessities. Sanctuary congregations helped by housing refugees, providing money for bonds, and locating individuals who could serve as legal guardians for detained minors. An attorney who worked for El Rescate in the mid-1980s recalled, "We knew that those who were deported could be killed, so that gave an urgency to our work. This was a cause! There were days when I didn't get out of the legal clinic until midnight. . . . People were in dire need. I had clients sleeping on my floor after they'd gotten out of detention." To address the root causes of refugees' suffering, refugee committees and service organizations lobbied Congress to extend temporary refuge to Salvadorans and Guatemalans, opposed U.S. military aid to El Salvador and Guatemala, denounced human rights abuses, and sought an end to the Salvadoran and Guatemalan civil wars. Refugee committees also sent delegations to El Salvador and Guatemala, publicized instances of human rights abuses, met with representatives from sister organizations in Central America, protested U.S. intervention in Central America, and formed sister city relations between towns in the United States and in El Salvador. Refugee committees' domestic efforts to obtain refugee status for Salvadorans and Guatemalans were connected to committees' attempts to end the civil war. Activists reasoned that drawing attention to human rights abuses might make it difficult for the U.S. government to continue military aid, which could, in turn, create conditions for a negotiated settlement.

Unlike political committees, refugee committees and refugee service organizations were able to apply for federal, state, and local funding, as well as for grants from foundations. Staff members acquired greater expertise, groups moved from houses to more formal offices, and participants sometimes began to dress more formally. Such shifts brought greater recognition on the part of local and federal authorities. Yet, due to the oppositional nature of their work, refugee organizations were also suspect. One activist claimed that his organization was infiltrated, a former CRECEN member received death threats and survived an assassination attempt, and a solidarity worker was abducted, tortured, and raped.

As refugee committees went through transitions, so too did activists. Many activists had immigrated during the late 1970s and early 1980s, often with no intention of remaining in the United States. Over time, however, their attitude changed, as one activist explained:

> The first years, we never thought that we would become residents, that we would stay. But . . . from '81 [when I arrived] to '86, when the amnesty occurred, it had already been five years. . . . The strategy of the U.S. in El Salvador changed. The FMLN was no longer as effective, and we said, "The war is going to be long-term. If we are going to stay in this country and an amnesty comes, let's legalize ourselves. . . ." So the great majority of those of us who came in '81 were fortunately able to legalize our immigration status.

Gaining status through the 1986 Immigration Reform and Control Act permitted activists to participate more visibly in political activities and travel more freely within and outside of the United States.

Refugee work was also affected by events in Central America and changes in U.S. immigration policy. In 1989, the FMLN launched a final offensive, during which six Jesuits, their housekeeper, and her daughter were assassinated by members of the Salvadoran right. These brutal killings increased U.S. awareness of the effects of the Salvadoran civil war, and in 1990, the legislation that Salvadorans had sought for almost a decade was passed. The 1990 Immigration Act awarded eighteen months of Temporary Protected Status (TPS) to Salvadorans who had entered the United States prior to September 19, 1990. Then in 1991, *American Baptist Churches v. Thornburgh* (known simply as ABC), a lawsuit that charged the U.S. government with discriminating against Salvadoran and Guatemalan asylum seekers, was settled out of court. The ABC agree-

ment granted some three hundred thousand Salvadorans and Guatemalans the right to apply or reapply for political asylum under special
rules designed to ensure fair consideration of their cases. As these benefits became available, organizations dedicated resources to registration
efforts. Such decisions were not uncontroversial, as a former El Rescate
staff member recalled:

> It was a tremendous drain of energy just to be able to agree on the
> importance of the domestic work. . . . I was one of the supporters, and
> sometimes the only person who, within the staff, supported whole-
> heartedly the domestic work. Not in opposition to the international
> work, but I always felt that it was as strategic and it was important,
> and it deserved much more attention than we were paying at the time.
> Not at the expense of the international work. But somehow find a
> balance.

Such dilemmas intensified in 1992, as peace accords were signed in El
Salvador and Salvadoran activists concluded that they could no longer
call themselves "refugees."

Phase III: Seeking Residency (1992–1997)

> We're calling ourselves immigrants because that's what we are; we're no longer
> refugees. There's no longer a war in El Salvador. We can't justify using that term,
> as we could during the war. "Immigrant" implies that we're staying, here, which
> is the reality. . . . We are an immigrant community.
> *(Interview with Salvadoran activist, June 18, 1996)*

The 1992 Salvadoran peace accords provoked dramatic shifts on the part
of Central American community organizations in Los Angeles. Activists
who had spent a decade opposing U.S. military aid to El Salvador and
advocating that Salvadorans and Guatemalans deserved refugee status
found that with the end of the Salvadoran civil war the issue around
which they had focused their organizing was transformed. Instead of
opposing human rights violations in El Salvador, activists turned to supporting reconstruction efforts following over a decade of political violence. And, instead of seeking refugee status on the grounds that they
would be persecuted if deported, they turned to claiming U.S. residency
on the grounds that they had set down roots in the United States. This

shift was reflected organizationally in the birth and/or renaming of numerous organizations. CARECEN—the Central American *Refugee* Center—became the Central American *Resource* Center; CRECEN, the Central American Refugee Committee, became CODDES, the Comite por la Democracia y el Desarrollo en El Salvador (Committee for Democracy and Development in El Salvador); the Santana Chirino Amaya Refugee Committee became CCCA, the Centro Comunitario Centroamericano (Central American Community Center), and El Rescate gradually closed its human rights department and opened a department of economic development.

Central American community organizations' work was affected not only by the signing of the peace accords in El Salvador, but also by legislative and legal developments in the United States. When the 1990 Immigration Act awarded eighteen months of Temporary Protected Status to Salvadorans, groups devoted resources not only to registering Salvadorans for this benefit but also to advocating that the eighteen-month period be extended. Within CARECEN, a committee called ASOSAL, the Association of Salvadorans of Los Angeles, formed to work on the TPS extension and then became an independent organization. In June 1992, President George H. W. Bush awarded Salvadoran TPS recipients the right to register for a new status, Deferred Enforced Departure. Organizations once again devoted resources to registration efforts and extension campaigns. Finally, the settlement agreement in the ABC lawsuit permitted Salvadorans and Guatemalans to apply or reapply for political asylum under special rules designed to ensure fair consideration of their cases. With the signing of peace accords in El Salvador in 1992 and in Guatemala in 1996, it was unlikely that most ABC class members' cases would be approved. Nonetheless, advocates reasoned that while their applications were pending, ABC asylum applicants would perhaps accrue the seven years of continuous presence that would make them eligible to ask to have their deportations suspended. In 1996, however, the U.S. Congress approved the Illegal Immigration Reform and Immigrant Responsibility Act (IIRIRA), which replaced suspension of deportation with cancellation of removal, a remedy that required ten years of continuous presence and that heightened the standard for proving that deportation would be a hardship. A national campaign to restore ABC class members' suspension eligibility resulted in the 1997 Nicaraguan Adjustment and Central American Relief Act (NACARA).

As community organizations redefined their goals, the Salvadoran community itself changed from a transient, undocumented, marginalized population, to a permanent, more established, and increasingly documented group. A San Francisco activist described these changes:

> The whole process through which this change occurred took place during the last five years of the 1980s, to arrive at the final change at the beginning of 1990. The community said, "This isn't a community that is trying to return to El Salvador," though there are always exceptions. . . . This is no longer . . . a typical refugee community. Many had acquired material possessions here; they had children born here, they'd gotten married. A series of factors that totally changed it, converting it into an immigrant community. And people would tell you, "I'll go to El Salvador, but to visit. I now live here."

With a reduced need for emergency social services, a continuing involvement in political advocacy, and a shift from claiming refugee status to seeking residency, community organizations developed interest in newly available forms of political empowerment, such as voter registration and civic involvement. The 1992 civil disturbances caused by the verdict in the trial of police officers accused of beating motorist Rodney King led many groups to conclude that local economic development efforts were needed. Moreover, as attention focused on Los Angeles, funding for economic development projects became available. El Rescate launched a community-based credit union, and CARECEN developed a short-lived market for vendors. Organizations added naturalization to their list of legal services, and new organizations—OSA, the Organization of Salvadoran Americans, and SALEF, the Salvadoran-American Leadership and Educational Fund—launched voter registration drives (see Coutin 2003). Activists considered the naturalization and civic involvement of Salvadorans to be key to countering what they perceived as anti-immigrant and racist attacks on immigrants' rights, affirmative action, and bilingual education. One activist explained:

> With this anti-immigrant wave, to develop, they [Salvadorans] are going to need political power, they are going to need to participate in the political system. And we still have to see who can run for political office, who can be a candidate for city council, who truly represents the people. Pico-Union doesn't interest us as much any more because now

there aren't as many Salvadorans there. We have to go to Huntington Park; we have to go to the [San Fernando] Valley.... And that's why it's important for the people who can become citizens to do so.

As some organizations promoted civic involvement in the United States, a new type of organization dedicated to aiding El Salvador arose: hometown associations (Baker-Cristales 2004; Orozco 2000). Made up of members of the same hometowns in El Salvador, these groups hold social events to raise money for specific projects, such as buying schoolbooks, for their hometowns. In 1996, some thirty-three hometown associations joined together to form COMUNIDADES (Comunidades Unificadas de Ayuda Directa a El Salvador—United Communities of Direct Assistance to El Salvador), an association of associations (the number of participating associations has fluctuated since its founding). Although some hometown association leaders had roots in the Salvadoran left or the Salvadoran right, the work of hometown associations is best described as humanitarian rather than political. At COMUNIDADES meetings, for example, participants stressed that their goals were humanitarian, not *negocio* (business) and that COMUNIDADES did not pursue political or religious ends.

Like hometown associations, other Salvadoran community organizations maintained some work in El Salvador. Organizations supported particular reconstruction projects, provided a forum through which Salvadoran leaders—including political candidates—could visit Los Angeles, and developed ties with Salvadoran government officials. Remittances, which in 2003 totaled 2.5 billion dollars (Banco Central de Reserva de El Salvador 2004), became increasingly important to El Salvador, and during the administration of Calderón Sol, a monument was erected to honor migrants for their contributions to Salvadoran society. New alliances became possible, as Salvadoran officials joined community groups in lobbying for legal remedies for former Salvadoran TPS recipients.

The Clinton administration was receptive to calls for restoring ABC class members' suspension eligibility, and with its backing, NACARA was approved in November 1997. NACARA permitted Nicaraguans who had entered the United States prior to 1995 to adjust their status to that of legal permanent residents, whereas Salvadorans and Guatemalans who had applied for asylum prior to April 1, 1990, registered for the benefits of the ABC settlement, or applied for TPS were permitted to apply for suspension of deportation. In contrast to the relatively automatic and straightforward process created for Nicaraguans, eligible Salvadorans and Guatemalans would have to individually prove that they had been in the United States continuously for seven years, that they had good moral character, and that deportation would be an extreme hardship. To meet these criteria, Salvadorans and Guatemalans would have to assemble documentation packets, pay application fees, and, in many cases, secure some form of legal assistance. In addition, the adjudication of Salvadoran and Guatemalan NACARA cases would be limited by INS scheduling constraints, which would in turn produce a lengthy delay for many applicants. Moreover, civil war continued in El Salvador until 1992 and in Guatemala until 1996. To include Nicaraguans who had entered the United States prior to 1995 but to exclude Salvadorans and Guatemalans who had entered after 1992 struck many Central American activists as preferential treatment for individuals who had fled a left-wing government and discrimination against those who had fled right-wing regimes. Despite NACARA's shortcomings, community organizations and Salvadoran authorities urged eligible Salvadorans to apply for NACARA, and the Salvadoran government printed a pamphlet describing the application process.

The increasing empowerment of Central American community groups, the shift from being a refugee to an immigrant community, the legislative gains achieved in the early to mid-1990s, the increase in the proportion of the Central American community that was eligible to vote in U.S. elections, and the new alliances that developed during the struggle to pass NACARA made it possible for Salvadorans to claim rights not only as refugees fleeing persecution or as immigrants seeking legal status, but also as constituents who deserved policymakers' attention.

Phase IV: Becoming a Constituency (1997–2001)

We need to understand citizenship more as a matter of participation, civic and democratic participation. A part of which happens to be . . . to become if you are qualified to do so . . . a so-called "naturalized U.S. citizen." But much more so than just becoming naturalized U.S. citizens, I think it's a matter of how do we make Salvadoreños in the U.S. be more engaged? Be more willing and more available to participate in every aspect of life that is affecting us? Economically, socially, politically, culturally, and so on. And to do [so] in a way that allows us to impact both places, El Salvador and the U.S.

Interview with Salvadoran activist, September 14, 2000

The passage of NACARA in 1997 boosted the morale of Salvadoran activists but also provoked dismay and outrage over the disparity in the remedies awarded to Nicaraguans, on the one hand, and to Salvadorans and Guatemalans, on the other. In response to this disparity, Central American organizations launched a campaign to create parity in remedies and in eligibility dates and to include similarly situated immigrants, such as Haitians and Hondurans. In seeking parity, advocates stressed the contributions that Salvadorans and Guatemalans had made to U.S. society through work, taxes, ties to U.S. citizen relatives, setting down roots, and becoming members of communities. In other words, advocates approached policy makers as constituents who deserved attention. As constituents, activists developed extensive connections to congressional staffers, White House aides, INS officials, Salvadoran embassy and consular staff, and leading immigrant and Latina/o organizations, such as the American Immigration Lawyers Association, the National Council of La Raza, the National Immigration Forum, and the United States Conference of Catholic Bishops' Office of Migration and Refugee Services. As organizations engaged in repeated lobbying efforts, nationally recognized leaders emerged. SANN, the Salvadoran American National Network, a coalition that had been founded in 1992 through the effort to obtain a permanent status for TPS recipients, became more visible on a national level, while in Los Angeles and other cities with large Salvadoran populations, activists sought to mobilize local leaders in support of their cause. In Los Angeles, SAL-PAC, the first Salvadoran American Political Action Committee, and SANA (the Salvadoran American National Association), a group dedicated to spiritual and civic involvement (such as recognizing and celebrating traditional Salvadoran holidays) were founded.

Efforts to empower Central Americans were affected by natural disasters that temporarily kept Central America in the national spotlight. In 1998, after the parity campaign was underway, Hurricane Mitch devastated Central American nations. The U.S. government responded by granting Temporary Protected Status to Honduran and Nicaraguan nationals who were in the United States as of December 30, 1998, but, because the damage in El Salvador was less severe, this protection was not extended to Salvadorans. Nonetheless, under pressure from activists and from the Salvadoran government, the Clinton administration argued that the NACARA regulations, which streamlined application procedures and granted applicants a presumption of hardship, provided some assistance to Salvadorans. Then, in January and February 2001, more disasters struck. On January 13 and again on February 13, massive earthquakes of 7.6 and 6.6 respectively rocked El Salvador, causing more than one thousand deaths and destroying over one hundred thousand homes (Moreno 2001). In response, the administration of President George H. W. Bush granted Salvadorans who had been in the United States on or before February 13 eighteen months of Temporary Protected Status.

By 2000, Salvadoran activists involved in the parity campaign had joined forces with other Latina/o and immigrant groups seeking a legalization program for undocumented immigrants in the United States. The mere fact that legalization was a viable option presented a sharp contrast to the early and mid-1990s, when, in a fervor of anti-immigrant sentiment, the United States adopted restrictive immigration policies (Perea 1997). Many also saw the viability of legalization proposals as a measure of the increasing empowerment of Latina/o and immigrant coalitions. During the summer of 2000, the Latino and Immigrant Fairness Act (LIFA), which would have permitted the legalization of many undocumented immigrants, was introduced in Congress. This act had three provisions: (1) changing the date of registry—a program through which anyone in the United States as of a certain date could seek legal permanent residency—from 1972 to 1986; (2) restoring 245(i)—a section of immigration law that permitted the beneficiaries of a family visa to pay a fine and adjust their status in the United States rather than returning to their country of origin; and (3) creating parity between Salvadoran, Guatemalan, and Nicaraguan NACARA beneficiaries, and extending immigration benefits to migrants from Honduras, Haiti, and possibly Liberia. LIFA had the backing of a broad coalition of immigrant, Latina/o, Asian, business, and labor groups, as well as the support of the Democratic leadership, but was opposed by key Republicans, who argued that any form of "amnesty" for illegal immigrants would simply encourage more illegal immigration (*Congressional Record* 2000, H11291). At the end of the fall session, when President Clinton was threatening to veto the Washington, D.C., appropriations bill if it did not include LIFA, the Republicans proposed and passed their own immigration legislation: LIFE, the Legal Immigration Family Equity Act. LIFE permitted the legalization of fewer individuals and did not include parity. Nonetheless, the fact that parity had been a central component of LIFA, a bill that some saw as a national priority, was an indication of the growing clout of Salvadoran and Guatemalan advocates.

As they sought remedies for undocumented and temporarily documented immigrants, Salvadoran activists also considered ways to remain involved in El Salvador. ASOSAL opened an office in El Salvador to provide immigration services and consultations; El Rescate opened an office there to distribute earthquake relief to hard-hit communities; and CARECEN-Houston established a San Salvador office to educate would-be migrants about the dangers of the journey, aid families of individuals who had died or been injured en route to the United States, and advocate with Salvadoran authorities on behalf of immigrants. All of these groups were involved in the effort to obtain NACARA parity. In addition, some argued that Salvadorans who live outside of El Salvador should be granted the right to vote in Salvadoran elections. Others favored alternative models of participation, such as using the remittances sent by hometown associations to foster development. The Salvadoran government has recently created a program called Unidos por la Solidaridad (United in Solidarity) to award funds to Salvadoran hometown associations that propose development projects in El Salvador.

Salvadoran activists' 2000–2001 efforts to claim political space created dilemmas that, with the events of September 11, 2001, have become more complex. If Salvadorans are positioning themselves as a new ethnic group in the United States, does this strategy reproduce or challenge dominant notions of race and ethnicity? As one Salvadoran activist noted:

> One of the things that in the U.S., the establishment doesn't like, is to acknowledge the complexity of, for example, Latinos in the U.S. I mean, the very fact that they bag us all together under the so-called "Hispanic" label or "Latino" label says it all! I mean, you speak to somebody from rural Mexico and then you speak to somebody from urban, you know, Buenos Aires. Both of them residing in the U.S. Both of them categorized as Latinos. But you're talking about day and night.

As this activist suggests, redefining dominant assumptions about what it is to be "Latina/o," and about the meanings of race and ethnicity within the United States might include securing recognition that Latinas/os are diverse, with differing histories, traditions, and social locations. To this end, some Los Angeles-based groups, such as SALEF, have been develop-ing curricula that school districts can use to teach students about Cen-tral American history and holidays. The importance of such curricula is demonstrated by one Salvadoran parent's experience when her daughter came home from elementary school on Cinco de Mayo and said, "Look Mother, here is our flag!" The flag that her daughter displayed was that of Mexico rather than of El Salvador. The teacher had apparently as-sumed that all of the Latina/o students in the classroom were of Mexican descent. Curricular and other efforts may also challenge dominant under-standings of "ethnic identities" and "multiculturalism," understandings that naturalize difference by depicting "immigrants as having 'roots' in other lands but [as] now [being] fully 'American'" (Schiller and Fouron 1999, 345). In contrast to such understandings, the economic, social, political, and organizational ties that migrants maintain to their coun-tries of origin define "difference" not as something that is commensur-able, private, and located in the past, but rather as particular, public, and ongoing. Thus, diverse Latina/o immigrant groups can coordinate their efforts not only through the development of a pan-Latina/o identity, or through identifying commonalities in their positioning within the United States, but also through regional efforts to mobilize political lead-ers in their countries of origin. An example of such regional efforts occurred in August 2001, when a delegation of labor and Central Ameri-can activists urged Central American leaders to join in Mexican president Vicente Fox's proposals for developing new legalization and immigration policies in the United States.

Since September 11, 2001, the scenario within which Salvadoran com-munity groups operate has undergone dramatic change. In the wake of attacks on the World Trade Center and the Pentagon and of the U.S. war on terrorism, Central American activists expressed fears of a new wave of anti-immigrant policy making, discrimination, and economic deprivation. With the passage of new antiterrorism legislation, the civil rights of non-citizens have been curtailed. Given such developments, ethnicity-based organizing and appeals to different histories and traditions may be neither popular nor effective. During the fall of 2001, at Central American events in Los Angeles, such as the Salvadoran and Central American indepen-dence day parades, which occurred shortly after September 11, U.S. flags far outnumbered those of Central American nations. National security has now become a key idiom in which immigration policies are assessed.

174 Susan Bibler Coutin

Any reform that permits legalization would have to be justified in security terms as, for example, permitting easier tracking of individuals within the United States. Not surprisingly, pending legislation that would grant parity to NACARA beneficiaries is entitled the "Central American Security Act." Similarly, President George W. Bush's January 2004 call for a new temporary worker program is listed on the White House web page under the heading, "National Security" (White House 2004). Nonetheless, the fact that, in 2004, both the Republican and Democratic parties have proposed some form of legalization and/or guest worker program suggests that the tide of immigration reform may be turning. In this shifting political context, Central American and other Latina/o groups are likely to develop new strategies for political empowerment and legal inclusion.

Conclusion

In 1987, a caravan of U.S., Salvadoran, and Guatemalan activists traveled from San Francisco to Oregon and back. The purpose of this caravan was to denounce human rights abuses in El Salvador and Guatemala, oppose U.S. involvement in the Salvadoran and Guatemalan civil wars, and seek refugee status for Salvadorans and Guatemalans in the United States. As the caravan traveled, interpreters (that was my role) spoke for Central Americans, many of whom were undocumented, as they gave "testimonies" to church and other groups along the route. This 1987 caravan contrasts sharply with the 2000 effort to pass LIFA. In 2000, Salvadoran activists from around the United States gathered in Washington, D.C., to meet with lobbyists and congressional staffers. Some of the individuals who participated in this effort had become legal permanent residents or U.S. citizens entitled to the ear of their representatives in Congress. Instead of seeking solidarity, these activists sought alliances with other powerful groups. Times had definitely changed.

The increased empowerment of Salvadoran immigrants and activists did not occur automatically, but rather was accomplished through complex and creative strategies. The solidarity and refugee work of the 1980s laid the groundwork for the immigration remedies of the 1990s. These remedies were implemented in a changed political context, in which peace accords were signed in El Salvador and Guatemala, restrictive immigration measures were adopted in the United States, and policies— such as bilingual education and affirmative action—that extended rights to minority groups were under attack. Political tensions were particularly heightened in Southern California, given the 1992 Los Angeles uprisings, the O. J. Simpson trial, and statewide initiatives that limited the rights of immigrants and of minority groups. In response to these changed conditions, Central American community organizations became involved in ethnicity-based political organizing, promoting naturalization, voter registration, and civic involvement. In so doing, they forged alliances with other Latina/o and immigrant groups and sought to claim politicians' attention as constituents with a right to a voice and presence in the United States but also with particular histories that shaped their messages and their needs. Until September 11, 2001, this strategy seemed headed for success, with President Fox of Mexico advocating for the legalization of Mexican nationals and with congressional leaders and members of the George W. Bush administration seriously considering new approaches to immigration, legalization, and border issues.

The experiences of Central American immigrants and activists suggest that Los Angeles will continue to be a crucible for national trends in immigration and ethnic relations. Most immigrant and ethnic groups in the United States are well represented in Los Angeles (Waldinger and Bozorgmehr 1996), and these groups participate actively in forging local, national, and transnational political discourses. Latina/o Los Angeles is incredibly diverse. It is differentiated not only along lines of national origin but also generation, immigration status, gender, socioeconomic status, and political affiliation. Salvadoran immigrants, for example, entered the United States at different times, have different legal statuses, are politically and economically diverse, identify with different communities within El Salvador, and have differing organizational goals. Diverse groups have mobilized around both particularistic and pan-Latina/o issues, uniting in support of legalization, better schools, and greater civic involvement, but sometimes prioritizing different concerns—such as NACARA parity. Given this history, Los Angeles is likely to continue to be a site in which the positioning of Latinas/os in the nation is worked out.

References

Bach, Robert L. 1990. "Immigration and U.S. Foreign Policy in Latin America and the Caribbean." In *Immigration and U.S. Foreign Policy*, edited by Robert W. Tucker, Charles B. Keely, and Linda Wrigley. Boulder, Colo.: Westview Press.

Baker-Cristales, Beth. 2004. *Salvadoran Migration to Southern California: Redefining El Hermano Lejano*. Gainesville: University of Florida Press.

Banco Central de Reserva de El Salvador. 2004. "Ingresos mensuales en concepto de remesas familiares." [Electronic table.] Available at http://www.bcr.gob.sv/. Accessed July 21.

Byrne, Hugh. 1996. *El Salvador's Civil War: A Study of Revolution*. Boulder, Colo.: Lynne Reinner.

Churgin, Michael J. 1996. "Mass Exoduses: The Response of the United States." *International Migration Review* 30(1): 310–25.

Congressional Record. 2000. 106th Cong., 2d sess. Vol. 146, p. H11291.

Coutin, Susan Bibler. 1993. *The Culture of Protest: Religious Activism and the U.S. Sanctuary Movement*. Boulder, Colo.: Westview Press.

———. 1995. "Smugglers or Samaritans in Tucson, Arizona: Producing and Contesting Legal Truth." *American Ethnologist* 22(3): 549–71.

———. 1998. "From Refugees to Immigrants: The Legalization Strategies of Salvadoran Immigrants and Activists." *International Migration Review* 32(4): 901–25.

———. 2000. *Legalizing Moves: Salvadoran Immigrants' Struggle for U.S. Residency*. Ann Arbor: University of Michigan Press.

———. 2003. "Cultural Logics of Belonging and Movement: Transnationalism, Naturalization, and U.S. Immigration Politics." *American Ethnologist* 30(4): 508–26.

Durand, Jorge, Emilio A. Parrado, and Douglas S. Massey. 1996. "Migradollars and Development: A Reconsideration of the Mexican Case." *International Migration Review* 30(2): 423–37.

Fiederlein, Suzanne L. 1991. "Interpreting International and Domestic Law Concerning Refugees: The U.S. Government vs. the Sanctuary Movement." *Journal of Borderlands Studies* 6(1): 23–50.

Hamilton, Nora, and Norma S. Chinchilla. 1991. "Central American Migration: A Framework for Analysis." *Latin American Research Review* 26(1): 75–110.

———. 2001. *Seeking Community in a Global City: Guatemalans and Salvadorans in Los Angeles*. Philadelphia: Temple University Press.

Harvey, David. 1989. *The Condition of Postmodernity*. Cambridge, Mass.: Blackwell.

Hondagneu-Sotelo, Pierrette, and Ernestine Avila. 1997. "'I'm Here, but I'm There': The Meanings of Latina Transnational Motherhood." *Gender and Society* 11(5): 548–71.

Itzigsohn, José. 2000. "Immigration and the Boundaries of Citizenship: The Institutions of Immigrants' Political Transnationalism." *International Migration Review* 34(4): 1126–54.

Menjívar, Cecilia. 2000. *Fragmented Ties: Salvadoran Immigrant Networks in America*. Berkeley: University of California Press.

Menjívar, Cecilia, Julia DaVanzo, Lisa Greenwell, and R. Burciaga Valdez. 1998. "Remittance Behavior among Salvadoran and Filipino Immigrants in Los Angeles." *International Migration Review* 32(1): 97–126.

Montes Mozo, Segundo, and Juan José Garcia Vasquez. 1988. *Salvadoran Migration to the United States: An Exploratory Study*. Washington, D.C.: Center for Immigration Policy and Refugee Assistance.

Montgomery, Tommie Sue. 1995. *Revolution in El Salvador: From Civil Strife to Civil Peace*. 2d ed. Boulder, Colo.: Westview Press.

Moreno, Sylvia. 2001. "Devastated by 2 Quakes, Salvador Pleads for Help." *Washington Post*, Feb. 16, A18.

Orellana Merlos, Carlos. 1992. "Migración y remesas: una evaluación de su impacto en la economía salvadoreña." *Política Económica* 1:2–23.

Orozco, Manuel. 2000. *Latino Hometown Associations as Agents of Development in Latin America*. Washington D.C.: Inter-American Dialogue.

Orozco, Manuel, Rodolfo de la Garza, and Miguel Baraona. 1997. *Inmigración y remesas familiares*. San Jose, Costa Rica: FLACSO.

Perea, Juan F., ed. 1997. *Immigrants Out! The New Nativism and the Anti-Immigrant Impulse in the United States*. New York: New York University Press.

Pirie, Sophie H. 1990. "The Origins of a Political Trial: The Sanctuary Movement and Political Justice." *Yale Journal of Law and the Humanities* 2(2): 381–416.

Poitras, Guy. 1983. "Through the Revolving Door: Central American Manpower in the United States." *Inter-American Economic Affairs* 36(4): 63–78.

Sassen, Saskia. 1989. "America's Immigration 'Problem': The Real Causes." *World Policy Journal* 6(4): 811–31.

———. 1996. *Losing Control? Sovereignty in an Age of Globalization*. New York: Columbia University Press.

Schiller, Nina Glick, and Georges E. Fouron. 1999. "Terrains of Blood and Nation: Haitian Transnational Social Fields." *Ethnic and Racial Studies* 2(2): 340–66.

Schiller, Nina Glick, Linda Basch, and Cristina Szanton Blanc. 1995. "From Immigrant to Transmigrant: Theorizing Transnational Migration." *Anthropological Quarterly* 68(1): 48–63.

Smith, Christian. 1996. *Resisting Reagan: The U.S. Central America Peace Movement*. Chicago: University of Chicago Press.

Taylor, J. Edward. 1999. "The New Economics of Labour Migration and the Role of Remittances in the Migration Process." *International Migration* 37(1): 63–88.

U.S. Committee for Refugees (USCR). 1986. *Despite a Generous Spirit: Denying Asylum in the United States*. Washington, D.C.: American Council for Nationalities Service.

U.S. House Committee on the Judiciary. 1984. Subcommittee on Immigration, Refugees, and International Law. *Temporary Suspension of Deportation of Certain Aliens*. 98th Cong., 2d sess., Apr. 12.

Waldinger, Roger, and Mehdi Bozorgmehr, eds. 1996. *Ethnic Los Angeles*. New York: Russell Sage Foundation.

White House. 2004. "Policies and Initiatives." Available at http://www.white house .gov/infocus/index.html. Accessed July 21.

Zolberg, Aristide R. 1990. "The Roots of U.S. Refugee Policy." In *Immigration and U.S. Foreign Policy*, edited by Robert W. Tucker, Charles B. Keely, and Linda Wrigley. Boulder, Colo.: Westview Press.

9 Negotiating Latinidade in Los Angeles

The Case of Brazilian Immigrants

Bernadete Beserra

In the United States, the label *Latino* generally refers to patterns of immigration and to social stratification. Its specific content, however, varies from place to place and from time to time (Hayes-Bautista and Chapa 1987; Muñoz 1989; Oboler 1995). Whereas in Los Angeles the category *Latino* is immediately associated with Mexicans, in Miami it is associated with Cubans, and in New York with Puerto Ricans. In all cases, it refers to a social identity produced by American history. The category *Latino* is a consequence of the civil rights movements in the 1960s and was mostly connected to struggle and resistance (Muñoz 1989). Despite the considerable number of meanings that may fall under the category today, in Los Angeles *Latino* generally means an immigrant from Mexico and Central America (Salvadorans and Guatemalans) and his/her descendants born in the United States. Thus, the label *Latino* is connected to a political economic determination, the Third World; to a historic destiny, immigration to the United States; and to a social fortune, low status in the United States.

Despite examples of more privileged Latinos, such as Cubans in Miami (Portes and Stepick 1993; Stack and Warren 1992), the low social status of Latinos is what shaped discrimination against them in the United States. In this sense, Castles and Kosack (1985, 2) propose that the problem of racist discrimination against immigrants must be interpreted as connected mainly to the function that immigrants generally have in the socioeconomic structure, and not the other way around. Color or ethnicity cannot be regarded as the determinants of immigrants' social position because their position has been already determined beforehand, as immigration is motivated to supply specific labor demands (Piore 1979).

Even coming from the same country, region, or continent, immigrants do not comprise a single social class and do not all migrate for the same reason. How different immigrants cope with discrimination is the broad issue of this chapter. Its aim is to discuss the class content of Latino identity in Los Angeles by exploring what is behind Brazilian immigrants' refusal to be identified as Latinos.

The Context: Brazilians in Los Angeles

Los Angeles is not the most common destination for Brazilian immigrants to the United States. The Brazilian Foreign Ministry estimates that about 90 percent of the Brazilian immigrant population in the United States is concentrated on the East Coast (New York, 300 thousand; Miami, 200 thousand; and Boston, 150 thousand).

In the metropolitan area of Los Angeles, the number of Brazilians is estimated at thirty-three thousand (MRE 2003). Although this community is far smaller than those in New York, Boston, or Miami, it shares some of the characteristics of larger communities (Margolis 1994 and 1995; Goza 1994; Sales 1995 and 1999; Assis 1995; Martes 2000; Beserra 2003). In Los Angeles, as in the other cities, Brazilians exist as one immigrant group among many in a diverse society where Latinos, defined broadly, form a significant demographic and economic force.

Distinct from many other immigrant populations, Brazilians in Los Angeles are not concentrated in one geographical region. Rather, there are a number of small communities. The largest geographic concentration of Brazilians in Los Angeles is in West Los Angeles around Venice Boulevard. My respondents estimate, however, that this concentration does not amount to more than five hundred people. Most of the Brazilians that I interviewed consider Venice a gateway community for newcomers, artists, or those who have been unable to buy a place elsewhere. One individual explained to me that "Venice represents more a lack of option than anything else."

There are several reasons why Brazilians comprise neither an ethnic enclave nor a geographically based community. First, Brazilians are not as numerous as Mexicans, Indians, Koreans, and Salvadorans. Second, because of racial diversity, Brazilian immigrants are not as physically distinguishable as those in some other immigrant groups. And third, they have a very recent immigrant history, and therefore have not yet built an immigrant "know-how," as many of these "classic" communities have (Ribeiro 1997a and 1997b). Although there is no visible Brazilian neighborhood, there are several clubs and associations of Brazilians that meet on a regular basis. One way of locating these gatherings is to browse the pages of Brazilian magazines on the Internet (Beserra 1998 and 1999). As a Brazilian, however, I learned about these associations through the Brazilians that I associated with, which were mainly those studying at the University of California, Riverside, and their families and acquaintances.

Research Methodology

The data presented here was collected between November 1997 and November 1999 as part of a larger study entitled "Brazilians in Los Angeles: Imperialism, Immigration, and Social Class" (2000). During this period, I observed and participated in the regular meetings and other social gatherings (such as birthday and wedding parties, baby showers, and so forth) of the Portuguese-speaking Seventh-day Adventist Church of Chino and the Brazilian Women's Group. I chose these groups because they represent different ways of Brazilian immigrant integration into Los Angeles. Whereas the Adventists of Chino more closely illustrate a community-based, working-class experience of integration, the Brazilian Women's Group represents the experience of the integration of Brazilian elites in Los Angeles. Although neither group is homogeneous in terms of the social position of its members, each group more closely represents either the experience of the working classes or the elites. Other aspects of each group were also salient for my choice. The Brazilian Women's Group is a gender-based group that has, among other goals, the mission of creating a different image of Brazilian immigrants in Los Angeles. These women want to disassociate themselves from the eroticized image of Brazilian women they believe Americans have, as well as distinguish themselves from an essentialized Hispanic and/or Latino identity. The Brazilian Adventist group of Chino, in comparison, was chosen for capturing a particular experience of Brazilian integration into Los Angeles that is different from the majority of Brazilians, who are Catholic. Members of this group were socialized as Protestants and always kept a closer bond with the United States than have other Brazilians.

I tape-recorded in-depth, open-ended interviews with fifteen members of each of the two associations and with ten Brazilians connected to other Brazilian associations and institutions, such as the Brazilian Consulate, the Brazil-California Chamber of Commerce, the Brazilian Socio-cultural Committee, the Cultural Gaucho Center, the Brazilian Evangelic Community-Salvation Army, the Hollywood Palladium Brazil *carnaval*, the MILA-Samba School, and the SambaLA-Samba School. Through face-to-face conversations or by telephone, I also collected socioeconomic data (age, time of immigration, state of birth in Brazil, level of education, type of job before and after immigration, marital status, and so forth) for 195 people, most of them connected to the two groups that I researched. In order to ensure my informants' privacy, I have altered all names, although I have retained the ethnic or American character of all given names and surnames.

Of the Brazilian immigrants in the greater Los Angeles area that I surveyed, 65 percent were women, 73 percent were married, 53 percent were between the ages of thirty and forty-five. Most migrated from the industrialized region in Brazil, the Southeast, mainly from the states of Rio de Janeiro (27 percent) and São Paulo (20 percent). However, there was also a significant number from the southern state of Rio Grande do Sul (14 percent), and northeastern Bahia (7 percent). The great majority (76 percent) immigrated between 1981 and 1999. The sharp difference between males (35 percent) and females (65 percent) in my sample has to do with the fact that one of the associations that I researched is for females only, and it does not reflect the reality of the Brazilian immigrant population in Los Angeles as a whole.

Coming from the middle classes, most of the interviewees attended college (52 percent) or had finished high school (32 percent). The percentage of those surveyed holding white-collar jobs is 48, which is just slightly less than expected. Some 32 percent hold blue-collar jobs, 13 percent are housewives, and 6 percent are students. Sixty-three percent of those who are married have a Brazilian spouse, whereas 30 percent are married to American citizens. The remaining 7 percent are married to Mexican, European, and other South American immigrants. Most of the Brazilians with whom I conducted in-depth interviews described migrating for reasons other than "making money." They came to work for Brazilian or American companies, to study, to marry, and so forth. They either arrived with their families or established families in Los Angeles, and although going back to Brazil is a dream for many, they struggle to become assimilated into U.S. society.

The Latino Fate

Although immigrant stereotypes are related to the role that immigrants generally have in the socioeconomic structure, immigrant integration is a result of a combination of the following factors: (1) color and social position of the immigrant in his country or city of origin; (2) the position of the country or city of origin in the national or international division of labor; (3) the relative position of each immigrant population in relation to other immigrant populations; and (4) specific needs of the job market in the host country or city (Beserra 2003, 60).

In general, however, the construction of a Brazilian identity in the United States, particularly in Los Angeles, can only be grasped within the broader context of a Latin American identity as it has been constructed in the context of globalization in which Latin Americans—and Third World people in general—have become the "other" in U.S. domestic and international politics (Larrain 1994, 156–57). It is, then, in this disadvantageous position that a Brazilian identity shifts between distinguishing itself from or allying itself with a Latino identity.

Brazilian immigrants relate differently to *Latinidade*—the Latino character or condition—as a consequence of how they combine this aspect of their identities with others, such as color, class position in Brazil, type of job, and place of residence in Los Angeles. Considering that Brazilian integration is individually processed and identities are individually negotiated, those immigrants who come from higher social positions in Brazil have better chances to negotiate to their advantage "negative" components of their identities, such as color and nationality. In contrast, when immigrants come from lower social positions and work in low-paid jobs, even color does not seem to matter much in defining identities and positions.

Marta Anderson, age forty-five and an immigrant since 1989, is an example of how Brazilians who come from higher social positions in Brazil may negotiate their Latinidade in Los Angeles:

> I'm going to speak of what I see at my children's school because that is the place where I interact with the largest number of people daily. Well, in general, all of them are white, upper-middle-class Americans. The first impression that they have is that I am a Brazilian, a Latina, an immigrant, have an accent, etc. . . . Even being white and having this

Anglo look I have . . . they keep me off. . . . I think [Latino] is sort of devalued. . . . When [European Americans] are going to say something that may involve social and economic status they even have a certain caution because this person is, poor thing, a Latina. They always think that we, Latinos, are poor, that we must have some sort of scholarship because it isn't possible that I, a Latina, could pay fifteen thousand dollars a year for an elementary school for my child. It's impressive how they change when they come here to my house. . . . Even so the first question they ask me is if my husband is American, as if to say, "Wow, this Latina was very lucky to marry an old rich man. But thank God my husband is young, my age, and he is very Brazilian!

Marta is also an example of how the classification forged by colonizing countries situates people differently based on their birthplace. Even though the position of Brazil in the international division of labor does not prevent Brazilians from relocating themselves in U.S society (in social spaces that suit their purchasing power), it certainly colors their movements, thus interfering with their integration, especially when "integration" means full integration into American White society.

Marta's case shows that regardless of their social position in Brazilian society, Brazilians in the United States have to deal with the consequences of being identified as Latinos, which means to be or to feel somehow "devalued." There is no question, however, that coping with discrimination as an upper-middle-class individual is quite different from coping with discrimination while being a maid for that same upper-middle-class family. For instance, Telma Haller, age forty-six, who, in 1975, migrated to Los Angeles, and currently works as a cook, observes:

I think that now, after all these years here, I ended up learning to see the people as the Americans [U.S.-born individuals] see them. I define quickly what they are. The race. It's not that I want to, I don't even like to! Here Americans always want to know if one is black or white. So I also began defining persons. I am even ashamed of saying so, and I don't even think I am racist, but I don't like it when anyone speaks in Spanish with me. Simply because I don't want people to think I'm Mexican, or from Guatemala because they are races that the Americans denigrate. They are . . . how can I say it? Latinos are like a lower class for the Americans.

There are clear differences in the ways Latinidade is experienced by Marta and Telma. Marta is connected to Brazil, a Third World country, only when she speaks and responds to questions about her place of birth. Otherwise, she has the option of passing as a European immigrant, or simply White American. Telma's case is different. She has a job that is nowadays typically held by immigrants, and she is physically closer to the stereotypical conception of the Mexican peasant than to the White American. The last sign of distinction left is her language, Portuguese, or her English with a non-Spanish accent. So, whereas Marta is included in the Latino category, when she chooses to declare her nationality, Telma is automatically included because of her job and physical appearance. Thus, when Telma says "Latinos are like a lower class for the Americans," she is saying that in Los Angeles her connection to the Latino label has assigned her a place with which she does not feel comfortable because of its connotation of poor immigrants, cheap labor, and low status. In Marta's case what comes first is the relationship to an economic region. When she says that she is Brazilian, Americans do not necessarily connect her immediately with a social fortune in the United States. She is from a Third World country, which in terms of general status is not good either, but she is not a Latina in the terms that Telma is because of her appearance and place in the job market. She is instead a Latin American, someone who is from Latin America and who is not necessarily connected to a low status in U.S. society.

Telma's quote also calls attention to the differences between the construction of racial categories in the United States and Brazil. She says that in the United States she learned to see people the same as U.S.-born individuals do: one is either Black or White and color alone is enough to ascribe someone a place in society. But when she says that she does not like to be thought of as Mexican or Guatemalan, she is also saying that the non-White category fits more races than just Black, and that being Latino is also having been ascribed a low rank in the American social hierarchy.

Aware of these meanings, Brazilians explain their Latinidade in a way that seeks to detach them from this image of Latinos, a pattern that is also apparent among other Latinos (see Oboler 1995; Ochoa 2000). Telma and other Brazilians I interviewed rarely stop to wonder why the Latino category has such a different meaning in Los Angeles than in Brazil. They more easily fall into the racist trap and prefer not to face their own

Latinidade, because they believe that Brazil, too, and consequently Brazilians, are superior to other Latinos. They believe that they can benefit from the same racist politics that discriminate against them, and many of them benefit from the countless hierarchies of power proposed and practiced by the imperialist regime. This confirms the observation that the political position of a nation in the international scenario is relative and that racism works hierarchically, as does exploitation and oppression. Borrowing Balibar's (1991, 89) words, "in a sense, every modern nation is a product of colonization: it has always been to some degree colonized or colonizing, and sometimes both at the same time." Thus, Brazilians see that in terms of the economy, Brazil is hierarchically inferior to the United States, but it is superior to many other countries that, broadly and ideologically speaking, make Brazilians feel superior to people from these nations.

Another way of understanding the discomfort of Brazilians with the Latino label in Los Angeles is to explore what being Latino means for a Brazilian in Brazil. Raquel Tavares, for instance, was a twenty-five-year-old Brazilian married to a Spaniard and taking English classes at UCLA when I interviewed her. While explaining her integration into Los Angeles, she began talking about her difficulties of approaching American citizens in general, as well as other nationalities, such as Indians and Japanese. In her experience, the contact with other Latinos had always been much easier. But then she explained that she was still using the word *Latino* with the meaning that it has in Brazil. She explains:

> When I say "Latinos" I do not mean only Mexicans as people in the United States do. I mean, instead, people from Portugal, Spain, France, Italy, and people from American countries colonized by them. In this sense, I am a Latina, but I don't feel comfortable being a Latina in Los Angeles. First, because there is way too much prejudice against Latinos here, and second, because I don't think that it is okay to lump into the same category people as different as Brazilians, Mexicans, and Argentines. Plus, I don't think that I am what American people expect a Latina to be.

She is calling attention to the fact that the term *Latino* in the United States has a general connotation very different from the connotation it has in Brazil. Despite Anglo-Saxon hegemony and its politics of misrepresentation of the Latin identity, the category *Latino* in Brazil still holds a generally positive connotation (Freyre 1975). Connected to the previous hegemonic colonizing powers, Portugal and Spain, Latino is everything that refers to the Latin world and its consequences, and, in principle, it encompasses all people connected to the Latin culture and tradition including its European creators. As one of the most important elements of the Brazilian national character, the Latin-Iberian tradition is a source of pride. It is also a source of shame and stratification when what is at stake is comparison between the political-economic positions of Brazil and the United States. Without taking into consideration important facts connected to international imperialist politics, Brazil and the United States are generally compared as if they were simply results of the adaptation of two different cultures (the Anglo-Saxon and Latin-Iberian) to a new environment, the American continent.

The fact is that because of the position of Brazil in the international division of labor, and the general conception and experiences of other Latinos, when Brazilians come to the United States their value is immediately decreased. This reduction of value occurs despite the social class to which one belongs. Even though different networks enable different forms of adjustment in Los Angeles, all Brazilians have to cope with discrimination during their integration, as exemplified in the case of Marta Anderson.

But the reasons why Brazilians immigrate, and the networks to which they are connected, matter as much as the conditions they find here. As Bourdieu (1986, 4) argues, connections and group networks are part of the resources that define class position, which means that different networks bring individuals to different social places and opportunities. A Brazilian who has a working-class background, for example, would hardly come to the United States through an upper-class network unless such mobility was already in progress in Brazil. For instance, in the case of menial laborers serving the Brazilian international diplomatic corps, even though they come through a network that is part of the Brazilian dominant classes' network, they have an inferior position within it. When deciding to stay in the United States, they hardly settle within the limits of the network that brought them here. They generally find and get along with Brazilians of a similar class background, and it is through these new relationships that they learn how to get around in Los Angeles.

Discovering that, in most cases, the Latino world is the world ascribed for Brazilians in the United States is a big disappointment for many Brazilian immigrants, as one sees in the statement of Omar Santana, age sixty, a retired nurse living in Los Angeles since 1963:

> There are lots of Brazilians who say that they don't like California because there are a lot of Mexicans, and they don't like the sound of the Spanish language because of the Mexicans, and all that nonsense. Because many people in the world speak Spanish, not just Mexicans. . . . The problem is that when you leave Brazil, you leave with a vision of the United States as a Caucasian race. When you get here and you enter a community where you go to the supermarket and the largest population is Mexican, you go to work and it is Mexican, you go to the university and it is Mexican. Then you say, well, I left Brazil to speak English, to meet the Americans, and so far I haven't seen an American!

Omar's quote sheds light on several important issues: It is by living in the United States that Brazilians learn that their vision of Americans as a Caucasian race is mistaken, and they realize that Americans are also Black Americans, Mexican Americans, Japanese Americans, and so forth. Generally guided by the images produced by Hollywood, when Brazilians go to Los Angeles they expect to find mostly blond people. Yet they are disappointed when they face the existing racial/ethnic variety and find their place in it. It is after coming to the United States that Brazilians learn that there is a connection between Latinos and low status, and it is precisely this connection that causes Brazilians to fear being identified as Latinos. Brazilians, therefore, avoid being identified with other Latinos in Los Angeles—not because of a perceived idea of Brazilian uniqueness, but in reaction to the meaning attached to Latinos.

It does not seem to matter whether Brazilians have or have not had good experiences with other Latinos. It seems that whenever they have to generalize their impressions, they are drowned by the same racist mainstream ideologies that discriminate against the so-called people of color. For instance, during the summer of 1998, I met a Brazilian woman who was moving to New York. She was regretting having to move because she would miss the Hispanic church where she had been a member for the last six to eight years. Although she had a positive experience with Mexicans in California, she ended up reproducing the mainstream discourse when comparing what is good and bad about Los Angeles and New York, saying, "At least New York does not have as many immigrants as here. I mean, to tell you the truth there is no place like here. The Mexicans are destroying California."

One can hypothesize that these discourses are not necessarily the product of American mainstream ideologies but must be connected first with Brazilian systems of classification and stratification. Indeed, immigrants quite generally process the understanding of the new culture through the eyes of their native culture (Thomas and Znanieck 1996). In this sense, they will impute old prejudices to new social actors, or they will renovate their anterior systems of stratification in light of the systems of stratification they find wherever they go. Brazilians see that the words *Hispanic* and *Latino*, which are the social categories that encompass them, refer to both an identity and a social position. It is an identity linked to negative social patterns, such as poor immigrants, gangs, high school dropouts, criminality, and so forth. But it is an identity whose negative content is mainly a consequence of its immediate relationship to the working class. This proves the thesis that any social segmentation, whether based on ethnicity, race, or gender, has to be understood within the limits of the capitalist need of producing and maintaining differences to justify inequality and exploitation (Bonacich 1973; Balibar and Wallerstein 1991; Stolcke 1995).

The Latino label does not cause only problems for Brazilian immigrants, nor does the negative content linked to it prevent Brazilians from establishing cooperative relationships with other Latinos. As a matter of fact, as Gimenez (1992, 13) proposes, there are some visible advantages of identifying oneself as Latino, particularly for middle- and upper-class Latinos:

> Latin Americans as a whole benefit if they choose to play the minority role. While civil rights legislation and affirmative action are indifferent to class, protecting everyone from illiterate peasants to scientists, professionals, and the wealthy from discrimination in economic, political and social activities, it is the upper strata that are likely to benefit the most. Working-class Central and South Americans are likely to be over-represented in low-paid, undesirable employment; affirmative action is not relevant to their chances of finding jobs. [Thus] it is possible to hypothesize, consequently, that while all Latin

American immigrants are potentially subject to stereotyping and racial discrimination, racism is likely to be most strongly felt among those who are working-class, poor, and/or of mixed non-European ancestry.

To Gimenez's assertion, I would add the following: loading the term *Latino* with negative connotation is a need of the international job market, which, as we have stressed before, benefits from these hierarchies of power. However, it is necessary to distinguish different roles played by different Latinos. Even though all Latinos are subject to the same general racist constraints, some of them benefit from playing a more valued role in the system, as Giménez pointed out. It is a mistake, however, to expect all components of an ethnic group or social class to benefit equally from the cleavage established between Brazil and the United States, or between upper middle classes and working classes. There is a hierarchy of advantages ranging from one position to the next, and, in their integration into American society, the Brazilians are always trying to negotiate their identities to their advantage. Thus, even though many Brazilians benefit from affirmative action and other specific protections for minorities, when they referred to the benefits of being Latino in Los Angeles they were also referring to other kinds of benefits. They suggested that Brazilians function as a bridge between White Americans and other Latinos—or as a sort of middlemen (Bonacich 1973). In this way, a few of them have been granted management positions in companies where the employees are mostly Spanish-speaking Latinos. This is the case of Anne Drummond, age thirty-six, living in Los Angeles since 1990:

> During the first two years, I worked making crafts with an American woman. I learned to speak Spanish before English, and I would only speak English and Spanish the entire time at work. I painted and taught the Mexican women. So I was an intermediary between the employees and my boss. . . . My boss didn't treat me like she treated the Mexicans, but I knew that I was also an employee. . . . I earned more than the others. My salary was different than theirs. The treatment was different from theirs. But I was the intermediary between these two worlds. My boss didn't speak Spanish and neither did the workers speak English. I think the first year I was the bridge between these two worlds. . . . A Mexican woman attained the same position as me, but she wasn't treated with the same respect. It makes a difference

the fact that I speak Portuguese, it makes a difference, to the Americans, that I am white. One thing that I felt, I also worked with a Jewish girl, and a higher value was also shown toward her.

I found other examples of Brazilians having been granted management positions in companies where the employees are mostly Spanish-speaking Latinos. The case of Claudiner Mockiuti, a former minister of a Portuguese-speaking Seventh-day Adventist church in the greater Los Angeles area is very revealing. He was invited by the Adventist congregation to serve a Hispanic church in Glendale because, according to the congregation, he represented the type of leadership that they needed for that moment. He explained, "The church congregates Latinos of varied nationalities including Brazilians, but mainly Mexicans. Brazilians are seen as ideal leaders because we are Hispanics, but we are different. So, sometimes it makes it easier to accept our leadership." Brazilians seem to have the privilege of passing as both insiders and outsiders of the imaginary Latino community in Los Angeles according to what the circumstances require. In this case, in principle, all Brazilians would be spared the discrimination that afflicts Mexicans, suggesting that Brazilians also benefit from not having taken part in the historic circumstances in which the existing prejudice against Latinos was created.

I want to insist that Brazilians distinguish themselves from other Hispanics or Latinos not only for the sake of Brazilian singularity, but also to protect themselves from being lumped under a category the mainstream clearly discriminates against. Consequently, they look for symbols that demonstrate Brazilian uniqueness.

The Carnavalesco Brazilians and the Limits of Exoticization

There are many elements that make Brazilians distinct from other Latin Americans. But the elements most commonly chosen by my respondents to express Brazilian identity are the ones connected to Carnaval. What I will be referring to hereafter as the *carnavalesco* stereotype is a set of qualities that Brazilians believe compose their character and distinguish them from Americans, Latinos, and people of other nationalities. Thus, according to several Brazilians that I interviewed, Brazilians are happy, playful, nice, warm, artistic, colorful, beautiful, and so on. These are the same elements that the exoticization of Brazilians, especially Brazilian women starting with Carmen Miranda, were based upon. I argue that, in Los Angeles, the Brazilians who cannot or choose not to pass as "Europeans" or "European-Americans" have to find their way between the Latino and the carnavalesco stereotype. Both are problematic, but the carnavalesco seems to be more malleable and more advantageous because the Brazilian referent is too far away to prove it right or wrong, as suggested by Ivan Becker, age forty-six, a journalist living in Los Angeles since 1990:

> The average Brazilian doesn't feel he is less than anyone. He thinks he is Brazilian. And when he gets to those areas where he is good, then no one else comes close. Be it in soccer, samba, music, sex, in those things that we believe we are good at, in our own positive image of ourselves. And the Brazilian, what do we believe the Brazilian is? We believe that all Brazilians are good ball players, every Brazilian is a good conversationalist, every Brazilian is good at sex, at music, at partying. We are hot! And the image that the world has of Brazil is that we are good with a ball, good at samba, good at fucking, good at everything! It's exotic! In a racist country such as this, the Brazilian even has a privileged position because we are not placed together with other Latinos. Brazilians are a separate category.

Ivan's quote brings out many issues, but I will explore only two of them. First, he is clearly aware that the qualities that distinguish Brazilians from other Latinos work to reinforce Brazilian exoticization, but I argue that this device is not really capable of escaping prejudice because exoticization is just a way of recasting it. As a matter of fact, the exoticization of the colonized is mainly a maneuver of the colonizer to keep the colonized in his place. It is interesting to notice that many Brazilians who want to distinguish themselves from other Latinos want to be differentiated from Brazilian immigrants as well (Beserra 2003, 74–75). In other words, by being a Brazilian, one is saved only from the prejudice against Latinos (meaning mainly poor, working-class people), but one immediately falls into another category of prejudice: the one against people from the Third World. Second, Brazilians may or may not be treated as a separate category, but it all depends on factors other than this abstract Brazilianness, as suggested above.

The following quote from Paola Ketterer, age thirty-six and a university professor living in the United States since 1989, offers some elements to help us understand what may allow Brazilians to be treated differently from other Latinos:

> Here in the United States, everything has a lot to do with appearances and Americans vary in their treatment towards Brazilians, or toward any foreigner, according to his color. If you are Brazilian and you have lighter skin, they treat you one way. If you are Brazilian and you have darker skin, they treat you a different way. It's always appearance. They think we are cute. They think Brazilians are interesting. But if the Brazilian has a darker skin, they already classify him as another Hispanic. When they are not classified as Hispanics, they receive the same treatment as a European. In that case, they find him interesting, fascinating, like they find the French and Italians fascinating.

Paola did not consider, however, that appearance is not only related to color but also to social position. Thus, I am led to believe that the Brazilian identity can be taken as a trump only when combined with other elements that allow one to rank different Brazilians into different social positions in American society. João Cândido, age fifty, who has been in the United States for eight years and worked mostly as a janitor or in similar jobs, says:

> By my brown color [moreno] and by the fact of being an immigrant here, I am classified as Latino, or as Hispanic. I relate well with them, the Latinos, the Mexicans. The only thing that I see in the Mexicans is that they don't know how to assert themselves. . . . Have you ever thought that they are the majority? If we were to consider merely their numbers, they would rule here in California. As such they work for free for everybody, and we lose our opportunities because of them. . . . We live badly here because of them. Because the American will never do the work that we do. . . . Look, there are Mexican babysitters who charge one or two dollars per hour! So if a Brazilian wants to work as a babysitter, she will have to fill her house with children because the people are already used to paying little to the Mexicans.

As an Adventist, working-class man, João Cândido cannot take full advantage of the carnavalesco stereotype. So he has to conform to identification as a Latino, which he thinks is fine in itself. What is hard, he says, is to accept and be happy with the lack of political organization among

Latino workers. This, according to him, makes wages go down to an unbearable level. So for João, the likelihood of some improvement in his lifestyle is all connected to more effective organization of working-class Latinos. In other words, it does not matter much if he insists on being identified as a Brazilian instead of Latino. In his social location, both identities seem to lead to the same place: low wages and experiences of discrimination.

Whereas life is generally much easier for those Brazilians who can prove that they are not "Latinos," for other Brazilians, as in the case of João, life is a bit harder. In those cases, skin color does not seem to matter much. I have talked to many "white" Brazilians working in low-paid jobs who feel like and are treated as Latinos as much as any Mexican who fits the stereotype of the "Latino." Thus, I am led to conclude that our "funny sort of French-sounding accent" (which is how many U.S.-born individuals refer to my accent) is taken positively only when combined with other symbols of status or distinction. In other words, European Americans and others will count our Brazilianness positively depending on what roles we are performing and where, which supports the proposition that racist discrimination against immigrants must be interpreted as connected mainly to the function that immigrants generally have in the socioeconomic structure, and not the other way around (Castles and Kosack 1985, 2).

Conclusions

Throughout this chapter, I have argued that the negative connotations attached to the Latino identity in Los Angeles are more likely to affect negatively those Brazilian immigrants who (1) are of color, (2) come from lower social positions in Brazil, and (3) work in low-paid jobs.

Although some may argue that the immigrants in this study, the majority of whom come from the middle classes, refuse Latino identity because it is connected to a social position with which they do not identify, even those who come from lower social positions refuse the label because of its negative connotations. In these cases, they tend to claim their Brazilian identity, which seems to offer them more alternatives. However, this claim does not prevent them from aligning or cooperating with other Latinos, nor does it prevent them from being discriminated against, because Brazilian identity also includes negative connotations related to the position of Brazil in the international division of labor.

Claiming either the Brazilian or Latino identity is much easier when one does not fit the economic or phenotypic stereotype. For instance, Brazilians who are located in higher social positions and have a Caucasian phenotype are more likely to claim their Latinidade without fear of discrimination. In contrast, Brazilians of color and those who look Caucasian but work in low-paid jobs have to bear the consequences of integrating into a new country through an identity that is discriminated against. This makes me believe that discrimination is not against Latinos or Brazilians for any essential characteristic they might possess. It is instead discrimination against their position in the domestic and international division of labor. Discrimination against them and against other immigrants in a similar position is comparable to discrimination against lower (working) classes in general.

References

Assis, Gláucia de Oliveira. 1995. "Estar Aqui, Estar Lá . . . uma Cartografia da Vida entre Dois Lugares." Master's thesis, Department of Anthropology, Universidade Federal de Santa Catarina.

Balibar, Etienne. 1991. "The Nation Form: History and Ideology." In *Race, Nation, Class—Ambiguous Identities*, edited by Etienne Balibar and Immanuel Wallerstein. London: Verso.

Beserra, Bernadete. 1998. "Keeping the Flame: Brazilian Gauchos in Los Angeles." *Brazzil* 10(156): 26–27.

———. 1999. "Move your Body! Brazilian Carnaval Takes over the World." *Brazzil* 10(158): 19–24.

———. 2000. "Brazilians in Los Angeles: Imperialism, Immigration, and Social Class." Ph.D. diss., Department of Anthropology, University of California, Riverside.

———. 2003. *Brazilian Immigrants in the United States: Cultural Imperialism and Social Class*. New York: LFB Scholarly Publishing.

Bonacich, Edna. 1972. "A Theory of Ethnic Antagonism: The Split Labor Market." *American Sociological Review* 37 (Oct.): 547–59

———. 1973. "A Theory of Middleman Minorities." *American Sociological Review* 38 (Oct.): 583–94.

Bourdieu, Pierre. 1986. "The Forms of Capital." In *Handbook of Theory and Research for the Sociology of Education*, edited by John G. Richardson. New York: Greenwood Press.

Castles, Stephen, and Godula Kosack. 1985. *Immigrant Workers and Class Structure in Western Europe*. London. Oxford University Press.

Freyre, Gilberto. 1975. *O Brasileiro entre os outros Hispanos: Afinidades, Contrates e Possíveis Futuros nas suas Inter-relações*. Rio de Janeiro: José Olympio Editora/ MEC.

Gimenez, Martha. 1992. "U.S. Ethnic Politics: Implications for Latin Americans." *Latin American Perspectives* 19(4): 7–17.

———. 1999. "Latino Politics—Class Struggles: Reflections on the Future of Latino Politics." In *Latino Social Movements—Historical and Theoretical Perspectives,* edited by Rodolfo D. Torres and George Katsiaficas. New York: Routledge.

Goza, Franklin. 1994. "Brazilian Immigration to America." *International Migration Review* 28(1994): 136–52.

Hayes-Bautista, and Jorge Chapa. 1987. "Latino Terminology: Conceptual Bases for Standardized Terminology." *American Journal of Public Health* 77(1): 61–68.

Larrain, Jorge. 1994. *Ideology and Cultural Identity—Modernity and the Third World Presence*. Cambridge, Eng.: Polity Press.

Margolis, M. 1994. *Little Brazil—An Ethnography of Brazilian Immigrants in New York City*. Princeton, N.J.: Princeton University Press.

———. 1995. "Brazilians and the 1990 United States Census: Immigrants, Ethnicity, and the Undercount." *Human Organization* 54(1): 52–59.

Martes, Ana C. B. 2000. *Brasileiros nos Estados Unidos: Um estudo sobre imigrantes em Massachusetts*. São Paulo, Brazil: Paz e Terra.

Ministério das Relações Exteriores (MRE). 2003. "2001 Brasileiros Residentes no Exterior—Tabelas." Available at http://www.mre.gov.br. Accessed Jan. 8.

Muñoz, Carlos Jr. 1989. *Youth, Identity, Power: The Chicano Movement*. London: Verso.

Oboler, Suzanne. 1995. *Ethnic Labels, Latino Lives: Identity and the Politics of (Re)Presentation in the United States*. Minneapolis: University of Minnesota Press.

Ochoa, Gilda Laura. 2000. "Mexican Americans' Attitudes toward and Interactions with Mexican Immigrants: A Qualitative Analysis of Conflict and Cooperation." *Social Science Quarterly* 81(1)84–105.

Piore, Michael J. 1979. *Birds of Passage: Migrant Labor and Industrial Societies*. New York: Cambridge University Press.

Portes, Alejandro, and Alex Stepick. 1993. *City on the Edge: The Transformation of Miami*. Berkeley: University of California Press.

Ribeiro, Gustavo. 1997a. "Street Samba: Carnaval and Transnational Identities in San Francisco." Paper presented at the fourth Conference of the Brazilian Studies Association, Washington, D.C.

———. 1997b. "Vulnerabilidade e Ambiguidade: Cidadania na Situação de Emigrante em São Francisco, Califórnia." Paper presented at the I Conferência sobre Imigrantes Brasileiros no Contexto das Novas Migrações Internacionais (First Conference on Brazilian Immigrants in the Context of the New International Immigration). Lisboa.

Sales, Teresa. 1995. "O Brasil no Contexto das Migrações Internacionais." *Travessia*. 8(21): 5–8.

———. 1999. *Brasileiros Longe de Casa*. São Paulo, Brazil: Cortez Editora.

Stack, John, and Christopher Warren. 1992. "Ethnicity and Politics in Miami." In *Miami Now! Immigration, Ethnicity, and Social Change*, edited by Guilhermo Grenier and Alex Stepick. Gainesville: University of Florida Press.

Stolcke, Verena. 1995. "New Boundaries, New Rhetorics of Exclusion in Europe." *Current Anthropology* 36(1): 1–24.

Thomas, W. I., and Florian Znanieck. 1996. *The Polish Peasant in Europe and America*. Urbana: University of Illinois Press.

10   Black Face, Latin Looks

Racial-Ethnic Identity among Afro-Latinos in
the Los Angeles Region

Anulkah Thomas

> Social meanings connect our faces to our souls.
> *Ian Haney Lopez, 1995*

The city of Los Angeles is the geographical index for a region that is
home to one of the largest Latino populations in the United States. According to the 2000 U.S. Census, Latinos make up 47 percent of the Los
Angelino population. Although Los Angeles is home to native- and
foreign-born U.S. Americans of various cultural and national origins, the
common understanding of race and ethnic categorizations does not truly
reflect the diversity of the Latino inhabitants of this region. Although
Latin America is very diverse, notions of a normative Latino phenotype
have favored a mestizo (mixed European and Native American heritage)
aesthetic. Although this conceptualization has been a source of identity
and solidarity for many Latinos, those who do not claim a mestizo identity may feel that their identity and existence are not acknowledged and
validated within the larger Latino community. Much like people of mixed
race, such individuals may face a metaphorical tug-of-war between the
overlapping communities to which they own membership.

The fluctuation of racial and ethnic categorizations throughout the
history of the U.S. Census highlights the continual reconceptualization
of race and ethnicity. Latinos, being a racially mixed group, may often
confront many of the issues other mixed-race individuals struggle with.
Although many Los Angelinos may not experience an internal conflict
when checking the boxes presented to them on the U.S. Census or other
paperwork, there are those who do. Most relevant attention has been paid
to the plight of multiracial U.S. Americans, who often do not want to
choose one or some heritages over others. Little known, however, is the
particular dilemma that Latinos of African descent face when pressed to
identify themselves in terms of race and ethnicity. This is largely due to
the fact that most U.S. Americans of all racial/ethnic backgrounds do not

realize that such a community exists. As a matter of fact, a lot more attention has been given to conflict between African Americans and Latinos, particularly in the Los Angeles region.

Given the fact that people of color have been the historically racialized "other" in relation to the normative White U.S. identity, people of mixed race and Afro-Latinos do not have as much freedom in how they identify in comparison to White ethnics. Sociologist Mary Waters explains that many Euro-Americans enjoy having a "symbolic ethnicity" in which they may link to their ethnicity in deliberate ways, such as celebrating a particular holiday, eating a certain dish, or knowing a few phrases of their grandparents' language (1990). These activities give them a sense of being part of a unique community. For people of color, such as U.S. Americans of African, Latin American, Asian, and Native American descent, their ethnic identity is experienced daily by virtue of their "other" status.

As the multiethnic population of Los Angeles grows and further diversifies, it is important to understand the dynamics of the many groups that inhabit this metropolis and its surrounding communities. In particular, this chapter focuses on how descendents of Afro-Latin American immigrants forge their identity in the U.S. racial landscape and how this is reflected in their experiences. The existence of Afro-Latinos who fall into two supposedly separate categories confounds and challenges the existing racial categorizations and highlights the socially constructed origins of these classifications. Most studies that have contributed to our understanding of the experiences of Afro-Latin Americans and other Black immigrants have been based on populations on the East Coast (Duany 1998; Ibrahim 1999; Kasinitz 1992; Torres-Saillant 1998; Waters 1994, 1999). Even fewer studies have focused on members of the second generation (Rumbaut 2001; Waters 1994, 1999).

Thus, the goal of this chapter is to explore how U.S. American youths with Afro-Latin American backgrounds negotiate their racial and ethnic identities within the geographical context of Southern California. Interviews with Afro-Latina/o Americans who have grown up in various U.S. locales highlight the role location, appearance, language, and situational context play in identity construction. The findings of this study show that geographical location, appearance, and daily encounters provide input for the formation of racial-ethnic identities. Of course, these identities are forged within a society in which the socially constructed and historically generated racial-ethnic categorizations already exist. The relative youth of the respondents—all young adults—serves to provide insight into contemporary experiences of racial-ethnic identity from the perspectives of individuals who have had enough life experience to draw and reflect upon.

Background Literature

Before delving deeper into this study of racial and ethnic identifications, it is important to outline exactly what these conceptual terms refer to. The terms *race* and *ethnicity* are used popularly with some overlap, often diverging from how they are defined and used in academia, particularly the social sciences. In this chapter, *race* is understood to be a group that shares biological characteristics considered to "set them apart from other groups, often in invidious ways" (Pincus and Ehrlich 1999, 12). Omi and Winant (1994) posit that the notion of race does not carry significance on a genetic level, but the social classifications that persist on the basis of this misperception have caused the existence of race as a social construct to continue to affect the life chances of individuals and groups on both personal and institutional levels. This results in structuring the nature of social relationships in such a manner that it creates problems like "social stratification, discrimination and prejudice, cultural domination and cultural resistance, state policy," and others (Omi and Winant 1995, 10). Ethnic identifications are also socially constructed. The essential elements sociologists use to define a group of people bound together by ethnicity, unlike race, do not include biological or phenotypic specifications, but rather cultural characteristics and a shared history. Although a shared past, whether real or imagined, is characteristic of ethnic groups, "the central defining characteristic of ethnic groups is the belief in their own existence as groups" (Kasinitz 1992, 4; Patterson 1975, 309).

It is instructive to apply these definitions to the racial and ethnic groups of the United States. The principal groups that make up the U.S. population are Asians/Pacific Islander Americans, White/European Americans, Native Americans, Black/African Americans, and Latino Americans. Whereas the first four groups are ethnically heterogeneous, Latinos are a racially heterogeneous ethnic group. This means that there are various ethnic groups among the people who trace their origins to Asia and the Pacific Islands, Europe, Africa, and the indigenous inhabitants of the Western Hemisphere. Latinos, who can also be broken into smaller ethnic groupings based on nationality or other criteria, can also trace their ancestry to all of the regions just named.

It is important to remember that racial and ethnic classifications in Latin America and the United States are quite different from each other. Whereas U.S. constructions are organized within a binary Black-White paradigm, Latin American racial classifications are conceptualized on a continuum. Latin American racial classifications are quite specific and numerous, especially when compared to the Black-White dichotomy concerning race in the United States. In both Spanish- and Portuguese-speaking Latin American societies literally hundreds of words are used that are meant to signify the phenotype and "blood mixtures" of those whom they describe. This extensive vocabulary (for example, *negro*, *mulatto*, and *trigueño*) racially classifies persons using such criteria as facial features, skin color, and hair texture (Comas-Diaz 1996, 171; Gómez 1998, 28, 62; Wade 1997, 15).

In comparison, U.S. racial categorizations are essentially based upon hypodescent. Also known as the infamous one-drop rule, hypodescent places an emphasis on "genetic," or inherited, race, rather than emphasizing phenotype (Omi and Winant 1994, 53; Duany 1998, 15; Wade 1997, 14). The so-called one-drop rule determined that an individual who could trace any African ancestry whatsoever was Black. Although biracial and multiracial identities have been historically acknowledged in the United States (mulattos, quadroons, and so forth), monoracial classifications have been normative (Spencer 1999, 4). A Black-White paradigm has always prevailed, a dichotomy in which multiracial individuals as well as Asian-Americans, Native Americans, and many Latino Americans have been marginalized. The diversity of one's ancestors has not been historically emphasized in the United States, as it has in other parts of the Americas.

Black immigrants from Latin America, as well as Africa, Europe, and the Caribbean, face particular social, structural, and consequently identification issues upon entering the United States. Popular notions of Black identity are constrained into a narrow and inaccurate description of a diverse group. Blacks in the United States are often viewed as both a racial and an ethnic group, meaning that this large group of people with a shared racial origin is also perceived to share one monolithic culture, not allowing for the existing variation in nationality, religion, language, and culture (Omi and Winant 1994, 22; Waters 1999, 45). Upon entry into the United States, Black immigrants face "a double process in being incorporated into American life, coming simultaneously into mainstream 'America' and 'Black America'" (Kasinitz 1992, 32). In his sociological work on Anglophone West Indians in New York, Kasinitz (1992) found that race played a dominant role in the life chances of Afro-Caribbean immigrants. Like the children of all immigrants, second-generation West Indians often found themselves conflicted with both "the urge to assimilate and feelings of [cultural] loss" (Kasinitz 1992, 53). Similarly, a study on the interrelation between identity and English language acquisition of continental African immigrants to Ontario, Canada, revealed that the adolescent respondents engaged in a process of "becoming black," in which they drew upon "Black popular cultural forms, rap and hip-hop, as sites of identification" (Ibrahim 1999, 365). Ibrahim (1999, 353) posited that in coming to North America these black immigrants entered "a discursive space" in which "they are already constructed, imagined, and positioned and thus are treated by the hegemonic discourses and dominant groups, respectively, as Blacks." Thus, how others see these Black immigrants and members of the following generations in terms of race—as well as how they are treated as a result—has produced an interesting effect. Upon entrance to the United States these individuals may have seen themselves as quite different from African Americans. However, with the passing of time often come experiences that provide an outlook more in line with many African Americans. As a result, many Black immigrants and their descendents identify with the African American community at large (Ibrahim 1999, 53).

Research Methodology

This research is based primarily on nine in-depth, open-ended interviews with college and graduate students in the Los Angeles area. The hour-long interviews were all conducted in person. The interview procedure is similar to a study conducted by Rodriguez, in which Latino participants were asked to answer a question identical to that which appeared in the 1980 U.S. Census (1992, 934). Before asking any questions, each respondent was given a replication of the 2000 U.S. Census ethnicity and race categories to fill out. One question inquired about the Latin American origin of the respondent, asking "Are you Spanish/Hispanic/Latino?" There were five possible choices. The first was "No, not Spanish/Hispanic/Latino." The next three were "yes" answers with specific national indications, namely "Mexican, Mexican Am., Chicano," Puerto Rican, and Cuban. The final option was for all other Latinos. All respondents also had the option of writing in the unlisted group(s) they identified with. The subsequent question asked, "What is your race?" The choices were White, "Black, African Am. or Negro," American Indian or Alaskan Native, with a space for writing in a tribe name; numerous Asian and Pacific Island nation groups, as well as an option of writing in a missed group; and finally "some other race," with the instructions to "Print race" in the space allotted for that purpose.

I started each interview with a discussion of why the respondent chose to answer how s/he did. I asked this question in order to gain an understanding of what the respondents take into consideration when filling out forms that ask for racially or ethnically identifying information. The remaining interview questions were designed to gain understanding of the way the participants' identities have changed over their lifetimes, as well as the experiences that have influenced their identity development.

The sampling method relied heavily on word-of-mouth and thus is a snowball sample. It involved formal measures such as contacting Latino and Pan-African student associations at Los Angeles-area colleges and universities, as well as more informal ones, such as contacting individuals I had previously learned were Afro-Latinos and asking peers if they had any Afro-Latino acquaintances I could contact for interviews.

Throughout the duration of this study, not to mention throughout my life, I have found that people often assume that someone who is Afro-Latino (or Black Hispanic, another popular descriptor) has one Latino parent with no African ancestry, and one African-descent parent with no connections to Latin America. However, scholars of the African diaspora and Latin Americanists have written extensively about past and existing communities of Black populations in Latin America. In a general sense, Afro-Latinos are the descendents of African slaves who toiled under the yoke of slavery in Latin America. The following exploration of Afro-Latino identity highlights how factors much more complex than ancestry factor into how the respondents define themselves in terms of race and ethnicity. This study reveals that Afro-Latinos in the United States form a quite varied group with complex origins, diverse family backgrounds, and different life journeys that bring them to different conclusions about race and their personal identities.

Before this chapter delves into the issues discussed in the interviews, it will be useful to briefly introduce each of the nine participants. In order to ensure the privacy of the respondents, fictitious names will be used. Table 10.1 summarizes basic demographic information about the respondents. The average age of the respondents is twenty-two years. Although all of the participants were attending or had already graduated from college at the time the interviews were conducted, on average the respondents were approaching their third year of undergraduate study. Six of the nine respondents, or two-thirds, are female. The final two columns reveal how they answered the census questions on Latino origin and racial heritage. The column preceding those two describes their parents' racial and national backgrounds.

As the U.S.-born daughter of Afro-Panamanian immigrants, I have a personal as well as academic interest in the experiences of Afro-Latinos in the United States. I felt that conducting in-depth interviews, rather than gathering quantitative data based on a survey, would allow for a deeper understanding of how my peers forge their racial-ethnic identities within the dichotomous and exclusive racial paradigms of the land in which they were born. Given the multifaceted and complex nature of racial-ethnic identity, the qualitative research approach applied in this study offers detailed information for analysis. These interviews provide revelations about the formation of racial-ethnic identity that could not have been accessed without the qualitative methodology employed here.

This study adds to the existing scholarship by highlighting the experiences and voices of members of an invisible racial-ethnic grouping. The interviews particularly illustrate how contextual factors, such as the geographical space in which one identifies oneself, can shape perceptions and performance of racial-ethnic identity. The findings presented here must be read with the understanding that African Americans, Latinos, and Afro-Latinos are underrepresented in higher education. Although the issues addressed in the interviews are relevant to all Afro-Latin Americans in the United States, the composition of this respondent pool causes the trends found in this work to belong particularly to this segment of the Afro-Latin American population of Los Angeles.

Table 10.1. Respondents' Biographical Information

Respondent	Sex	Age	Education	Hometown	Parental Background	Latino Origin	Race
Shona Brown	F	22	Senior	Los Angeles, Calif.	Afro-American father; mestiza Chicana mother	Yes; Mexican	Black
Joanne Fox	F	26	B.A. completed in English	Los Angeles, Calif.	Afro-Panamanian	Yes; other	Black
Elton Harvey	M	19	First-year undergraduate	Newark East Woodland Park, Calif.	Afro-American father; mother half Afro-American, half Afro-Puerto Rican	Yes, Puerto Rican	Black
Lanisha Hernandez	F	21	Junior	Seattle, Wash.	Afro-Mexican father; Afro-American mother	Yes; Mexican	Black
Yolonda Herrera	F	22	Fifth-year senior	Queens, N.Y.	Afro-Panamanian	Yes; other (Panamanian)	Black

Michael Johnson	M	19	Sophomore	Pomona, Calif.	Afro-Panamanian father; Afro-American mother	No	Black
Dolores Lopez	F	18	First-year undergraduate	Montclair, Calif.	Afro-Cuban mother; White Puerto Rican father	Yes; other (Cuban and Puerto Rican)	Other (Latin American)
Sabrina Manting	F	18	First-year undergraduate	Boston, Mass.	Afro-Honduran father; Afro-American mother	Yes; other (Black Hispanic-Honduran)	Black
David Swenson	M	31	Doctoral student	Harlem, N.Y.	Afro-Puerto Rican father, Afro-American mother	Yes; Puerto Rican	Black

Conflating and Separating Race and Ethnicity

Overall, the findings indicate that racial and ethnic identities are situational, intersecting, and always changing. The life experiences of the respondents demonstrate how their individual identities are shaped by the historically constructed ways of defining race and ethnicity. In effect, this discussion illustrates just how and why the current racial and ethnic categorizations are highly insufficient and exclusive. Ultimately, the research findings support the conjecture that racial and ethnic groupings are based on socially determined, historically contingent criteria.

Marking the Box

The participants filled out the 2000 U.S. Census ethnicity and race categories in a similar fashion; there were only a couple of exceptions. Almost all of the respondents checked one of the "Yes" options for the question "Are you Spanish/Hispanic/Latino?" The differences among the "Yes" answers selected were a matter of national origin. In response to the race question all respondents except one identified themselves as "Black, African Am., or Negro."

All of the respondents drew upon U.S. conceptions of race and ethnicity in defining their identities, albeit they did not all do this in the same way. Most of the respondents acknowledged both their Latin American backgrounds and African origins on the form. This illustrates some sense of being able to separate the ethnic and racial identifications. Of course, this was encouraged by the setup of the census, in which the two are deliberately set apart. As the following discussion will show, the experiences of the respondents have caused them to realize that since they do not fit norms for African Americans or Latinos/as, their identifications with both of these groups have at times been interpreted differently.

Michael Johnson, a nineteen-year old college sophomore, was the one respondent who did not indicate his Latin American background on the census form. He explained that he did not indicate his Panamanian background because his Panamanian father had always instructed him not to do so "because it cuts down on confusion." The fact that Michael's father came to the United States at a young age (ten years) and has had strained relations with many members of his family on racial grounds has most likely provided him with experiences that explain his current stance on how he identifies himself. Michael's father is darker than his siblings and was treated differently for this reason. He also had to deal with being a black person in a region of Panama heavily influenced by Jim Crow-based racial doctrines due to its proximity to the U.S.-run Panama Canal. Thus, both within and outside of his home country, Johnson's experiences were very much shaped by the social status allotted individuals with dark skin. Although both Michael and his father primarily highlight their identities as Black men, they both seem to value their Panamanian background, as evidenced by the fact that Michael's father still speaks Spanish fluently and Michael regrets that his father did not pass on the language. For this reason, Michael has made efforts to learn and practice it on his own, particularly since he would like to visit Panama someday.

One respondent evaded racial descriptors when filling out the census forms. Dolores Lopez, an eighteen-year-old college freshman, also could have described her identity differently than she did. Her father is a White Puerto Rican and her mother a Black Cuban. She made sure to acknowledge the nationalities that made up her background for the Latin American origin question by checking "Yes, other Spanish/Hispanic/Latino" and writing in "Cuban and Puerto Rican," but she did not relate to any of the options provided for racial identification. While she was examining the race options, she remarked, "they don't even have Latin American" as a choice. Dolores opted to check "Some other race" and wrote in "Latin American." It seems that her understanding of her identity fits the pattern discussed by Rodriguez (1992), in which many Latinos in the United States disassociate themselves from U.S. racial groups because of cultural differences that take precedence over racial similarities. Given Rodriguez's theory, it is possible that Dolores may have chosen to identify racially as Latin American because her cultural background prevented her from identifying with European and/or African Americans.

The multiracial backgrounds of several of the respondents also influenced how they identified themselves. The diversity of Sabrina Manting's maternal ancestry (African, Native American, and European) in combination with her proximity to Afro-Honduran relatives caused Sabrina's primary identification to fall toward that of her Afro-Latino side. However, she did mention that she wants to learn more about her mother's ancestry, particularly the Native American part since she has a substantial number of Blackfoot forebears. Also, Dolores's binational, biracial background has allowed her to identify in many ways throughout her life.

Michael Johnson has always identified as African American, not seeming to see himself as mixed on a cultural level. Lanisha Hernandez offered an interesting comparison between herself and a friend whose father is Afro-Mexican and whose mother is Euro-American. Lanisha feels that her friend's fair-skinned appearance gave her the privilege of being able to identify as Chicana, which Lanisha does not feel she can easily do because of her dark complexion. (This is not to say that she does not identify herself as Mexican or Latina, for she does.) Presumably, the *perceived* ambiguity of her friend's racial appearance allows her, from Lanisha's perspective, a different range of possible identifications.

The fact that many of the respondents filled out the census form in a similar fashion does not mean that they all conceptualized their identities in the same way or that they necessarily had similar backgrounds. It is understandable that many of the respondents conflated race with ethnicity since they are socialized in a country in which these terms and concepts are often used interchangeably. This shows that although the respondents may have challenged the existing ways of describing their racial-ethnic identities by not always necessarily choosing their Blackness over their *Latinidad* (Latinness) (or vice versa), they never completely separate themselves from the socially established categories.

Language and Performing Racial-Ethnic Identity: From the Mouths of the U.S.-Born Generations

Many of the respondents spoke of Spanish language fluency without my prodding, indicating that it is a crucial link to Latin American culture and identity. Although all of the respondents had varying degrees of familiarity and comfort with the Spanish language, none of them considered their Spanish language skills to surpass or equal their competency in English. None of the nine respondents considered themselves truly fluent in Spanish. This finding differs from other studies that find that most children of immigrants are bilingual (Fishman 1964; Valdes 1988). The fact that four of the six members of the second generation have one parent who is not Latino probably plays a role in this situation. Although most of the respondents are not native speakers of Spanish, all except one had enough exposure to the language that they have some level of comprehensive or spoken ability.

Language, along with other factors, can play into how one "performs" his/her cultural identity. Dolores Lopez and Yolonda Herrera were clearly the most proficient in the Spanish language, according to their accounts. They both expressed a high level of comfort in conversing in Spanish if a situation called for it. But at the same time, Yolonda emphasized that she felt quite Americanized and preferred speaking in English:

> If I'm in a Spanish country I'd definitely just spit out the Spanish and it's just like second nature if I know that no one can speak English. But then once I know that someone can speak English, I don't speak Spanish to them at all. I might throw in a word to explain something better. . . . But I'm sort of skittish about speaking Spanish.

Yolonda explained that this hesitation to speak Spanish is at least partially related to the variety of Spanish she speaks. Her grandmother has teased her for speaking "very proper Spanish" as a result of taking Spanish courses and spending a year in Spain during high school, and Yolonda added, "it's sort of embarrassing that a year in another country could change my Spanish more than living with my parents and my family all my life." Dolores also described a situational aspect to the contexts in which she is most likely to speak Spanish: "I think it comes out more when I'm at parties and stuff, family parties. I'll just start speaking Spanish, and it comes so easily. You just have to be in the environment for a certain amount of time." Both Yolonda and Dolores exhibited interesting personal connections to certain aspects of the Spanish language. Yolonda only knows lullabies in Spanish, and Dolores remarked, "a lot of sayings sound better in Spanish than they do in English . . . it's so much clearer than it is in English."

The interviews revealed that individuals do use language to establish one's ethnic identity and group membership. David Swensen, a thirty-one-year-old doctoral student, complained that although he biologically belonged to his father's family, which is Afro-Puerto Rican, they—including his own father—often wrote him off as "the American." He explained:

> [L]ooking back on it I was deprived because, it's like, they saw me as the American kid . . . my father sees me as his child, but sees me also as an American. 'Cause I was raised in the United States around

American people and so when I'd be around his family he'd be around his people. Yet biologically I was their people, but I didn't speak the language, I didn't do this—so I wasn't 100 percent there.

Lanisha Hernandez found herself in an even more uncomfortable family situation. Her paternal grandfather has children by two different women. When she moved from Seattle to Southern California to go to college, she met her father's half-siblings and their children, who live in Los Angeles. Lanisha was clearly ostracized because of her obvious African ancestry in comparison to the mestizo appearances of the Los Angeles branch of the family. Her improved Spanish skills after spending a semester in the Dominican Republic have dissuaded them from speaking about her in Spanish in her presence. Now they have even found themselves in situations in which Lanisha has to speak for them, since their Spanish skills are not very strong. Lanisha's and David's experiences combine to exemplify the connection between language and ethnic identity. For example, Bucholtz (1995) found that her respondents pursued learning one of their "family's languages of heritage" in order to "construct ethnic authenticity through language" (362). The experiences of the respondents also illustrate just how language can be a powerful source of authenticating ethnic identification, whether for acceptance, or in Lanisha's case, some sort of protection. In sum, the experiences of the respondents illustrate just how language plays a role in the formation as well as performance of racial-ethnic identity.

Black Face, Latin Looks: Notions of a Latino Aesthetic

The appearance of the respondents also factored in to how they identified themselves as well as how they believed others perceived them. All of the respondents addressed the power of an exclusive Latino aesthetic that is favored in the United States. As dark-skinned Latinos, their claims of Latinidad were often challenged and disbelieved. Interestingly, however, some respondents noticed a regional difference in how others perceived them in terms of race and ethnicity. Yolonda, David, and Sabrina—who are all originally from the East Coast—asserted that due to the highly Caribbean composition of New York and Boston Latino communities, there is generally a darker conception of who is a Latino than there is in Southern California. This is attributed to the fact that the Latin American population in New York and Florida, as well as other parts of the Eastern Seaboard, tend to be inhabited by Caribbean, dark-skinned Latinos in comparison to the predominantly Mexican and Central American mestizo and indigenous populations in the West, particularly in California, where this study took place (Haslip-Viera 1996, 12).

Sabrina, David, and Yolonda, who are all from the East Coast, provided compelling insights into the difference between West and East Coast conceptions of a normative Latino aesthetic. Sabrina, a Bostonian, explained that many Mexicans (using the reference point of her time spent in California) are not dark enough to fit the Latino aesthetic of her region. She explains that this is because of the large number of East Coast Dominicans and Puerto Ricans, whom she describes as looking "very [racially] mixed." For this reason, Sabrina, who has a medium brown complexion, and her fair-skinned Salvadoran friend are not usually perceived as Latinas by their fellow Bostonians. David elaborated upon his observations of notions of "Latinidad" in California in comparison to New York City, where he grew up:

> There's almost no such thing as Black Latin out here. Latin out here is Mexican, El Salvadorean, that's it. Panamanian, Puerto Rican, Dominican, Cuban, you know, just does not exist out here. . . . I go to New York City, okay? I could be taken as African American, I could be taken as Puerto Rican, I could be taken as Dominican, I could be taken as Cuban, I could be taken as anything. I'm considered any category over there. . . . [C]ome over here, you're black and that's it.

David's account serves to portray the East Coast, or particularly New York, conception of Latinos as being quite inclusive in opposition to the more narrowly defined conceptions of a Latino aesthetic he has observed while living in Southern California. Yolonda also described her observations of the differing Latina/o aesthetics on the East and West Coasts, saying that there is "a browner standard on the East Coast for Hispanics," again attributing this to the large Puerto Rican and Dominican populations in that region. Overall, these observations serve to emphasize again the socially constructed nature of racial and ethnic classifications and highlight the role environment plays in forming those conceptions.

Two respondents from the West Coast, Lanisha Hernandez, who is from Seattle, and Shona Brown, who is from Los Angeles, were cognizant of this dichotomy as well. In Seattle, the people around Lanisha knew of her Mexican heritage, and she would have peers ask her to help them with their Spanish homework. But there were differences in Southern California, where she had to establish a new presence. She commented that "Southern California's a whole different aspect 'cause people would just assume that [Hernandez] was my married name." Shona's words reinforce the observations of the other respondents:

> On the East Coast, it's totally different. Everyone speaks Spanish. Like you can't look at someone and just because they look Black to you, you would assume that they didn't speak Spanish. . . . [B]ut over here, people don't expect you—they expect you not to speak Spanish if you're Black. . . . [W]hen I speak [people] would look at me. Like, why are you speaking Spanish type of thing.

A considerable number of the respondents also noted that how others perceived them often seemed contingent upon the environments they found themselves in. This again highlights the contextual and socially constructed nature of these group identities, not to mention an ever present inconsistency that signals how problematic they are.

Most respondents recounted an incident in which they had to react to how others (mis)interpreted their racial and ethnic backgrounds. Dolores narrated an experience where, because of her appearance, a Mexican family assumed she was not Latina. She was waiting for her mother at a chiropractor's office and realized that members of this family were talking about her in Spanish, confident that she did not understand:

> These people really didn't think I understand what they're saying, and I'm just staring at them and they're saying . . . "look at her, look what she has, look what she has." And I turned around, and I just whipped out in Spanish. I was like, "Yeah, what do I have?" Their eyes just bugged out, and their mouths were down to the ground and then my mom came out and I was like [in a low voice] "talk to me in Spanish, talk to me in Spanish." [She] busted out with Spanish and everybody was [really surprised and] the guy apologized and everything.

Dolores's narrative of this incident, in which she was perceived and treated as an outsider to a group in which she proudly claims membership, is quite representative of the experiences of the respondents. This example speaks to a normative identity within the Latina/o community in Los Angeles that in effect marginalizes those who do not fit the aesthetic created by the historical construction of racial-ethnic identification.

Respondents also experienced other scenarios in which their racial-ethnic identities were challenged. Examples abounded of instances in which their Afro-Latino identity was somehow established and then disputed. Lanisha remembers instances in which her identity as a Latina was "put to the test." More than once people have demanded that she somehow prove her "Mexican-ness," usually by conversing in Spanish, which she does not speak natively. Lanisha provided the most intriguing example concerning a night in which she and her Mexican boyfriend, a fluent Spanish speaker who many would perceive as Latino by his appearance, went to a comedy club. Seated near the front, Lanisha did not want to bring attention to herself by raising her hand when the African-American comedian asked all the Latinas in the club to identify themselves. Her boyfriend nudged her to do so, and as she feared, the comedian turned his attention to them, asking, "Are you raising your hand for your boyfriend or for you?" When she answered that she had raised her hand for herself the comedian asked, "What are you?"

Despite Lanisha's Mexican pride, her quick thinking told her that the fastest way to get through the situation was to give the answer that she thought would be most believable; she told him she was Dominican. Lanisha named two specific reasons for doing this. First, she figured both he and the audience would at least have the example of dark-skinned Sammy Sosa, who is undoubtedly of African descent, to draw upon. Secondly, she has never actually been to Mexico, but has detailed knowledge of the Dominican Republic since she spent a semester abroad there. Thus, if her Latina identity continues to be challenged she has the evidence to, well, "prove it." Lanisha's comedy club incident exemplifies another aspect of the racial-ethnic identity conflict that respondents face. For it is not only her Latinidad that others might question, but also the fact that she traces her Latin background to a country that has a small population of African descendents rather than one that is known to have a population with a darker complexion.

The interviews also revealed how the respondents at times adhered to the existing racial classifications and in other instances challenged them. Lanisha, for example, described her mother as "just Mexican, Chicana." There were no overt racial indicators in her description of her mother's background, which signaled a normative view in which a mestizo/a ancestry is the norm for Mexicans, if not all Latinos. This is in direct opposition to David's critique of the racialized identity many Latinos embrace. David, whose father is Afro-Puerto Rican and mother is African-American, commented, "a lot of Latinos, in my opinion, they see Latinos as a separate race. . . . [F]or myself Latino is cultural." Here David's views are aligned with the academic distinctions between race and ethnicity outlined earlier, as opposed to Shona's statements, which imply that mestizos represent the normative aesthetic for a Latino race.

Both Shona's and David's ways of describing race are understandable given their backgrounds. The fact that David's identification as a bicultural Black male did not come into existence until he was a young adult illustrates just how he sees his identity. David grew up around family and community members who were not Latino. He was exposed to his mother's African American family members, as well as the Black community where he grew up in Harlem. He later embraced Puerto Rican culture after visiting the island during his undergraduate years and taking Black Studies courses in that same period. Although Shona's father has emphasized African diaspora studies in her home, her particular background apparently contributed to how she views, or at least describes, her understanding of racial and ethnic classifications. Black Studies or Diaspora Studies envision people of African descent as sharing racial origins, but being diverse in place of birth, language, and culture.

The specific racial, ethnic, and national backgrounds of the respondents influenced their identities and experiences. Only two respondents, Joanne Fox and Yolonda Herrera, had two Afro-Latino parents. Their parents all happened to originate from Panama. Four respondents— Sabrina, Dolores, David, and Michael—had one parent who was Afro-Latino. Of these Afro-Latin American parents, all except one was married to someone who identifies him- or herself as an African-American. Dolores's Afro-Cuban mother is married to a White Puerto Rican.

Two of the respondents did not exactly fit the profile I had in mind when designing my project. However, the content of their interview sessions begged for inclusion in this study because they drove home the theme of this research: that racial and ethnic classifications are socially constructed. Neither of Shona's parent are Afro-Latin American; her father is African-American and her mother is a mestiza Chicana. Elton Harvey's father is African-American and his mother *might* be part Afro-

Puerto Rican. Elton's story is so fascinating; it must finally be told here. His maternal grandfather is African American and his maternal grandmother "is a bunch of stuff, but she identifies—she has a strong heritage in the Puerto Rican background. So, that's what she identifies with." For nineteen years of his life, Elton has grown up with the understanding that his grandmother is Puerto Rican. It was not until the end of the interview that Elton discussed a recent revelation regarding his ancestry. An intoxicated aunt at a family gathering told him that his grandmother had lied about her heritage. He exclaims:

> I mean, this came out of the blue and I'm like, "What are you talking about?" She goes, "You, you're not Puerto Rican. They just said that 'cause they don't . . . like admitting that they're—that they're Indian and White."

The next day the relative stuck to her story after sobering up. Elton has continually tried to talk to his grandmother about the subject, but she remains unwilling. Elton explained that racial mixtures are quite stigmatized within the African American community. However, his grandmother's identification as Puerto Rican, rather than White and Native American, is preferable within the African American community because of the legacy of slavery. This is not so surprising considering the taboo nature the subject of miscegenation carries in the African-American community (Cunningham 1997; Waters 1999). Although admittedly confused and frustrated by the situation, Elton adamantly justifies his identification as Puerto Rican, explaining that it is "a little late to be telling me this kind of stuff" after nineteen years. Although he unwaveringly claimed his Puerto Rican heritage in the interview, Elton explained that he is quite guarded about who he shares this information with in the African American community, explaining that many people are often skeptical or wary of people who don't "say they're just Black." Elton's unique background and experiences highlight the intangibility of identity, that one's sense of self is shaped not so much by biological heritage as the social realities born of the resulting group membership.

This example indicates just how individuals with dissimilar backgrounds may still share similar experiences on some general level because of externally imposed identifications. Both Shona and David overtly identified their black identity as that of primary significance, yet emphasized that their Latin background was also essential to their identities. Shona stated, "basically I consider myself Black just because that's how people perceive me, but I'm Mexican too. . . . So I consider myself an African Latina." Although Shona's explanation of her self-identification directly acknowledges the role the perceptions of others plays, she does not allow this to nullify her Latina identity. Although Shona grew up identifying with both of these identities, David did not consciously embrace his Puerto Rican identity until his early twenties. He maintains his African-American identification and emphasizes the Blackness of his Puerto Rican side. Thus, both Shona and David try to achieve some sort of balance between these two major components of their identities. They both take into account how society views them, but do not allow that view to completely shape their own understanding of their identities.

The roles of geographical location, social situations, appearance, and language are just a few factors that influence how we understand our identities. The interview setting and the marks made on the census forms captured only a moment in the lives of these respondents. The interviews revealed that most of the respondents have understood and described their racial-ethnic backgrounds in different ways throughout their lives, often depending on aspects such as who they want to be friends with, what their parents have taught them about their background, and what they think the government will do with the information they gather in the census. Ultimately, the findings of this study not only emphasize the socially constructed nature of identity, but also highlight how historically contingent notions of "who is who" shape daily lives.

Conclusion

Conducting this study in the Los Angeles region offered different experiential and situational contexts than studies that have been done on Afro-Latino identity on the East Coast. The differing compositions of California and New York Latino populations in combination with the experiences of many of the respondents highlighted the distinctive notions of a Latino aesthetic in the two regions. Perhaps the most intriguing revelation of this study was that notions of how Latinos (should) look differed notably between the East and West Coasts. Many of the respondents had observed that East Coast conceptions of a Latino aesthetic allow for darker-skinned Latinos, whereas the West Coast conception generally favors comparatively lighter-skinned individuals. In both cases, a normative aesthetic dominates these regions, still serves to exclude many Latinos, and ultimately denies the international racial origins of Latin Americans. This serves to further emphasize the contextual nature of the social meanings we assign to life's realities.

Ultimately, this study supports what social scientists from varying disciplinary backgrounds have been saying for many years now: race is a social construct that conceals historically contingent contradictions, such as class, gender, and so forth. Furthermore, all of these group identities (race, ethnicity, nationality) are based on socially defined criteria that vary from place to place and era to era, not to mention the discrepancies among interpretations on an individual level.

The participants showed various levels of awareness about the fact that these classifications had social rather than scientific origins. The respondents both adhered to and rebelled against the racial and ethnic categories that socialization in the United States has obligated them to draw upon. Some were more critical of U.S. racial classifications than others, but all respondents had encountered experiences that forced them to reevaluate their racial-ethnic identity from one point to another in their lives. Nevertheless, the respondents are products of their environments. Even those who criticized the racial-ethnic identification norms in other instances used language or drew upon notions that reinforced normative, and thus, exclusive identities.

Although the findings presented here are significant in their contribution to a miniscule body of literature on Afro-Latino identity in the United States, there is still an undeniable need for more research. Although working with a small pool of respondents did allow for a richness in data that can only be attained with in-depth interviews, it is important to acknowledge that the experiences they shared were filtered through a lens somewhat skewed from the broader Afro-Latin American population in the United States. Since all of the participants in the study had managed to elude or traverse the barriers that prevent many of their peers from entering the higher education system, their views and experiences cannot be considered to be all-inclusive. Nonetheless, the conclusions drawn from this study still manage to serve the ultimate objective to contribute to and diversify a historically narrow discourse on race and ethnicity in the United States.

How long will Black Latinos continue to be an invisible "other" category? Forms that ask for racial/ethnic identity information often attempt to set apart Whites and Blacks who are not of Latin American ancestry by providing the choices "White (not of Hispanic origin)" and "Black (not of a Hispanic origin)" along with "Hispanic." Such forms also include a stipulation that only one option should be selected. Thus, respondents encounter the same dilemma that bi-/multiracial individuals confront: being instructed to choose between their identities. Naturally, this presents a problem for individuals who want to explicitly acknowledge both their African and Latin American origins. In the words of one respondent, "I don't wanna just mark one sometimes!" The existing conceptions of race and ethnicity within the regions the respondents have lived and attended college have provided for the daily, lifelong experiences in which the social order has ascribed an identity to these Afro-Latinos. This is in contrast to White ethnics, whom Waters (1990) asserts can choose the time and place in which to associate with a particular ethnic identity; the young people of color in this study did not enjoy such a liberty. Although survey designers usually mean for the terms *Hispanic* and *Latino* to represent a multiracial category, some respondents still felt uncomfortable selecting that option instead of "Black" or "African-American," as well as the other way around. David Swenson feared that by marking "Hispanic" or "Latino" to represent his Puerto Rican background, he might lead the interpreters of his response to envision someone very different than himself. Thus, although many institutional structures might have a clue as to the diversity of the populations they monitor and observe, their data gathering methods are not necessarily designed to reflect the complete identities of these populations. Furthermore, the general U.S. population's understanding of race and ethnicity does not usually allow for the overlap of African descent and Latin American identifications.

The relative youth of these respondents, who are all the children or grandchildren of immigrants, allows us to examine the views and perceptions of an up-and-coming generation. Although their narratives suggest the clear invisibility of Afro-Latinos in the Los Angeles racial-ethnic landscape, the ever diversifying nature of the region and the movements for "multicultural awareness" may make their existence known to more people than in their parents' generation. As the number of people who consider themselves multiracial continues to grow, it is possible that future generations of Los Angelinos and U.S. Americans in general may come to view racial and ethnic identities through a less rigidly defined looking glass.

Whether or not the respondents have even been to Latin America, whether or not they speak or understand Spanish, their experiences as part of this little-known immigrant community have shaped their identities as individuals as well as family and community members. My desire to conduct this research project comes out of my own experiences as a U.S.-born daughter of Afro-Panamanian immigrants. My ultimate goal was a selfish one: to talk to people who might have had experiences that I can relate to and learn from—for there are surely as many dissimilarities as there are commonalties. Shona Brown, in particular, voiced one of my concerns, stating, "It really upsets me that Black Latinos are not really recognized in the . . . overall Latino community because they're there, . . . they exist." Hopefully, studies like my own and collections like *No Longer Invisible*, an edited book on Afro-Latin Americans published by the Minority Rights Group (1995), will add to a body of literature that recognizes and validates the existence of Afro-Latinos in the United States and Latin America. In fact, *No Longer Invisible* provided me with my first encounter with Black pride in Spanish literature. Although in my own personal experiences I have learned just how incomprehensible the notion of Black people speaking Spanish is to many people, reading the words of Afro-Ecuadorian poet Nelson Estupiñan Bass (1954) for the first time affirmed a part of my Black identity exactly *because* it was written in Spanish—the Panamanian part it often seems that no one knows about.

References

Bass, Nelson Estupiñén. 1954. "Canción del niño negro y del incendio." In *Canto Negro Por La Luz: Poemas para Negros y Blancos*. Esmeraldas, Ecuador: Casa de la Cultura Ecuatoriana.

Bucholtz, Mary. 1995. "From Mulatta to Mestiza: Passing and the Linguistic Reshaping of Ethnic Identity." In *Gender Articulated: Language and the Socially Constructed Self*, edited by Kira Hall and Mary Bucholtz. New York: Routledge.

Collins, Patricia Hill. 1991. *Black Feminist Thought: Knowledge, Consciousness, and the Politics of Empowerment*. New York: Routledge, Chapman, and Hall.

Comas-Diaz, Lillian. 1996. "LatiNegra: Mental Health Issues of African Latinas." In *The Multiracial Experience*, edited by Maria P. Root. Thousand Oaks, Calif.: Sage.

Cunningham, Julie L. 1997. "Colored Existence: Racial Identity Formation in Light-Skin Blacks." *Smith College Studies in Social Work* 67:375–400.

Duany, Jorge. 1998. "Reconstructing Racial Identity: Ethnicity, Color, and Class among Dominicans in the United States and Puerto Rico." *Latin American Perspectives* 25(100)3: 147–72.

Fishman, J. A. 1964. "Language Maintenance and Language Shift as Fields of Inquiry." *Linguistics* 9:32–70.

Gómez, Christina. 1998. "The Racialization of Latinos in the United States: Racial Options in a Changing Society." Ph.D. diss., Harvard University.

Haslip-Viera, Gabriel. 1996. "The Evolution of the Latino Community in New York City: Early Nineteenth Century to the Present." In *Latinos in New York: Communities in Transition,* edited by Gabriel Haslip-Viera and Sherrie L. Baver. Notre Dame, Ind.: University of Notre Dame Press.

Ibrahim, Awad El Karim M. 1999. "Becoming Black: Rap and Hip-Hop, Race, Gender, Identity, and the Politics of ESL Learning." *TESOL Quarterly* 33(3): 349–69.

Kasinitz, Philip. 1992. *Caribbean New York: Black Immigrants and the Politics of Race.* Ithaca, N.Y.: Cornell University Press.

Lopez, Ian Haney. 1995. "The Social Construction of Race." In *Critical Race Theory,* edited by Richard Delgado. Philadelphia: Temple University Press.

Minority Rights Group. 1995. *No Longer Invisible: Afro-Latin Americans Today.* London: Minority Rights.

Omi, Michael, and Howard Winant. 1994. *Racial Formation in the United States: From the 1960s to the 1990s.* New York: Routledge.

——. 1995. "Racial Formations." In *Sources,* edited by Adalberto Aguirre Jr. and David Baker. Guilford, Conn.: Dushkin.

Patterson, Orlando. 1975. "Context and Choice in Ethnic Allegiance: A Theoretical Framework and Caribbean Case Study." In *Ethnicity: Theory and Practice,* edited by Nathan Glazer and Daniel P. Moynihan. Cambridge, Mass.: Harvard University Press.

Pincus, Fred L., and Howard J. Ehrlich. 1999. *Race and Ethnic Conflict.* Boulder, Colo.: Westview Press.

Rodriguez, Clara E. 1992. "Race, Culture, and Latino 'Otherness' in the 1980 Census." *Social Science Quarterly* 73(4): 930–37.

Rumbaut, Ruben G., and Alejandro Portes. 2001. *Ethnicities: Children of Immigrants in America.* Berkeley: University of California Press, 2001.

Spencer, Rainier. 1999. *Spurious Issues: Race and Multiracial Identity Politics in the United States.* Boulder, Colo.: Westview Press.

Torres-Saillant, Silvio. 1998. "The Tribulations of Blackness: Stages in Dominican Racial Identity." *Latin American Perspectives* 25(100)3: 126–46.

Valdes, Guadalupe. 1988. "The Language Situation of Mexican Americans." In *Language Diversity: Problem or Resource?* edited by Sandra Lee McKay and Sau-Ling Cynthia Wong. New York: Newbury House.

Wade, Peter. 1997. *Race and Ethnicity in Latin America*. London: Pluto Press.

Waters, Mary. 1990. *Ethnic Options: Choosing Identities in America*. Berkeley: University of California Press.

——. 1994. "Ethnic and Racial Identities of Second-Generation Black Immigrants in New York City." *International Migration Review: The New Second Generation* 28(4): 795–820.

——. 1999. *Black Identities: West Indian Immigrant Dreams and American Realities*. New York: Russell Sage Foundation.

Part III   Labor Organizing and Political Activism

Respect Latinos

Karen Yamileth Salazar Barrera
(written at age sixteen)

They talk bad about Latinos
Saying that we're ghetto
living in torn-down houses
not having stable jobs
but then again we have more fun
Telling jokes *vulgares*
We might be poor
but you don't say that
when you are eating
pupusas
tacos
bahos
be moving your ass to
salsa
cumbia
mereingue
You'll be talking bad
about the ones who *no pueden hablar inglés*
those who can't defend themselves
can't even understand you
But why can't you talk to people like me
Salvadoreña Americana
who can speak English
and can understand you
and won't shut the hell up
when you rub the subject
in my face
Is it that y'all scared
because y'all know I'll tell the truth

how hard we be working
cleaning your toilets
burning our fingers with bleach
washing your dirty clothes
now you try to kick us out of the country
say we're taking your jobs
that we don't do nothing
treat us like trash
You won't be doing what we do
like getting dirty
breaking our backs
building your houses
bussing your plates and cups
nah . . . y'all just be working in offices
typing on computers
sitting around
thinking you guys are killing yourselves
working "so hard"
but what about us
who die middle-aged from the hard work
without seeing our children grow
our grandchildren born
So the next time you see a Latino
Give much respect

11 Justice for Janitors Latinizing Los Angeles

Mobilizing Latina(o) Cultural Repertoire

Maria A. Gutierrez de Soldatenko

This chapter explores the characteristics, cultural elements, and strategies used by Service Employees International (SEIU) Local 399 Justice for Janitors (JfJ) to mobilize successfully Latinas and Latinos in California. Its organizing tactics make its struggle more visible, and in the course of taking this action it has made the city of Los Angeles into its stage. Latino/a janitors, using their cultural repertoire, contest and construct urban spaces in their struggle for union recognition. They often replicate rituals, practices, and spectacles from their countries of origin to serve their organizing interests. Much of the success of JfJ has been its recognition and ability to work with Latino/a's cultural practices to advance the organizational agenda.

This chapter examines four main topics to explore Latino uses of cultural practices in the struggle for labor rights. Cultural repertoire in this chapter refers to the different strategies, rituals, and practices Latinos/as employ in their protests and organizing efforts to assert their rights and to claim visibility in Los Angeles. First, I will consider the way Delgado (1993) has explained Latino union participation since he accounts for cultural nuances and language usage. This cultural knowledge that Latinas/os bring has not been recognized in recent research. Second, we must be able to see how Latinas/os are forming ethnic niches in the service sector occupations in Los Angeles. These ethnic niches facilitate the coming together at work of Latinas/os who share certain cultural practices and commonality of language that facilitate union organization. Also, gender represents an important aspect when considering ethnic niches in the service industry. Among the janitors in the union, both men and women are represented. Styles of participation among Latinos and Latinas in JfJ points to the strong presence and leadership of Latinas. Women are the expressive voice of the union; they integrate their families and children into labor mobilizations and become radicalized in the process of participating in struggle. Third, by briefly reviewing how SEIU JfJ has developed nationally and locally we learn about community unionism. While planning, leaders claimed to be more inclusive and attentive to demographic changes in union membership. In following their plans, JfJ delineated guidelines that inadvertently invited, in the case of Los Angeles, an infusion of Latinas/os working-class culture that impacted organizational tactics and outcomes. Fourth, in Los Angeles the deployment of Latinos' cultural repertoire has entailed reclaiming urban spaces outside Latino barrios. Also, JfJ's use of public space in its protests unveils Latino service workers' ongoing resistance against invisibility in Los Angeles. Through a case study of a JfJ campaign at Warner Center, I identify some of the cultural aspects of the Latino/a cultural repertoire set in motion through its struggle for a union contract.

I have used three sets of sources in my research of the union: (1) interviews, participant observations during meetings, marches, and campaigns; (2) newspaper accounts and union files in order to obtain a picture of the day-to-day incidents in a campaign; and (3) an analysis of the cultural repertoire of Latinos/as and uses of space. This data enables me to provide an analysis of the cultural politics of JfJ. However, the effective incorporation of Latinas and Latinos in Justice for Janitors has not come by chance. Union officials make Latino/a immigrant workers an integral part of their organization. Latinas and Chicanas also form part of the staff of the union, and, together with culturally aware Anglo leaders, they have worked to make this union possible. Thus, Latino and Latina workers are able to participate effectively and to identify strongly with the union. As a result, Justice for Janitors membership in downtown Los Angeles has risen from 30 percent to 90 percent.

Latinos in Unions

Except for Rudolfo Acuña's (1996) brief account of JfJ and its problems when placed under receivership in 1995, no researcher has systematically collected firsthand accounts from Latino and Latina workers in Justice for Janitors. Cynthia Cranford (2000) makes a compelling case for doing so while calling for a new way to organize immigrant workers and understanding the roles of gender, racialized power relations, and economic restructuring. Cranford calls for a more contextualized analysis of workers' lives. She writes, "In order to understand the new labor movement and its implications for inequalities of gender, we need to contextualize women's experiences within race and class relations." In her interesting study, she uses qualitative and cohort analyses to understand the way Latino/a immigrants participate in a class-based movement that is racialized. The most compelling insights of Cranford are her clear understandings of gender, race, and class divisions in the lives of Latino/a immigrant workers.

The participation of Latino/a immigrant workers in several other union campaigns in Los Angeles has been documented. Chicana/o historians have presented rich evidence of the active participation of Mexican American communities in labor organization. The work of Hector Delgado (1993) has debunked the myth that undocumented Latino/a immigrant workers do not fight for union recognition. Instead, Delgado demonstrates the combative spirit and persevering stance of Latinas and Latinos in Los Angeles. He also explains the need for organizers who are cognizant of cultural nuances and able to communicate effectively with immigrant communities in their own languages.

In contrast to Delgado and Cranford, some researchers argue that Latinos in JfJ have unionized only because they have a strong class consciousness (Waldinger et al. 1998). This argument dismisses the possible role of identity politics or cultural practices behind Latinas/os in labor struggles. Latinas/os practice panethnic solidarity at the same time that they confront interethnic conflicts, aware of their gender and class positions in Los Angeles. Latinas experience sexism, racism, and class exploitation simultaneously. In a racialized and gender-divided society, we cannot pretend to suspend racism and sexism in order to explain class struggle. However, mainstream researchers, although pretending to be rigorous in terms of class analysis, refuse to deal with gender, race/ethnicity, and culture. In the few instances when researchers detect a hint of cultural or racial/ethnic difference, they take note only of the "backwardness" of the Latino population for refusing to learn English and assimilate. If gender is mentioned, they do so only to point out the docility of Latinas and the prevalence of machismo among Latinos.

My work departs from these previous conceptualizations. Latinas/os, I argue, come together in JfJ because it blends their multiple identities as gendered/racialized individuals with ethnic/cultural repertoires and a social class interest. Their class consciousness is embedded in their cultural practices as Latinos in the United States. For these immigrant workers, their "Latinoness" (Padilla 1985; Oboler 1995; Flores and Benmayor 1997) is reenacted for affirmation and survival precisely because they live in an anti-Latino and anti-immigrant society. The way in which the labor market is segmented along the lines of gender, race, and ethnicity in Los Angeles explains the position Latino/as occupy in low-paying jobs such as those in the service industry.

Janitorial Work as an Ethnic Niche

The janitorial occupation in the private sector could be considered one of the ethnic niches for Latino/a immigrant workers. Latinas/os dominate this sector in Los Angeles. Researchers have tried to attribute the crowding of Latino/a immigrants in it to family networks. During my interviews, Latinas/os spoke of the practice of recommending their kin to work in the same buildings, their cousins, compadres, brothers, and sisters working closely beside them in many instances. However, we must understand that the domination of Latino/as in this sector is not simply the result of a choice to be with kin, but rather a result of limited job opportunities available for immigrant Latinos elsewhere in Los Angeles. In contrast, janitorial work in the public sector is better paid and provides benefits, yet it continues to be one of the ethnic niches of African Americans (Grant, Oliver, and James 1997). Thus, within the janitorial occupations, Latinos occupy the lowest strata, where working for the private sector gives them lower wages and benefits are rarely granted.

Latina/o janitors who work in ethnic niches have the option of organizing with friends and kin. Companies understand the importance of bilingual staffs to represent their interests, and the janitors' supervisors are often Latinos, as well. In this context, the work place is marked by gender and social class differences between workers and managers within a Latino cultural space. The workers communicate in Spanish, and there is a firm understanding of the boundaries within which people "belong." However, supervisors can demand and act as if they have absolute power over workers. It is not uncommon for bosses to verbally abuse janitors and to demand more work from them. Also, women workers complain of sexual harassment as part of their day-to-day interaction with supervisors.

Janitors are not isolated. They work as a group, and they communicate with each other. For janitors who work on the same premises, the possibility exists for the development of solidarity and union organization. What is also empowering for them is the possibility of comparing notes about managers, salaries, and work tasks. In case of a labor dispute, this shared information becomes a great organizational tool.

Service Employees International Union (SEIU) Justice for Janitors Campaign

According to union documents, Justice for Janitors started in Denver in 1985, but researchers tell a different story. Hurd and Rouse (1989) trace the beginning of Justice for Janitors to Pittsburgh in 1985. In that year, Mellon Bank decided to replace a unionized cleaning company with a nonunion firm, which triggered a series of events that culminated in a strike and a victory for the union workers. The National Labor Relations Board (NLRB) ruled for the unionized janitors, named the bank as a coemployer, and ordered it to pay back wages. In their struggle, the janitors had challenged the business owner rather than the contracted cleaning firm. This was a strategy that would be repeated in other campaigns. Other important lessons were the need to forge community alliances and the importance of the media to publicly expose corporate greed and lack of ethics (Banks 1991).

Justice for Janitors is a community based organization. Thus, community members and leaders are involved in its efforts. Andy Banks (1991) lists the different elements of community unionism: (1) community grassroots groups working for minority rights, civil rights, and church organization; (2) active involvement of both union and nonunion workers in organizing; (3) unions that are not defined by the narrow rules dictated by the NLRB; (4) campaign resources and a large budget committed to organize workers; (5) a sense of solidarity with other unions; and (6) an overall strategy to fight the battle for unionization in the "court of public opinion."

Justice for Janitors in Los Angeles

Latinos account for a high percentage of the population in Los Angeles (Lopez and Feliciano 2000). They live in communities scattered throughout Los Angeles and are clustered around the inner city. In 1995, the union's eight thousand janitors in the city were mainly concentrated in four areas: Pico Union (32 percent), South Central (20 percent), Holly-wood (17 percent), and Watts (10 percent) (SEIU 1995). Many of these janitors work in the area of downtown Los Angeles.

Morales and Ong (1993) argue that, as a result of restructuring in Los Angeles, jobs available for Latinos have changed. The service industry in Los Angeles increased in size 109 percent from 1973 to 1989. This afforded a place for Latino/a immigrants in one of the largest of all the sectors in Los Angeles. As a result, African Americans no longer dominate the service industry; Latinos are the majority now. But they also face increased inequality and poverty.

According to Schimek (1989), many janitors belonged to unions in the late 1970s and early 1980s. In 1983, they experienced a decline in wages while the cost of living, including the cost of housing, increased in Los Angeles. Real estate profits improved downtown, while janitors' wages decreased even further. Compared to other cities, Los Angeles ended up paying the lowest wages for janitorial services (Schimek 1989). By 1995, most janitors lived in poverty, and the majority did not receive health insurance. The cost of workers' health care was passed on to taxpayers at the cost of 2.7 million dollars a year (SEIU 1995). Overall, janitors' wages in Los Angeles decreased by 40 percent from 1979 to 1995. In 1995, the majority lived in the highest poverty areas of the city.

Stephen Lerner (1991), director of the Building Service Division of the SEIU, proposed that the union pay more attention to the new demographics in terms of organizing different sites. Lerner noted in 1991 that the majority of the new workforce was comprised of immigrants and people of color and that these changes should be taken seriously. According to Lerner, if unions faced the challenge of these changes creatively, their membership would increase. He had a vision of being more inclusive, but his plan did not foresee the possibility of including Latinos at the top leadership levels. Fallout from this lack of vision at JfJ surfaced in 1995, when the union faced unrest from a group of dissident immigrant Latino workers called the Reformistas and was placed under receivership. As Rudy Acuña states (1996), "the union needs immigrants as much as the immigrants need the union" (188).

The staff of JfJ recognized the need to create new strategies to appeal to and accommodate Latinos/as by way of encouraging their involvement in labor organizing. Even if Lerner did not spell out cultural specificity as a need, the people JfJ hired filled the gap effectively. Latinos and non-Latinos who were bilingual and bicultural transformed the union by embedding new strategies with a clearly Latino/a cultural repertoire. The first step was the hiring of bilingual organizers and other staff members who had gained experience previously in Latino communities in the United States and/or had knowledge of social movements in Latin America. The influx of young, energetic, and bright staffers had a tremendous impact on the the union. Examples of such individuals include Rocio Saenz, who became one of the most celebrated union organizers in Los Angeles (Milkman and Wong 2000), Miguel Menjives, Patricia Recinos, and Ana Navarrete (Acuña 1996).

Many of the staff members, some non-Latinos, have also acquired knowledge about Latinidad and know how to act biculturally and bilingually. Among these are Jono Schafer, in charge of organizers, and Triana Silton, who acted as community liaison. As defined by Padilla (1985), Ladinidad means an ethnic consciousness that develops in the everyday practices of Latinos. Latinos who work with each other in political mobilizations to improve their lives and communities put their Latinidad into practice. Cultural citizenship as explained by Rosaldo (1997), a related concept, allows us to appreciate the important role of culture in terms of empowerment and political mobilization among Latinos in the United States. Within this context, Rosaldo identifies the demand Latinos make for recognition as full-fledged citizens. Thus, a demand for *respeto* (respect) is a demand for cultural citizenship (Rosaldo 1997).

We can easily observe the improvements that emerged four years after Lerner presented his plan in the work of Lisa Hoyos among Latinos in the Silicon Valley. Lisa Hoyos (1994), the community organizer in the Campaign for Justice, emphasizes the work of JfJ with immigrant workers. She states, "Effort[s] need to deal directly and forthrightly with the linguistic and cultural challenges of organizing such a diverse workforce." JfJ's placement of Latinos/as at the center of organizing efforts and its implied cultural infusion has had an impact on JfJ organizational tactics by transforming the face of the union.

Latinas as the Expressive Voice and Leader

Throughout the JfJ campaigns many Latinas came to occupy key positions. It has been assumed that Latinas are passive, yet research on labor mobilization and Latinas tells a different story, which the JfJ experience supports. In the United States, struggles by Chicano- and Latino-origin farm workers (Leeper Buss 1993), cannery workers (Zavella 1987), garment workers (Ching Yoon Loui 2001; Soldatenko Gutierrez 2002), restaurant and hotel workers (Milkman and Wong 2000) and community organizations (Pardo 1991) have always included strong women. Also, throughout Latin America there is a long tradition of women and mothers who have mobilized their communities, such as COMADRES in El Salvador, las Madres de la Plaza de Mayo in Argentina, las Madres de Los Desaparecidos in Mexico, and the women in the Zapatista movement.

For some young Latina immigrant women working in the United States, joining a union is a first-time experience, but they enthusiastically integrate themselves in the cause. There are women in JfJ who stand out, such as the celebrated Rocio Saenz, a staffer, and Rosa Ayala, a rank-and-file member. Ayala, a Salvadoran, is intelligent, unflinching, witty, and loved by everyone. I met many women like Rosa who were quite outspoken *peleoneras* (fighters) for the labor struggle in general and in organizing their particular buildings. Women not only led and made decisions, they also learned to negotiate with cleaning contractors and became impassioned public speakers. Many women are at the forefront of union campaigns, and they assert themselves with poise. Some women have expressed the belief that mobilizations have transformed their lives forever. In some instances, women transformed themselves from silent submission to outspoken militancy in all aspects of their lives. Many of these women are also single mothers, in sole charge of their families.

The Warner Center: A Case Study

Since the fall of 1994, I have conducted fieldwork research following JfJ in its organizing campaigns. During the spring of 1995, I observed janitors in their campaign at the Warner Center in Woodland Hills. In February 1995, I met the janitors from that area for the first time. The meeting took place shortly before their work shift change at around five o'clock in the afternoon. The park next to the building complex offered a perfect space to meet and relax.

Woodland Hills is, for the most part, a White middle-class suburb in the San Fernando Valley. East of the Warner Center is Canoga Park, a working-class community that is racially mixed. Many of the janitors who clean the Warner Center live in Canoga Park. The main JfJ organizer at the time was Miguel Menjives.

About fifty people attended the initial meeting. Everyone in attendance was Latino/a, and about 60 percent of them were women. The women varied in age; they appeared to be between the ages of thirty and forty-five, whereas the men looked substantially younger, in their twenties and thirties. The young members kept cracking jokes about everyone in attendance and even those who were absent.

Miguel skillfully gave workers the union rap in beautiful Spanish. He insisted that they remain united and invite more people to join. He also mentioned that the struggle would be long and arduous. He told workers that they could win, but that he could not promise them anything. He also explained that their bosses were at the negotiation table with the union. Miguel announced that JfJ was devising a plan of action. He asked everyone during these negotiations to wear their union buttons and stickers announcing April first as the big day the contract would be signed. Miguel exhorted them to talk to secretaries and other workers in the office buildings when they saw them, to promote the coalition the union was building and to get community support.

Working Conditions for Janitors at Warner Center

Workers began to enumerate a list of complaints. They explained that they always leave the offices spotless, yet are always pressured and harassed to do extra work. These workers saw themselves at the mercy of their supervisors. They are supposed to take a break at ten o'clock at night and eat their meals, but in reality there are no breaks and they cannot finish all their tasks in the allotted time. Sometimes, workers are able to eat a snack while working, however, there is no time to sit and eat a decent meal. Recently, supervisors had demanded that janitors do more tasks without a wage increase. Some of the workers mentioned that they had worked in the same place for ten years, and they still earn only $4.25 an hour. They were recently granted a 25-cent hourly increase, but management had revoked it. One supervisor explained, "tengo que ver por mis propios huesos" (I have to look after myself) to get a promotion by saving the company some money. The same supervisor also claimed that he could do all the tasks in less than eight hours. One worker named

Maria said that she had cleaned for a month and gotten an award for her efficiency. But she was later told that more was expected from her since she had proven to be so good. According to management, she should do even better despite not getting a raise.

In their interviews, all of the workers mentioned the size of the spaces they were required to clean in eight hours. They start at six o'clock in the afternoon and end their shift at three o'clock in the morning, with one break for dinner. During this time Mela, for instance, was expected to clean three complete floors, including the office spaces, two sets of rest rooms, and three kitchens. But before the new manager arrived, she was required to clean only two floors. She also had to dust all surfaces, and now her boss wanted her to clean window frames with a rag rather than a duster, which made the task take longer. After the supervisor checked her work, she had to vacuum floors and leave a pinecone pattern marking called a *pineado* on the carpet. Mela showed me the callous where the vacuum cleaner rested on her thumb. She had to empty all the trash accumulated on the three floors and take it to the dumpsters downstairs. In some instances, she asked for help to take the heavy trash bags downstairs, but other times she managed on her own. During the winter, the heating was off, and workers kept warm only with the heavy burden of work. However, in the summer the air conditioner was turned off. Thus, the janitors clean in a sauna, for temperatures may reach one hundred degrees Fahrenheit in the San Fernando Valley and there is no air circulation since the windows remain shut. Adding to these poor working conditions, the supervisor wants them to wear slacks and the buttoned logo shirt so that they look neat in their company uniforms. This is the case even though few people other than the supervisor actually see the cleaning crew at night. This and other absurd policies make the work janitors do difficult to tolerate.

Organizing Challenges

To complicate matters, the last supervisor in the Warner Center had been abusive. He believed that in order to keep worker discipline it was necessary to push people around. His conduct had inadvertently helped the union effort, because he made workers see that they were exploited. Miguel, the union organizer, insisted that this abuse was not a personal matter, and that people should not deviate from the main objective of getting a union contract. Nevertheless, workers constantly joked about the supervisor. He gave them comic relief. They changed his name to sound like the Spanish word for "killer dog," which caused everyone to laugh.

Miguel asked the workers to be patient with other janitors who had refused or were afraid to join the union. He reminded them that in the past they had also been fearful and that it takes time to become aware of injustices. Carla interjected to remind everyone that in the past she had hidden from the union people whenever they had come around. The points were also raised that janitors in Los Angeles make a better wage compared to janitors in Warner Center because they have joined the union and that the union had been calling on this group for almost five years before this meeting. But this time the workers had called the union. Miguel also tried to impress upon the workers that they needed only to work at their own pace and complete only those tasks they could finish. They did not need to speed up their jobs only to satisfy "killer dog."

Resisting Invisibility

It is in the context of Los Angeles as a city of immigrants, many from the Third World, that creative forms of protest are enacted and practiced. In this urban landscape, Latinos and Latinas are usually only part of the background. Latinas and Latinos are there to serve and clean in bars and restaurants, to keep tables free of clutter, to cook in all types of food businesses, from fast food establishments to expensive restaurants. Latinos/as clean buildings, malls, airports, stores, museums, hospitals, stadiums, and so forth. Office workers go to sparkling environments every morning without suspecting who has made it possible for them to have clean spaces, windows, desks, phones, chairs, floors, blinders, bathrooms, ceilings, and doors.

Latinas and Latinos in Los Angeles are not seen or heard; their labor is assumed and rarely gets noticed. Lawns are trimmed and buildings always look well maintained, but nobody thinks a person or group does the job. In the interviews, janitors expressed concern for the level of invisibility that occurs in connection to their work, for janitors labor overnight, when office workers are absent and they do not have to interact with the the janitors.

Janitors are invisible to the well-groomed business community of Los

Angeles. Business people expect a clean environment without knowing who does the work, the conditions under which it is done, or the costs. Some office workers who put in overtime are kind and greet janitors. However, some ignore them. They slam doors in their faces and generally see through them. The janitors' experience of erasure is similar to what Romero (1992) and Rollins (1985) found with housekeepers, who are considered nonpersons, just one more fixture or piece of furniture in the homes they clean. Thus, part of the job of the union is to make Latinos/as visible in Los Angeles.

Latinos are "othered" in the cultural landscape of Los Angeles. However, they assert themselves in different ways by creating their own spaces in neighborhoods earmarked for Latino/a consumption (Rocco 1997) or in such public spaces specified for Latinos as Broadway, in downtown Los Angeles; The Alley, in the garment district; La Placita Olvera; Central Market; el Mercado, in East Los Angeles; and the now-defunct theater, El Million Dollar.

In many of the JfJ campaigns Latinos/as take over public spaces not intended for their use. These spaces demand the services of Latinos who are not there for their everyday use and enjoyment. These are the buildings they clean; occupying them is the janitors' way of making their presence known. Janitors clean these buildings every night, yet they are not supposed to enjoy them and be there in the daytime. The presence of Latinos/as in their red union T-shirts in broad daylight disrupts the flow of non-Latino and middle-class patrons in certain areas of the city.

During the day, the most luxurious building complexes are available to middle-class Whites and other non-Latinos for consumption, occupancy, day work, and leisure. Latinos might be present yet hidden from public view in kitchens, basements, and storage areas. Thus, when Latinas/os make their appearance in business centers during the day as janitors without mops, brooms, or vacuum cleaners, the sight is shocking to many viewers. By appearing there during the day, demanding higher wages at places they are not welcome, these Latinos symbolically subvert the space. They furthermore appear at these sites making noise, with drums, rattles, whistles, and guitars, all to the amazement of passersby. Janitors scream, they chant, they demand, and they do it all in Spanish! Thus, janitors challenge the assumptions of a monolingual and homogeneous America.

Circo, Maroma y Teatro: Justice for Janitors and Latino/a Cultural Repertoire in Motion

As stated in the strategic plan of JfJ, the way to influence the conditions under which contract cleaners work is by pressuring building owners. Janitors stage protests targeting them and their tenants. They promote negative press about selected companies, for instance, identifying them as the "Top Trash Company of the Year," and call for boycotts of products sold or manufactured at nonunion buildings. A good example of this strategy is the campaign launched against FAO Schwartz in New York for selling products made by Mattel, which had contracted the services of a cleaning company called ABM (Advanced Building Maintenance) in El Segundo, California (Ybarra 1994). As a result of that campaign, JfJ was challenged in court, which resulted in a ban on secondary boycotts (Fisk, Mitchel, and Erikson 2000).

The most effective strategy that JfJ has used to accomplish its ambitious plan in Los Angeles has been to mobilize Latinos and Latinas using their cultural repertoire while reclaiming public spaces. This does not necessarily mean that the union leaders have outlined a plan with the use of that repertoire in mind. However, the end result has been to make use of a long tradition of marches, processions, fiestas, and carnivals in Latin America. By using language and music familiar to the union membership, JfJ mobilizes Latino/as effectively. Some of the union's performances are no different from guerilla theater and street theater performances; the actors are not trained, they participate spontaneously. This approach brings to mind the important influence of El Teatro Campesino under the direction of Luis Valdez in the farm worker struggles (Broyles 1994). El Teatro was the politicizing arm of the UFW and Cesar Chavez to keep workers' spirits high and to raise consciousness. El Teatro draws from a long Mexican tradition of *La Carpa* (popular theatre performance in tents) and *merolicos*, or street performers, who make their pitches in Mexico City's public spaces. Guillermo Gómez-Peña, a famous Mexican performance artist in Los Angeles, embellishes the performances of merolicos in his soliloquies. His use of Spanish and English, and sometimes Spanglish and Ingleñol, in a quick-paced political satire is empowering. In his performances, Gómez-Peña speaks about the plight of Latina/o immigrants and the new cultural hybrid formed when they cross the border.

Justice for Janitors does not have a Teatro Campesino, as the UFW did, but it has made use of performance art, changing the Los Angeles urban landscape. Even if only for brief moments, JfJ has made sensational appearances in some of the city's most posh neighborhoods and shopping centers, such as Century City, Glendale, Warner Center, and exclusive areas of downtown Los Angeles. JfJ has mastered a performance art that gives a politicized voice to Latina/o immigrants in a very creative way.

Reconstituting Space in Los Angeles

Several authors have noted the ways in which Chicanos construct a sense of place in their communities (Villa 2000). Latinos in JfJ take these social constructions of space outside their own barrios, teaching "barriology" to the rest of Los Angeles. Latino influences go beyond the creation of Latino restaurants and curio shops or the commercialization of Latino fiestas. Through its organizational practices, JfJ politicizes its cultural expressions.

The affirmation of Latinoness is embedded in the JfJ struggle for a living wage and in its assertion of the right to organize as a union. To accomplish these goals and to fight abuses, Latina/o workers have made use of their rich cultural repertoire and construction of space (Rocco 1997). Thus, Justice for Janitors has succeeded in organizing Latinos where other unions have failed, despite arguments from some journalists and scholars that it is impossible to mobilize and effectively organize Latino/a immigrant workers. The main barrier, according to some, is the immigration status of many Latinos/as. However, JfJ is one union that has been able to incorporate a large number of documented and undocumented Latinos in its ranks.

One of the most salient aspects of the union in Los Angeles is its predominantly Latino/a immigrant composition. The union's picket lines in Westwood and Century City are festive and combative; chants in Spanish and English fill the streets and rattles made with empty soda cans and pebbles are shaken to Latin rhythms and songs. Thus, Latino/a workers Latinize the streets where they hold their protests and the vibrancy of Latino street life is momentarily exported to White suburban areas. We observe in JfJ protest class consciousness, an affirmation of Latina/o identities, and Latino revitalization of an otherwise moribund labor movement. As seen in this strategy, Latinos have defied the belief that workers organize or want union jobs only if they become assimilated or Americanized (Waldinger and Demartirosian 2000).

Subverting the Media

Justice for Janitors has been able to subvert the media, gain free publicity, and win public support. Among the more interesting ways it has called public and media attention to itself has been through production of a short video, *Sí Se Puede* (Yes We Can), and the recent film *Bread and Roses* (2000), whose screenplay was done by Paul Laverty, and that was directed by Ken Loach. In 1993, a group of JfJ supporters came up with a bilingual *fotonovela*, a form of magazine common in Latino popular culture that uses pictures and bubbles to tell stories of romance and drama, which they titled *The Big Sweep* (1993). In this magazine, they creatively combined bilingual bubbles to tell stories that included factual information at the bottom of each page. The magazine was published to teach lessons, to explain the plight of janitors in Los Angeles, and to make their story accessible to workers.

Justice for Janitors actively plans ways to attract media attention. A newspaper advertisement in *Variety*, for instance, announced the plight of janitors in Century City with a display of a miner's picture next to the caption, "Remember Pittston Miners?" Another well-done advertisement, in the *New York Times* on April 30, 1995, was a full-page picture taken during International Women's Day that shows a peaceful sit-in with women wearing red union shirts and surrounded by menacing Los Angeles Police Department officers on horses and in full riot gear. JfJ never misses a photo opportunity to advance its union demands. The image remains in our minds of a powerful display by a state and police force against a powerless group of striking Latina janitors demanding fair pay for hard work, on the day we celebrate as International Women's Day.

The union's strategy to command public and media attention in Los Angeles and to capitalize on the use of city streets and public spaces as a stage has been very effective. Some critics consider its tactics closer to a show than to part of the union's struggle, as *Wall Street Journal* writer Michael Ybarra (1994) explains:

At the time when traditional U.S. labor union influence continues to fade, the decidedly unconventional SEIU is flourishing thanks largely to a combination of zany, obnoxious and occasionally illegal techniques that seem more borne for the burlesque hall than the union hall.

Even though Ybarra makes a valid point regarding the innovative techniques of JfJ, he wrongly assumes that when the powerless take to the streets and make use of popular culture the result must be a grotesque spectacle and not a definitive political tool.

Justice for Janitors uses street theater to please and shock audiences. Among some of the most outrageous performances has been the street theater debut of *Barbie and Mopman*. One of the memorialized performances of *Barbie and Mopman* was staged in front of the Mattel office building in El Segundo. Peter Olney, a chief organizer at the time, dressed in red tights and a JfJ T-shirt à la Superman. Holding a mop and wearing a mask, Olney as Mopman tried to convince Barbie to abandon Ken because of unfair labor practices against janitors at Mattel.

The participation of Latino/a janitors in marches and street theater points to the cultural repertoire Latinos bring with them. They recreate, transform, and develop it while becoming more active in union campaigns. Included among some of the cultural aspects set in motion to promote unity and resistance are the centrality of family and children; the use of Spanish in songs, messages, and double meaning; and the use of humor. Humor and resistance in Spanish is embedded in cultural practices, in different manifestations of improvisation and quick responses and challenges, such as *hechando relajo* (having fun) and *choteo* and *cabula* (teasing), as described by Yolanda Broyles (1994) in *El Teatro Campesino*.

Family and Children

Children are an integral part of the marches and protests that members of the union stage. Children are present to affirm that the reason parents need higher wages is to support their children and families and to deter violent responses by the police. Women push strollers with babies and toddlers hold signs that read, "Can you support a family on $4.25?" Women and men carry children on their shoulders and children are specially dressed for the occasion in their Sunday best. The media loves the images they are able to capture of women and children. Women know that pictures will be taken and that the video cameras will be focused on them, and they know how to respond. For children, this is an outing with their mothers; it is quality time in the best possible way. Children sing and know the union songs, chants, and slogans, and they scream as loudly as they can "Que queremos? Justicia! Cuando? Ahora!" (What do we want? Justice! When do we want it? Now!) "Queremos un contrato, nos pagan muy barato!" (We want a contract, they pay us too cheaply!) "Estamos en huelga que limpien los ricos!" (We are on strike let rich people do the cleaning!). The members welcome the presence of children. They understand the importance of their role, and recreational vehicles are set up to transport children and mothers if they get tired.

Spanish Use and Bilingualism

Chants, slogans, and songs in Spanish and English are repeated throughout the marches. When the chants and slogans are in Spanish, the language of the majority, participants respond loudly in unison. Slogans are repeated in English for the benefit of those who do not understand Spanish. Only a few dare to shout out in English, except when the marchers chant "No justice, No peace!" in remembrance of the Los Angeles race riots of 1992. Workers also sing union songs adapted to the sound of the Nueva Canción, a Latin America cultural movement in the 1970s. In the manner of El Quilapayun's "No Nos Moverán!" these include "La Union hace la fuerza, no nos moverán! Porque estamos bien organizados no nos moverán!" (The union makes strong, we will not be moved! Because we are well organized, we will not be moved!) The use of noisemakers crafted out of empty milk bottles or soda cans makes for a wonderful experience, and the use of drums, guitars, voices, and rhythms adds to the carnivalesque atmosphere. For non-Latino spectators, who may accept and read union leaflets, this is a colorful sort of protest. For those who hold anti-immigrant feelings, however, this may be their worst nightmare, and some frown at the marchers and refuse to accept any literature.

Humor as Resistance

Throughout the marches, there are spontaneous performances and loud statements that are quite humorous. When we formed our line for the Warner Center, the organizers tried to direct first-time marchers from the Woodland Hills area. Latino/a janitors were shy and nobody wanted to carry a big banner. Finally, some women agreed to carry it. The organizer then announced that we should get our partners and dance; we should either dance or make the company dance to our tune. Someone in the crowd suggested that we should do *el baile del perrito* (the doggie dance), which in Latin America is sung and danced with a double picaresque meaning.

At one of the workers' meetings in Warner Center, union representative Miguel Menjives advised janitors to fight to the end and get ready to go on a hunger strike if necessary. Jorge, one of the young janitors, stood behind Miguel so we could not miss his theatrics. He made faces of terrible pangs of hunger and shook all over as if having a seizure. He knelt, begging Miguel not to make him go through with the strike. Meanwhile, Miguel looked at us without understanding why we were laughing. On another day, the workers planned a Valentine's Day march that would walk around the center with a list of demands. Someone suggested creating a big heart-shaped Valentine card, signed by all of the union activists with love for "killer dog," the manager. Others jokingly suggested that Menjives should lure "killer dog" toward the parking lot, where they would give him his Valentine present, *una buena chinga*, which roughly translates into beating the hell out of him. Everybody laughed since they would not dare get violent, but the thought was enticing. In the Century City campaign, workers took over happy hour in various bars and restaurants. They appeared donning their red T-shirts and ordered sodas. They raided the hors d'oeuvres and *botanas* (appetizers) to the discomfort and disbelief of patrons and owners, who felt violated in their own urban dominions, for Latinas/os, who are poor and working class, are not expected to mingle with the middle classes on the Westside. Yet in a humorous way, Latinos/as were able to disrupt and penetrate leisure spaces not designated for Latinos in the same buildings they clean every night for miserable wages.

Conclusion

I have tried to demonstrate the strong influence of Latinos/as' cultural repertoire in the JfJ's efforts to organize a large workforce in an anti-immigrant city where Latinos/as are invisible. Latinas/os' language, cultural memory, and street theater have activated a political voice among

Latinos/as in Los Angeles that enriches and transforms labor organization throughout the United States. Other immigrant groups in the past have acted similarly and transformed their cultures as part of the movement to organize workers in the United States, so Latinos are not the only ones. However, we must be careful to recognize and seriously note how unique cultural repertoires and language use help any organizing campaign among immigrant workers. Latino immigrants in Los Angeles experience a class consciousness embedded in their own cultural practices and social location as workers of color in a racialized and gender stratified society.

The struggles within JfJ continue. By the time I stopped my fieldwork and left for Arizona State University in the summer of 1995, things had worsened in the union. Before I left, the Reformistas asked me to meet with them, but I could not. There was discontent within the union and the air was tense. The official leadership of the union, despite all the planning and progressiveness, did not know how to work with a strong wing of Latino workers and organizers who perceived that the union could eventually be led by Latinos/as.

We need to study the successes and contradictions that non-Latino progressive union leaders have confronted along the lines of gender, race, and class. Are Anglo leaders in JfJ and other unions in Los Angeles ready to step down from their comfortable positions and work with Latinos/as as equals? Furthermore, will we ever see a Latina in the highest position of JfJ, as we see with Maria Elena Durazo in HERE (Hotel Employees and Restaurant Employees) Local 11, and with Cristina Ramirez Vazquez in Unite (Union of Needletrades, Industrial Textile Employees) (Milkman and Wong 2000). These and other questions remain open for future research on Justice for Janitors in Los Angeles.

References

Acuña, Rudolfo F. 1996. *Anything but Mexican: Chicanos in Contemporary Los Angeles*. London: Verso.

Banks, Andy. 1991. "The Power and Promise of Community Unionism." *Labor Research Review* 18 (fall): 17–31.

Broyles, Yolanda. 1994. *EL Teatro Campesino: Theatre in the Chicano Movement*. Austin: University of Texas Press.

Callis, Stephan, Leslie Ernst, Sandra Ramirez, and Ruben Ortiz Torres. 1993. *La Gran Limpieza (The Big Sweep)*. Los Angeles: California Classic Books.

Ching Yoon Loui, Miriam. 2001. *Sweatshop Warriors: Immigrant Women Workers Take on the Global Factory*. Cambridge, Mass.: South End Press.

Cranford, Cynthia. 2000. "Economic Restructuring, Immigration and the New Labor Movement: Latino/a Janitors in Los Angeles." Working Paper No. 9, Center for Comparative Immigration Studies, University of California, San Diego.

Delgado, Hector. 1993. *New Immigrants Old Unions: Organizing Undocumented Workers in Los Angeles*. Philadelphia: Temple University Press.

Fisk, Catherine L., Daniel J. B. Mitchel, and Christopher L. Erickson. 2000. "Union Representation of Immigrant Janitors in Southern California: Economic and Legal Challenges." In *Organizing Immigrants: The Challenge for Unions in Contemporary California*, edited by Ruth Milkman. Ithaca, N.Y.: ILR Press.

Flores, William B., and Rina Benmayor, eds. 1997. *Latino Cultural Citizenship: Claiming Identity Space and Rights*. Boston: Beacon Press.

Grant, Davis, Melvin Oliver, and Angela D. James. 1997. "Two Black L.A.s: Social and Economic Bifurcation in Los Angeles Region, 1970–1999." In *Ethnic Los Angeles*, edited by Roger Waldinger and Mehdi Bozorgmehr. New York: Russell Sage Foundation.

Hoyos, Lisa. 1994. "Workers at the Center." *Crossroads*, July/Aug., 24–27.

Hurd, Richard W., and William Rouse. 1989. "Progressive Union Organizing: The SEIU Justice for Janitors Campaign." *Review of Radical Political Economics* 21(3): 70–75.

Leeper Buss, Fran, ed. 1993. *Forged Under the Sun: The Life of Maria Elena Lucas*. Ann Arbor: University of Michigan Press.

Lerner, Stephen. 1991. "Let's Get Moving." *Labor Research Review* 18 (fall): 1–15.

Lopez, David, and Cynthia Feliciano. 2000. "Who Does What? California's Emerging Plural Labor Force." In *Organizing Immigrants: The Challenge for Unions in Contemporary California*, edited by Ruth Milkman. Ithaca, N.Y.: ILR Press.

Milkman, Ruth, and Kent Wong. 2000. *Voices from the Frontlines: Organizing Immigrant Workers in Los Angeles*. Los Angeles: Center for Labor Research, UCLA.

Morales, Rebecca, and Paul Ong. 1993. "The Illusion of Progress: Latinos in Los Angeles." In *Latinos in a Changing U.S. Economy: Comparative Perspectives on Growing Inequality*, edited by Rebecca Morales and Frank Bonilla. Newberry Park, Calif.: Sage.

Oboler, Suzanne. 1995. *Ethnic Labels, Latino Lives: Identity and the Politics of Representation in the United States*. Minneapolis: University of Minnesota Press.

Padilla, Felix. 1985. *Latino Ethnic Consciousness: The Case of Mexican Americans and Puerto Ricans in Chicago*. Notre Dame, Ind.: University of Notre Dame Press.

Pardo, Mary. 1991. "Creating Community: Mexican American Women in Eastside Los Angeles." *Aztlán: A Journal of Chicano Studies* 20, nos. 1–2 (spring–fall): 39–71.

Rocco, Ray. 1997. "Citizenship, Culture and Community: Restructuring in South-east Los Angeles." In *Latino Cultural Citizenship: Claiming Identity, Space and Rights,* edited by William V. Flores and Rina Benmayor. Boston: Beacon Press.

Rollins, Judith. 1985. *Between Women: Domestics and their Employers.* Philadelphia: Temple University Press.

Romero, Mary. 1992. *Maid in the U.S.A.* New York: Routledge.

Rosaldo, Renato. 1997. "Cultural Citizenship, Inequality and Multiculturalism." In *Latino Cultural Citizenship: Claiming Identity, Space and Rights,* edited by William V. Flores and Rina Benmayor. Boston: Beacon Press.

Savage, Lidia. 1998. "Geographies of Organizing Justice for Janitors in Los Angeles." In *Organizing the Landscape: Geographical Perspectives on Labor Unionism,* edited by Andrew Herod. Minneapolis: University of Minnesota Press.

Schimek, Paul. 1989. "From the Basement to the Boardroom: Los Angeles Should Work for Everyone." N.p.: Service Employees International Union.

Service Employees International Union (SEIU). 1995. "A Penny for Justice." N.p.

Soldatenko Gutierrez, Maria A. de. 2002. "International Ladies' Garment Workers' Union Labor Organizing: Chicana and Latina Leadership in the Los Angeles Garment Industry." *Frontiers: A Journal of Women's Studies* 23(1):46–66.

Villa, Raul Homero. 2000. *Barrio Logos: Space and Place in Urban Chicano Literature and Culture.* Austin: University of Texas Press.

Waldinger, Roger, and C. Demartirosian. 2000. "Immigrant Workers in American Labor: Challenge . . . or Disaster?" In *Organizing Immigrants: The Challenge for Immigrants in Contemporary California,* edited by Ruth Milkman. Ithaca, N.Y.: ILR Press.

Waldinger, Roger, Chris Erickson, Ruth Milkman, Daniel J. B. Mitchell, Abel Valenzuela, Kent Wong, and Maurice Zeitlin. 1998. "Helots No More: A Case Study of Justice for Janitors in Los Angeles." Unpublished paper, Lewis Center for Regional Policy Studies, UCLA.

Ybarra, Michael J. 1994. "Waxing Dramatic: Janitors' Union Uses Pressure on Theatrics to Expand Its Ranks." *Wall Street Journal,* Mar. 21.

Zavella, Patricia. 1987. *Women's Work and Chicano Families: Cannery Workers of the Santa Clara Valley.* Ithaca, N.Y.: Cornell University Press.

12 Constructing Chicana and Chicano Studies

1993 UCLA Conscious Students of Color Protest

Michael Soldatenko

I was awakened from my intellectual and ethical slumber by protests that occurred on various college campuses in the 1990s. I had grudgingly come to accept Chicano student politics within the paradigm of nationalist politics that was traditional at UCLA and other campuses in California. I continued to perceive Chicano student practices through the lens of *El Plan de Santa Bárbara* (Chicano Coordinating Council on Higher Education 1970). I therefore retained an urban, Marxist, nationalist, and male-centered perception of Chicano students and their politics. This meant that I concurred that Chicano student politics was about control and autonomy within the academic institution and hoped to use the university as a base for action in the wider social and political world. The vision of *El Plan* permeated my comprehension of Chicano student practices and my own political behavior. The 1993 UCLA Conscious Students of Color Protest released me from these assumptions and presented new political possibilities.

The UCLA student protest made me aware of two important issues that were central to the protest's objectives. First, UCLA activism reinforced a concern that my students at Santa Monica College (SMC) had begun to raise in my classes: the notion of a fixed Chicano identity. Although my students may not have had the language to express their frustrations, it was clear to me that they rejected a Chicano politics that was determined by the interests of supposed homogeneous non-immigrant male Mexican Americans. My SMC students conceived of a different student politics based on the diversity within the Latino(a)/Chicano(a) community. Mexican Americans and Latinos(as) had to accept the heterogeneity of the community and links with students from other racial/ethnic and immigrant groups in order to challenge academic practices.

The generation of the 1993 protest was part of the demographic transformation of Los Angeles. By 2000, Mexicans and Mexican Americans had replaced African Americans as the dominant minority in the city and, together with other immigrants from Latin America, had formed the largest ethnic group in the city. Although some people spoke of a homogeneous community of Latinos(as), most recognized the dissimilarities within the group that were further accented by national, religious, political, and economic differences, together with the discrepancies in U.S. policies toward these immigrants and their home countries. For instance, the El Salvadorans, Nicaraguans, and Guatemalans arriving at my campus challenged my courses on Chicanos(as) and Mexican history. Furthermore, these students transformed SMC's Movimiento Estudiantil Chicano de Aztlán (MEChA). These Central American students demanded a widening of the concept of Chicano Studies and the creation of courses on Latinos(as) in United States and Central American history. Although UCLA's enrollment figures do not provide corresponding demographic details of its student population, I believe parallels exist that allow us to hypothesize a similar change of the Latino(a) student body at UCLA as at SMC. Clearly, demographic changes could influence the existing intellectual practices that formed Chicano Studies.

At the same time, Chicano Studies also faced challenges from women and the gay community. Intellectually, many Chicanas had confronted the male construction of Chicano Studies since its inception. Furthermore, they continued to battle student organizations, especially MEChA, that sustained a patriarchal politics. On the UCLA campus, this defiance resulted in alternative organizations during the 1980s, like Raza Women or Latinas Guiding Latinas. By the early 1990s, these and other organizations had established deep roots on the campus and were keeping an eye on the gendered politics of MEChA. Possibly influenced by Chicanas, gay Chicano(a) students also came together outside of MEChA and established La Familia in the early 1990s. These organizations exemplified the heterogeneity of the Chicano(a)/Latino(a) community at UCLA. For these reasons, when UCLA Chicano(a)/Latino(a) students protested in 1993, it was impossible to speak of a typical Chicano(a) student or of a representative organization.

The second issue present in the protest was a recognition that the battle at universities and colleges was not about academic or administrative positions, control, or autonomy, but about the mechanisms that the academy utilizes to construct and implement knowledge of the world. The problem with earlier student protests was their ignorance of the "hidden curriculum" and its disciplining of all within the academy

(Margolis 2001). In contrast, the UCLA protesters demanded that we reconceptualize ethnic and women's studies by encouraging epistemological and ethical questions that could both confound and subvert institutional practices. The students, furthermore, put a mirror to the face of us academics who have been engaged in Chicano Studies, and questioned our dealings with them and one another.

The 1993 protest was the outcome of growing student dissatisfaction with UCLA policies toward ethnic and gender studies as well as with the larger University of California system's inability to articulate an alternative to the rising tide of anti-immigrant and anti-affirmative action rhetoric in California. On May 11, students challenged UCLA with a rally and sit-in at the UCLA Faculty Center. The response of campus management was to deploy the largest use of police power at UCLA since the May 1970 protest. For the following two weeks, students organized demonstrations, marches, vigils, and so forth to stress their demands that the administration deal with issues of ethnic and gender studies, in particular a Chicano(a) Studies department, as well as the use of force on the campus and with the sit-in arrestees. The 1993 protest demanded new political and intellectual directions. The UCLA students moved beyond traditional Chicano student politics and advanced a different form of Chicana and Chicano politics. For these students, the events of spring had the potential to revive a moribund movement by students who no longer accepted "Chingon politics" as Chicano politics—with its sexism, machismo, and narrow nationalism (Martinez 1998). They also initiated a curricular reformation of ethnic studies, in particular the discipline of Chicano Studies at UCLA. The students presented a potentially new Chicana(o) intellectual agenda and political practice that would be simultaneously open, critical, oppositional, and progressive.

Sadly, the protest took a different turn on May 25 when a small group of individuals, ostensibly to increase pressure for the demands, decided to begin a hunger strike. This group manifested the presence of a male-centered, patriarchal, homophobic, nationalist, and traditional political agenda and curricular vision. These activists, always a minority, redirected the struggle toward preservation of traditional Chicano political values, practices, and curricular vision—always clothed in the language of community action. Their practice shifted the emphasis of the protest into an ultimatum for a Chicano/a Studies department that reflected their particular vision. This marked a major change in the protest. During the following weeks, the initial open-ended and participatory protest gave way to a nationalist and patriarchal political exercise that introduced exclusion into the movement. When the UCLA administration began to negotiate an end to the protest, the hunger strikers and their allies asserted their vision and subverted the earlier hope for a different style of ethnic and gender studies. Thus, the final accords and the endeavors to structure a new department resonated with the return of an old-fashioned form of Chicano academic politics. By the end of the struggle, Chingon politics had survived the students' endeavor for transformation.

To untangle all these issues in a single chapter would be impossible. Therefore, I have chosen to leave the intellectual concerns and issues for a later discussion. In this essay, I recount the struggle at UCLA to detail the two contrasting visions for Chicano(a) Studies. (We often write as if Chicano(a) Studies is singular—this has never been the case.) On one side, some students built a movement that sought a nonnationalist approach to ethnic studies and identity politics. They sought a campus politics that could bring together the various national, racial, ethnic, and gender groups on the campus to create an oppositional intellectual agenda. On the other side were students whose nationalist approach was driven by traditional Chingon politics that articulated everything in the language of *El Plan*, albeit with indigenous overtones.

"Genesis" of a Protest

When one looks for a beginning to the 1993 UCLA Conscious Students of Color Protest, most commentators construct a continuum linking all prior Chicano UCLA protests with 1993. The 1993 protest appears as part of the long history of Chicano protests at UCLA whose goal had been to establish an autonomous Chicano Studies department and whose purpose was to wage battle with the university and society in general. Thus, in a recent conference at UCLA the organizers placed the 1993 protest in a chain of events that began with the first organizational efforts by Chicanos(as) on the campus and continues today. From this reading, the same political language, practices, and goals have animated Chicano protests at UCLA over the past thirty years (Organizing Committee n.d.).

To accept this reading is to create a caricature of the 1993 UCLA Conscious Students of Color Protest. In 1993, protestors engaged in a politics that both challenged and overcame traditional Chicano campus politics. By working together with other students of color and looking beyond the instrumentalism of earlier Chicano politics, they sought a different articulation of epistemology and ethics in academic practices. To engage in academic knowledge production and transmission, based on institution building, was simply unacceptable. Instead, influenced by an assortment of new theoretical visions, these students sought to engage in an oppositional production of knowledge and pedagogy that could not, at least temporarily, be incorporated into the academy. Their practices rejected the academic politics of the Chicano movement and *El Plan de Santa Bárbara* that narrowly focused on institution building.

Although there was no beginning to this protest, there was a particular historical setting that shaded the 1993 protest. For this reason, I sketch a story of Chicano Studies at UCLA without imposing a necessary political link between the events. By doing so, I hope to sharpen the oppositional vision offered by the 1993 protestors.

When one looks back to the creation of Chicano Studies programs in California, two events stand out: student protests and the establishment of an academic program for Chicano Studies. Although these two activities often coincided, they did not necessarily determine one another. The high school walkouts in Los Angeles in March 1968 and the San Jose State College graduation protest a couple of months later, together with the Third World strikes at San Francisco State College and the University of California at Berkeley, during the school year 1968–69, were the political foreground to the formation of Chicano Studies in California. Among the protesters' demands was the creation of Chicano Studies programs. For some, these programs were to deal with student services; for others, to teach about the Chicano experience. Frequently, the protestors mixed the two. Yet, all participants agreed on the political purpose of these programs—self-determination. *El Plan de Santa Bárbara* articulated the political vision that all activists should endeavor to practice on all their campuses through their student organization, MEChA.

Contemporaneously, a handful of faculty, staff, and graduate students at particular University of California campuses began the process of institutionalizing Chicano Studies as an academic program. This often had to be done under the auspices of liberal Anglos who managed these programs and through academic senates and other administrative hurdles. On campuses where activism was high, students struggled with Chicano(a) and Anglo faculty, administrators, and staff because they felt that the process of institutionalization could remove the political orienta-tion of Chicano Studies. The result was a mishmash of programs, depart-ments, and research centers that rarely found backing from activists. On campuses where militancy was mute, student participation was kept at a minimum. Although this may have resulted in stronger institutional and/or academic programs, it did little to deal with the political concerns expressed in *El Plan.*

At UCLA, the style of Chicano campus protest resulted in the more appealing development of four ethnic studies research centers under the auspices of the Institute of American Cultures in 1969. The new Chicano Studies Research Center (CSRC), finalized in 1973, although dedicated to research, was also expected to develop and coordinate a teaching program in Chicano Studies. To run this program, the center was dependent on traditional departments to sustain courses and hire faculty. At best, the center and traditional departments shared newly hired faculty. Unfortu-nately, the allegiance of faculty might be to her/his home department, since that department determined tenure. Thus, Chicano Studies was hobbled from the start. In the following years, Chicanos(as) did not chal-lenge the structure or practice of Chicano Studies at UCLA and did little to halt its bureaucratization and ossification. This remained the situation at UCLA for the next twenty years.

By the end of the 1980s, Chicano Studies classes and the future of the Chicano Studies major were in crisis at UCLA. Although the program was never well embedded in proper institutional procedures, UCLA poli-cies sharpened the misfortune. First, there was the inconsistent history of hiring Chicano(a) and Latino(a) faculty at UCLA. Second, the coordina-tion of Chicano Studies classes was not working well, since the university consistently underfunded the program and kept its academic status un-clear. Thus, by early 1990, no new admissions to the Chicano Studies ma-jor were to be accepted. Furthermore, UCLA was looking to suspend the Chicano Studies major and possibly disestablish the program (Gómez-Quiñones 1979, 1985, 1987; Weber 1979; Roy and Campbell 1988; Healy and Miech 1990; Hayes-Bautista 1990; Miech 1990; Hagstrom 1990d). It was in this context that UCLA Chicanos(as), together with MEChA, organized protests against UCLA's policies in the spring of 1990 (*UCLA Daily Bruin* 1990a, 1990b; Hayes-Bautista et al. 1990).

The program also was suffering from an academic crisis. What did it mean to engage in teaching Chicano Studies? How could research and teaching be oppositional if they needed to find acceptance within the academy? For some, Chicano Studies had become an apolitical, uncritical, bureaucratic program; it resembled other traditional programs. This situation was made worse by its gendered academic and political work. Sadly, most students did not see the links between the first set of problems and this intellectual crisis. In most cases, they felt satisfied to blame whoever was in charge of the CSRC (Muñoz 1989, 159; *La Gente* 1974, 1979, 1981; Cruz 1981; Haro 1981; Una Voz 1990).

Although the protest was small, MEChA engaged UCLA and its chancellor, Charles Young, on the issue of the Chicano Studies major (Orbach 1990a, 1990b). Keeping within earlier Chicano political practices, MEChA simply stipulated that faculty who specialized in Chicano Studies should be housed in a Department of Chicano Studies; it also presented a timetable to establish this department (Suk 1990; Hagstrom 1990a; *UCLA Daily Bruin* 1990a). Though the UCLA administration was not in agreement ("Provost's Committee" 1990a, 1990b, 1990c, 1990d, 1990e; Anima 1990a; *UCLA Daily Bruin* 1990a; Hagstrom 1990b, 1990c), Provost Raymond Orbach called together a special committee on restructuring the major, which led to the establishment of a subcommittee to administer it. Students participated in both committees (Ortiz 1990a, 1990b). After a summer of meetings, the provost decided to retain and increase support for the Chicano Studies program, though he left the discussion about the subject to a later date (Ramos 1991; *UCLA Daily Bruin* 1990a). In response to these administrative moves, MEChA prepared its proposal for a department and presented it in December 1990 (Anima 1990a, 1990b; "Minutes" 1990a; MEChA and United Community and Labor Alliance 1990).

When the institution resisted, MEChA initiated two tactical moves. First, it raised public awareness about the issue by organizing campus protests. These public displays, it hoped, would put pressure on the UCLA administration. Second, it developed a community organization whose concern was the struggle for a new department at UCLA. Thus, the United Community and Labor Alliance (the Alliance), organized at UCLA, was to serve as the community representative. Although this organization had ties to the Olvera Street Merchants Association, most participants in the Alliance already had prior ties to UCLA. Although some researchers accept the notion that the Alliance was a "community-based organization" with community roots (Rhoads and Martinez 1998; Campbell n.d.), the organization had few real organic links to the community it claimed to represent. Neither tactic was successful.

At the same time, some UCLA Chicano(a) and Latino(a) faculty showed interest in working with students to establish a department. Throughout the school year 1990–91, as Professor Vilma Ortiz reconstructed the major and rebuilt a functioning program, now called the Chicana and Chicano Studies Program (Ortiz 1991, 1992), some faculty worked on a proposal for the creation of a Chicana and Chicano Studies department ("Proposal for the Creation of a Department of Chicana and Chicano Studies at UCLA" 1991; Magner 1991). While reorganizing the major, Ortiz and Professor George Sanchez arranged a "curriculum transformation project" for Chicano Studies. They set up faculty seminars to develop new courses and think through the meaning of these courses in Chicano and Chicana Studies beginning in the winter of 1991. Unfortunately, UCLA administration blocked any real discussion of establishing such a department. Though the associate chancellor of ethnic affairs, Raymond Paredes, held a couple meetings with Chicano(a) and Latino(a) scholars and students, there was a clear understanding that the administration was not interested in a Chicano(a) Studies department (Anima 1990a, 1990b, 1990c; Mitchell 1991; Marquez 1992a). The administration felt that the department would "ghettoize" instructors and remove responsibility for hiring more Chicano(a) and Latino(a) faculty from traditional departments. Furthermore, using an apparent split within Chicano(a) and Latino(a) faculty on whether to develop a department quickly or slowly, administrators decided to go slowly—if ever (Sears 1991; Moran 1991). After consulting with his departments, the dean of social science concluded: "[t]he faculty is not persuaded that a department is the appropriate organizational structure for those efforts, for a wide variety of reasons. I share that view as well" (Sears 1991). Seymour Feshbach, chair of the Academic Senate, agreed: "They were also unanimous in expressing the view that departmental status is not appropriate at this time" (Feshbach 1991). Provost Orbach was also in accord that the university should continue to develop the current program and see what happened (Orbach 1992, 7). Even when UCLA Chicano(a)/Latino(a) faculty presented their proposal for a department early in 1992 (Teaching Faculty of Chicana and Chicano Studies 1992; "Proposal for the Creation of Chicana and Chicano Studies Department" 1992; Ramos 1991, 1992), the administration had already rejected the idea (Sears 1992; Ramos 1992; Magner 1991; Marquez 1992b). A year later, a new dean of social science again rejected the idea of a department (Waugh 1993).

Why was UCLA unresponsive to Chicano(a) student and faculty requests for a department? In reading these administrators' letters one is struck by their limited vision. Some felt that the issue was "excessively politicized" (Sears 1991, 3). For others, a separate department "implie[d] that a separate epistemology is called for and that would reduce the comparative nature of most sociological studies," thus resulting in the department becoming narrow and restricted and causing a "ghettoizing problem" (Morony 1991). Others noted the fiscal issue or the possibility that other interdepartment programs (IDP) might demand their own departments, thus leading to further marginalization (Waugh 1991). Most administrators agreed on the need to build the program, but none accepted the need for a department (Sears 1991; Orbach 1992; Feshbach 1991; Morony 1991; Miech 1991; Nicol 1991; Sheats 1991; Dorr 1991). UCLA's administration never offered an intellectual rebuttal—nor, by the way, did the Chicanos(as) provide an intellectual defense.

Though the chancellor promised to make a final decision quickly, none came. Instead the administration's behavior served to antagonize the students, create splits among the faculty, and pit students against faculty (Marquez 1991a, 1991b; Wolowiec 1991). Whether through chance or by design, the administration manipulated divisions within the Chicano(a) community and then waited (Gordon 1992a).

Administration policies worked. In early 1993, the Academic Senate voted to strengthen the current IDP structure while rejecting the creation of a department. Student activism around the department issue had quieted down (Koppelman 1993; Loza 1993; Karimi 1993). MEChA, following traditional tactics, found it difficult to find support on campus or from outside groups and individuals. Given this silence, the administration's response finally came on April 28, 1993. Chancellor Young stated that the program structure was fine. There was no need to create a department; Chicano Studies lacked integrity to become a department and would lead to ghettoizing the faculty. Therefore student and faculty demands for a department were dismissed—all stated, of course, in the most cordial and academic language.

Chancellor Young and his administration seemed oblivious to the fact that their decision to reject the creation of a Chicano(a) Studies department coincided with the eve of Cesar Chavez's funeral. Young's act came to symbolize UCLA's policies toward minorities. As one student poignantly noted in the campus newspaper: "The only diversity on this campus is the fact that Mexicans and Africans are gardeners, janitors or food service workers, who are forced to take a pay cut at that" (Barragan 1993; Ramirez 1993).

In looking back at MEChA's position, one finds few differences with earlier Chicano Studies politics. For students who followed *El Plan*, the department was to exist as an autonomous structure within the academy that could serve to transform the Chicano(a) and Mexican community. In a draft of a proposal for a department, MEChA saw this as a program about and for Mexicans:

> Our vision of the Chicana and Chicano Studies degree program, is one which would encompass all aspects of Mexican culture and history, from our pre-European indigenous civilizations to the effects of north american capitalism and state on the present day Mexican community. (MEChA and United Community and Labor Alliance 1990, 4)

Moreover, the authors further insisted that any model of ethnic studies would not work. For this reason, many read the resulting protest as part of the continuum of struggle at UCLA.

I would like to present another reading of these events. The previous history had little to say about the development of the 1993 protest. UCLA students ignored MEChA's politics. For these new activists, the issue of the department was not at the center of their political practice, but part of a larger program. Although the action of Chancellor Young might have led to protest, other issues had overtaken the demand for a department. At the forefront of these concerns were the various cutbacks at UCLA. California was undergoing an economic downturn that resulted in legislative cuts in funding for the University of California. State Senator Tom Hayden notes that appropriations for the University of California had declined by $342 million since 1990 (Hayden 1993; Mercer 1993; Gordon 1993). UCLA needed to cut about $8 million a year from its budget. One area that UCLA decided to cut was in the various ethnic studies and women's studies programs. In particular, the CSRC proposed to cut the CSRC's library budget to the point that it would "call the integrity of the Library into question" (Chabran 1993; Lopez 1993). It appeared to many that UCLA was trying to fix its budgetary problems on the back of what some considered "questionable" programs.

Simultaneously, UCLA's Academic Senate rejected a plan to establish an ethnic and gender studies requirement for UCLA students. The University of California at Berkeley had already debated and established such a requirement on its campus. The rejection of such a requirement was particularly striking since Los Angeles had just suffered a major social upheaval in the spring of 1992. The Los Angeles rebellion highlighted social, economic, and political tensions articulated through class, race, space, ethnicity, and immigrant status. The rebellion asserted a much more complex Los Angeles than those who lived in West Los Angeles and Santa Monica wanted to understand. This must also be put in light of contemporary fraternity problems at UCLA, where "Mexican" theme parties had been organized. Yet the UCLA Academic Senate had decided that UCLA students did not need to understand their campus, city, state, or nation. This was interpreted as another example of UCLA's lack of interest in issues of importance among students of color.

This lack of concern struck a chord in a student body that had undergone significant demographic changes in the decade 1985–95 and before implementation of SP-1, SP-2, and Proposition 209, which, together, ended affirmative action in the University of California system (Shah 1999; University of California Board of Regents 1995a, 1995b). Although the percentage of Whites on campus had declined by 33 percent, that of Chicanos(as) had increased by 84 percent, Asian Americans by 100 percent, Filipinos by 32 percent, and Latin Americans by 40 percent. From a different angle, the decade witnessed an increase in the proportion of students of color, from 34.1 percent in 1985 to 57 percent in 1995. African Americans, unfortunately, saw little significant change. These demographic changes provided a background, though not an explanation, to a student politic that was increasingly based on multinational/racial identity politics. Students of all ethnic, racial, and immigrant statuses were trying to bridge the artificial gap among communities of color, especially in light of public policies and media constructions that occurred in the wake of the 1992 rebellion. In other words, organizations like MEChA found themselves in a very different political environment facing more nuanced issues with outdated (often nationalist) political tools.

The 1993 UCLA Conscious Students of Color Protest

Budget cuts, rejection of an ethnic studies requirement, rebuff of the department, and the rising tide of anti-immigrant rhetoric (building up to a push for passage of Proposition 187) (Diamond 1996) drew students who were critical of UCLA's policies together from different communities. The budget cuts and possible disaffiliation of the CSRC Library from the center sparked some of these students to create a new organization in early 1993—Conscious Students of Color (CSC) (Martinez 1993a; Mora-Ninci 1999, 320–27). They organized a protest for Tuesday, May 11, to demand an end to cuts in the library budget, a freeze on cuts in the budgets for Ethnic and Women's Studies programs, the establishment of a Chicano(a) Studies department, and student participation in the search for a permanent replacement for the director of the CSRC. More importantly, CSC transformed the issue of simply demanding the establishment of a Chicano(a) Studies department into a critique of the academy and its policies toward students of color. Establishment of the department was no longer a Chicano(a) issue; the concern was the nature of education.

About 150 students staged a rally at the UCLA Faculty Center. After a series of presentations, the plate window on the door broke and some of the students entered the Faculty Center and decided to conduct a sit-in. (Rhoads and Martinez 1998, 124, argue that the sit-in was premeditated.) As the students entered the center, faculty and guests evacuated. Acting chancellor Andrea Rich apparently panicked and ordered campus police and the Los Angeles Police Department to respond in full riot gear. About 250 officers arrived and closed off the area as students within the center decided to follow through with a large-scale sit-down protest. The police cordoned off the center, antagonizing the crowd outside. Many students complained of verbal and physical abuse by the authorities. The police moved into the Faculty Center about 5:00 P.M. and began to arrest students who had decided to remain; by 1:00 A.M., eighty-nine had been booked on the premises and then bussed to Los Angeles County Jail and the Sybil Brand Institute, a detention facility for women. The students were not processed and released quickly, apparently due to UCLA obstinacy (UCLA Public Information 1993; UCLA African Gay Revolutionary Activist 1993).

On the day of the protest and arrests, a MEChA notice in the UCLA campus paper called for a rally to be held on May 12 against Chancellor

Young's decision concerning a Chicano(a) Studies department. This rally was not connected to the one called by CSC. This demonstrated the tension between MEChA and CSC (Mora-Ninci 1999, 436). Mora-Ninci suggests that "conservative" elements in MEChA expressed a lack of interest in working with CSC and other groups because they believed that the groups had different visions. MEChA was concerned with the departmental issue alone, whereas CSC wanted to focus on the reduction of the library's budget as a symbol of the differential allocation of budget restrictions (Mora-Ninci 1999, 445–47). Nevertheless, due to the Tuesday arrests, the MEChA protest drew over one thousand people. MEChA benefited from the organizational work of CSC. Though MEChA distanced itself from the events of the day before, it demanded release of the students arrested. This protest was made livelier by the arrival of a large and vocal contingent of Justice for Janitors members, who were protesting at the Federal Building in Westwood. When they heard of the student protest at UCLA, they decided to join. One of their spokesmen told the crowd of the need to link campus activism with worker issues. She invited students to join the janitors in their protest at the Federal Building later in the week. Many of the speeches were directed against Chancellor Young's attitude toward Chicanos(as) and Latinos(as) at UCLA and his response to the issue of a Chicano Studies department.

CSC called for a silent march the following day, May 13. "We had a demonstration on Tuesday, on Wednesday and we're having one today," said Shiva Abdul of CSC. "Until our demands are met, we will not stop, but no one has to get arrested" (Mabalon 1993c). CSC presented four demands: an end to the proposed cuts in ethnic and gender studies programs, more student representation on committees making decisions about these programs, implementation of a Chicano(a) Studies department, and the dropping of charges against the arrested students. Again, the goal was not merely resolution of these issues but also their use as symbols of the contradictions in higher education. On the same day, a series of groups appeared to support the arrested students and the CSC's issues, and the *Los Angeles Times* came out with an editorial calling for the establishment of a Chicano(a) Studies department (1993b).

After another protest on Friday, May 14, a group of local politicians, actor Edward James Olmos, and some UCLA faculty, staff, and students met with Young, Rich, and other administrators. It was clearly not a fruitful gathering. "Hayden said the meeting served only 'to clarify the differences that were already there'" (Farley 1993). In the afternoon, about two hundred faculty and students gathered for a review of the situation with some of the politicians. Olmos made a very dramatic call for a large peaceful demonstration the following week. Meanwhile, the students who had been initially arrested were returning to campus. The university accused them of vandalism and of causing some fifty thousand to seventy-five thousand dollars worth of damage at the Faculty Center.

During the following week, several protests were held throughout the campus. A political vacuum, however, developed over the direction of the protest. Students seemed divided. On one side was a small group that wanted to focus the protest on the formation of a department. On the other side were CSC and its allies, whose concerns included not only the department but also the policies of UCLA against students of color ("Statement of the Ethnic Staff and Faculty Association" 1993). Furthermore, the issue of UCLA's decision to address its financial crisis by balancing its budget on the backs of students was also called into question. Chicano(a) and Latino(a) faculty, furthermore, did not present a united front. In this context, a small group of students connected with Mexica Cuahtemoc dance group decided to stage a hunger strike to force UCLA to establish the department. The *danzantes* sought a nationalist Chicano Studies department that would stress "northern Aztlan culture" (Rhoads and Martinez 1998, 124).

On Friday May 21, CSC gathered about two thousand people to protest UCLA's policies and reaffirm its demands. Again, local politicians appeared and offered support for the ongoing protest. Various student groups and organizations spoke about the need to support the struggle and build democratic organizations among students. A group of UCLA Chicano(a)/Latino(a) faculty stepped forward to present their encouragement. Community organizers and activists came to pledge their support. Even local gang members from Culver, Sotel, and Venice noted the link between peace in their communities and student activism. What was striking was the diverse character of the crowd. "Speaker after speaker applauded the crowd's diversity, which included representatives from the Asian-American and African-American spectrum" (Frazier and Weston 1994). During the presentation, Professor Jorge Mancillas informed the crowd that on Tuesday of the following week, May 25, he and a group of students were going to begin a hunger strike and would continue until the demands were met. CSC acquiesced to this change in tactics. Mora-

Ninci suggests that a small group within the committee essentially took over and promoted the hunger strike. He sees this as one of the first "splits in the movement" and an example of the "power struggle" within the student movement (Mora-Ninci 1999, 472).

On May 25, the hunger strike began as an effort to force the administration to create a Chicana(o) Studies department (Mancillas 1993). The other issues that CSC had promoted became less important. Whatever the rhetoric, the struggle had been progressively reduced to one over establishment of the department alone (Roemer 1993). Unfortunately, most research on the UCLA protest also reduces the movement to a strike for a department; even Rudy Acuña misses the larger picture proposed by CSC about the nature of education and the new politics necessary to challenge the academic leviathan (Acuña 1996, 304–8). In the process, the protest became "Mexicanized." All the hunger strikers were Mexicans or Mexican Americans who viewed the struggle as one solely for establishment of the department of Chicano Studies.

Although the number of hunger strikers varied over time, altogether there were five-six UCLA students, a high school sister of one UCLA striker, two community leaders, a concerned parent, and one professor. The strikers set themselves up in a large tent in an open space facing the administrative offices of UCLA. Initially, the hunger strike was not well organized or attended. Active support was at best sparse. Furthermore, the strike began before a long weekend, which left the strikers isolated. But thanks to the support of a large group of well-organized and hardworking women, mostly from CSC, the hunger strike was turned into the media event it needed to be to achieve success. For anyone who went to the growing tent city, one could not escape the power and activity of these women. Women like Blanca Gordo, Claudia Sotelo, and Gabby Valle were everywhere; they made everything work. If you needed information, you asked them. When the hunger strikers needed something, they got it. If the media needed directions and information, they were there. Without doubt, the success of the hunger strike was due to their work. They, unfortunately, have not been sufficiently praised for their accomplishments. Contemporaneously, many non-Chicano(a) and Latino(a) student activists, many active in CSC, worked hard to make the struggle successful.

On the third day, the hunger strikers decided to accelerate the protest. They decided that they would take only water. This decision reflected a new trend in the struggle. The hunger strikers and their close supporters now presented themselves as the vanguard of a resurrected Chicano/Chingon politics. Although the early phase organized by CSC had been open, democratic, and slightly chaotic, this next phase witnessed a shift in decision making to the hunger strikers and their allies. This was evident in the media attention that was now directed toward the hunger strikers; they displaced the wider UCLA movement. In this situation, many student organizations, like MEChA and CSC, were checked or excluded. Although the activists continued their work, their leadership role was declining. The CSC women, some of whom had been arrested, were progressively ignored by the development of events. Information became scarce; decision making was more secretive. The open process gave way to small meetings by preselected people in the main tent. "Most strategy sessions during the hunger strike were open only to actual participants, select faculty members and invitees" (Acuña 1996, 306). Rumors quickly replaced discussion and decisions. Discontent over decisions grew.

Up to this point, the protesters had spoken about the possibity of a new conceptualization of student politics on campus. Many had hoped for a politics that would bring together diverse voices with many particular agendas sharing the same strategic goal: the creation of a democratic, open, and diverse space in the academy. The attitudes of Asian American students exemplified the new possibilities that the protest had fostered. Unity among different ethnic/racial/immigrant student groups was seen as central to opening up the university. Mora-Ninci (1999, 481) quotes one student:

> Though I am Asian, Chicano Studies had become my struggle. . . . I'm also fighting in this struggle for my people, the Asian people, for African people . . . for all people of color who need to know about Chicano Studies, Mexican struggles. . . . I need to know about [the] Mexican struggle and the African struggle and the struggle of all people of color. . . . [O]nly then can I see the commonalities in our struggle and link our movement together to fight as a united community of people of color towards real change.

Such Asian American students linked the struggles at UCLA with those on other campuses, like the rotary hunger strike for the development of an Asian American Studies department at the University of California at Irvine (De Tran 1993; Chung 1993; Moon 1993; "Why Asian Students"

1993; Bui 1993; "The Role of Asian Pacific" 1993). White women activists also supported the protest as part of the struggle to challenge patriarchical society (Hagstrom 1993). But the hunger strikers' vision unfortunately gave way to old-style Chingon student politics.

The change in the character of the struggle reflected the increased influence of the ideology of the Mexica Cuahtemoc dancers, since four of the strikers belonged to that group (Chavira 1993, 108), and the arrival of old Chicano *veteranos*. The difference between the first couple weeks of struggle and the hunger strike period was startling. The area around the tent that the strikers occupied was marked off as a sort of sacred place, with semireligious/indigenous features surrounding the tent. These features included the Mexican flag, images of the Virgin, the burning of copal, and security/warrior guards. This arrangement divided the tent city between the land of the strikers and those who were organizing and working for the strike. This arrangement also reflected the shift of power and decision making from CSC and the women organizers to the hunger strikers. The division was further accelerated by the arrival of old Chicano activists and their so-called "community" connections. The Chingon dinosaurs came to bless the event as the Chicano Movement returned. For some, it was an opportunity to continue political agendas from the 1960s and 1970s; they returned to the language of earlier protests. These activists reasserted the rhetoric of autonomy, as expressed in *El Plan de Santa Bárbara*, together with *El Plan's* assumptions of politics and the academic world. The strikers' influence was further solidified by the appearance of politicians who desired to resolve the strike and receive media attention. In this new political context, we see the assertion of a nationalist, male, hierarchical, and closed political process (Acd n.d.).

Ruben Martinez and Bill Boyarsky, in two very different pieces written for the *Los Angeles Times*, mentioned this nationalist trend (Martinez 1993; Boyarsky 1993). Martinez was initially worried about the nationalist symbolism, whereas Boyarsky was put off by the religious attitudes expressed at the tent city. Nevertheless, they both *hoped* that the protest would go beyond these limitations. Their hope rested on the participation of people from a wide variety of ethnic/racial/immigrant backgrounds. Thus, Martinez wrote: "Rather than a narrow ethnocentrism, what I hope has been born through the UCLA fight for Chicano Studies is the beginning of an 'international' nationalism—a coalition that fights for equal representation for all of the city's histories." Elizabeth Martinez shared this hope for a new political movement that would avoid reactionary nationalism, sexism, and homophobia by building "serious, non-sectarian coalitions with other progressive students of color and whites" (Martinez 1993a, 52). Unfortunately, their hope was misplaced. Elizabeth Martinez hinted at possible contradictions that threatened to return the UCLA movement to traditional Chicano politics, increasingly shrouded in spirituality and *indigenismo*. The "international nationalism" that both Martinezes hoped to see unfortunately faded into a virulent nationalism that was exclusive. Even the endeavor to read the protest as a continuation of the ideals of Cesar Chavez reinforced the patriarchal, hierarchical, and nationalist turn of the protest (Sotomayor 1993a, 1993b).

On Tuesday, the eighth day of the hunger strike, a committee of parents and students met with UCLA's administration. By this time, an amorphous negotiating committee was structured. Who belonged to this committee and what it represented were unclear. Some students insisted that they were not "negotiating" but "discussing" issues with the administration—they were "opening lines of communication with the university" (Mabalon 1993d). Initially Olmos and Professors David Hayes-Bautista and Juan Gómez-Quiñones appeared as part of the negotiating team. Later, Professors Cynthia Tellez, Steve Loza, Leo Estrada, and Visiting Professor Gina Valdez were present. California legislators Art Torres and Tom Hayden also participated in the negotiating process. As the process unfolded, certain self-identified "community representatives" came into the picture to negotiate for the students. Among them were Arturo Díaz López of *Danza Azteca*, Arturo "Paztel" Mireles of *Danza Mexica Cuahtemoc*, Juan José Gutierrez of One Stop Immigration and the Alliance, Vivien Bonzo of the Alliance, and Gilbert Cedillo from Local 660. Closed meetings were held with Chancellor Young and his administrators. Rhoads and Martinez argue that the initial meetings were long and confused, with increasing numbers of participants and onlookers. After three days of meetings, the hunger strikers decided to join the discussions as well. Rhoads and Martinez claim that the hunger strikers feared that the people negotiating with UCLA were not sufficiently tough. Their participation altered the negotiations, often turning them into times of "emotional venting." Given the slow pace of negotiation, tempers became increasingly short (Rhoads and Martinez 1998, 130–31).

By this time, thanks to the work of the women organizers, the tent area had grown and was constantly full of people. These women built the community support that went beyond organizations like the Alliance. Students from other campuses set up tents. On June 3, a large demonstration took place that extended from Westwood to UCLA with about two thousand participants. From another direction, the UCLA Academic Senate began to put pressure on the chancellor to compromise. At the same time, the *Los Angeles Times* called for mediation "to bridge the chasm between the protesters and UCLA Chancellor Charles E. Young" (*Los Angeles Times* 1993a).

It is hard to understand the negotiating process, since there appears to have been the formal negotiating process and several informal ones on the side. Young would not accept any Chicano Studies department; he would not budge. To resolve this impasse Professor Archie Kleingartner, chair of the Executive Board of the Academic Senate, followed up on an idea of Professor David Kaplan and proposed a Center of Interdisciplinary Instruction (Rhoads and Martinez 1998, 131–32; Kleingartner 1993). In a letter to Young, Kleingartner acknowledged the central role that faculty FTEs (full-time equivalents) played in department autonomy and recommended a mixed model that incorporated parts of a department and parts of an IDP. The new center was presented as a natural development of the current program structure, "when the centrality and maturity of the subject matter is deemed sufficient to warrant the increased allocation of resources." It would have all the features of a department without the name. Meanwhile, the administration continued being very tough on the arrested students and the "vandalism" at the Faculty Center, in particular two CSC students who had been marked as "instigators" of violence.

To continue pressure on Young, a major march and rally were held on Saturday, June 5. In overcast and at times rainy weather, two thousand marchers made their way from downtown Los Angeles to the UCLA campus (some fourteen miles) for a rally at the tent city. Eventually, negotiations were concluded. Following Kleingartner's proposal, the university created the Cesar Chavez Center for Interdisciplinary Instruction in Chicana and Chicano Studies instead of a Chicano Studies department. "Stopping just short of calling it a department, the compromise would give the enhanced program power to hire its own professors and allow professors from other departments to transfer into it" (Gordon and Nazarion 1993). This was a significant change from the model of an interdepartmental program that has little control over budgets and faculty hiring. Moreover, the administration agreed to hire six faculty members, provide an appropriate budget for the center, freeze cuts on all ethnic and Women's Studies centers, and deal leniently with the ninety arrested protestors. On the issue of the arrested students, charges against eighty-four were dropped; seven students who were accused of damages to the Faculty Center would not be charged if restitution were made. Thus, on the fourteenth day, the hunger strike came to an end with chants of "Chicano Power." "For many within the Chicano community at UCLA the resolution was a victory," so concludes Rhoads and Martinez (1998, 133). Identity politics had prevailed to everyone's benefit. But was this really the case?

With the end of the hunger strike, concerns that had been suppressed during its course flooded to the fore. What was achieved on the issue of a Chicano Studies department? Was the new center simply another space for Chingon Studies? A group of women, unhappy with the politics of the hunger strike, called for a town meeting on June 9 to reflect on what had occurred over the past two weeks and what it meant for Chicanas and Latinas. Gabby Valle states that "not all students agreed with the choice of indigenous symbolism," but once the strike was on, all had to support it (Lee 1993). A clear misogynistic and homophobic character had arisen during the strike. Many of the women were torn between the joy of victory and concern over Chingon politics. There was clear tension. Did criticizing the movement mean disloyalty? The women decided it was necessary to hold a public town meeting to discuss the issues of inclusiveness and unity, and to prepare the process for implementation of the new center. Maybe the dream of a new Chicano Studies department could be saved. For this reason, they demanded that the question "what is Chicano(a) Studies about" needed to be considered. If the CSRC had not been successful, if many Latino(a)/Chicano(a) faculty were *vendidos* (sell-outs), then what purpose did Chicano(a) Studies serve? To those who asked these questions, it became important to open a public dialogue over Chicano(a) Studies before the center was set up and individuals hired. Saul Sarabia of *La Gente* pointed out the need to think of the hunger strike as more than simply a protest about establishment of the Chicano Studies department. Rather, it "represent[ed] an opportunity to challenge the sincerity of the rhetoric about rebuilding and democraticizing the city in the wake of last spring's unrest" (Sarabia 1993).

Unfortunately, the hope of having a discussion about the goals and future of the movement never occurred. The level of antagonism, rumor, accusation, and *chingonismo* limited dialogue. Since the hunger strikers had been unable to force the administration to agree to the organization of the center, they pushed other issues to the fore instead. These included who the director would be, how the center would be governed, what roles students and the community would have in the new center, and how these categories were to be defined. In other words, the organizational issue of Chicano(a) Studies and who would run the new center became the bones of contention. Epistemological and ethical questions were dismissed as divisive. No space was allowed for discussion of what Chicano(a) Studies was about. In fact, differences of opinion were dealt with by the art of "jamming." The women's agenda was stifled from the start. The hunger strikers and their associates rejected any attempt to think outside traditional institutional hierarchies and procedures.

The lack of an open democratic process during the hunger strike and the resurgence of Chingon politics made the aftermath of the strike problematic. The initial town meeting became a more-or-less permanent process throughout the summer, with biweekly meetings and the creation of a "General Assembly." The hunger strikers and their allies pushed their agenda (Implementation Committee Student Members n.d.). The assembly quickly consumed itself in distrust, attack, jamming, and rhetoric. Students began to abandon the meetings, so by the end of the summer less than a dozen remained.

The UCLA administration simply waited. Since most of the faculty refused to think politically, they allowed themselves to be used and maligned. The administration then further undercut what little faculty unity existed (Olmos 1993; Paredes 1993). Professor Ortiz observes that, although many UCLA departments suffer from long histories of factionalism and internal competition, the administration typically tries to maintain an evenhanded approach. But when it came to Chicana and Chicano Studies, this was not the case. "Instead, incompetence is rewarded and promoted; academic success is devalued; teaching and research plans developed along sound academic criteria are not allowed to develop; success at raising funds from external sources is not rewarded; and outspokenness and voicing one's own opinion—the very cornerstone of academic life—are punished" (Ortiz 1993b, 8). Thus, the administration's active interference in faculty self-management strengthened the hand of the most conservative Chicano(a) forces on and off campus. Furthermore, the administration did little to protect the faculty from threats and intimidation (*UCLA Daily Bruin* 1994). This situation permitted one or two Chicano faculty to push their particular agendas, in conjunction with the Alliance and hunger strikers, while painting the rest of the faculty as vendidos (Young 1993; "Framework for a Center for Interdisciplinary Instruction in Chicana and Chicano Studies" 1993; Hsu 1994a, 1994b, 1994c, 1994d, 1995; Hsu and Silva 1994; Lebo 1993, 1994; Grijalva 1994; "Report of the Student Representatives" 1994; Burger 1995).

As the administration dragged its feet on the accords, anger and frustration mounted. It was not until mid-January 1994 that an interim director (Assistant Dean Carlos Grijalva) was appointed to the Chavez Center and the search for six positions announced—amid much discontent and distrust. The conflict among the students, the politics of Chicano(a)/Latino(a) faculty, the split between students and faculty, the rhetoric of who really is a Chicano activist—all made work impossible (Nuñez 1994). The administration inflamed the situation by capitalizing on these divisions. It never provided the space and support for a resolution. Rather, it consistently undercut the faculty who worked for a resolution, played games with students' issues, and then portrayed itself as a concerned participant.

The Politics of Chingon Studies

The hunger strike allowed chingonismo to return to UCLA. Patriarchy, nationalism, and an exclusionary form of indigenismo stifled the possibility of a new form of Chicana and Chicano Studies. These three obstacles made any debate about a different kind of Chicano(a) Studies unattainable. The protestors' demand for a dialogue over alternative epistemic and ethical practices never took place; rather, traditional academic institutional procedures created another academic discipline. The Cesar Chavez Center was simply one more academic program that had to establish its space within UCLA.

The role of patriarchy within the Chicano movement is not new, nor is it gone. One need only observe the works of contemporary Chicana and Latina writers, the Chicano(a)/Latino(a) academic community, and our own homes and communities to note the prevalence of patriarchy within the Chicano movement. During the hunger strike, a macho style of politics asserted itself. Men spoke for the struggle; male practices permeated the overt leadership and style of doing politics. When the old Chicano activists came to the campus with their Jurassic politics, women were further brushed aside. These women demanded their space, but as in many other cases, they were reminded of the need for a united front. When women were granted space, it was to provide support for the *movimiento*. When large sketches of "heroes" were placed throughout the tent city, they were of Zapata, Chavez, and Che—which reinforced the narrow image of the Chicano movement. There was no escaping the patriarchal politics of tent city.

This sexist behavior was often explained away as the result of ignorance, unintended consequences, or individual mistakes. For the hunger strike supporters, feminism, at best, had a secondary role in Chicano Studies. It was as if the Chicano failures of the 1970s and 1980s had never occurred. When women voiced their unhappiness, a "feminist activist" with the Alliance stated: "We will make sure that the number of men and women on the committees are equal." The audience to this statement accepted it since among nationalists and others the code words for feminism at UCLA were simply "gender balance" (Ortiz 1993b, 7). When women brought up the point that the only intellectual basis for the future of Chicana and Chicano Studies was feminism (Ortiz 1993b, 9), that in fact without a feminist position Chicano(a) Studies was dead, the same female "community activist" stated, "Oh, we all care about women, but we first need to organize for Chicano Studies." When women continued to focus on a feminist agenda, they were accused of playing "the gender card." Some were threatened and intimidated. By controlling feminism, the activists allowed the return of an invigorated Chingon Studies.

Patriarchy at UCLA was made stronger by a virulent and narrow nationalism (Ortiz 1993b, 5). Nationalism has been at the heart of the Chicano movement. What that meant, however, has differed among individuals and groups. In the case of the hunger strike, instead of providing a tool for unity and struggle, the politics of nationalism was used to exclude and attack those whose perspectives of the future program did not coincide with their own. The commitment and activism of Central and South Americans, mixed Latino(a)-Other, and non-Chicano(a) supporters were questioned. It appeared that only those that were really *Mexicano* could understand the issues at hand. In fact, some of the hunger strikers spoke about hiring only "Mexican faculty." Professor Ortiz has recalled that often students rejected her arguments because of her Puerto Rican background: "These students felt no responsibility to develop their arguments. . . . Rather their 'correct' nationalism and my 'incorrect' nationalism was sufficient justification" (Ortiz 1993b, 6). Mora-Ninci has presented another example of these exclusionary politics. In one of the first assembly meetings of the summer, Vivian Bonzo of the Alliance rejected the notion that the assembly spend time on the defense campaign of the seven students charged during the Faculty Center takeover in May. It was suggested that, since most were from CSC and not Mexican Americans, their legal problems were not central issues of concern— only the establishment of the new Chavez Center was important. Mora-Ninci has concluded that this same nationalist attitude severed UCLA Chicanos(as) from the larger proimmigrant movement that followed (Mora-Ninci 1999, 489–90 and 498).

What made this nationalism more exclusionary and strengthened the link to patriarchy was the abuse of indigenismo. The period of the hunger strike was marked by a heavy dose of indigenous rhetoric and imagery. Although I found the emphasis on native spirituality questionable, this was not a crucial problem. My concern was the danzantes' political use of native traditions. They utilized native symbols, images, and practices to exclude others. Native spirituality served to transform the strikers into semireligious figures, legitimated their separation from the community, and reenforced their dominance. Instead of allowing native practices and symbols to create community, it undercut unity. The use of security/warriors further isolated the strikers and, in turn, became a force of intimidation. By these practices, indigenismo fed patriarchal and nationalist tendencies. Martinez (1993a, 56) adds that indigenismo could further be used to counter feminism.

Therefore, it should not be considered paradoxical that the end result of the hunger struggle was preservation of traditional academic practices. The intellectual vision offered by the hunger strikers and their friends simply acquiesced to traditional academic practices. This lack of intellectual foresight allowed the academy to become the determining factor in the development of Chicano Studies at UCLA. The demand for a department did not question the operation of the university. The creation of the Chavez Center therefore reinforced the hand of the university. Without a debate over the nature of Chicano(a) Studies within the academy, without acknowledging the control of the institution, without redefining the form and practice of a discipline, without speaking to politics and feminism, the struggle resulted only in the constitution of a department that was defined (and confined) by the institution. The result of the hunger strike and its aftermath was creation of a department that operated in accordance with administrative procedures. It was neither more nor less political than any other academic program—in which most of us academics function. In the end, without problematizing the university and academic work, as proposed by CSC, the struggle for the Chavez Center reinforced the logic of the institution.

Epilogue: Questioning Chicano Studies

Most research on the 1993 UCLA Conscious Students of Color Protest fails to recognize the two distinct political visions present during the struggle. For most scholars, the hunger strike for a department of Chicano Studies was the purpose of the movement and reflected the "new" identity politics on U.S. campuses. Thus, Rhoads and Martinez argue that the protest produced a multiculturalism that challenged given educational structures. Campbell adds that the UCLA protesters were able to use Chicano nationalism and ethnicity to successfully challenge UCLA by integrating them into American public discourse (Rhoads and Martinez 1998; Rhoads 1998; Campbell n.d.). These writers ignore the more radical position taken by CSC and its call for an epistemic revolution in Chicano Studies and U.S. higher education in general. Rather, much like the hunger strikers, they acquiesce to the instrumentalist logic of Chicano politics as represented in *El Plan de Santa Bárbara*. Ironically, Mack, in an undergraduate essay, demonstrates greater sensitivity to the real possibilities of the 1993 protest. She points to the epistemological assumptions that lie behind all academic departments. Therefore, Chicano(a) Studies cannot be reconstituted as simply another department; it must be a department that departs from an understanding of the restrictions imposed by institutional structures and power distribution (Mack n.d.). Unfortunately, this possibility was lost; the hunger strike and its resolution derailed the transformative hope of the UCLA 1993 protest.

Five years later, a few UCLA Chicano(a) students were still fighting for the control and direction of the Chavez Center (Valenzuela et al. 1998; Serna 1998). Sadly, they had little interest in the epistemological and ethical issues the 1993 protest had brought to the fore. Although the nomenclature had changed much, the practice of Chicano Studies remained untouched. Yet hope remains. Although some Chicano(a) students may have returned to an autarchy politics, others are struggling to bridge nationalism and identity politics in order to fight for immigrant rights, in favor of affirmative action, and against globalization. At the same time, the 1993 protest left the seeds for a potential rethinking of Chicano Studies. Although this might mean the sublimation of Chicana and Chicano Studies, it does not in any way mean they will be mainstreamed into traditional disciplines. Rather, Chicano Studies will have served its purpose when all disciplines face the same transformation. Thus, hope for an epistemic break as proposed by the 1993 protest remains.

Sources

References

Acuña, Rudolfo F. 1996. *Anything but Mexican: Chicanos in Contemporary Los Angeles*. London: Verso.

Aguilar, Dahlia. 1993. "Protest for Progress." *Hispanic* 6:7.

Anima, Tina. 1990a. "Committee Agrees Chicano Studies Needs a Department." *UCLA Daily Bruin*, June 7.

——. 1990b. "Community Derides Chicano Administrator for Views." *UCLA Daily Bruin*, Nov. 19.

——. 1990c. "Conference to Focus on Chicano Studies." *UCLA Daily Bruin*, Nov. 30.

Barragan, Ramiro. 1993. "Chicana/os Ill-treated." *UCLA Daily Bruin*, May 10.

Boyarsky, Bill. 1993. "UCLA Strike Grew from Deep Historical Roots." *Los Angeles Times*, June 9.

Bui, Thien-An. 1993. "What Is the Chicana/o Studies Debate About?" *Pacific Ties*, June.

Burger, Leslie. 1995. "Case Underlines Chicano Studies Struggle." *Los Angeles Times*, Dec. 3.

Campbell, Christopher D. n.d. "Cultural Components of Civil Action: Discourse and Narrative in Student Protest." Master's thesis, Department of Sociology, UCLA.

Chabran, Richard. 1993. "Chicano Studies Trapped in UCLA's Ghetto." *UCLA Daily Bruin*, May 3.

Chavira, Adriana. 1993. "UCLA Struggles for Chicano Studies Program." *Lowrider* 15:9.

Chicano Coordinating Council on Higher Education. 1970. *El Plan de Santa Bárbara: A Chicano Plan for Higher Education*. Santa Barbara, Calif.: La Causa Publications.

Chung, Carol. 1993. "It Is Time for Change." *Hwet Bool* 1:4.

Comesaña Amado, Pablo. 1993. "No se necesita departamento de estudios chicanos: Young." *La Opinion*, May 25.

——. 1994. "Hector Calderon dirigá el Centro Interdisciplinar de Estudíos Chicanos de UCLA." *La Opinion*, Nov. 20.

Cruz, Sylvia. 1981. "Chicano Studies Center." *La Gente*, Jan.–Feb.

Dean, Jon. 1993. "We Fast, They Feast." *UCLA Daily Bruin*, June 1.

De Tran. 1993. "UCI Protestors Win Guarantee on Asian Studies." *Los Angeles Times*, June 11.

Diamond, Sara. 1996. "Right-wing Politics and the Anti-immigrant Cause." *Social Justice* 23:3.

Farley, Giles. 1993. "Protestors Gain Legislative Allies." *UCLA Daily Bruin*, May 17.

Frammolino, Ralph. 1993. "A New Generation of Rebels," *Los Angeles Times*, Nov. 20.

——. 1994. "UCLA Picks Interim Head for Chicano Studies." *Los Angeles Times*, Jan. 28.

Frazier, Joanna, and Ivy Weston. 1994. "Protestors Rally for New Dept. at UCLA." *Daily News*, May 24.

Fuentes Salinas, José. 1993. "Huelga de hambre. . . ." *La Opinion*, July 4.

Gordon, Larry. 1992a. "On Race Relations, Colleges Are Learning Hard Lessons." *Los Angeles Times*, Jan. 4.

——. 1992b. "UC Regents Debate Fallout from Audit." *Los Angeles Times*, Sept. 18.

——. 1992c. "UC Riverside Chancellor to Be Named." *Los Angeles Times*, Mar. 20.

——. 1993. "UCLA Resists Forming Chicano Studies Department." *Los Angeles Times*, Apr. 29.

Gordon, Larry, and Sonia Nazarion. 1993. "Fasters, UCLA Officials Meet to Defuse Protest." *Los Angeles Times*, June 6.

Grijalva, Carlos V. 1994. "Update: Faculty Searches for the Cesar Chavez Center." *UCLA Daily Bruin*, June 9.

Hagstrom, Christine. 1990a. "Committee Wants More Chicano Faculty." *UCLA Daily Bruin*, July 30.

——. 1990b. "Students Barred from Chicano Studies Meetings." *UCLA Daily Bruin*, July 2.

——. 1990c. "Students Rally for Chicano Studies Major Today." *UCLA Daily Bruin*, May 7.

——. 1990d. "UCLA Students Protest Threatened Suspension." *UCLA Daily Bruin*, Apr. 25.

——. 1993. "Mobilize Behind Chicana/o Studies, Revolutionize Feminism." *Together*, June 1.

Haro, Carlos. 1981. "Chicano Studies Center: A Rebuttal." *La Gente*, May.

Haro, Guillermo. 1993. "UCLA Latinos Press Demands for Chicano Studies Program." *Wave Newspaper*, May 19.

Hayden, Tom. 1993. "Amid Cash Crisis, Hispanics Win a Historic Victory." *Chronicle of Higher Education*, June 30.

Hayes-Bautista, David, Guilermo Hernandez, George Sanchez, and Edit Villareal. 1990. "To UCLA Students, Faculty and Staff." *UCLA Daily Bruin*, Apr. 25.

Hsu, Nancy. 1993a. "Montañez Draws Strength from Family Support." *UCLA Daily Bruin*, Dec. 9.

———. 1993b. "Progress on Chicana/o Studies Center Lags." *UCLA Daily Bruin*, Oct. 21.

———. 1993c. "Students Call for Young's Resignation." *UCLA Daily Bruin*, Dec. 9.

———. 1994a. "Chicano Center Starts Taking Shape." *UCLA Daily Bruin*, Apr. 13.

———. 1994b. "Fast Protests Chavez Center Faculty Hiring." *UCLA Daily Bruin*, June 9.

———. 1994c. "Many Still Concerned about Center." *UCLA Daily Bruin*, Apr. 18.

———. 1994d. "Students to Fast, Protest Chavez Center Recruiting." *UCLA Daily Bruin*, June 6.

———. 1995. "C. Chavez Head Aims to Enrich Community." *UCLA Daily Bruin*, Jan. 19.

Hsu, Nancy, and Julie Ann Silva. 1994. "Chavez Center Director Named." *UCLA Daily Bruin*, Jan. 28.

Jimenez, Carlos M. 1994. "A Forum for Community Issues." *Los Angeles Times*, Feb. 21.

Karimi, Robert. 1993. "Proponent Argues for Chicana/o Studies." *UCLA Daily Bruin*, Jan. 14.

Koppelman, Carrie-Andrea. 1993. "Chicano/a Studies Will Break Barriers." *UCLA Daily Bruin*, Jan. 14.

La Gente. 1974. "Ex-Director Alvarez . . . Again." Oct.–Nov.

———. 1979. "Chicano Studies: MEChA Critique." June.

———. 1981. "A Question of Priorities." Jan.–Feb.

Lebo, Harlan. 1993. "Chavez Center Begins Search for Faculty." *UCLA Today*, Dec. 9.

———. 1994. "Progress Noted in Chicano Studies." *UCLA Today*, Apr. 21.

Lee, John H. 1993. "UC Meets LA." *LA Weekly*, June 18–24.

Los Angeles Times. 1993a. "It's Time for Mediation at UCLA." June 3.

———. 1993b. "Reassessment, Please, in UCLA Controversy." May 13.

Los Angeles Times Metro Desk. 1993. "Monthly Report." *Los Angeles Times*, July 2.

Loza, Steve. 1993. "Chicana/o Studies Issue is Academic, Not Ethnic." *UCLA Daily Bruin*, Jan. 14.

Mabalon, Dawn B. 1993a. "Chicano Studies Department Denied." *UCLA Daily Bruin*, Apr. 30.

———. 1993b. "Chicano/a Studies Suffers Upset." *UCLA Daily Bruin*, Feb. 4.

———. 1993c. "Students, Local Leaders Meet with Young." *UCLA Daily Bruin*, June 4.

———. 1993d. "Students March Silently to Chancellor's Office." *UCLA Daily Bruin*, May 14.

Magner, Denise K. 1991. "Proposal to Revise Chicano Studies Divides UCLA." *Chronicle of Higher Education*, May 1.

Mancillas, Jorge R. 1993. "At UCLA: The Power of the Individual." *Los Angeles Times*, June 11.

Margolis, Eric, ed. 2001. *The Hidden Curriculum in Higher Education*. New York: Routledge.

Marquez, Letisia. 1991a. "Freshman Talk Marred by Protest." *UCLA Daily Bruin*, Oct. 11.

———. 1991b. "MEChA Letter Attacks Chicano Administrator, Staffer." *UCLA Daily Bruin*. Apr. 18.

———. 1992a. "Program's Alumni Fight for Creation of Department." *UCLA Daily Bruin*, Apr. 13.

———. 1992b. "University Demands Full-time Commitment from Faculty." *UCLA Daily Bruin*, Apr. 13.

Martinez, Elizabeth. 1993a. "Seeds of a New Movimiento." *Z Magazine*, Sept.

———. 1993b. "UCLA: A Time to Celebrate." *Crossroads* (July/Aug.): 12.

———. 1998. "'Chingon Politics' Dies Hard: Reflections on the First Chicano Activist Reunion." In *Living Chicana Theory*, edited by Carl Trujillo. Berkeley: Third Woman Press.

Martinez, Ruben. 1993. ". . . The Emergence of L.A.'s True Identity." *Los Angeles Times*, June 9.

McCurdy, Jack. 1993. "UCLA's 'No' on Chicano Studies Dept. Brings Violent Protest." *Chronicle of Higher Education*, May 19.

Mercer, Joye. 1993. "UCLA, Under Pressure from State Budget Cuts, Stirs Anxiety and Anger with Plan to Close 4 Schools." *Chronicle of Higher Education*, June 16.

Mitchell, John L. 1991. "Coalition Backs Call for Chicano Studies Dept." *Los Angeles Times*, Feb. 7.

Moon, Paul. 1993. "Students Combine Efforts for Curricular Reform." *Hwet Bool* 1:4.

Moran, Julio. 1991. "UCLA Faculty Split on Chicano Studies Department." *Los Angeles Times*, Apr. 19.

Mora-Ninci, Carlos. 1999. "The Chicano/a Student Movement in Southern California in the 1990s." Ph.D. diss., University of California, Los Angeles.

Mostkoff-Linares, Aida. 1993. "Chicanas/os Show Strength." *UCLA Daily Bruin*, July 12.

Muñoz, Carlos, Jr. 1989. *Youth, Identity, Power: The Chicano Movement*. London: Verso.

Nuñez, Berenice. 1994. Letter to *UCLA Daily Bruin*, Apr. 26.

Pacific Ties. 1993. "The Role of Asian Pacific Americans in the Chicana/o Studies Struggle." June.

Ramirez, Jerry. 1993. "Young's Timing Very Insensitive to Chicana/os." *UCLA Daily Bruin*, May 20.

Ramos, George. 1991. "UCLA Cuts in Chicano Studies Hit Education." *Los Angeles Times*, Jan. 9.

———. 1992. "Plan Unveiled for UCLA Department of Chicano Studies." *Los Angeles Times*, Jan. 29.

———. 1993. "Courage, Not Caution." *Los Angeles Times*. Nov. 15.

Revolutionary Worker. 1993. "UCLA Student Takeover Demands Chicana/o Studies." May 23.

Rhoads, Robert A. 1998. "Student Protest and Multicultural Reform: Making Sense of Campus Unrest in the 1990s." *Journal of Higher Education* 69:6.

Rhoads, Robert A., and Julio G. Martinez. 1998. "Chicana/o Students as Agents of Social Change: A Case Study of Identity Politics in Higher Education." *Bilingual Review/Revista Bilingüe* 23:2.

Rodriguez, Roberto. 1993. "Battle over UCLA's Chicano Studies Program Ends." *Black Issues in Higher Education,* June 17.

Sarabia, Saul. 1993. "Chicano Studies Fight Involves a Bigger Issue." *UCLA Daily Bruin,* May 20.

Serna, Elias. 1998. "Chicano Studies Now." *La Gente,* May.

Shah, Andy. 1999. "Students Rally to Restore Affirmative Action." *UCLA Daily Bruin,* May 21.

Sotomayor, Frank O. 1993a. "Ideas de Chavez nutrieron lucha de estudiantes." *Los Angeles Times,* July 1.

———. 1993b. "UCLA Strikers Keep Alive Cesar Chavez's Flame." *Los Angeles Times,* July 1.

Suk, Sarah. 1990. "Troubled Major's Future Discussed." *UCLA Daily Bruin,* Apr. 30.

Tocoztli. 1998. "Read between the Lies." *La Gente,* June.

UCLA African Gay Revolutionary Activist. 1993. "Eye on the Storm." *Ten Percent,* June.

UCLA Daily Bruin. 1990a. "Chicano Studies Deserves Own Department." Sept. 24–27.

———. 1990b. "MEChA Position Paper on Chicana/o Studies." May 29.

———. 1990c. "Students Locked Out of Meeting." July 2.

———. 1994. "Open Letter to the UCLA Community." June 9.

UCLA Public Information. 1993. "Statement Regarding Arrests at UCLA on May 11." May 12.

UCLA Today. 1993. "Framework for a Center for Interdisciplinary Instruction in Chicana and Chicano Studies." June 24.

University of California Board of Regents. 1995a. "Policy Ensuring Equal Treatment—Admissions"(SP-1). July 20. Available at http://aad.english.ucsb.edu/docs/SP-1html.

———. 1995b. "Policy Ensuring Equal Treatment-Employment and Contracting" (SP-2). July 20. Available at http://aad.english.ucsb.edu/docs/SP-2html.

Wolowiec, Chris. 1991. "Gardner and Young Receive Grilling." *UCLA Daily Bruin,* Oct. 25.

Worker Vanguard. 1993. "Protests Rock UCLA." May 21.

Archival Sources

UCLA Chicano Studies Research Center Library Collection

Acd. N.d. "Chican(o), The Name That's Not Tame."

Chabran, Richard. 1993. Letter to David Lopez. Apr. 13.

Dorr, Aimee. 1991. "Graduate Council Response to the Report of the Committee on Structure of Chicana and Chicano Studies." Dec. 6.

Feshbach, Seymour. 1991. Letter to Academic Senate Chair. Dec. 30.

"Framework for a Center for Interdisciplinary Instruction in Chicana and Chicano Studies." 1993. June.

Gomez-Quinoñes, Juan. 1979. Letter to Eugene Weber. Apr. 27.

———. 1985. Letter to Ray Orbach. June 26.

———. 1987. Interview. Feb. 20.

Hayes-Bautista, David. 1990. "Review Document." Apr. 2.

Healy, Charles, and Ronald J. Miech. 1990. "1989–90 Committee on Undergraduate Courses and Curricula: Out of Phase Review of the Interdepartmental Program in Chicano Studies." Feb. 9.

Implementation Committee Student Members. N.d. "Cesar Chavez Center for Xicana/o Studies Chair Nomination."

Kleingartner, Archie. 1993. Letter to Charles E. Young. June 2.

Lopez, David. 1993. Letter to Claudia Mitchell-Kernan. Apr. 1.

Mack, Katherine. N.d. "Chicano/a Studies: A Fight over the Shaping of California's Future."

MEChA and United Community and Labor Alliance. 1990. "Proposal for the Department of a Chicana and Chicano Studies Department at UCLA—Working Draft."

Miech, Ronald J. 1990. "Academic Senate Chair Sidney Roberts." Apr. 26.

———. 1991. "Creation of a Chicano Studies Department." Dec. 4.

"Minutes of the Committee to Administer the Major in Chicano Studies." 1990. Sept. 18.

Morony, Michael. 1991. Letter to Academic Senate Chair. Nov. 27.

Nicol, Malcolm F. 1991. "Comments on Report of the Committee on Structure of Chicana and Chicano Studies." Dec. 6.

Olmos, Edward James. 1993. E-mail message to UCLA Chicano/Latino Faculty and Other Concerned Faculty. May 31.

Orbach, Raymond L. 1990a. "Current Status of the Chicano Studies Program." Sept. 4.

———. 1990b. Letter to Antonio Serrata. May 8.

———. 1992. Letter to unknown recipient. Jan. 16.

Organizing Committee. N.d. "El Movimiento en UCLA 30 Years of Chicana and Chicano Student Activism: Youth, Power, Change."

Ortiz, Vilma. 1990a. Letter to Colleague. Sept. 12.

———. 1990b. "Meeting of the Committee." Sept. 4.

———. 1991. "Curriculum for Chicana and Chicano Studies Major-Revised Version." Feb. 21.

———. 1992. "OID Proposal for Year 3." Mar. 2.

———. 1993a. E-mail message to unknown recipient. May 13.

———. 1993b. "Reflections of a Puerto Rican Woman in Leadership in Chicana and Chicano Studies." Nov. 29.

Ortiz, Vilma, and George Sanchez. 1991. "Chicano Studies Curriculum Transformation Project."

Paredes, Raymond. 1993. Letter to unknown recipient. June 16.

"Proposal for the Creation of a Department of Chicana and Chicano Studies at UCLA." 1991. Mar. 18.

"Proposal for the Creation of Chicana and Chicano Studies Department." 1992. Jan. 25.

"Provost's Committee on the Restructuring ot the Chicano Studies Major." 1990a. May 21.

——. 1990b. June 6.

——. 1990c. June 22.

——. 1990d. July 27.

——. 1990e. Aug. 21.

"Report of the Student Representatives of the Cesar Chavez Chicana/o Studies Center Implementation Committee, 1993 Hunger Strikers, & May 11th Faculty Center Occupiers on the Implementation Process for 1993–94." 1994. June 2.

Roemer, Ruth. 1993. Letter to Chancellor Young and the Students and Faculty Member Engaged in a Hunger Strike. June 2.

Roy, William, and Russell Campbell. 1988. "1987–88 Committee of Undergraduate Courses and Curricula; Review of the Interdepartmental Program in Chicano Studies." Apr.

Sears, David O. 1991. "Structure of Chicana/Chicano Studies." Dec. 13.

——. 1992. Letter to P. Newman, A. Leijonhufvud, N. Entrikin, S. Waugh, L. Binder, J. Alexander, M. Alkin, J. Post, and C. Johnson. May 20.

Sheats, Paul D. 1991. Letter to Academic Senate Chair. Dec. 6.

Teaching Faculty of Chicana and Chicano Studies. 1992. Open letter. Jan. 23.

"UCLA Students and Community Members Fast to Stop Corruption of Implementation Process in the Cesar Chavez Center for Chicana/o Studies." 1994. June 3.

Una Voz. 1990. Open letter. Jan. 5.

Valenzuela, Abel, Gaspar de Alba, Eric Avila, and Otto Santa Ana. 1998. Open letter. Feb. 25.

Waugh, Scott L. 1991. "Chicana/o Studies Program." Dec. 18.

——. 1993. "Chicana/o Studies." Jan. 19.

Weber, Eugen. 1979. Letter to Juan Gomez-Quinoñes. June 11.

"Why Asian Students Should Join the Chicana/o Studies Struggle." 1993.

Young, Charles E. 1993. Letter to Claudia Mitchell-Kernan and David Lopez. June 7.

13   Organizing Immigrant Workers

Action Research and Strategies in
the Pomona Day Labor Center

José Z. Calderon, Suzanne F. Foster, and Silvia L. Rodriguez

After a local ordinance was passed in the city of Pomona, California, to get day laborers off street corners, a city policeman confronted a day laborer about his inability to read an antisolicitation ordinance in English. Asking a student to interpret for him, the policeman shook his finger as he scolded the day laborer:

> He is in violation of the law. If he is going to sit here now and say "I don't, understand, I don't speak English," he has to make a decision. That decision is, you can either learn to speak English to function in society, because that's what the signs are, they are in English, or find himself in violation of the law. It's that simple . . . learn English or go to jail. (Beetley-Hagler 2000)

The action of this policeman, captured on videotape by then-Pitzer College student Andy Beetley-Hagler, is not an isolated case. It is how city officials and law enforcement agencies have responded in many urban and suburban communities where Latino day laborers, known as *jornaleros*, congregate on street corners to seek jobs. Groups of men can be found gathering on urban street corners, hardware store parking lots, and truck rental facilities looking for work. These are men who do not have permanent jobs but are driven to work by circumstances on a day-to-day basis. According to a study conducted by Abel Valenzuela (1999), director of UCLA's Center for the Study of Urban Poverty, "Day laborers are overwhelmingly Latino, predominately from Mexico."

Changes in immigration laws and regional economic restructuring are credited for the thousands of Latino immigrants from Mexico, Guatemala, El Salvador, and other Central American countries entering the United States and accepting jobs in the low-wage and low-skill service sector (Soja and Scott 1996). The passage of the Hart-Cellar Act in 1965 increased the total number of immigrants admitted to the United States and inadvertently gave opportunities to approximately five million immi-

grants in the service sector (Waldinger and Bozorgmehr 1996). As described by Myrna Cherkoss Donahoe in this volume, the deindustrialization of Los Angeles led to a loss of jobs in the manufacturing sector, a
restructuring process of growth in "high-skill, high-tech" employment,
and the rise of a service sector based on low-wage workers and an informal
economy (Pastor 2000; Valle and Torres 2000; Soja and Scott 1996; Waldinger and Bozorgmehr 1996). As Los Angeles deindustrialized with the
loss of steel, automobile, and tire manufacturing between 1965 and 1992,
new jobs were generated in the informal and service sectors that paid
low wages, were nonunionized, and offered few protections and benefits.
These transformations have contributed to a growth in both the Latino
population and the low-wage manual labor pool that is used to advance
economic growth (Soja 1996; Milkman 2000; Milkman and Wong 2000).

Some of these Latino immigrants have become part of the informal
economy as day laborers or workers who are hired on a temporary basis in both the service and commercial sectors. The informal economy
is characterized by low wages, usually paid by an employer in cash,
and working conditions that are unregulated (Sassen 1994, 2001; Pardo
1998). In the Southern California region, it is estimated that there are
twenty thousand day laborers looking for work on a daily basis (Añorve,
Osborn, and Salas 2000). Of this number, 78 percent are Mexican, 20 percent Central American, 1 percent U.S.-born, and 1 percent born elsewhere (Valenzuela 1999).

With an increase of day labor sites and corners, thirty cities in the Los
Angeles region have adopted some type of municipal ordinance against
the solicitation of work in public spaces (Toma and Esbenshade 2000,
57). Some of these ordinances have been in response to complaints by
local residents and businesses. Others have been as a result of an anti-
immigrant sentiment that has been propagated by right-wing organizations and politicians who have blamed immigrants for everything from
the loss of jobs and social services to the cyclical downturns in the U.S.
economy (Waldinger and Bozorgmehr 1996, 445–55; Acuña 1996, 158–
64). Pomona's Ordinance 3814, approved in June 1996, fines workers up
to one thousand dollars and/or places them in jail for up to six months if
they solicit employment on any street, public area, or parking lot. The
city of Ontario, California, passed a similar ordinance prohibiting the
solicitation of employment on public streets and at unauthorized commercial and industrial parking areas (Clark 2000, A1).

Unions affiliated with the American Federation of Labor-Congress of Industrial Organizations (AFL-CIO) have responded to these attacks by organizing immigrant workers and supporting legislation to give complete amnesty to undocumented workers. However, they held back on organizing day laborers. Hence, other grassroots groups, organizations, and individuals have recognized the need to fill that void (López-Garza 2000, 162–63; Toma and Esbenshade 2000; Acuña 1996, 197–98; Hondagneu-Sotelo 2001, 221–29; Valenzuela 1999; Jones-Correa 1998).

This chapter focuses on a collaborative effort in the city of Pomona, where college students, a faculty member, community advocates, and day laborers joined together to establish an official site from which day laborers could negotiate employment. This case study is part of a larger story taking place throughout the Los Angeles metropolitan area and the United States, where workers are creating partnerships and coalitions to build power and defend their rights.

Our findings show that day laborers are difficult to organize. Unlike other low-wage workers such as janitors and gardeners who are more established in specific locations with specific employers, day laborers are highly mobile and dependent on different employers on a daily basis. These difficulties have manifested themselves in the use of various strategies to organize day laborers. One strategy depends on a top-down (business-union-type) model that excludes the voices of the workers and simultaneously uses antisolicitation city government ordinances and law enforcement agencies to force day laborers off the streets. Another strategy, the participatory model, focuses on improving the long-term conditions of day laborers by advancing services aimed at improving their quality of life and involving them in the policy making and leadership building. This chapter, inasmuch as it is about building collaborative relations, is also about the different strategies that are being used to organize day laborers.

The Pomona Day Labor Center

The Pomona Day Labor Center is situated in the city of Pomona, which is located thirty miles east of downtown Los Angeles. Similar to the demographic changes taking place in Los Angeles, Pomona's overall population has grown from 131,723 in 1990 to 149,473 in 2000, a 13.5 percent change. The population changes between 1990 and 2000 have resulted in the proportion of Latinos in the city's population growing from 54 percent (77,776) to 65 percent (96,370); Asian/Pacific Islanders remaining at about 7 percent (from 9,846 to 10,765); African Americans decreasing from 14 percent (19,013) to 10 percent (14,398); and Whites decreasing from 26 percent (36,687) to 17 percent (25,348) (U.S. Census Bureau 1990, 2000).

Since opening its doors on January 5, 1998, the center has been located in a business center west of downtown and east of the Corona Freeway. A Contractor's Warehouse is located on the south side of the business center. Employers gather materials at the Contractor's Warehouse and then proceed to hire workers who congregate in the parking lot. *La esquina*, as the corner in front of the center where some workers wait for employers is called, has an eighteen-year history of serving as a gathering place for day laborers.

On entering the center, a long bar-shaped table awaits the employer or employee. From this table a staff member greets employers and registers day laborers for employment on a first-come and first-serve basis. A roster is used to keep records about who works on any given day, the hours worked, the salary received, and the employer's information, such as license plate numbers. The day laborers who do not go on a work assignment for the day are given priority on the roster the following day.

Behind the table are some filing cabinets and office supplies, which are next to a used computer that sits on a desk. A plain wall, constructed by the day laborers, separates the front desk from a long room. The walls, painted a plain green by the student interns and day laborers, display various posters, including one with a United Farm Workers' Union flag. On any given day, one can see workers watching television at one corner of the room as others work diligently at a table of computers. At the other corner, half a dozen workers are observed sitting around a folding table playing cards. This room is also the site for various Pitzer College student-led efforts, which include language training, health care referral, and immigration rights services.

Campus/Community Partnership

A partnership between Pitzer College and the day laborers in Pomona developed out of a common interest in community building. Pitzer College, a coeducational liberal arts college located in the city of Claremont with an enrollment of approximately 850 men and women, has had a history of encouraging social responsibility through student participation in community service learning projects.

The authors of this article reflected this ethos by carrying out research and participating in various organizing efforts alongside the day laborers in Pomona. As part of a course in the spring of 1997 called "Restructuring Communities," Professor José Z. Calderon had college students interning in various local movements so that they could work with community activists. One of the student groups began to work with Fabian Nuñez, a community activist and Pitzer student (who is now the speaker of the California State Assembly). Meanwhile, Pomona city officials were debating ways to implement the municipal ordinance approved in 1996 to remove day laborers from public streets. Professor Calderon and his students joined Nuñez, day laborers, and other Pomona community organizers in packing city hall to protest the ordinance. When city officials defended their actions by claiming that all day laborers were undocumented, Pitzer students presented evidence proving that permanent residents also made up a portion of those who solicited work on the street corners. Using Valenzuela's aforementioned 1999 study on day laborers, the students showed the council that a portion of day laborers had resided in the United States for ten years or more.

In addition, Pitzer students explored other alternatives to the punishment and incarceration proposed by city officials. Pitzer students visited day labor centers organized by the Coalition for Humane Immigrant Rights of Los Angeles (CHIRLA), which receive more than one hundred thousand dollars each from the city of Los Angeles. They gathered crucial information on the success of well-established day labor centers, which led to a funding proposal for a similar center in Pomona. The funding information in particular has been extremely useful in the struggle to receive more financial support from the city of Pomona and from private foundations for the Pomona Day Labor Center.

Ultimately, the Pomona City Council supported the establishment of a day labor center near the most popular day laborer corner. Although calling it "unlawful" to solicit work in public spaces, Ordinance 3814 proclaimed that a "designated day labor center" was the only "lawful" place to solicit work in the city. Subsequently, a coalition of community organizers and students formed a nonprofit organization, the Pomona Economic Opportunity Center (PEOC), which received fifty thousand dollars in seed money from the city of Pomona's Community Development Block Grant (CDBG) program to establish a day labor center (Tresaugue 1997). The city also appointed a board of directors that included city commission members, some independent consultants, and community representatives. Resulting from the college's involvement, the city council also appointed Professor Calderon and various students to the board.

An on-site director was hired to oversee the daily operations of the center. A lawyer on the board who had organized a day labor center in Glendale, California, suggested that the PEOC hire directors from outside the center. Unfortunately, due to high overhead costs and a lack of consistent financial resources, the PEOC was unable to pay the director a substantial wage or offer adequate benefits. This placed most of the pressure on the site director, because he worked 7 days a week and 365 days a year. Without adequate funds to hire a staff that could take care of the operational needs of the center, the burden of administering the nonprofit organization fell on the shoulders of the board of directors.

Embedded in the allocation of the seed money was the city's expectation that the center would be able to become self-sufficient. As a way to achieve self-sufficiency, the original organizers of the center encouraged the workers to pay dues of thirty dollars per month. Although the dues collections were sporadic, with many workers not paying at all, the dues eventually dropped to twenty dollars and then to ten dollars. The initial seed money and workers' dues, although helping to sustain the center's operation for two years, was not enough to cover the total costs. With the help of Pitzer College's Center for California Cultural and Social Issues (CCCSI), Professor Calderon urged more of his students to use their research at the center to write funding proposals to the city and various private foundations. Although the grants were relatively small and not enough to hire a full-time executive director, they were instrumental in keeping the center in operation.

Promoting Social Change through Participatory Research

The summer of 1999 served as a critical turning point in the development of the center. Under the direction of José Calderon, Pitzer students Suzanne Foster and Silvia Rodriguez (along with fellow student Jill McGougan) served as participants and researchers at the Pomona Day

Labor Center from June 1999 until April 2000. They talked to the day laborers and listened closely to their experiences, including their transition from the corner to the center and their life stories. The methodology of participant observation was used in order to collect information about the center and to build a successful organization. The three students taught English as a Second Language (ESL) classes, trained new student interns working at the center, helped to advance the development of a health project, and wrote proposals to foundations for funding. Suzanne Foster, co-vice president of the center's board of directors in 2000, wrote a senior thesis entitled "Empowerment Services and Social Change at the Pomona Day Labor Center." Jill McGougan, who has served on the center's board of directors since 2000, also wrote a senior thesis entitled "The Internal and External Factors Impacting a Day Labor Center."

In contrast to traditional research methods, our research team focused its inquiries on those issues that primarily benefited the day laborer community. Rather than setting ourselves apart from the community that we were researching, we sought to participate alongside the day laborers in finding solutions to the problems that they were facing (Nyden et al. 1999). We applied aspects of the action research method, where both the researchers and community participants collaborate to produce knowledge with the express purpose of taking action to promote social change and analysis (Greenwood and Levin 1998). The kind of change that this methodology refers to is one that is pragmatic and involves the community participants in the decision-making process so that they can negotiate having more control over their lives. Our research team participated in all aspects of the day labor center's activities. We informed the workers about our research and shared our findings as a means of advancing collaboration around grant proposals, policy changes, and board decisions. Because of the highly mobile character of day laborers based on their fluctuating opportunities for work, we were not able to involve them directly in the research methodology on a daily basis. Nevertheless, we shared our research processes, findings, and written work with them.

In seeking to apply a methodology that could involve the workers in the research process, the research team began with the premise that trust had to be an essential component of a just relationship with the day laborer community and that this could only be accomplished through equal participation and compassion. Raúl Gomez, an ex-day laborer who visited the center in June 1999, expressed to Foster the importance of having mutual respect as a foundation for the success of any project at the center. He commented that "the workers are very sensitive to being talked down to or to being made to feel stupid," and that without respect on the part of all the participants, the researchers "shouldn't volunteer, nor should anyone else."

The research team took this advice into serious consideration as it met with CHIRLA, the Institute of Popular Education of Southern California (IDEPSCA), and the Community Learning Network (CLN) in order to assess their methods of organizing day laborers and use of popular education. Based on our meetings with these groups, our research team determined that the so-called top-down model of organizing is an ineffective way to organize day laborers and that a more effective model is one that emphasizes "worker participation, confrontation, pressure from arenas other than the worksite itself, and strategic planning" (Sherman and Voss 2000, 84).

Top-Down Organizing Model

The top-down model of organizing day laborers can be compared to the traditional models of unionism that rely primarily on dues in exchange for a staff that handles the problems of the members (Sherman and Voss 2000). This type of organizing places the primary power in the hands of the staff and treats the worker as a secondary participant.

This business-unionism model best characterized the practice of two consultants working on day laborer issues for a national hardware supply company. The consultants (whose names have been changed) began their participation with the Pomona Day Labor Center when the nonprofit board of directors was in its developmental stages. Alice Smith, one of the consultants, described herself as a student from the University of California, Los Angeles (UCLA) carrying out research on day laborers. The other consultant, Winston Nelson, introduced himself as a lawyer who volunteered his services to help establish day labor centers in the region. Both of the consultants immediately moved into leadership positions at the center by claiming that they had created models for establishing day labor centers in other Los Angeles area cities like Glendale and El Monte.

When the center first opened, Smith and Nelson implemented a membership structure in Pomona that they had used in other cities. This structure defined members as those who used the services of the center and paid the thirty dollar dues. Smith and Nelson originally imposed the dues component as a means of persuading the workers to follow the center's rules and to develop a basis for self-sufficiency. They negatively labeled those day laborers who chose not to become members of the center as *piratas* (pirates), a name that workers at the center continue to use to this day. Further, they persuaded some of the first directors of the center to portray the piratas publicly as being drug and alcohol users. The directors were also trained by Smith and Nelson to enforce the ordinance and use the police to force the piratas to register as members of the center. This tactic involved getting members of the center to distribute fliers at the parking lot entrance that spoke negatively about the piratas, advising employers of the city's ordinance, and calling on employers to hire day laborers only from the city-sanctioned center. Smith used cameras and two-way radios to pinpoint the so-called piratas. The center's director was instructed to call the police to report fights and disturbances, even when such activities were not happening. Later, the police officers realized that the calls were placed solely to instill fear and to force the workers to become members of the center and to generate revenue. Two police officers were present at a board of directors' meeting on August 18, 1999. They announced that they would no longer respond to what they called "fraudulent calls." Even after the police department took this position, Smith and Nelson insisted that the phone calls were necessary to implement the ordinance and to stop the growing concentration of day laborers on the corner.

The strategies used under the direction of Smith and Nelson divided the day laborers, created conflict between those who were considered members of the center and those who were not, and increased animosity between the day laborers and the center's board of directors. Subsequently, the board of directors began to question Smith and Nelson on criticisms raised by the day laborers about the workers' lack of representation in the center's decision-making processes. For example, pursuant to the recommendations of Smith and Nelson, the board of directors agreed to charge the day laborers thirty dollars per month in dues. According to Smith and Nelson, these were the wishes of the day laborers themselves. Later, through a meeting between members of the board and the day laborers, the board learned that the workers had never voted or reached a consensus on paying this amount. According to the workers, the idea of paying dues and the amount were imposed on them by Smith and Nelson.

The board also questioned Smith concerning the reason that worker representatives no longer attended the board meetings, as prescribed by the bylaws of the organization. She reported that the worker representatives had problems with their board membership and "had decided to resign." Smith did not explain the reasons for the workers' resignations nor did she attempt to recruit more day laborers to the board. Instead, Smith committed herself to being present at all the meetings and serving as a liaison between the board and the day laborers. Meanwhile, Nelson proposed a change in the organization's bylaws to have a five-member board instead of the original eleven to thirteen members, five of which were designated as day laborers. Although Nelson's proposed bylaw change was never voted on, the day laborers stopped coming to the meetings and Smith took the liaison position.

By January 1999, Nelson and Smith had moved into the positions of president and treasurer of the board of directors. Since the other board members did not have the time to devote to these positions, no one objected to their appointments. Their role as liaisons, however, resulted in a lack of communication between the board of directors and the day laborers. Further, the day laborers began to raise questions about the center's expenditures and, in particular, how their dues were being used.

The Needs of the Workers

Although recent studies of new immigrants have found a high rate of labor force participation and a low usage of public assistance, this does not mean that they do not have needs related to quality-of-life issues (Pastor 2000). Largely because of their undocumented status, day laborers turn to places such as day labor centers to help provide employment and education opportunities.

The research team soon learned of the day laborers' criticism of Smith for her failure to implement the English classes she had promised for at least a year. From the day laborers' perspectives, English was essential for gaining employment, negotiating a decent wage, and contesting mistreatment. Manuel Gonzalez, one of the day laborers at the center, emphasized this point at a general membership meeting. He said that the day laborers had all agreed to come to the center in the beginning because it promised job training, English classes, and other benefits, but the workers never received these services. He was angry because the workers had been promised these programs and services but had received only an organized system of work distribution, shelter, and a bathroom. As reported in Foster's July 1999 field notes, the workers didn't even have any drinking water.

Smith and Nelson's strategy centered more on meeting employers' needs for workers who worked hard and did not question anything or complain. This exemplifies the situation that some studies describe where employers prefer immigrant workers as a "controllable labor force" that works hard and keeps quiet about working conditions for fear of deportation (Ong and Valenzuela 1996).

The desire of the day laborers to improve their quality of life required a move beyond the marketplace strategies of supply and demand. It demanded that the workers be treated as "subjects," not as "objects," in the process (Freire 1993). This was a difficult transition to implement, particularly when the workers were caught in the immediacy of survival. Author Henry Giroux proposes that the "notions of critical thinking, culture and power disappear under the imperatives of the labor process and the need of capital accumulation" (1983). The necessity of trading labor for wages becomes the primary focus of many people's realities, although critical thinking, culture, and power are perhaps equally significant. The labor process does not freely allow access to education and critical thinking because of its strong demands on people. Although gaining employment is an essential piece of the puzzle, attaining empowering education and services significantly aids a strategy for organizing workers.

The urgent requests of the members of the center for certain services demonstrated that, although employment was a priority, it certainly was not the only valued goal. For example, several men wrote "*superar*" (to advance, or succeed) when asked what they most wanted on their membership application for the center. Although an equal number, if not more, answered "work" to this question, it could not be denied that these men had additional goals and dreams that deserved to be addressed. One man, Miguel Venustiano, answered the same question on July 5, 1999, in this way: "Quiero triunfar, para sacar adelante a mi familia, y asi devolverles la felicidad y la paz que ellos me ofrecen" (I want to triumph, to move my family forward, and by doing this return to them the happiness and peace that they have given me).

The experience of a seventy-five-year-old immigrant worker at the center exemplifies this issue. Originally a farmer in Mexico, Pepe Sánchez is considered a grandfather by the day laborers and placed in honor at the top of the roster list for jobs daily. Realizing that Sanchez was getting too old to work, the site director looked into the possibility of obtaining some type of social services for him. As with other immigrant workers, the case has become entangled in the bureaucratic process of proving permanent resident status. The day may well come when Sánchez is physically unable to work but has no one to look out for him. This elderly day laborer's case brought forward the need to move beyond employment services to also provide immigration rights, education, and health care services at the center. The center now emphasizes community building along with employment and encourages everyone to look out for each other.

The men at the center have a wide range of skills and educational levels. Some have not completed a sixth-grade level of education, whereas others have earned their university degree in their country of origin. Some have completed or almost completed high school in the United States. Others have received training all of their lives, in different areas like manufacturing, construction, or agriculture. Although there is no lack of skills at the center, there is a lack of knowledge regarding local resources and services that would allow the workers to improve and build on what they already know or even earn a more advanced degree. Some workers, like Tomás Rios and Antonio Guerrero, do not feel that they can attain their goals in a system that is not in their language, or in a country that is not officially their own. Attaining these skills or knowledge can improve their socioeconomic status, improve their outlook on life, and help them find permanent employment. This knowledge and provision of services are essential to their empowerment as human beings and as working immigrants.

Smith and Nelson pitted the need for employment against the need for other types of services. Calderon's field notes from June 22, 1999, reflect a meeting between our research team and Smith in which she claimed that the most effective strategy for running a day labor center was to implement what she called a "union" model. This model, according to Smith, allows the workers to restrict the supply of their labor and to force the employers to pay a living wage above the minimum. Smith suggested that the union model was currently used at the center. She added that this strategy had resulted in the day laborers agreeing collectively on a minimum hourly wage of $7.00 to charge employers. She stated that other day labor centers (particularly those directed by the organization CHIRLA) implemented the "social service agency model that do[es] not have a collective minimum wage" and "will accept paying the workers only $5.00 an hour, and even below." Smith went on to explain that the service model practiced by CHIRLA resulted in the day laborers using the centers primarily for the free services and not to reach financial stability. "The day laborers protest against freebies," said Smith during our meeting. Our research of CHIRLA day labor centers revealed that they do have an established collective minimum wage of $8.00 an hour and, as described later in this chapter, that they provide access to an array of services.

One Pitzer student researcher, Heather Miller, found that some day laborers shied away from available services, but not for the reasons stated by Smith. As the Pomona Day Labor Center began to sponsor health screenings and eye exams, it was noted that some day laborers hesitated because of their immigration status and because of their need to make work the primary focus of their lives. Others openly mentioned a lack of trust in established institutions (Miller 2001).

The Participatory Model for Day Laborer Organizing

Jeremy Brecher and Tim Costello, in *Building Bridges*, propose that successful organizing strategies among workers, in addition to ensuring their full democratic participation, involve the advancement of coalitions between worker and community organizations "that go beyond the traditional limits of collective bargaining" (1990, 196).

CHIRLA and IDEPSCA are carrying out all aspects of this participatory model when organizing day laborers. In mid-1999, the research team met with two CHIRLA representatives, Day Laborer Project coordinator Pablo Alvarado and Worker's Rights Project coordinator Victor Narro. They introduced their projects and their methods to involve day laborers in all facets of the organizing effort. Alvarado explained that in 1989, CHIRLA assisted the city of Los Angeles in opening the first day laborer site in the nation, located in Harbor City. CHIRLA organizers assisted in the creation of the site, but did not get directly involved in the operation of the center. Rather, the Harbor City site was considered a pilot project and was first operated by the city of Los Angeles. In 1990, the city opened another site in North Hollywood. Between 1989 and 1996, both centers were operated by the Los Angeles Community Development Department. The department viewed the day laborers' presence primarily as a health and safety issue, and therefore did not allow the workers to organize or to initiate marketing campaigns about the center.

CHIRLA soon began to move beyond informal organizing at street corners to organizing around the issues that affected day laborers throughout Los Angeles. During this time, CHIRLA's efforts were concentrated at one corner in the Ladera Heights community, where there was a local movement to criminalize day laborers. Here, CHIRLA organized a multiracial coalition to defend the rights of day laborers and to protest against a citywide initiative targeting day laborers. In 1994, the Los Angeles County supervisors passed a local ordinance, similar to the one later passed in the city of Pomona, against labor solicitation on public and private property in unincorporated areas. Rather than calling for any specific penalty, the supervisors left it up to property owners to implement the ordinance. In response, CHIRLA developed a "free speech zone" where collaboration occurred among the police, local residents, Home Depot, community organizations, and the day laborers. The Los Angeles County Human Relations Commission facilitated collaborative meetings where a number of conflict resolution sessions were held between the residents and day laborers. These sessions resulted in policies that benefited the status of day laborers in other areas throughout the county. In addition to ensuring respect for free speech areas for day laborers, it advanced the implementation of similar "human relations models" in places such as Woodland Hills, the area centered in Maria A. Gutierrez de Soldatenko's discussion of Justice for Janitors in this volume. Here, government officials sought to stop the concentration of day laborers on corners by employing police on horseback. CHIRLA proposed the alternative of organizing day labor centers as community-based organizations that included the voices of day laborers. According to the CHIRLA representatives, the city of Los Angeles began receiving a great deal of criticism for not finding solutions to day laborers gathering on corners, an issue that some city officials categorized as *el patito feo* (the ugly duckling), or a problem that no one wanted. In 1996, the city of

Los Angeles sought to address this issue by releasing requests for proposals (RFPs) and inviting community organizations interested in administering the various day laborer centers to submit bids. In the first round of RFPs, CHIRLA and IDEPSCA were the only agencies that applied. City officials opened up another round of RFPs with the intention of getting more applications, with no result. In the absence of other interested organizations, CHIRLA and IDEPSCA were given a contract to operate the various sites and to implement various conflict mediation programs. According to Calderon's field notes from July 6, 1999, CHIRLA and IDEPSCA were then receiving up to $112 thousand from Community Development Block Grant funds annually for each of four different centers.

Moving beyond the health and safety models developed by the city of Los Angeles, CHIRLA introduced three participatory components for organizing day laborer centers:

1. Ensure the basic civil, labor, and human rights of day laborers by involving them in advocacy efforts on issues that directly affect them.
2. Develop employment opportunities through outreach and marketing strategies organized by day laborers.
3. Advance a practice of civic engagement by involving day laborers in their communities (initiating volunteer community cleanups, remodeling old housing, organizing soccer leagues, and so forth).

In contradistinction to the perspective of Alice Smith, the CHIRLA representatives rejected the idea of day laborer organization being narrowly configured along the lines of a service agency model. Mayron Payes, a CHIRLA organizer, explained that CHIRLA uses "different approaches" to ensure the "full participation" of the day laborers. CHIRLA provides services such as assistance with wage claim cases both to encourage participation in the center and to defend workers' rights. He added that these services do not make workers more dependent, but improve the conditions of their lives so that they can fully participate in all aspects of civil society. Since the majority of the day laborers are Latino, CHIRLA has sought to tap the cultural aspects of this particular community. Payes gave various examples of this approach, including the organization of a soccer team, a *teatro* (theater) group, and a musical group. In addition, a group of workers was collaborating at that time to produce a newsletter for day laborers. Other day laborers join in a yearly day labor conference where organizing strategies are discussed. For Payes, these "nontraditional" approaches to organizing allow "day laborers to participate, to grow as persons and as a community, and to reduce their alienation." In terms of empowerment, the CHIRLA representatives also spoke about another group of day laborers organizing themselves into a union, El Sindicato de Jornaleros. The workers have also organized themselves and lobbied their state representatives to pass a bill supporting the right of undocumented workers to obtain driver's licenses or state-sanctioned identification cards. In this way, CHIRLA representatives claim, day laborers move beyond the individual needs of getting a job and securing good wages to organizing around the policies that affect their everyday lives.

CHIRLA supported this process of empowerment by holding a day laborer leadership school. The leadership school provided a forum for discussion and education on how institutions function in the United States, how the global economy affects day laborers, and how they can become participants in the decision-making process. The success of the leadership school could be seen at the day labor centers and corners, where the workers take the lead in implementing their own rules, devising their own processes of distributing work each morning, holding general decision-making assemblies, and participating in monthly advisory board meetings.

CHIRLA's strategy of organizing has been implemented in the approximately 150 corners throughout Los Angeles where day laborers gather. Since it is impossible to acquire funding for so many day labor centers, Pablo Alvarado states that CHIRLA has found an alternative by building collaborative relationships among residents, city officials, and day laborers at these various sites:

> With a little organizing and conflict mediation, we have been able to turn tense situations at some of these corners into places where the workers have negotiated their responsibilities to these communities by developing agreed-upon rules of conduct and designated employment pickup sites.

CHIRLA and IDEPSCA utilize a participatory model based on popular education in the delivery of their services and in their organizing principles. Similar to various workers' rights centers organized in Los Angeles, the work of CHIRLA and IDEPSCA goes beyond social services. Their organizing principles empower the workers. The workers understand the world around them. In addition, they receive leadership training to create changes in their conditions (Bonacich 2000, 146). According to the CHIRLA representatives, this holistic approach serves the needs of the day laborers and advances the goal of creating "self-sustaining communities."

Pomona's Day Labor Center: Building the Participatory Model

An effort to duplicate the participatory model at the Pomona Day Labor Center faced a serious challenge. The research team discovered that Smith and Nelson had been writing fraudulent progress reports to the city of Pomona claiming to be implementing various services at the center, including ESL classes; translation and mediation services between workers and employers; referring workers to appropriate agencies for services; and conducting tax workshops (City of Pomona 1999). This same report revealed some important figures that the day laborers had no knowledge about:

> A help to the Pomona program are the materials and expenses donated by [a national hardware supply company] of $9,280.40 in the last year, and the two consultants paid by the [company] to facilitate the program, a lawyer [Nelson] and a day laborer organizer [Smith] who organized [a nearby city's] program as well as others ($55,532.50 in the last year, actual billed hours). (City of Pomona 1999)

Smith and Nelson were asked by the center's board of directors to account for these funds. As noted in Calderon's field notes from November 17, 1999, a board member requested an itemized budget reflecting how the consultant fees were spent, the conditions under which the funds were granted, and the actual use of the funds in relation to the center. Nelson's response to the request was that the consultant fees were not anyone's business but his own, and that he didn't ask where anyone else's "personal paychecks came from."

Under fire from the day laborers and the board, both Smith and Nelson resigned their positions as treasurer and president, respectively. Their resignations gave way to a more democratic process in which workers were involved in decision making at the center, the development of partnerships was strongly emphasized, and the particular services that the workers had been asking for were finally implemented.

A partnership developed that, like the participatory model, sought to use a holistic approach with a combination of employment opportunities, leadership training, various services, projects, meetings, and organizing efforts to sustain the center. Through a collaborative effort with the Community Learning Network (CLN), an organization based at Claremont Graduate University, several Pitzer students (including the co-authors) began to develop an ESL curriculum for the center. CLN's organizers advised the Pitzer students on implementing a participatory action model of education and organization that focused on the community's assets rather than its deficiencies (Kretzmann and McKnight 1993). The model CLN used seeks to overcome the practices of many community initiatives, which, rather than advancing a "positive capacity-building venture," serve only to perpetuate "feelings of dependency" (Kingsley, McNeely, and Gibson 1997). CLN sought to advance this community-building process by assessing the needs of the community, connecting to its skills and resources, and working on common issues.

The CLN organizers and the Pitzer students used focus groups as the primary vehicle to gather information on the needs and assets at the center. The focus groups identified the needs for work, ESL classes, and information on immigrants' rights. The focus groups also determined that the men had a vast amount of personal knowledge about their experience as immigrants, crossing physical and political borders, and trading their labor for wages. The ESL classes, then, were taught in such a way that acknowledged the workers' experiences and areas of expertise. Further, the curriculum helped to draw out the workers' opinions on issues at the center and other needed resources.

This participatory model of communication and education was implemented with the intention of empowering the workers to examine critically the issues in their realities, to connect them with other issues in a process of problematizing their similarities, and to reflect upon their common themes for social change (Freire 1993, 89). Through the process of dialogue, the students and teachers together created a curriculum that focused on experiences and themes that were important to them, including employment, tools, and health (Bentley 2001).

A health project emerged after a student found out that a worker was very ill and did not have access to health care. After the student took this individual to a doctor, many other workers asked for similar help. A partnership was soon created between the center and the Western University of Health Sciences in Pomona and regular health screenings and health referrals were implemented. More than thirty medical interns and doctors from Western University's Pomona Community Health Action Team (PCHAT) performed physical exams at the center. Eighty workers attended the health fair and more than fifty workers received physicals—some for the first time in many years.

Presently, Pitzer students continue to expand the health project to include eye and dental care. One man, in his sixties, had experienced difficulty with his vision for ten years. When the students took him to get an eye exam and bought him glasses through the program, he related that a whole new world had opened up to him. Now he could see things around him that he had never seen before.

An immigration rights project was also launched at the center. An immigration rights lawyer held a workshop on recent changes in immigration laws. Some student interns were involved on various legal cases, including one where an employer refused to pay three workers a total of three thousand dollars owed to them. Through the simple process of training and educating the workers on how to prepare and file a small claims suit, the full amount was eventually retrieved.

Transforming Los Angeles through Coalition Building

With the transformation of the Los Angeles region to a postindustrial urban economy there has been an expansion of high-wage professionals, on one end, and low-wage unorganized manual laborers, on the other. These developments have led to an increase of day laborers in the informal economy, which has resulted in various efforts aimed at organizing them.

Some initiatives, led by conservative anti-immigrant groups, have sought to abolish various services and programs, such as bilingual education and adult literacy programs, that can help build the economic and political capacity of immigrant workers (Ono and Sloop 2002; Crawford 1992; Calderon 1989). There are others who promote municipal ordinances either to criminalize day laborers or to promote their exploitation as a cheap labor force. What these groups have in common is a top-down strategy that aims at dividing immigrant workers from the working class and excluding them from the growing political voice and clout of a growing Latino and "minority majority" population.

The story of the implementation of participatory strategies through collaborative partnerships described in this chapter shows that there is no contradiction between the use of education as a service and an organizational form that is inclusive of the day laborers' voices and leadership. Through the use of nontraditional methods that allow for critical dialogue and the involvement of the participants, the goals of an empowering education can be achieved. Ira Shor, a pacesetter in the field of critical education, defines the goals of an empowering education as relating "personal growth to public life, by developing strong skills, academic knowledge, habits of inquiry, and critical curiosity about society, power, inequality, and change" (1992, 15). The collaboration between Pitzer College and the Pomona Day Labor Center, although confronting many obstacles, has advanced the development of a participatory action model between the day laborer and campus communities, a culture of bottom-up decision making by all the partners involved, and a connection between the needed services of day laborers and an organizational form to advocate for their rights.

References

Acuña, Rodolfo. 1996. *Anything but Mexican*. New York: Verso.

Añorve, Raúl, Torie Osborn, and Angélica Salas. 2000. "Jornaleros Deserve Dignity." *Los Angeles Times*, Aug. 27.

Beetley-Hagler, Andy, dir. 2000. *La Lucha de Trabajar en Pomona*. Pitzer College.

Bentley, Sarah. 2001. "English-as-a-Second-Language (ESL) Curriculum Development and Implementation at the Pomona Day Labor Center." Senior thesis, Pitzer College, Claremont, Calif.

Bonacich, Edna. 2000. "Intense Challenges, Tentative Possibilities: Organizing Immigrant Workers in Los Angeles." In *Organizing Immigrants: The Challenge for Unions in Contemporary California*, edited by Ruth Milkman. Ithaca, N.Y.: Cornell University Press.

Brecher, Jeremy, and Tim Costello. 1990. "American Labor: The Promise of Decline." In *Building Bridges: The Emerging Grassroots Coalition of Labor and Community*, edited by Jeremy Brecher and Tim Costello. New York: Monthly Review Press.

Calderon, José. 1989. "How the English Only Initiative Passed in California." In *Estudios Chicanos and the Politics of Community*, edited by Mary Romero and Cordelia Candelaria. Oakland, Calif.: Cragmont.

City of Pomona. 1999. "Pomona Day Labor Center Quarterly Report." Sept.

Clark, Deborah. 2000. "Day Laborers Fate Debated." *Ontario, Calif., Daily Bulletin*, Sept. 18, A1.

Crawford, James. 1992. *Language Loyalties*. Chicago: University of Chicago Press.

Foster, Suzanne. 2000. "Empowerment Services and Social Change at the Pomona Day Labor Center." Senior thesis, Pitzer College, Claremont, Calif.

Freire, Paulo. 1993. *Pedagogy of the Oppressed*. Rev. ed. New York: Continuum.

Giroux, Henry. 1983. *Theory and Resistance in Education: A Pedagogy for the Opposition*. New York: Bergin and Garvey.

———. 1992. *Border Crossings: Cultural Workers and the Politics of Education*. New York: Routledge.

Greenwood, Davydd J., and Morten Levin. 1998. *Introduction to Action Research: Social Research for Social Change*. Thousand Oaks, Calif.: Sage.

Hondagneu-Sotelo, Pierrette. 2001. *Doméstica: Immigrant Workers Cleaning and Caring in the Shadows of Affluence*. Berkeley: University of California Press.

Jones-Correa, Michael. 1998. *Between Two Nations: The Political Predicament of Latinos in New York City*. Ithaca, N.Y.: Cornell University Press.

Kingsley, Thomas G., Joseph B. McNeely, and James O. Gibson. 1997. *Community Building Coming of Age*. Washington, D.C.: The Urban Institute.

Kretzmann, John P., and John L. McKnight. 1993. *Building Communities from the Inside Out: A Path Toward Finding and Mobilizing a Community's Assets*. Evanston, Il.: Acta.

López-Garza, Marta. 2000. "A Study of the Informal Economy and Latina/o Immigrants in Greater Los Angeles." In *Asian and Latino Immigrants in a Restructuring Economy: The Metamorphosis of Southern California*, edited by Marta López-Garza and David R. Diaz. Stanford, Calif.: Stanford University Press.

McGougan, Jill. 2000. "The Internal and External Factors Impacting a Day Labor Center as Part of a Social Movement." Senior thesis, Pitzer College, Claremont, Calif.

Milkman, Ruth. 2000. Introduction to *Organizing Immigrants: The Challenge for Unions in Contemporary California*, edited by Ruth Milkman. Ithaca, N.Y.: Cornell University Press.

Milkman, Ruth, and Kent Wong. 2000. "Organizing the Wicked City: The 1992 Southern California Drywall Strike." In *Organizing Immigrants: The Challenge for Unions in Contemporary California*, edited by Ruth Milkman. Ithaca, N.Y.: Cornell University Press.

Miller, Heather. 2001. "Culture and Gender-Based Internal Barriers to Health Care among Latino Day Laborers." Senior thesis, Pitzer College, Claremont, Calif.

Nyden, Philip, Anne Figert, Mark Shibley, and Darryl Burrows. 1999. *Building Community: Social Science in Action*. Thousand Oaks, Calif.: Pine Forge Press.

Ong, Paul, and Abel Valenzuela Jr. 1996. "The Labor Market: Immigrant Effects and

Racial Disparities." In *Ethnic Los Angeles*, edited by Roger Waldinger and Mehdi Bozorgmehr. New York: Russell Sage Foundation.

Ono, Kent A., and John M. Sloop. 2002. *Shifting Borders*. Philadelphia: Temple University Press.

Pardo, Mary. 1998. *Mexican American Women Activists: Identity and Resistance in Two Los Angeles Communities*. Philadelphia: Temple University Press.

Pastor, Manuel, Jr. 2000. "Economics and Ethnicity: Poverty, Race, and Immigration in L.A. County." In *Asian and Latino Immigrants in a Restructuring Economy: The Metamorphosis of Southern California*, edited by Marta Lopez-Garza and David R. Diaz. Stanford, Calif.: Stanford University Press.

Sassen, Saskia. 1994. "The Informal Economy: Between New Developments and Old Regulations." *Yale Law Journal* 103, no. 8 (June): 2289–304.

———. 2001. *The Global City: New York, London, Tokyo*. Princeton, N.J.: Princeton University Press.

Sherman, Rachel, and Kim Voss. 2000. "Organize or Die: Labor's New Tactics and Immigrant Workers." In *Organizing Immigrants: The Challenge for Unions in Contemporary California*, edited by Ruth Milkman. Ithaca, N.Y.: Cornell University Press.

Shor, Ira. 1992. *Empowering Education: Critical Teaching for Social Change*. Chicago: University of Chicago.

Soja, Edward W. 1996. "Los Angeles, 1965–1992: From Crisis-Generated Restructuring to Restructuring-Generated Restructuring." In *The City: Los Angeles and Urban Theory at the End of the Twentieth Century*, edited by Allen J. Scott and Edward W. Soja. Berkeley: University of California Press.

Soja, Edward W., and Allen J. Scott. 1996. "Introduction to Los Angeles: City and Region." In *The City: Los Angeles and Urban Theory at the End of the Twentieth Century*, edited by Allen J. Scott and Edward W. Soja. Berkeley: University of California Press, 1996.

Toma, Robin, and Jill Esbenshade. 2000. *Day Laborer Hiring Sites: Constructive Approaches to Community Conflict*. Los Angeles: Los Angeles County Human Relations Commission.

Tresaugue, Matthew. 1997. "Pomona OKs Labor Center." *Los Angeles Times*, July 31, A1, A6.

U.S. Bureau of the Census. 1990. *Statistical Abstract*. Washington, D.C.

———. 2000. *Statistical Abstract*. Washington, D.C.

Valenzuela, Abel. 1999. "Day Laborers in Southern California: Preliminary Findings from the Labor Survey." Working Papers Series, Center for the Study of Urban Poverty, UCLA.

Valle, Victor M., and Rodolfo D. Torres. 2000. *Latino Metropolis*. Minneapolis: University of Minnesota Press.

Waldinger, Roger, and Mehdi Bozorgmehr. 1996. "The Making of a Multicultural Metropolis." In *Ethnic Los Angeles*, edited by Roger Waldinger and Mehdi Bozorgmehr. New York: Russell Sage Foundation.

Review of Contemporary Latina/o
Scholarship and Resources

14   Latinos in Los Angeles

Select Review of Latino/a Scholarship and Resources

Ester E. Hernández

As the Latino population in Los Angeles has grown dramatically in the past few decades, so, too, has scholarship on this population. This review highlights selected ethnographic studies, literature, and audio/visual material on Latino Los Angeles that foreground Mexican and Central American populations negotiating with the larger society and with each other. The works under review examine the events of the 1980s and 1990s, focusing on Latinos/as negotiating social spaces at school, at work, and in their neighborhoods. This review is intended as a resource for teachers and teachers-in-training and will be useful for those preparing courses on comparative Latino populations.

Although Los Angeles Latinos share important cultural commonalities, as the chapters in this volume attest, there are various factors— such as generation, immigration status, language, home ownership, and income—that differentiate the groups (see Pardo 1998a). Therefore, Chicanos, Mexicans, and Central Americans in Los Angeles negotiate distinctions of class, gender, ethnic and national histories, and political ideologies and practices that construct their identities as Latinos in relationship to each other and to non-Latinos. Whether through migration or as indigenous minorities, Latinos are bound up within the mechanisms of a larger international economic system (Robinson 1992) and the linkage between forces of globalization and transnationalism (Kearney 1995).

Immigration Policies and Conceptions of Citizenship

The Los Angeles region has been one of five major U.S. metropolitan destinations for Mexican and Central American immigrants during the past two decades according to census data. As a backlash to this migration, immigration legislation has increasingly restricted the rights of undocumented immigrants to obtain work. For example, the U.S. Immigration Act of 1986 imposed sanctions on those who employed undocumented immigrants and in 1993 California state law curtailed their right to obtain driver's licenses. Until 2001, undocumented students were charged exorbitant out-of-state tuition to attend the state's public colleges and universities. Furthermore, in 1996 federal enactment of the Welfare Act and the Illegal Immigration Reform and Immigrant Responsibility Act restricted the rights of legal aliens to state and federal forms of economic assistance. This latter measure disproportionately targeted women, the elderly, and documented and undocumented children (Hondagneu-Sotelo 1995; Chavez et al. 1997).

Citizenship is of central concern for understanding Latinos. Although citizenship is a legal concept, it shapes dynamics of belonging and political participation in society. Despite the fact that undocumented people are not recognized as full participants in society, as the chapters in this volume on Justice for Janitors and day laborers discuss, undocumented immigrants have been engaged in grassroots activism, protests, and labor organizing (see also Pincetl 1994; Chincilla and Hamilton 1999). These activities promote a form of "Latino cultural citizenship." That is, culture interprets and shapes notions of citizenship. Although legal definitions have primacy in formal institutional settings, Latinos in Los Angeles develop practices of citizenship that are anchored in everyday life and recognition of common struggles (Flores and Benmayor 1997; Flores 1997). Pincetl (1994), for example, has demonstrated that Latino grassroots participation in the Pico-Union area, with a large population that originated in Central America and Mexico, involves "street demonstrations, lobbying, testifying in public hearings, mobilizing community support, letter writing, using the media and establishing networks and coalitions of allies" (897). In so doing, they exercise citizenship—they transform and (re)create local democratic practices as engaged members of communities. It is in these citizen-like activities that the undocumented join others to shape the conditions of everyday life in Los Angeles.

Although Mexican and Central American immigrants share many commonalities, as Kristine M. Zentgraf and Susan Bibler Coutin illustrate in this volume, Central Americans differ in their experiences of political repression (see also Loucky and Moors 2000). Many have left their homes as a result of direct persecution, whereas others have fled armed conflict supported by U.S. foreign policy (Hamilton and Chinchilla 1991). Two widely available films, *El Norte* (Nava 1984) and *Romero* (Duigan 1989), can be used to explore the histories of Salvadorans and

Guatemalans and their experiences in U.S. cities such as Los Angeles. Many have experienced posttraumatic stress disorder, suffering anxiety and depression as a result of witnessing or going through traumatic events (Dorrington 1995; Suarez-Orozco 1989). Scholarship on these groups has focused on their economic adaptation, their unrecognized refugee status, and their transnational connections to the home country (Chinchilla and Hamilton 1999; Coutin 2000). Much of the earlier scholarship on this wave of migration, shaped by U.S. immigration policy, tried to clarify the issue of whether Central Americans were refugees fleeing the Central American wars or economic migrants like their Mexican counterparts (Zolberg 1995; Stanley 1987).

As Coutin explains in this volume, Central Americans, in particular Salvadorans, have established organizations both to affect the course of events in Central America and to alleviate the hardships that have confronted refugees upon arrival (see also Hamilton and Chinchilla 2001). Guatemalan refugees in many cases have formed organizations based on ethnic identity, with indigenous Mayans creating their own support networks (Loucky 2000). Central Americans have shifted their political activism from strategies directed at influencing U.S. policy in the Central American region to a more permanent, locally driven orientation (Chinchilla and Hamilton 1999; Hamilton and Chinchilla 2001; Coutin 2000; Loucky 2000).

Economy: Manufacturing and Informal Economy

The economy of Los Angeles and U.S. immigration policy provide a useful lens through which to view Mexicans and Central Americans from the 1980s onward. Many Central Americans who arrived in Los Angeles in the late 1970s and 1980s were refugees from violence, and they, like a great number of newcomers from Mexico, confronted constraints because a high proportion were undocumented, employed in low-paying jobs, and challenged with problems in housing, schooling, and neighborhoods that were negatively affected by economic restructuring. Immigrants and refugees alike worked in predominantly labor-intensive, low-paying, nonunionized industries, including manufacturing and services. The labor conditions new immigrants have encountered in Los Angeles are related to these larger forces that structure local economies.

Bonacich et al. (1994) have examined the growth of the garment industry and the concomitant increase in migration levels to the area. As a result of economic restructuring, the garment industry relies on immigrant labor to maintain high profit levels. Because the income from jobs in this industry is very limited, workers resort to other ways of supplementing their income. In a succinct analysis of the structure of the garment industry, Sarmiento (1996) notes that Mexican and Central American women who labor in this industry often work at home doing piecework. She observes an increasing reliance on "flexible" production that leaves workers at a disadvantage. They earn little, forcing many to live in overcrowded conditions due to expensive housing costs in their area. Among the Maya in Los Angeles, for example, the garment industry is an important source of employment, as is street vending (Loucky 2000).

Vending of food and convenience items on the street provides income for many immigrants even though many city ordinances prohibit it. In the documentary *Por la Vida* (Olea 1994), local police confiscate the merchandise of informal street vendors and fine them. In contrast to law enforcements' rejection of informal street vending, however, ethnographic accounts of street vending note that it often revitalizes economically depressed communities. Notably, Moore and Vigil (1993) have examined the importance of the informal economy as it affects the residents of East Los Angeles. In their ethnographic analysis of four neighborhoods, they note that Mexicans are more likely to take part in this kind of work, but that Chicanos also use informal work as part of their survival strategy. In these studies, the authors illustrate that theories of the underclass do not neatly fit Latinos because the informal economy provides important economic benefits to people who would not otherwise have access to jobs in the formal economy.

The informal economy can be a creative economic solution to reduced employment opportunities. Other benefits, Chinchilla, Hamilton, and Loucky (1993) suggest, ensue when Latino families' use of public space makes streets safer. These issues need further study; the street is a space where Latinos and the larger society meet. Besides vending goods, as recounted by José Z. Calderon, Suzanne F. Foster, and Silvia Rodriquez in this volume, day laborers, mostly men, seek employment in construction, gardening, and other related areas of employment. Malpica (1996) has explored the processes of getting a job at two day labor sites. Street vending, domestic work, and day labor all require the use of the street as a public space and as a site for making a livelihood. High levels of participation in informal economic strategies are related to the disappearance of high-paying manufacturing jobs and the abundance of low-paying, "flexible" manufacturing jobs and service sector jobs. Similarly, Valle and Torres (2000) have analyzed the growth of service sector jobs in restaurant and hotel industries and found that these industries offer low pay and few benefits in terms of training and promotion.

Schools and Neighborhoods

Debates about the relationship of immigration and the use of state services, bilingual education, and affirmative action programs in schools directly and indirectly affect newcomers, sometimes in ways that they see themselves. There has been growth surrounding some of these issues in ethnographic studies that focus on Latino experiences in Los Angeles-area schools. For example, Diego Vigil has examined youth identity in two high schools in *Personas Mexicanas* (1997). He notes that retention of Mexican identity and bilingual skills has a positive impact on the education of Mexican American youths. In addition, he considers their prospects for social mobility by comparing the labor market opportunities available to them and those available to their parents.

Also examining neighborhoods and labor market conditions, Suarez-Orozco (1989) observes students in Los Angeles schools where Mexicans and Central Americans predominate. He follows fifty Central American students to assess their school progress and motivations for achievement. This ethnographic study illustrates how the students overcame traumatic situations and how these experiences compelled many to "be somebody," someone who finished school and pursued a path toward economic stability. The students, however, did not arrive at "safe havens." Many of the schools they attended were overcrowded, teachers often did not want to work at them, and there was a lot of violence among the students formed along ethnic lines. Furthermore, some of the students faced pressure to work to help support their families. The Central American students formed their identities and opinions of themselves in opposition to negative stereotypes of other students in the school. It will be important for future studies to compare how students from different ethnic backgrounds deal with these issues. In addition to violent interactions within the schools, the students faced violence in their surrounding communities. Gangs organized themselves along ethnic/national identifications, and circulation and use of drugs were problems in their neighborhoods, as were overcrowded living conditions. Diego Vigil (2002) analyzes the proliferation of gangs and the escalation of policing in these neighborhoods, the use of injunctions to control them, and the incidence of police brutality.

Focusing on younger children, Dorrington (1995) provides important background information regarding refugee youths in Los Angeles schools. Central American newcomers, particularly in the early 1980s, when Salvadorans and Guatemalans began to appear in the Los Angeles landscape, faced many problems in school. One of Dorrington's informants, a community activist, related the sense of displacement found among children who had suffered through war:

> So, there's problems with knowing who they are. They have a lot of wisdom in a sense and a lot of awareness, probably more than a child should have, a lot of maturity. . . . There's just a lot of denial here of those experiences or people have never heard of El Salvador or Guatemala, which is a lot different than for, say, Russian immigrants. Every American knows where Russia is. The [Central American] children have the sense of not being known at all. (122–23)

These children had to define who they were in relationship to others.

A useful film regarding some of the experiences of undocumented youths and the socioeconomic conditions in their neighborhoods is *Fear and Learning at Hoover Elementary* (Simon 1997). The film examines young children dealing with the fear of Proposition 187, neighborhood violence, and school staff attitudes. The film argues that the fear extends to documented and undocumented youths, with negative effects on the education of both. The film questions whether it is wise social policy to block educational opportunities to this disenfranchised sector.

From the voices of youths, an important collection of stories, entitled *Izote Vos* (Kim, Serrano, and Ramos 2000), examines identity among young Salvadorans. Through poems, essays, and other reflections, Salvadoran youths explore their identities and family histories in relationship to ethnic community and neighborhood concerns. The collection includes material from youths residing in Los Angeles and San Francisco.

Within neighborhoods, the interactions between recent immigrants and more established Latinos do not always occur smoothly, despite the fact that certain communities are 80 percent Latino or more. Exaggerating differences rather than commonalities, for example, gang affiliations and disputes over territory often form along national lines (Vigil 2002). Among the few sources that focus on newcomers and established residents, Pardo (1998c) suggests that, although Latinos may have opportunities for observation of each other at schools and at work, little interaction or integration might actually take place. When interaction does occur, it may be highly hostile or derogatory. According to Pardo's study, newcomers and established immigrants sometimes hold hostile or negative views of each other. Their encounters highlight class differences and opposition between city folk and rural folk.

Recent work by Ochoa (2004) examines how Mexican Americans and Mexican immigrants become neighbors in the city of La Puente. Ochoa examines mobilization efforts in response to Proposition 227 on bilingual education. Moreover, her work considers how Mexican Americans—instead of adopting a position of distance, conflict, and competition—demonstrate group solidarity with Mexican immigrants and work together with them to improve educational opportunities for the newcomers. More research needs to be done on the ways in which Latinos come together to effect change in their communities.

Gender Patterns and Incorporation

Research on Latinas often looks at their participation in society in terms of changing gender relations, that is, from restrictive dynamics in the country of origin to less restrictive ones in the new place of residence. For example, Hondagneu-Sotelo (1995) has coined the term *gendered transition* to describe how Mexican immigrant families reconfigure relations of authority within the family when Mexican immigrant women enter the workforce. Although this gendered transition may mean that these women enter the workforce, it does not necessarily mean that changes in gender relations occur or that those changes are intrinsic to migration. In fact, Segura (1994) shows that workforce participation may not produce a shift in gender relations from restrictive to nonrestrictive.

Pardo's (1998a) important work on mothers in East Los Angeles looks at the grassroots activism of women and the ways in which gender and activism are linked. The mothers of East Los Angeles, Pardo maintains, were concerned with two issues usually left to mothers: the education of children and the safety of the surrounding community. They reacted to a proposal for a state prison in their area by mobilizing and protesting. By using motherly imagery and wearing scarves in the tradition of devout Catholic mothers, they used family and community for political ends. Like the mothers of Plaza de Mayo in Argentina, who mobilized the symbolic sacredness of mothers to prevent the military from retaliating against them, East Los Angeles mothers used a politically charged imagery to attract media attention and visibility. Whereas Argentinean mothers mobilized against a brutal military regime that threatened their families, East Los Angeles women mobilized to protect their families and community against such powerful interests as the California governor and the state prison complex. However, Pardo describes how greater activism in their community did not necessarily restructure the women's domestic responsibilities. Many of the women activists that Pardo interviewed and observed performed their homemaking duties as a prerequisite to their outside, or community, activities. Thus, this research calls attention to the fact that increased participation in public spaces does not intrinsically change gender relations.

Research that attends to gender dynamics has provided further insights into macro-micro linkages. One tendency of immigration scholarship has been to emphasize gender relations as sites of struggle with macrostructural forces and to deemphasize or ignore politically charged relations at the family or household levels (Hondagneu-Sotelo 1998). This structural emphasis produces a simplified notion of power that may prevent analysis of differences and negotiation among family members. Negotiations occur at many different levels. They are mediated through institutions, relations between different classes, and their intersections with gender.

Another reason to attend to the effects of structural factors on the people we study is provided by Soldatenko (1999). She analyzes the story of a Latina garment worker in Los Angeles who insisted on recounting her story as a narrative of opportunity. By paying attention to the woman's voice, Soldatenko presents complex layers of accommodation and resistance. She aims to show that looking only at the global garment industry silences such women's experiences and their struggles to make sense of their situation. She shows that women identify and seek access to power with varying degrees of success. These issues are important because they contribute to notions of identity and illustrate the intersections of gender, class, and racialized identity. More research has been produced about women from a gendered perspective than about immigrant men. We still need to learn more about the experiences of day laborers, who are mostly men, for example, to understand how gender structures notions of masculine and feminine in a racialized context. Few published studies have focused on how Latino men's experiences differ from women's or even how notions of masculinity affect political activism.

Political Activism

Throughout the 1990s, unionization efforts and political mobilization among drywallers and janitors brought attention to Latino activism. Even labor unions that once saw immigrants as unfair competitors who depressed wages—and as a population difficult to organize—now publicly support a proimmigrant stance. These campaigns have included a call by the AFL-CIO to offer a blanket amnesty to immigrants in the country illegally in recognition of the potential vitality that these workers could provide to the labor movement.

Delgado's (1993) analysis of a union of workers in the Los Angeles furniture industry offers insights into the dynamics of immigrant organization. Activists believed that organizing undocumented immigrants was impossible. Yet the union drive tended to encourage and affirm their status as workers rather than immigrants. The strategy was successful and benefited from the fact that many of the Central Americans had considerable unionization experience. The campaign had to overcome Mexican workers' negative views of unions in Mexico, as well as company-led efforts to discredit unions. The feature length video, *Bread and Roses* (Loach 2001), is useful in classes that examine labor organization among Latinos in Los Angeles.

Similarly, Hondagneu-Sotelo (1998) chronicles efforts to unionize domestic workers. These efforts have been largely undertaken by the Coalition for Humane Immigrant Rights of Los Angeles (CHIRLA), a network of immigrant advocates. This network provides legal advocacy in congressional settings on behalf of immigrants, and it provides legal training to facilitate naturalization and family reunification procedures.

Hondagneu-Sotelo's (2001) ethnography about primarily Central American domestic workers provides an in-depth analysis of this important service job in Los Angeles.

As described by Calderon, Foster, and Rodriguez in this volume, day laborers have also organized to create centers to protect themselves from arrests and harassment for soliciting work in public areas. In addition to CHIRLA, organizations such as the Day Laborer Union of Los Angeles County, and the Institute of Popular Education of Southern California (IDEPSCA) have been instrumental in such organizing campaigns. A musical group of day laborers, Los Jornaleros del Norte, has compiled and produced music in CD format.

Among Central Americans, community organizations and/or centers offer important spaces for political activism. These community organizations create opportunities for economic development and provide community services (Hamilton and Chinchilla 2001). Loucky (2000) shows that, in lieu of official mechanisms of assistance, these organizations have been crucial to Guatemalan immigrants' negotiations with local institutions such as schools.

Pardo's (1998a) analysis of Mexican American women's political activism notes that their energies have been focused on promoting community improvements in schools, health care facilities, park facilities, and community-police relations through such established organizations as the PTA and ethnic associations. Therefore, the range of political mobilizing among Latinos/as is dynamic. Similar research will advance knowledge about coalitions that form in response to the demographics of particular neighborhoods.

Reflections and New Directions in Scholarship on Latinas/os in Los Angeles

During the 1980s, immigrants from Mexico and Central America arrived in the Los Angeles region in large numbers. Early research of Central Americans tended to contrast the political turmoil that compelled many of them to migrate with economic factors behind the larger inflow of immigrants from Mexico. In the labor market of the Los Angeles region, however, whether Central Americans were political refugees or labor migrants, they joined the labor force in jobs that tended to compensate them very poorly and offered few or no benefits, in areas of work such as the garment industry and street vending. Central Americans arriving into Los Angeles in the past few decades have not had extensive ties to the area, as did their Mexican counterparts. Their migration patterns and engagement with communities of origin are different. For instance, a great proportion of Central Americans have not enjoyed travel to and from their countries of origin due to war and/or the constraints of legal status.

Immigration policies, employment, education, and community conditions have been among the most visible and important points of convergence for political activism among Mexicans and Central Americans. Already sharing the same space in neighborhoods, schools, and work, the immigrants have common experiences that have helped to bridge national and historical differences in many cases and promote grassroots mobilization. Future research on Latinos in Los Angeles might examine the subgroups in regard to education, politics (formal and informal, panethnic and national), class, and cohort of arrival. Furthermore, we need to know more about recent arrivals and longtime residents and interactions between them.

In Los Angeles, Chicanos, Mexicans, and Central Americans bring to their encounter distinctive notions of identity based on nationality, ethnicity, and class distinction. It will be important to explore comparative research that examines the construction of panethnic identity. Given the inter- and intraethnic diversity of newcomers, coming together to advocate for their communities and to form or join unions is neither automatic nor intrinsic to the commonalities they share. This review has highlighted resources that allow for comparisons between Mexicans and Central Americans. In this volume, Daniel Melero Malpica's work on indigenous Mexicanos/as, Bernadete Beserra's on Brazilians, and Anulkah Thomas's on Afro-Latinos/as expose important areas of research and contribute to future comparative analysis. In sum, research on Latinos and their intra- and intergroup dynamics must attend to common struggle as racialized groups that must strive to attain full civil rights.

Sources

References

Bonacich, Edna, Lucie Cheng, Norma Chinchilla, Nora Hamilton, and Paul Ong, eds. 1994. *Global Production: The Apparel Industry in the Pacific Rim*. Philadelphia: Temple University Press.

Chavez, Leo R., Hubbel, F. Allan, Shiraz Mishra, I. Valdez, and R. Burciaga. 1997. "Undocumented Latina Immigrants in Orange County, California: A Comparative Analysis." *International Migration Review* 31, no. 1 (spring): 88–107.

Chinchilla, Norma, and Nora Hamilton. 1989. "Central American Enterprises in Los Angeles." New Directions for Latino Public Policy Research, Interuniversity Program for Latino Research and the Social Science Research Council, University of Texas at Austin.

———. 1998. "Ambiguous Identities: Central Americans in Southern California." Working Paper Series 1998, Paper No. 14, Chicano/Latino Resource Center, University of Californa, Santa Cruz.

———. 1999. "Changing Networks and Alliances in a Transnational Context: Salvadoran and Guatemalan Immigrants in Southern California." *Social Justice* 26, no. 3 (fall): 4.

Chinchilla, Norma, Nora Hamilton, and James Loucky. 1993. "Central Americans in Los Angeles: An Immigrant Community in Transition." In *In the Barrios: Latinos and the Underclass Debate,* edited by Joan Moore and Raquel Pinderhughes. New York: Russell Sage Foundation.

Coutin, S. B. 2000. Legalizing Moves: Salvadoran Immigrants' Struggle for U.S. Residency. Ann Arbor: University of Michigan Press.

Delgado, H. 1993. *New Immigrants, Old Unions: Organizing Undocumented Workers in Los Angeles.* Philadelphia: Temple University Press.

Donato, K. 1993. "Current Trends and Patterns of Female Migration: Evidence from Mexico." *International Migration Review* 27(4): 748.

Dorrington, C. 1995. "Central American Refugees in Los Angeles: Adjustment of Children and Families." In *Understanding Latino Families: Scholarship, Policy and Practice,* edited by R. E. Zambrana. Thousand Oaks, Calif.: Sage.

Flores, William V. 1997. "Citizens vs. Citizenry: Undocumented Immigrants and Latino Cultural Citizenshio." In *Latino Cultural Citizenship: Claiming Identity, Space, and Rights,* edited by V. W. Flores and R. Benmayor. Boston: Beacon Press.

Flores, William V., and R. Benmayor. 1997. *Latino Cultural Citizenship: Claiming Identity, Space and Rights.* Boston: Beacon Press.

Hamilton, Nora, and Norma Chinchilla. 1991. "Central American Migration: A Framework for Analysis." *Latin American Research Review* 26(1): 75–110.

———. 1995. *Central Americans in California: Transnational Communities, Economies and Cultures.* Los Angeles: Center for Multiethnic and Transnational Studies, University of Southern California.

———. 2001. *Seeking Community in a Global City: Guatemalans and Salvadorans in Los Angeles.* Philadelphia: Temple University Press.

Hondagneu-Sotelo, Pierrette. 1995. *Gendered Transitions: Mexican Experiences of Immigration.* Berkeley: University of California Press.

———. 1997. "The History of Mexican Undocumented Settlement in the United States." In *Challenging Fronteras: Structuring Latina and Latino Lives in the U.S.,* edited by M. Romero, Pierrette Hondagneu-Sotelo, and V. Ortiz. New York, Routledge.

——. 1998. "Latina Immigrant Women and Paid Domestic Work." In *Community Activism and Feminist Politics: Organizing across Race, Class, and Gender*, edited by Nancy A. Naples. New York: Routledge.

——. 2001. *Domestica: Central Americans Cleaning and Caring in the Shadow of Affluence*. Berkeley: University of California Press.

Hondagneu-Sotelo, Pierrette, and E. Avila. 1997. "I'm Here, But I'm There; The Meanings of Latina Transnational Motherhood." *Gender and Society* 11(5): 548–71.

Hondagneu-Sotelo, Pierrette, and M. Romero. 1997. "Challenging Fronteras: Immigration Coming From the Americas." In *Challenging Fronteras: Structuring Latina and Latino Lives in the U.S.*, edited by M. Romero, Pierrette Hondagneu-Sotelo, and V. Ortiz. New York, Routledge.

Kearney, M. 1986. "From the Invisible Hand to Visible Feet: Anthropological Studies of Migration and Development." *Annual Review of Anthropology* 15:331–61.

——. 1995. "The Local in the Global: The Anthropology of Globalization and Transnationalism." *Annual Review of Anthropology* 24:547–65.

Kim, Katherine C., A. Serrano, and L. Ramos. 2000. *Izote Vos: A Collection of Salvadoran American Writing and Visual Art*. San Francisco: Pacific News Service.

Lopez, David E., Eric Popkin, and Edward Telles. 1996. "Central Americans: At the Bottom, Struggling to Get Ahead." In *Ethnic Los Angeles*, edited by R. Waldinger and M. Bozorgmehr. New York: Russell Sage Foundation.

Lopez-Garza, M., and D. Diaz. 2001. *Asian and Latino Immigrants in a Restructuring Economy*. Stanford, Calif.: Stanford University Press.

Loucky, J. 2000. "Maya in a Modern Metropolis: Establishing New Lives and Livelihood in Los Angeles." In *The Maya Diaspora: Guatemalan Roots, New American Lives*, edited by J. Loucky and M. Moors. Philadelphia, Temple University Press.

Loucky, J., and M. Moors, 2000. "The Maya Diaspora, Introduction." In *The Maya Diaspora: Guatemalan Roots, New American Lives*, edited by J. Loucky and M. Moors. Philadelphia, Temple University Press.

Malpica, Daniel. 1996. "The Social Organization of Day Laborers in Los Angeles." In *Immigration and Ethnic Communities: Focus on Latinos*, edited by Refugio Rochin. East Lansing, Mich.: Julian Samora Research Institute, Michigan State University.

Moore, J., and D. Vigil. 1993. "Barrios in Transition." In *In the Barrios: Latinos and the Underclass Debate*, edited by J. Moore and R. Pinderhughes. New York, Russell Sage Foundation.

Moore, J., and R. Pinderhughes, eds. 1993. *In the Barrios: Latinos and the Underclass Debate*. New York, Russell Sage Foundation.

Morales, R., and P. Ong. 1993. "The Illusion of Progress: Latinos in Los Angeles." In *Latinos in a Changing U.S. Economy: Comparative Perspectives on U.S. Inequality*, edited by R. Morales and F. Bonilla. Newbury Park, Calif.: Sage.

Ochoa, G. 2004. *Becoming Neighbors: Power Conflict and Solidarity*. Austin: University of Texas Press.

Ong, P., and R. Morales. 1992. "Mexican Labor in Los Angeles." In *Community Empowerment and Chicano Scholarship*, edited by M. Romero and C. Candelaria. Cheney, Wash.: Eastern Washington University.

Pardo, Mary. 1998a. "Creating Community: Mexican American Women in Eastside Los Angeles." In *Community Activism and Feminist Politics: Organizing across Race, Class, and Gender*, edited by Nancy A. Naples. New York: Routledge.

———. 1998b. *Mexican American Women Activists: Identity and Resistance in Two Los Angeles Communities*. Philadelphia: Temple University Press.

———. 1998c. "Mexican American Women in Eastside Los Angeles." In *Community Activism and Feminist Politics: Organizing across Race, Class, and Gender*, edited by Nancy A. Naples. New York: Routledge.

———. 1999. "Gendered Citizenship: Mexican American Women and Grassroots Activism in East Los Angeles, 1986–1992." In *Chicano Politics and Society in the Late Twentieth Century*, edited by D. Montejano. Austin: University of Texas Press.

Pincetl, S. 1994. "Challenges to Citizenship: Latino Immigrants and Political Organizing in the Los Angeles Area." *Environment and Planning* 26(6): 895–914.

Robinson, William I. 1992. "The Global Economy and the Latino Populations in the United States: A World Systems Approach" *Critical Sociology* 19(2): 29–59.

Sarmiento, Socorro T. 1996. "Who Subsidizes Whom? Latina/o Immigrants in the Los Angeles Garment Industry." *Humboldt Journal of Social Relations* 22(1): 37–42.

Sassen, Saskia. 1988. *The Mobility of Labor and Capital: A Study in Transnational Investment and Labor Flow*. Cambridge, Eng.: Cambridge University Press.

———. 1991. *The Global City: New York, London, Tokyo*. Princeton, N.J.: Princeton University Press.

———. 1994. *Cities in a World Economy*. Thousand Oaks, Calif.: Pine Forge Press.

Sassen-Koob, Saskia. 1984. "From Household to Workplace: Theories and Survey Research on Migrant Women in the Labor Market." *International Migration Review* 18(4): 1114–67.

Segura, D. A. 1994. "Working at Motherhood: Chicana and Mexican Immigrant Mothers and Employment." In *Mothering: Ideology, Experience and Agency*, edited by E. Glenn, G. Chang, and L. R. Forcey. New York, Routledge.

Soldatenko, M. A. G. 1999. "Berta's Story: Journey from Sweatshop to Showroom." *Women's Untold Stories*, edited by M. Romero and A. J. Stewart. New York: Routledge.

Stanley, William. 1987. "Economic Migrants or Refugees from Violence? A Time-Series Analysis of Salvadoran Migration to the United States." *Latin American Research Review* 22(1): 132–54.

Suarez-Orozco, M. M. 1989. *Central American Refugees and U.S. High Schools: A Psychosocial Study of Motivation and Achievement*. Stanford, Calif.: Stanford University Press.

Valle, V. M., and R. D. Torres. 2000. *Latino Metropolis*. Minneapolis, University of Minnesota Press.

Vigil, J. D. 1997. *Personas Mexicanas: Chicano High Schoolers in a Changing Los Angeles*. Fort Worth, Tex.: Harcourt Brace College Publishers.

——. 2002. *Street Cultures in the Mega City: A Rainbow of Gangs*. Austin: University of Texas Press.

Zolberg, A. R. 1995. "From Invitation to Interdiction: U.S. Foreign Policy and Immigration since 1945." In *Threatened People, Threatened Borders: World Migration and U.S. Policy,* edited by M. Teitelbaum and M. Weiner. New York: W.W. Norton.

Instructional Feature Films and Documentaries

Duigan, John. 1989. *Romero*. Los Angeles: Vidmark Entertainment.

Loach, Ken. 2001. *Bread and Roses*. London: Parallax Productions.

Los Jornaleros del Norte. 2000. Los Angeles: CHIRLA/IDEPSCA Day Laborer Project.

Nava, Gregory. 1984. *El Norte*. Farmington Hills, Mich.: CBS/Fox.

Olea, Olivia. 1994. *Por la vida: Street Vending and the Criminalization of Latinos*. Riverside, Calif.: Salsa Productions.

Sayles, John. 1997. *Hombres Armados/Men with Guns*. N.p.: Columbia Tri-Star.

Simon, Angelica. 1997. *Fear and Learning at Hoover Elementary*. N.p.: Josepha Producciones.

Contributors

Bernadete Beserra is an associate professor at the Federal University of Ceará, Brazil. She is the author of *Brazilian Immigrants in the United States: Cultural Imperialism and Social Class* (New York: LFB Scholarly Publishing, 2003) and an associate editor of *Latin American Perspectives*.

José Zapata Calderon is a professor of sociology and Chicano Studies at Pitzer College, in Claremont, California. He has a long history of connecting his academic work with community organizing, student-based service learning, participatory action research, critical pedagogy, and multiethnic coalition building. As a participant ethnographer, he has published numerous articles and studies based on his community experiences and observations.

Susan Bibler Coutin is associate professor in the Department of Criminology, Law, and Society at the University of California, Irvine. She is the author of *Legalizing Moves: Salvadoran Immigrants' Struggle for U.S Residency* (Ann Arbor: University of Michigan Press, 2000) and *The Culture of Protest: Religious Activism and the U.S. Sanctuary Movement* (Boulder, Colo.: Westview Press, 1992). Her research for this paper was funded by the National Science Foundation (Awards SBR-9423023, SES-0001890, and SES-0296050). She is grateful to the many individuals and groups who participated in this project.

Myrna Cherkoss Donahoe is professor emeritus of Interdisciplinary Studies at California State University, Dominguez Hills. She also served as coordinator of the university's Women's Studies and Labor Studies programs. She has authored numerous articles on labor/community movements, ethnic studies, women's studies, and Los Angeles history. She is an active member of labor/community organizations and the Associations of Southwest Labor Studies and California Faculty.

Suzanne Filion Foster, program manager for the day laborer project at the Instituto de Educación Popular del Sur de California (IDEPSCA), received her M.A. in urban planning from UCLA in 2003. She is grateful to José Calderon for first bringing her to the Pomona Day Labor Center and for always encouraging her. She extends her utmost gratitude to the *jornaleros* of the Pomona Day Labor Center for sharing their lives with her, teaching her more than any book, and bringing her along with them on their organizing journey.

Ester E. Hernández is currently an assistant professor in the Department of Chicano Studies at California State University, Los Angeles. She received her Ph.D. from the University of California at Irvine. Her research interests include immigration and the political economy of Salvadoran families and their transnational households. She is coeditor of the anthology *Chicanos, Latinos and Cultural Diversity* (Dubuque, Iowa: Kendall-Hunt, 2004).

Daniel Melero Malpica is a Ph.D. candidate in the Department of Sociology at UCLA. His research interests include race and ethnic relations, immigration, and the working poor. His latest publications include "Making a Living in the Streets of Los Angeles: An Ethnographic Study of Day Laborers," *Migraciones Internacionales* 1, no. 3 (July 2003): 125–48. His dissertation focuses on how social networks and social capital influence the incorporation of indigenous Mexican migrants into the United States. He thanks Steven Gold, Leslie Howard, Ivan Light, Felipe Lopez, Edward Telles, and especially Edith Chen and Vilma Ortiz, for their extensive comments and suggestions. He is also grateful to Gilda Ochoa and Enrique Ochoa for inviting him to participate in this volume. All errors are the author's.

Enrique C. Ochoa is professor of history at California State University, Los Angeles. Born and raised in the Los Angeles area, his research has focused on Latin American economic history, the welfare state, revolution, critical pedagogy, and transnational Latino/a communities. His recent publications include *Feeding Mexico: The Political Uses of Food Since 1910* (Wilmington, Del.: S.R. Books, 2000); and "Education for Social Transformation: The Intersection of Chicana/o and Latin American Studies with Community Struggles," in *Latin American Perspectives* 31, no. 1 (Jan. 2004): 59–80. Enrique would like to thank Julie, Elisa, and Ricky for the love and support that they have given him throughout this project.

Born and raised in Los Angeles County, Gilda L. Ochoa is an associate professor of sociology and Chicana/o Studies at Pomona College. Her interests include Latinas/os and education, race and ethnicity, and Los Angeles communities. In her research and in the classroom, she is seeking to combine personal lives with macroissues and research with social change. She has written several articles on Mexican American-Mexican immigration relations, parent organizing, and service learning, and is the author of *Becoming Neighbors in a Mexican American Community: Power, Conflict and Solidarity* (Austin: University of Texas Press, 2004). She would like to acknowledge Mariela Garcia, Pei-Pei Ketron, and Anulkah Thomas, who assisted in organizing a conference through the Pomona College Sociology Department on Latinas/os in Los Angeles. She also thanks Eduardo Ruiz for his continued support.

Silvia Rodriguez-Sánchez is a native of Guatemala and was raised in Los Angeles. She received her degree in sociology from Pitzer College in May 2000. Presently, she is completing her graduate studies in public policy and administration at California State University, Sacramento. She resides in Sacramento County with her husband and two children.

Richard Roman was a professor of sociology from 1974 to 2003 at the University of Toronto, where he also taught in the Latin American and Canadian Studies programs. He is a fellow of the Centre for Research on Latin America and the Caribbean at York University and has been a visiting professor in Japan and Argentina. He is completing a book with Edur Velasco Arregui on the Mexican working class in continental perspective.

Maria A. Gutierrez de Soldatenko is an associate professor in Chicana/o Studies and gender feminist studies at Pitzer College. Her research and publications focus on the lives of immigrant Latina garment workers in Los Angeles. She has been the Chicana Caucus chair for the National Association of Chicano and Chicana Studies since 2003.

Michael Soldatenko's most recent article was "The Mexican Student Movements: Los Angeles and Mexico City, 1968: La imaginación al poder," *Latino Studies* 1, no. 2 (2003): 284–300. He thanks his many friends who participated in the 1993 UCLA Conscious Students of Color Protest, in particular Richard Chabran, Raoul Contreras, William De La Torre, and Angelina Soldatenko. To shorten this chapter for publication, he limited his citation of articles from the *UCLA Daily Bruin*, *Los Angeles Times*, *Outlook*, *UCLA Today*, and *La Opinion* during the period from May 12 to June 10, 1993. He dedicates this chapter to Angel, the *pug-nuestra gran campañera y amiga*.

Anulkah Thomas was born to Afro-Panamanian immigrant parents and grew up on Camp Pendleton, the Southern California military base where her father served most of his career as a U.S. Marine. After his retirement, the family moved to Oceanside, California, a popular settling spot for both active-duty and retired military families. Anulkah graduated from Pomona College in 2001 with a degree in Ethnic Studies. She worked as a program assistant for a nonprofit foundation in Los Angeles and is currently a graduate student at Harvard University.

Martin Valadez Torres was born in Mexico and grew up in Los Angeles from the age of seven. After graduating from UCLA, he went on to study Latin American history at Stanford University and is currently in the process of completing his dissertation on railway workers in Porfirian Mexico. Martin's research interests include Chicano history, Mexican immigration to the United States, and the economic and labor history of modern Mexico.

Zulema Valdez, a sociologist specializing in race and ethnic relations, economic sociology, and immigration, received her Ph.D. from UCLA in 2002. Currently, she is a postdoctoral research fellow at the National Poverty Center, University of Michigan, where she is completing a book manuscript entitled *Economic Strategies of Survival and Mobility: Ethnic Entrepreneurship in the United States*. She thanks Vilma Ortiz and Ivan Light for comments on a previous draft of this paper. This research was funded by the SSRC International Migration Program and the Center for Comparative Immigration Studies.

Edur Velasco Arregui is an economics professor at the Universidad Autónoma Metropolitana in México City and an activist in worker and peasant struggles. He was the secretary general of the Sindicato Independiente de Trabajadores de la Universidad Autónoma Metropolitana from 1994 to 1996 and one of the leaders and founders of the Coordinadora Intersindical Primero de Mayo (May First Inter-Union Coordinating Committee) in 1995. He has a Ph.D. in economics from UNAM and is completing a book with Richard Roman on the Mexican working class in continental perspective.

Kristine M. Zentgraf is an associate professor in the Department of Sociology at California State University, Long Beach, where she teaches classes on race, class and gender inequality, immigration/migration, social stratification, and sociological theory. Currently, she is working on a project that focuses on immigrant family separation, in particular the impact of family separation and reunification on immigrant children and their adaptation to U.S. society.

Index